Lecture Notes in Computer Sc

T0237783

Commenced Publication in 1973
Founding and Former Series Editors:
Gerhard Goos, Juris Hartmanis, and Jan van Leeuwen

Alex Gray   Keith Jeffery   Jianhua Shao (Eds.)

Sharing Data, Information and Knowledge

25th British National Conference on Databases, BNCOD 25
Cardiff, UK, July 7-10, 2008
Proceedings

 Springer

Volume Editors

Alex Gray
Jianhua Shao
Cardiff University, School of Computer Science
5 The Parade, Cardiff CF24 3AA, UK
E-mail: {w.a.gray, j.shao}@cs.cf.ac.uk

Keith Jeffery
Rutherford Appleton Laboratory, Science and Technology Facilities Council
Harwell Science and Innovation Campus, Didcot OX11 0QX, UK
E-mail: kgj@rl.ac.uk

Library of Congress Control Number: 2008930155

CR Subject Classification (1998): H.2, H.3, H.4

LNCS Sublibrary: SL 3 – Information Systems and Application, incl. Internet/Web and HCI

ISSN   0302-9743
ISBN   978-3-540-70503-1 Springer Berlin Heidelberg New York

Springer is a part of Springer Science+Business Media

springer.com

© Springer-Verlag Berlin Heidelberg 2008

Typesetting: Camera-ready by author, data conversion by Scientific Publishing Services, Chennai, India
Printed on acid-free paper   SPIN: 12322770   06/3180   5 4 3 2 1 0

Preface

Since 1981, the British National Conferences on Databases (BNCOD) have provided a forum for database researchers to report the latest progress and explore new ideas. Over the last 28 years, BNCOD has evolved from a predominantly national conference into one that is truly international, attracting research contributions from all over the world.

This volume contains the proceedings of BNCOD 2008. We received 45 submissions from 22 countries. Each paper was reviewed by three referees, and 14 full papers and 7 posters were accepted. All the research papers and posters are included in this volume, and they are organized into five sections: data mining and privacy, data integration, stream and event data processing, query processing and optimization, and posters.

The keynote was delivered by Monica Marinucci, EMEA Programme Director for Oracle in R&D. She has been involved in various advanced developments concerning Oracle, and participated in EC-funded projects as an expert, especially the CHALLENGERS special support action to propose the future of grid computing. In her keynote presentation, she addressed the audience on the topic of the power of data, emphasizing that the ability to store, handle, manipulate, distribute and replicate data and information can provide a tremendous asset to organizations. She also explored some of the latest directions and developments in the database field, and described how Oracle contributes to them partnering up with other leading organizations in different sectors.

BNCOD 2008 marked a special occasion in the BNCOD history – it was the 25th conference in the BNCOD series (BNCOD was not held in 1987, 1997 and 1999 when VLDB and ICDE were held in the UK). To mark this 25th anniversary, an International Colloquium on Advances in Database Research was held as part of the BNCOD main conference. Leading researchers were invited to the colloquium, and they presented and shared their latest research with the audience. The invited papers or the abstracts of the talks presented at the colloquium are included in this volume.

Two workshops were held alongside BNCOD 2008. The Workshop on Teaching, Learning and Assessment of Databases continued to address, as in the previous years, the issues concerning the educational aspects of databases. The papers from this workshop were published separately, and were not included in this volume. The Workshop on Biodiversity Informatics: Challenges in Modelling and Managing Biodiversity Knowledge aimed at advancing understanding in the challenges involved in this important, multi-disciplinary research area. The two best papers from this workshop are included in this volume.

Finally, we would like to thank all the authors for contributing their papers to BNCOD 2008, the referees for their effort in reviewing the papers, the EPSRC for their support of the International Colloquium on Advances in Database

Research, the Welsh Assembly Government for hosting the reception, and the Organizing Committee at Cardiff University for making this conference possible.

July 2008   Alex Gray
                                                            Keith Jeffery
                                                            Jianhua Shao

Conference Committees

Programme Committee

Alex Gray (Chair)	Cardiff University, UK
David Bell	Queen's University, Belfast, UK
Stefan Böttcher	University of Paderborn, Germany
Peter Buneman	University of Edinburgh, UK
Sharma Chakravarthy	The University of Texas at Arlington, USA
Richard Cooper	University of Glasgow, UK
Alfredo Cuzzocrea	Universita della Calabria, Italy
Barry Eaglestone	University of Sheffield, UK
Suzanne Embury	University of Manchester, UK
A. Fernandes	University of Manchester, UK
Mary Garvey	University of Wolverhampton, UK
Georg Gottlob	University of Oxford, UK
Jun Hong	Queen's University, Belfast, UK
Ela Hunt	Swiss Federal Institute of Technology, Switzerland
Wendy Ivins	Cardiff University, UK
Mike Jackson	Birmingham City University, UK
Anne James	Coventry University, UK
Keith Jeffery	Rutherford Appleton Laboratory, UK
Andrew Jones	Cardiff University, UK
Graham Kemp	Chalmers University, Sweden
Jessie Kennedy	Napier University, UK
Kavin Lu	Brunel University, UK
L MacKinnon	University of Abertay Dundee, UK
Nigel Martin	Birkbeck, University of London, UK
Ken Moody	University of Cambridge, UK
David Nelson	University of Sunderland, UK
M Norrie	ETH Zurich, Switzerland
Werner Nutt	The Free University of Bozen-Bolzano, Italy
Norman Paton	University of Manchester, UK
Alex Poulovassilis	Birkbeck, University of London, UK
Mark Roantree	Dublin City University, Ireland
Alan Sexton	University of Birmingham, UK
Jianhua Shao	Cardiff University, UK
Paul Watson	Newcastle University, UK
Richard White	Cardiff University, UK
John Wilson	University of Strathclyde, UK
Jian Yang	Macquarie University, Australia

Steering Committee

Lachlan Mackinnon (Chair)	University of Abertay Dundee, UK
Richard Cooper	University of Glasgow, UK
Barry Eaglestone	University of Sheffield, UK
Jun Hong	Queen's University, Belfast, UK
Anne James	Coventry University, UK
Keith Jeffery	Rutherford Appleton Laboratory, UK
David Nelson	University of Sunderland, UK
Alex Poulovassilis	Birkbeck, University of London, UK
Jianhua Shao	Cardiff University, UK

Organizing Committee

Nick Fiddian (Chair)	Cardiff University
Mikhaila Burgess	Cardiff University
Wendy Ivins	Cardiff University
Andrew Jones	Cardiff University
Jianhua Shao	Cardiff University
Gareth Shercliff	Cardiff University
Alysia Skilton	Cardiff University
Richard White	Cardiff University

25th Anniversary Colloquium Organization

Keith Jeffery	Rutherford Appleton Laboratory, UK
Jianhua Shao	Cardiff University, UK

Additional Referees

Mikhaila Burgess	Iadh Ounis
Grigorios Loukides	Punitha Swarmy

Table of Contents

Keynote

Data Mining and Privacy

Data Integration

Stream and Event Data Processing

Query Processing and Optimisation

Poster Papers

25th Anniversary Colloquium on Advances in Database Research

Best Papers from the Workshop on Biodiversity Informatics: Challenges in Modelling and Managing Biodiversity Knowledge

The Power of Data

Monica Marinucci

EMEA Oracle in R&D Programme
ORACLE Corporation
monica.marinucci@oracle.com

Abstract. From raw data to knowledge discovery, the ability to store, handle, manipulate, distribute and replicate data and information provides a tremendous asset to organisations, both in the commercial and scientific and academic sector. As IT infrastructures become more and more reliable, dynamic and flexible, applications and services require a modular, distributed, functionality-driven and secure environment.

Continual improvements and advancements are needed to meet these requirements and Oracle constantly innovates and pushes the limits of the technology to make data, information and knowledge available and exploitable. For Oracle to continue leading the database sector and to contribute to the development of ICT, it is crucial to engage with the R&D sector, both industrial and scientific, where existing and new challenges can be explored and novel and ground-breaking solutions found.

The talk will explore some of the latest directions and developments in the database field and describe how Oracle contributes to them partnering up with other leading organisations in different sectors. Highlights from some of the R&D projects across Europe Oracle is part of will be also presented.

A. Gray, K. Jeffery, and J. Shao (Eds.): BNCOD 2008, LNCS 5071, p. 1, 2008.

Efficient Mining of Frequent Itemsets
from Data Streams

Carson Kai-Sang Leung* and Dale A. Brajczuk

The University of Manitoba, Winnipeg, MB, Canada
{kleung,umbrajcz}@cs.umanitoba.ca

Abstract. As technology advances, floods of data can be produced and shared in many applications such as wireless sensor networks or Web click streams. This calls for efficient mining techniques for extracting useful information and knowledge from streams of data. In this paper, we propose a novel algorithm for stream mining of frequent itemsets in a limited memory environment. This algorithm uses a compact tree structure to capture important contents from streams of data. By exploiting its nice properties, such a tree structure can be easily maintained and can be used for mining frequent itemsets, as well as other patterns like constrained itemsets, even when the available memory space is small.

Keywords: Data mining, frequent itemset mining, frequent patterns, tree structure, limited memory space.

1 Introduction

Data mining aims to search for implicit, previously unknown, and potentially useful *information* and *knowledge*—such as frequent itemsets—that might be embedded in *data* (within traditional static databases or continuous data streams). The mining of frequent itemsets from large traditional static databases has been the subject of numerous studies since its introduction [1]. These studies can be broadly divided into two categories focusing *functionality* and *performance*. Regarding functionality, the central question considered is *what* (kind of patterns) to mine. While some studies [3,10] in this category considered the data mining exercise in isolation, some others explored how data mining can best interact with the human user. Examples of the latter include constrained mining [4,16,19,20,21] as well as interactive and online mining [13].

Regarding performance, the central question considered is *how* to mine the frequent itemsets as efficiently as possible. Studies in this category focused on fast Apriori-based algorithms [2] and their performance enhancements. Note that these Apriori-based algorithms depend on a generate-and-test paradigm. They compute frequent itemsets by generating candidates and checking their frequencies (i.e., support counts) against the transaction database. To improve efficiency of the mining process, Han et al. [11] proposed an alternative framework, namely a tree-based framework. The algorithm they proposed in this framework (the FP-growth algorithm) constructs an extended prefix-tree structure, called the *Frequent Pattern tree* (*FP-tree*), to capture the content of the

---

* Corresponding author.

A. Gray, K. Jeffery, and J. Shao (Eds.): BNCOD 2008, LNCS 5071, pp. 2–14, 2008.

transaction database. Rather than employing the generate-and-test strategy of Apriori-based algorithms, the FP-growth algorithm focuses on frequent pattern growth—which is a restricted test-only approach (i.e., does not generate candidates, and only tests for frequency). In the past few years, some other structures—such as the *Co-Occurrence Frequent-Item tree (COFI-tree)* [6,7]—have been proposed to further reduce the memory consumption of the FP-tree.

Moreover, over the past decade, the automation of measurements and data collection has produced tremendously huge amounts of data in many application areas. The recent development and increasing use of a large number of sensors has added to this situation. Consequently, these advances in technology have led to a flood of shared data. We are now drowning in streams of data but starving for knowledge. In order to be able to make sense of the streams of data, algorithms for extracting useful *information* and *knowledge* from these streams of *data* are in demand. This calls for *stream mining* [8,12,18,19].

In recent years, several stream mining algorithms have been proposed, and they can be broadly categorized into exact algorithms and approximate algorithms. Exact algorithms (e.g., Moment [5]) find truly frequent itemsets (i.e., itemsets with frequency not lower than the user-defined minimum frequency/support threshold *minsup*). However, these algorithms usually aim to mine some *special subsets* of frequent itemsets (e.g., maximal, closed, or "short" itemsets) instead of *all* frequent itemsets. On the contrary, approximate algorithms (e.g., FP-streaming [9], FDPM [22]) mine all "frequent" itemsets. They do so by using approximate procedures, which may lead to some false positives or false negatives. In other words, these algorithms may find some infrequent itemsets or may miss (certain frequency information of) some frequent itemsets.

When comparing with mining from traditional static databases [1,14,15,17,20,21], mining from data streams is more challenging due to the following *properties* of data streams:

1. *Data streams are continuous and unbounded.* To find frequent itemsets from streams, we no longer have the luxury of performing multiple data scans. Once the streams flow through, we lose them. Hence, we need some techniques to capture the important contents of the streams (e.g., recent data—because users are usually more interested in recent data than older ones) and ensure that the captured data can fit into memory.

2. *Data in the streams are not necessarily uniformly distributed, and their distributions are usually changing with time.* A currently infrequent itemset may become frequent in the future, and vice versa. We have to be careful not to prune infrequent itemsets too early; otherwise, we may not be able to get complete information such as frequencies of certain itemsets, as it is impossible to recall those pruned itemsets.

Hence, some natural questions are: How can we effectively capture the important contents of the streams? Can we design a data structure that helps finding frequent itemsets from streams of data? To this end, we previously proposed a tree structure—called the *Data Stream Tree (DSTree)* [18]—to capture the contents of the streaming data. Like much other existing work [9,23], we made the same realistic assumption about enough memory space that the tree can fit into the main memory. While this assumption holds in many real-life situations, it may not hold in some other situations due to various factors (e.g., the nature of the streams, the window size, the *minsup* value). When the amount

Table 1. Our proposed DSP-tree vs. the most relevant work

	FP-tree [11]	COFI-tree [6,7]	DSTree [18]	Our proposed DSP-tree
Goal	For mining traditional static DBs	For mining traditional static DBs	For mining data streams	For mining data streams
No. of components in each tree node	2 (item & its frequency)	3 (item, its frequency, & a participation counter)	2 (item & a list of frequencies)	2 (item & a counter)
Contents of the tree	Entire DB or projected DBs	DB for an item	Current batches of transactions from data streams	Current batches of data stream content for an item

of available memory space is small, the DSTree may not be able to fit into the main memory. Hence, we need a data structure that can work in environments with sufficient memory as well as insufficient memory space. We also need an algorithm that can use such a data structure to mine frequent itemsets for data streams.

The **key contributions of this work** are (i) the proposal of a simple, yet powerful, tree structure for capturing and maintaining relevant data found in the data streams; and (ii) the development of an efficient novel algorithm, which makes use of the developed tree structure, for mining frequent itemsets from streams of data in a limited memory environment. Experimental results in Section 5 show the effectiveness of our developed algorithm using our proposed tree structure in mining frequent itemsets from data streams. Table 1 summarizes the salient differences between our proposed DSP-tree and the most relevant alternatives.

This paper is organized as follows. In the next section, related work is described. Section 3 introduces our DSP-tree for stream mining in a limited memory environment. In Section 4, we discuss the applicability of the DSP-tree. Section 5 shows experimental results. Finally, conclusions are presented in Section 6.

2   Related Work

In this section, we discuss two groups of existing structures that are relevant to our work: (i) the COFI-tree [6,7] for mining static databases, and (ii) the DSTree [18] for stream mining.

2.1   Mining with the COFI-Tree

El-Hajj and Zaïane [6,7] proposed a *Co-Occurrence Frequent-Item tree* (*COFI-tree*) for mining frequent itemsets from traditional static databases. The key idea of mining with the COFI-tree can be described as follows. First, we scan the static database twice. The first database scan is to find frequencies of all domain items. These items are then sorted in *descending* frequency order. (As a preview, this global order of domain items will determine how the items are arranged in the COFI-tree.) The second database scan is to build a global tree (more precisely, a global FP-tree) to capture the contents of the database. Once the global tree is built, it can be used for constructing a COFI-tree for each frequent domain item x, from which frequent itemsets containing x can be mined. More precisely, given a user-defined *minsup* threshold, we construct a COFI-tree for each domain item with frequency greater than or equal to *minsup*, starting

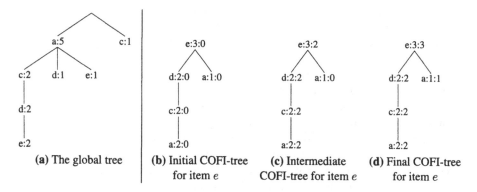

Fig. 1. The global tree and the COFI-tree for item e (Example 1)

from the least frequent item. Items with frequency less than *minsup* are ignored. The COFI-tree for item x is constructed as follows. We extract the captured transactions from the global tree, and form a conditional database (i.e., a collection of transactions containing x). Any locally infrequent (i.e., infrequent w.r.t. the conditional database) items are removed. From the resulting conditional database, we build a COFI-tree for item x. In the COFI-tree, items are arranged in *ascending* global frequency order of domain items (i.e., the reverse of the global frequency order of domain items). Each tree node contains three components: (i) the item, (ii) its frequency, and (iii) its participation counter. The participation counter, which keeps track of the number of times a node is participated in the mining of itemsets, is initialized to 0 and is incremented whenever the node participates. For all non-root nodes of any COFI-tree, the values of their participation counters match their corresponding frequencies at the end of the mining process for the COFI-tree. At that time, all frequent itemsets containing item x are found and the COFI-tree can be discarded. Note that frequent itemsets can be found without recursive calls (as were required in FP-growth). To gain a better understanding, let us consider the following example.

Example 1. Consider the following traditional static database transactions:

Transactions	Contents
t_1	$\{a, c, d, e\}$
t_2	$\{a, d\}$
t_3	$\{a, b\}$
t_4	$\{a, e\}$
t_5	$\{a, c, d, e\}$
t_6	$\{c\}$

Let *minsup* be 2. Then, this database is scanned twice for the construction of a global tree. The first database scan finds frequencies of all domain items (a:5, c:3, d:3, e:3, and b:1). Here, a:5 represents an item a having frequency of 5. The second scan extracts transactions from the database and puts the database contents into the global tree. See Fig. 1(a) for the resulting global tree.

Given a user-defined *minsup* threshold of 2, the mining process constructs a COFI-tree for each of the items that has a frequency $\geq$ *minsup* $= 2$ (i.e., items

e, d, c, and a). The COFI-tree for item e is shown in Fig. 1(b). Note that the root node $e{:}3{:}0$ represents item e with frequency of 3 and an initial participation value of 0. By traversing the left path $\langle e, d, c, a \rangle{:}\mathbf{2}$, we generate non-singleton itemsets $\{e, d, c, a\}, \{e, d, c\}, \{e, d, a\}, \{e, c, a\}, \{e, d\}, \{e, c\}$, and $\{e, a\}$ with their frequency counts set to **2** so far. Then, we increment the participation values for all the nodes in this path by **2**, and obtain an updated COFI-tree as shown in Fig. 1(c). For all non-root nodes on the left path, their participation values match their corresponding frequencies (meaning that these nodes have completed their participation in the mining process). So, we then traverse the right path $\langle e, a \rangle{:}1$, increase the frequency of an existing item-set $\{e, a\}$ by 1, and increment the participation counter of $\{e, a\}$. Now, the participation values for all non-root nodes in this COFI-tree match their corresponding frequencies (see Fig. 1(d)). This indicates the end of the mining process for this COFI-tree. We found all frequent itemsets $\{e, d, c, a\}{:}2$, $\{e, d, c\}{:}2$, $\{e, d, a\}{:}2$, $\{e, c, a\}{:}2$, $\{e, d\}{:}2$, $\{e, c\}{:}2$, and $\{e, a\}{:}3$, and this COFI-tree can be discarded. Afterwards, we construct and mine the COFI-trees for items d and c in a similar fashion. □

When comparing the above (which uses the global tree and a COFI-tree for each item) with the traditional FP-growth algorithm [11] (which recursively uses FP-trees), the former requires less memory space because at any time during the mining process, at most one COFI-tree (together with the global tree) is kept in the main memory. In contrast, the usual FP-growth algorithm requires recursive construction of FP-trees (say, for $\{e\}$-projected database, $\{e, d\}$-projected database, and then $\{e, d, c\}$-projected database, etc.). However, the COFI-tree was designed for traditional mining, but *not* for stream mining. So, using it for stream mining leads to the following problem (especially when available memory is limited): *Each node of the COFI-tree contains three components*, which take up memory space. This problem is serious when the available memory space is limited.

2.2   Mining with the DSTree

Unlike the COFI-tree, our previously proposed *Data Stream Tree* (*DSTree*) [18] is designed for *stream mining*. Moreover, unlike the construction of the FP-tree, the construction of the DSTree only requires *one* scan of the streaming data. The DSTree captures the contents of transactions in each batch of streaming data (in the current window).

The key idea of mining with DSTree can be described as follows. We first construct a DSTree, and then use this DSTree (as the global tree) to generate smaller FP-trees for projected databases. Note that the construction of a DSTree requires only *one* scan of the data streams. The contents of the streams are captured in the DSTree. Recall from Section 1 that data in the streams are not necessarily uniformly distributed. Because of this and of the dynamic nature of data streams, frequencies of items are continuously affected by the insertion of new batches (and the removal of old batches) of transactions. Arranging items in frequency-dependent order may lead to swapping—which, in turn, can cause merging and splitting—of tree nodes when frequencies change. Hence, in the DSTree, transaction items are arranged according to some *canonical order* (e.g., lexicographic order), which can be specified by the user prior to the tree construction or the mining process. In the DSTree, (i) the frequency of a node is at least as high as the sum of frequencies of all its children and (ii) the ordering of items is unaffected by the continuous changes in item frequencies.

To record and update the frequency information at each tree node, the DSTree keeps *a list of frequencies* (instead of just one frequency). Each entry in this list captures the frequency of an item in each batch. By so doing, when the window slides (i.e., when new batches are inserted and old batches are deleted), frequency information can be updated easily. Specifically, whenever a new batch of transactions flows in, the frequency count of the node Y in the current batch is appended to the frequency list for Y. In other words, the last entry of the list at node Y shows the frequency count of Y in the current batch. When the next batch of transactions comes in, the list is shifted forward. The last entry shifts and becomes the second-last entry; this leaves room (the last entry position) for the newest batch. At the same time, the frequency count corresponding to the oldest batch in the window is removed. This has the same effect as deleting from the window the transactions in the oldest batch.

With the DSTree, mining is "delayed" until it is needed. In other words, once the DSTree is constructed, it is always kept up-to-date when the window slides. Consequently, one can mine frequent itemsets from the updated DSTree in a fashion similar to FP-growth (using *minsup*). More specifically, we employ a divide-and-conquer approach. We form projected databases (e.g., $\{e\}$-projected database, $\{e, d\}$-projected database, $\{e, d, c\}$-projected database, etc.) by traversing the paths *upwards only*. Since items are consistently arranged according to some canonical order, one can guarantee the inclusion of all *frequent* items using just upward traversals. There is also no worry about possible omission or doubly-counting of items during the mining process. As the DSTree is always kept up-to-date, all frequent itemsets in current streams can be found effectively. To gain a better understanding of the DSTree, let us consider the following example.

Example 2. Consider the following stream of transactions:

Batch	Transactions	Contents
first	t_1	$\{a, c, d, e\}$
	t_2	$\{a, d\}$
	t_3	$\{a, b\}$
second	t_4	$\{a, e\}$
	t_5	$\{a, c, d, e\}$
	t_6	$\{c\}$
third	t_7	$\{a\}$
	t_8	$\{a, b, e\}$
	t_9	$\{a, c, d\}$

Let *minsup* be 2 and let the window size w be two batches (indicating that only two batches of transactions are kept). Then, when the first two batches of transactions in the streams flows in, we insert the transactions into the DSTree and keep frequency counts in a list of $w = 2$ entries at each node. Each entry in the list corresponds to a batch. For example, the node a:[3,2] in Fig. 2(a) indicates that the frequency of a is 3 in the first batch and is 2 in the second batch.

Afterwards (at time T'), when subsequent batches (e.g., the third batch) of streaming data flow in, transactions in those batches are then inserted in the DSTree. The list of frequency counts shifts, the frequent counts for the oldest (i.e., the first) batch are removed—leaving room for the frequency counts for the second and the third (i.e., the

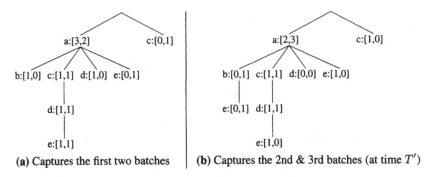

(a) Captures the first two batches   **(b)** Captures the 2nd & 3rd batches (at time T')

Fig. 2. The DSTrees (Example 2)

two newest) batches of transactions. See Fig. 2(b) for a DSTree capturing the second and the third batches. (Note that the node d:[0,0] can be removed.)

Note that, once the DSTree is constructed, one can easily form an $\{x\}$-projected database for some frequent item x. At any subsequent time, the usual FP-tree based mining process (e.g., FP-growth) can be applied to these $\{x\}$-projected databases to find frequent itemsets (i.e., itemsets with frequency counts $\geq minsup = 2$). $\square$

While the DSTree is a novel tree structure for stream mining of frequent itemsets, it uses FP-growth mining process for mining the projected databases. As a result, it inherits problems from FP-growth (which is an algorithm not designed for stream mining). It may suffer from the following problems when trying to mine with limited memory:

1. Depending on the length and distribution of items in transactions, the number of projected databases that need to co-exist (e.g., $\{e\}$-projected databases, $\{e,d\}$-projected databases, $\{e,d,c\}$-projected databases, etc.) may be large.
2. The assumption that all the above trees (including the DSTree and FP-trees for recursive projected databases) fit into the memory may not always hold. There are situations in which only some—but *not* all—of the trees can fit into the main memory.

3   Mining with Our Proposed DSP-Tree in a Limited Memory Space Environment

Recall from Section 2.1 that mining with the COFI-tree reduces memory consumption because it does not require recursive construction of COFI-trees for sub-databases. In other words, COFI-trees are only built for items. However, the COFI-tree was designed for mining traditional static databases, but *not* data streams. As for the DSTree, it was designed for stream mining. However, its success is partially based on a realistic assumption that memory is sufficient to hold the (global) DSTree and all recursive trees for projected databases. What if these recursive trees for projected databases do *not* fit into the memory? In other words, the DSTree does not deal with limited memory space. However, there is demand for mining streaming data with limited memory. So, our questions are: Can we take advantage of these structures? If so, how can we integrate techniques and benefits of both COFI-tree and DSTree? More specifically, we consider the following questions: (i) Given that the COFI-tree was designed for mining static databases, can it be used for mining data streams? (ii) Given that the COFI-tree was designed to extract projected/conditional databases from the global tree, can it be used to extract the data from paths in the DSTree? (iii) On the one hand, the COFI-tree reduces memory consumption by not creating any subsequent trees for projected databases; on the other hand, each node in the COFI-tree consists of three components (instead of the two components as in the FP-tree). Can we avoid creating lots of trees and not introduce an extra counter?

As a solution to the above questions, we propose a variant of combined COFI-tree and DSTree—which we call *Data Stream Projected tree (DSP-tree)*. Our proposed DSP-tree extracts data stream information from the global DSTree. For each frequent item, we extract transactions from batches of transactions in the current window and form a DSP-tree capturing the transactions in each projected database.

In the DSP-tree, items are arranged in descending local frequency order (cf. ascending global frequency order of domain items in the COFI-tree) w.r.t. the projected database. Note that the use of *local* frequency order is just a heuristic. We are not confined to just this order. One can use some other ordering (e.g., canonical order, some other user-defined ordering or constraints used in constrained mining). Regardless of which item order do we pick, the frequency of any node in our DSP-tree is at least as high as the sum of frequencies of its children.

Like the COFI-tree, our DSP-tree is built for a projected database for an item x. However, unlike the COFI-tree, each tree node in our DSP-tree contains only two components—namely, the item and a counter (cf. the three components required by the COFI-tree). The value of this counter for each node representing an item y is initially set to the frequency of y on that tree path, and its value is decremented during the mining process until it reaches 0. It is important to note that the DSP-tree for an item x will be discarded once all frequent itemsets containing x are found. Hence, it is not important to have the frequency values at each tree node at the *end* of the mining process on the tree. What is important is the frequency value of each node *during* the mining process. By carefully decrementing the counter value (which can be done easily), DSP-tree does not need to keep both the frequency and the participation value (as in the COFI-tree) for each node.

To mine frequent itemsets from the DSP-tree for an item x, we start from the least frequent item y in this DSP-tree. We locate a node containing y and follow the tree path from y to the root. This tree path gives us an itemset $\{x, y\} \cup Z$, where Z is an itemset comprised of items on such a tree path. The frequency of the itemset $\{x, y\} \cup Z$ equals the value of the counter of y. Not only do we generate the itemset $\{x, y\} \cup Z$, we also generate all its non-singleton subsets. The frequencies of these subsets also equal the value of the counter of y. For each subset, if it has not been generated, we add it to the list; otherwise (i.e., the subset has already been generated), we increment the frequency of such a subset. Then, we subtract the value of the counter of y from the counter for each of the nodes along this tree path. By so doing, not only do we *eliminate the need for recursive constructions to trees for projected databases*, we also *reduce the number of*

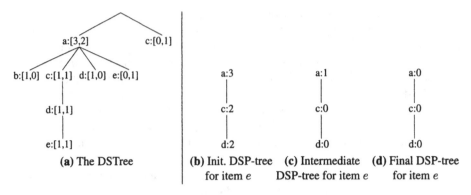

Fig. 3. The DSP-trees (Example 3)

counters needed for each node in the tree (i.e., remove the participation counter, which was required by the COFI-tree). See the following example for deeper understanding.

Example 3. Consider the sample stream of transactions as in Example 2. We use the same mining parameters: *minsup* of 2 and the window size w of two batches. The DSTree for the first two batches is copied from Fig. 2(a) to Fig. 3(a).

Then, we start constructing a DSP-tree for item e by extracting relevant tree paths from the DSTree. Note, from Fig. 3(b), that we do not need to put e in the DSP-tree for e because all itemsets generated from this DSP-tree must contain e. We traverse the path $\langle a, c, d \rangle$:2 from this tree, and generate all its seven subsets containing e—namely, $\{e, a, c, d\}$:2, $\{e, a, c\}$:2, $\{e, a, d\}$:2, $\{e, c, d\}$:2, $\{e, a\}$:2, $\{e, c\}$:2, and $\{e, d\}$:2. The frequency counter of each node in the path $\langle a, c, d \rangle$ is then decremented by 2, and results in the intermediate DSP-tree shown in Fig. 3(c). Then, we traverse the path $\langle a \rangle$:1 and properly update the frequencies of itemsets (e.g., $\{e, a\}$:2+1=3) that have already been generated. Finally, the DSP-tree for e (as shown Fig. 3(d)) is then discarded.

Next, we construct the DSP-tree for d and then the DSP-tree for a in a similar fashion, and find frequent itemsets $\{d, a, c\}$:2, $\{d, a\}$:2+1=3, $\{d, c\}$:2, and $\{c, a\}$:2.   □

On the surface, our proposed DSP-tree may look similar to the existing COFI-tree. However, there are several differences. First, each node in the DSP-tree consists of only two components (items and its counter), whereas each node in the COFI-tree consists of three components (items, frequency counter and participation counter). Hence, the latter requires 50% more memory space than the former. Second, the DSP-tree for an item x does not contain the node x, whereas the COFI-tree for an $\{x\}$-projected database contains x. Hence, the DSP-tree again saves some memory space. Third, the DSP-tree uses the heuristic of arranging items in descending local frequency w.r.t. projected database along the tree path, whereas the COFI-tree arranges items in ascending global frequency. Hence, the DSP-tree is more likely to require less memory space than the COFI-tree because putting items in descending frequency order is more likely to increase the chance of path sharing.

4 Discussion

In this section, we briefly discuss the applicability of our proposed DSP-tree. First, by using our DSP-tree, only the global DSTree and at most one DSP-tree are required to keep in the main memory at any time during the mining process. We are able to find all frequent itemsets (including frequent subsets) without the need for recursive construction of trees for projected databases. Moreover, we keep our DSP-tree small by (i) keeping only two components (i.e., item and its counter) in each DSP-tree node and (ii) removing x from the DSP-tree for an item x. Hence, having the DSP-tree is helpful when the available memory space is limited.

Second, if we have sufficient memory space to store the global DSTree and the subsequent FP-trees produced recursively for projected databases, we can use the DSTree/DSP-tree combination as an alternative to DSTree/FP-trees combination. Due to the compact representation and the non-recursive nature of DSP-tree, mining with DSTree/DSP-tree usually requires less time than that with DSTree/FP-trees. Hence, *mining with DSTree/DSP-tree is a good mining alternative* even we have sufficient memory space.

Third, although we proposed the DSP-tree for mining frequent itemsets from data streams in a limited memory environment, the DSP-tree can be applicable to mine other patterns such as maximal itemsets, closed itemsets, and constrained itemsets. Let us elaborate. A frequent itemset is *maximal* if none of its proper supersets is frequent. One way to find maximal frequent itemsets is to apply additional check to ensure a frequent itemset X satisfies this extra condition/requirement that none of the proper supersets of X is frequent. Hence, our proposed DSP-tree can be easily adapted to mine maximal frequent itemsets from data streams in a limited memory environment.

Similarly, a frequent itemset Y is *closed* if none of the proper supersets of Y has the same frequency as Y. Again, our proposed DSP-tree can be easily adapted to mine closed frequent itemsets from data streams in a limited memory environment by applying additional check to ensure a frequent itemset Y satisfies the extra condition/requirement during the mining process.

Regarding *constrained itemsets*, the use of constraints in mining permits user focus and guidance, enables user exploration and control, and leads to effective pruning of the search space and efficient discovery of frequent itemsets that are interesting to the user. Over the past few years, several FP-tree based constrained mining algorithms have been developed to handle various classes of constraints. For example, the FPS algorithm [16] supports the succinct constraints (e.g., $C_{succ} \equiv max(S.Price) \geq 50$ which finds frequent itemsets whose maximum item price is at least £50); the $\mathcal{FIC}$ algorithms [21] handle the so-called convertible constraints (e.g., $C_{conv} \equiv avg(S.Price) \leq 20$ which finds frequent itemsets whose average item price is at most £20). The success of these algorithms partly depends on their ability to arrange the items according to some specific order in the FP-trees. More specifically, FPS arranges items according to order $\mathcal{M}$ specifying their membership (e.g., arranges the items in such a way that mandatory items below optional items for C_{succ}); $\mathcal{FIC}$ arranges items according to prefix function order $\mathcal{R}$ (e.g., arranges the items in ascending order of the price values for C_{conv}). Recall from Section 3 that our proposed DSP-tree provides users with flexibility to arrange items in any canonical order. Hence, our proposed DSP-tree can be easily adapted to mine constrained frequent itemsets from data streams in a limited memory environment.

5   Experimental Results

The experimental results cited below are based on data generated by the program developed at IBM Almaden Research Centre [2]. The data contain 1M records with an average transaction length of 10 items, and a domain of 1,000 items. We set each batch to be 0.1M transactions and the window size to be $w = 5$ batches.

We have also experimented with some other datasets (e.g., Mushroom data) from UC Irvine Machine Learning Repository as well as Frequent Itemset Mining Implementations Repository. The results of these datasets were consistent with those cited below. For lack of space, we only showed our results on the IBM data.

All experiments were run in a time-sharing environment in a 1GHz machine. The reported figures are based on the average of multiple runs. Runtime includes CPU and I/Os; it includes the time for both tree construction and frequent-pattern mining steps. In the experiments, we mainly evaluated the accuracy and efficiency of the DSP-tree.

In the first experiment, we measured the accuracy of the two combinations: (i) DSTree/FP-trees and (ii) DSTree/DSP-tree. Experimental results show that mining with any of these two combinations gave the same mining results.

While these combinations gave the same results, their performance varied. In the second experiment, we measured the space consumption of our proposed DSP-tree. Results presented in Fig. 4(a) show that DSTree/DSP-tree combination required less memory space. This is partially due to the non-recursive nature of the DSP-tree. To elaborate, when mining with DSTree/DSP-tree, only a total of one DSTree and $f - 1$ DSP-trees (where f is the number of frequent domain items) need to be generated in the entire mining process. Only two trees—namely, one DSTree and one DSP-tree—are present in the main memory at any time during the mining process. The size of each DSP-tree is similar to that of the FP-tree generated for a domain item. In contrast, when mining with DSTree/FP-trees, usually more than two trees—one DSTree and d FP-tree (where d is the depth of the DSTree, and thus $d \leq f$)—are present in the main memory at many time moments during the mining process. Summing all these trees, the total number of trees that are generated in the entire mining process can be as high as $1 + \frac{f(f-1)}{2}$.

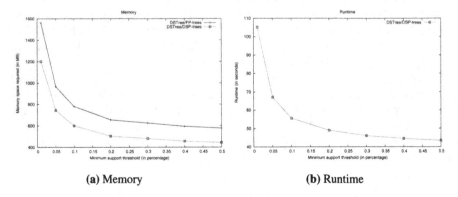

(a) Memory   (b) Runtime

Fig. 4. Experimental results of our proposed DSP-tree

Moreover, we performed some additional experiments. In the third experiment, we measured the time efficiency of our proposed DSP-tree. Fig. 4(b) shows the runtime of mining with our proposed DSP-tree.

In the fourth experiment, we tested with the usual experiment (e.g., the effect of *minsup*). As expected, when *minsup* increased, the runtime decreased.

In the fifth experiment, we tested scalability with the number of transactions. The required runtime appeared to be linearly proportional to the number of transactions in the current window.

6   Conclusions

A key contribution of this paper is to provide the user with an algorithm for mining frequent itemsets for streams of data, even when the available memory space is limited. The algorithm uses a compact tree structure, called the Data Stream Projected tree (DSP-tree), to mine frequent itemsets.

It is important to note that, when the available memory space is limited, the DSTree/DSP-tree mining process allows the user to find frequent itemsets from data streams in this limited memory environment. When the available memory space is sufficient, mining with the DSP-tree can be considered as an alternative to the DSTree/FP-trees mining process. Moreover, in addition to efficient mining of frequent itemsets from data streams, our proposed DSP-tree can also be used for efficient stream mining of maximal itemsets, closed itemsets, and constrained itemsets.

Acknowledgement. This project is partially supported by NSERC (Canada) in the form of research grants.

References

1. Agrawal, R., et al.: Mining association rules between sets of items in large databases. In: Proc. ACM SIGMOD, pp. 207–216 (2003)
2. Agrawal, R., Srikant, R.: Fast algorithms for mining association rules. In: Proc. VLDB, pp. 487–499 (1994)
3. Bashir, S., Baig, A.R.: Max-FTP: mining maximal fault-tolerant frequent patterns from databases. In: Cooper, R., Kennedy, J. (eds.) BNCOD 2007. LNCS, vol. 4587, pp. 235–246. Springer, Heidelberg (2007)
4. Bucila, C., et al.: DualMiner: a dual-pruning algorithm for itemsets with constraints. In: Proc. ACM KDD, pp. 42–51 (2002)
5. Chi, Y., et al.: Moment: maintaining closed frequent itemsets over a stream sliding window. In: Proc. IEEE ICDM, pp. 59–66 (2004)
6. El-Hajj, M., Zaïane, O.R.: COFI-tree mining: a new approach to pattern growth with reduced candidacy generation. In: Proc. FIMI (2003)
7. El-Hajj, M., Zaïane, O.R.: Non-recursive generation of frequent k-itemsets from frequent pattern tree representations. In: Kambayashi, Y., Mohania, M., Wöß, W. (eds.) DaWaK 2003. LNCS, vol. 2737, pp. 371–380. Springer, Heidelberg (2003)
8. Gaber, M.M., et al.: Mining data streams: a review. ACM SIGMOD Record 34(2), 18–26 (2005)

9. Giannella, C., et al.: Mining frequent patterns in data streams at multiple time granularities. In: Data Mining: Next Generation Challenges and Future Directions, ch. 6. AAAI/MIT Press (2004)

10. Guo, Y., et al.: A FP-tree based method for inverse frequent set mining. In: Bell, D.A., Hong, J. (eds.) BNCOD 2006. LNCS, vol. 4042, pp. 152–163. Springer, Heidelberg (2006)

11. Han, J., et al.: Mining frequent patterns without candidate generation. In: Proc. ACM SIGMOD, pp. 1–12 (2000)

12. Jin, R., Agrawal, G.: An algorithm for in-core frequent itemset mining on streaming data. In: Proc. IEEE ICDM, pp. 210–217 (2005)

13. Lakshmanan, L.V.S., Leung, C.K.-S., Ng, R.T.: Efficient dynamic mining of constrained frequent sets. ACM TODS 28(4), 337–389 (2003)

14. Leung, C.K.-S., et al.: A tree-based approach for frequent pattern mining from uncertain data. In: Washio, T., et al. (eds.) PAKDD 2008. LNCS (LNAI), vol. 5012, pp. 653–661 (2008)

15. Leung, C.K.-S., et al.: CanTree: a canonical-order tree for incremental frequent-pattern mining. KAIS 11(3), 287–311 (2007)

16. Leung, C.K.-S., et al.: Exploiting succinct constraints using FP-trees. ACM SIGKDD Explorations 4(1), 40–49 (2002)

17. Leung, C.K.-S., et al.: FIsViz: a frequent itemset visualizer. In: Washio, T., et al. (eds.) PAKDD 2008. LNCS (LNAI), vol. 5012, pp. 644–652. Springer, Heidelberg (2008)

18. Leung, C.K.-S., Khan, Q.I.: DSTree: a tree structure for the mining of frequent sets from data streams. In: Proc. IEEE ICDM, pp. 928–932 (2006)

19. Leung, C.K.-S., Khan, Q.I.: Efficient mining of constrained frequent patterns from streams. In: Proc. IDEAS, pp. 61–68 (2006)

20. Ng, R.T., et al.: Exploratory mining and pruning optimizations of constrained associations rules. In: Proc. ACM SIGMOD, pp. 13–24 (1998)

21. Pei, J., et al.: Mining frequent itemsets with convertible constraints. In: Proc. IEEE ICDE, pp. 433–442 (2001)

22. Yu, J.X., et al.: False positive or false negative: mining frequent itemsets from high speed transactional data streams. In: Proc. VLDB, pp. 204–215 (2004)

23. Zaki, M.J., Hsiao, C.-J.: CHARM: an efficient algorithm for closed itemset mining. In: Proc. SDM, pp. 457–473 (2002)

An Empirical Study of Utility Measures for k-Anonymisation

Grigorios Loukides and Jianhua Shao

School of Computer Science
Cardiff University
Cardiff CF24 3AA, UK,
{G.Loukides,J.Shao}@cs.cf.ac.uk

Abstract. k-Anonymisation is a technique for masking microdata in order to prevent individual identification. Besides preserving privacy, data anonymised by such a method must also retain its utility, i.e. it must remain useful to applications. Existing k-anonymisation methods all attempt to optimise data utility, but they do so by using measures that do not take application requirements into account. In this paper, we empirically study several popular utility measures by comparing their performance in a range of application scenarios. Our study shows that these measures may not be a reliable indicator of data utility for applications in practice, and how to use these measures effectively must be considered.

1   Introduction

Data about individuals (often termed *microdata*) is being increasingly used in many applications, ranging from location-based services to data mining systems [1]. However, publishing such microdata may lead to breach of privacy [2]. In response, a number of techniques which attempt to mask microdata in a way that individuals' privacy is protected and yet data utility is preserved [3] have been proposed. K-anonymisation is one such technique [2].

Assume that we have a table T consisting of three types of attribute: *identifiers* (IDs), *quasi-identifiers* (QIDs) and *sensitive attributes* (SAs). IDs contain information that may be used to identify individuals directly (e.g. phone numbers). QIDs are seemingly innocuous, but can potentially be linked with other data to identify individuals (e.g. age and postcode). SAs contain sensitive information about individuals (e.g. their shopping preferences or diagnosed diseases). Normally, IDs are removed from microdata, but QIDs and SAs are released to applications. Thus, it is important to consider how individual identification through QIDs may be prevented. K-anonymisation achieves this by deriving a view T' of T such that each tuple in the view is made identical to at least $k-1$ other tuples w.r.t. QIDs [2].

A typical k-anonymisation process involves an algorithm that performs *data grouping* and *value recoding* (to form groups of at least k tuples and to make QID values in each group identical), and a *utility measure* (to assess utility

A. Gray, K. Jeffery, and J. Shao (Eds.): BNCOD 2008, LNCS 5071, pp. 15–27, 2008.

of anonymised data). Many algorithms have been proposed in the literature [4, 5, 6, 7, 8, 9, 10], all attempting to optimise data utility by using measures that aim to minimise information loss (a consequence of having to recode QID values) incurred during anonymisation. However, these utility measures do not take application requirements into consideration, and as such they may not be a reliable indicator of how useful anonymised data is for applications in practice.

In this paper, we study some commonly-used utility measures empirically by investigating their performance in applications. We applied several popular methods on real data, considered aggregate query answering as an indicative application, and constructed a range of scenarios in experiments. Utility of the resultant anonymisations was then measured by quantifying query answering accuracy. Contrary to existing works [8, 11], we found that these commonly-used measures can be misleading about the level of data utility provided by anonymised data, and thus how they may be used effectively in practice must be considered.

The paper is organised as follows. Section 2 gives preliminaries for k-anonymisation. Section 3 introduces several popular utility measures. We show that these measures fail to capture utility in many application scenarios and suggest possible remedies in Section 4. Finally, we conclude in Section 5.

2   Preliminaries

All k-anonymisation algorithms employ a heuristic for grouping data [8,10,7,5,4] and a model for recoding QID values [5,8]. Different data grouping and recoding strategies are shown in Figure 1. *Global recoding* maps the entire domain of QIDs into generalised values, and it can be either single-dimensional (applied to the domain of a single QID) or multi-dimensional (applied to the multi-attribute domain of QIDs). *Local recoding*, on the other hand, maps values of individual tuples into generalised ones on a group-by-group basis. Data grouping strategies are essentially search methods that attempt to form optimal groups for recoding by partitioning or clustering data according to some heuristics, or by following a principle similar to the Apriori used in association rule mining. For our study,

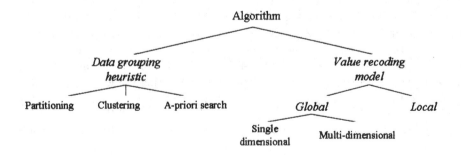

Fig. 1. Classification of k-anonymisation algorithms

we used three popular methods which are representative of these strategies: a variation of the Incognito algorithm [4] that employs an a-priori search heuristic and single-dimensional global recoding, the Mondrian algorithm [8] that uses median-based partitioning and multi-dimensional global recoding, and the K-Members algorithm [10] that adopts greedy clustering and local recoding.

There are also several ways to evaluate utility of anonymised data. Some measures are based on group size [6, 8]. Intuitively, larger anonymised groups incur more information loss, as more tuples are made indistinguishable. Other measures consider how QID values are generalised. Interval-based QID values are typically generalised by replacing the values in a group with their range, while discrete QID values are replaced by a more general value specified by generalisation hierarchies [5] or by the set of values appearing in the group [7]. Thus, the size of range (set) or the height of hierarchy used to recode values can be used to capture data utility [9, 10, 7]. Intuitively, groups that contain similar QID values (e.g. values with a small range or set size) are preferable, as less information loss is incurred when values are recoded or generalised this way. Finally, how well anonymised data supports an intended task such as aggregate query answering [8, 9, 11] or classification [12] can also be used to assess data utility. Being able to perform a task accurately using anonymised data implies that this data is useful to this specific task. We used three popular utility measures in our study: Discernability Measure (DM) [6] (based on group size), Utility Measure (UM) [7] (based on range size), and Relative Error (RE) [8] (based on support for task using aggregate query answering as an indicative application).

3   Utility Evaluation Based on Anonymised Data

Existing work on k-anonymisation measures utility of anonymised data largely by considering the data alone and without considering application-specific requirements. This may lead to unreliable assessment of utility in practice. In this section, we introduce three commonly-used utility measures and show that they may deliver inconsistent utility verdicts. In the following section, we analyse how different applications may affect the accuracy of these measures, and suggest how to use them effectively.

Definition 1 (Discernability Measure (DM) [6]). *Assume that T' is a k-anonymised table consisting of h groups $c_1, \ldots, c_h$ such that $|c_i| \geq k, i = 1, \ldots, h$, $\bigcap_{i=1}^{h} c_i = \emptyset$, $\bigcup_{i=1}^{h} c_i = T'$, and tuples of c_i have the same values in each QID. Discernability Measure of T' is defined as*

$$DM = \sum_{i=1}^{h} |c_i|^2$$

where $|c_i|$ denotes the size of group c_i.

Definition 2 (Utility Measure (UM) [7]). *Assume that T' is a k-anonymised table as defined in Definition 1 and has m QIDs, $a_1, \ldots, a_m$. Utility*

Measure *of T' is defined as*

$$UM = avg(\frac{1}{m} \times \sum_{i=1}^{m} qd(c_1.a_i), \ldots, \frac{1}{m} \times \sum_{i=1}^{m} qd(c_h.a_i))$$

where $c_j.a_i$ denotes the set of a_i values in group c_j and $qd(c_j.a_i)$ is calculated by

$$qd(c_j.a_i) = \begin{cases} \frac{max(c_j.a_i)-min(c_j.a_i)}{max(D_{a_i})-min(D_{a_i})} & \text{interval values} \\ \frac{s(c_j.a_i)}{|D_{a_i}|} & \text{discrete values} \end{cases}$$

where D_{a_i} is the domain of a_i, and $max(c_j.a_i)$, $min(c_j.a_i)$, $max(D_{a_i})$ and $min(D_{a_i})$ denote maximum and minimum values in $c_j.a_i$ and D_{a_i} respectively. If a hierarchy H exists for a_i, then $s(c_j.a_i)$ is the number of leaves of the subtree of H rooted at the closest common ancestor of the values in $c_j.a_i$. Otherwise, $s(c_j.a_i)$ is the number of distinct values in $c_j.a_i$. $|D_{a_i}|$ is the size of domain D_{a_i}.

Definition 3 (Relative Error (RE) [8]). *Assume a table T containing microdata, a k-anonymisation T' of T as defined in Definition 1, and COUNT(*) query q. Relative Error of T' is defined as*

$$RE = \frac{|\sum_{t\in T} p - \sum_{t'\in T'} p'|}{\sum_{t\in T} p}$$

where p is the probability of a tuple t in T being in the answer to q and p' is the probability of a tuple t' in T' being in the answer to q. The probability p is 1 when t is retrieved by q and 0 otherwise, while $p' = \frac{Rq\cap R}{R}$, where R_q and R denote the areas covered by q and the qualifying tuples in T', respectively, and $Rq \cap R$ denotes the overlap between R_q and R.

To illustrate these measures, consider Tables 1 and 2 below.

Table 2 consists of two groups of two tuples, so $DM = 2^2+2^2 = 8$. For UM the qd scores for the first and second group of Table 2 are $\frac{23-20}{27-20} = \frac{3}{7}$ and $\frac{27-25}{27-20} = \frac{2}{7}$ respectively. So $UM = \frac{\frac{3}{7}+\frac{2}{7}}{2} = \frac{5}{14}$. Finally, assume that our query is *count(*)* where *Age=25 and disease=HIV*. When q is applied on Table 1 the answer is 1,

Table 1. Original data

Table 2. A 2-anonymisation of Table 1

Age	Disease
20	HIV
23	Cancer
27	Obesity
25	HIV

Age	Disease
[20-23]	HIV
[20-23]	Cancer
[25-27]	Obesity
[25-27]	HIV

Table 3. Utility measures for the CENSUS dataset

	DM	UM	Avg RE	Max RE	StDev RE
Incognito	234166	0.553	0.65	1.10	0.28
Mondrian	293216	0.20	1.27	7.80	2.19
K-Members	200000	0.17	3.56	43.17	4.91

since only one tuple qualifies this query's predicates with a probability $p = 1$. When q is applied on Table 2, only the last tuple in the second group of this table qualifies q with a probability of $p' = \frac{1}{27-25+1} = \frac{1}{3}$ (since *Age* can be 25,26 or 27). Thus, the answer to q is $p' = \frac{1}{3}$, and the RE score for q is $\frac{|1-\frac{1}{3}|}{1} \approx 0.67$. This suggests that 67% less tuples are likely to be retrieved from Table 2 as answers to q, compared to the number of tuples that would have been retrieved if q was applied on Table 1.

To see how useful these utility measures are, we applied our three benchmark algorithms to the CENSUS dataset[1] [11, 13]. We configured this dataset as in [11] and fixed k to 2. The version of Incognito we used includes a (c, l)-diversity control which was configured to have c and l set to 2, and K-Members was configured to optimise UM. For query answering accuracy, we considered a workload of 10000 queries which retrieved random values uniformly from the domain of a random QID and the SA as in [11]. Table 3 shows the resultant DM, UM and RE scores.

As can be seen, these measures have not delivered consistent utility verdicts. For example, Incognito outperformed the other two methods w.r.t. RE, but appeared to be the worst according to UM; K-Members was the worst w.r.t. RE but was the best for DM and UM; and Mondrian had the worst DM, but its UM and RE scores were not the worst. Note that aggregate statistics based on RE [8, 11] may not capture utility accurately either, as they assume that the whole dataset is used in answering queries. Many applications often only need a small subset of the entire anonymised dataset to answer their queries, and unfortunately an algorithm which performs well on the whole dataset according to some aggregate RE statistics may perform poorly on its subsets.

4 Utility Evaluation Based on Application Scenarios

In this section, we investigate three interesting cases of COUNT(*) query of the form shown in Figure 2, where $q_i, i = 1, ..., m$ denotes a QID selected at random, r_i a randomly selected range of values from its domain, and u is a single value from the SA *Income*.

These three cases are constructed to study how well the utility measures will perform in some realistic application scenarios. First, we examine how query answering accuracy is dependent on QIDs by using a single QID in queries

---

[1] http:// www.ipums.org

```
select COUNT(*)
from anonymised table
where q₁ = r₁, ..., qₘ = rₘ and Income= u
```

Fig. 2. A COUNT(*) query

(e.g. how many individuals aged 23 earn more than 20K). We then study query answering accuracy for retrieved (subsets) of anonymised data, and we do so by considering queries that represent "rare" cases (e.g. how many individuals aged 20 earn more than 50K). These correspond to individuals whose demographic profile is not usual, which are expected in applications involving outlier detection, e.g. bank fraud detection or epidemiology research. Finally, we examine how dimensionality affects query answering accuracy by using queries involving different numbers of QIDs (e.g. how many single males aged 23 earn 30K).

4.1 Query Attribute Selection

To see how QID selection may affect query answering accuracy, consider the anonymised table given in Table 4. This table contains two QIDs *Age* and *Education* (number of years spent in school or university). Suppose that we have a query (q_1) similar to the one shown in Figure 2, which asks how many individuals aged below 24 earn 10K. q_1 can be accurately answered from the first group (the first two tuples) of Table 4. Now suppose that we have another query (q_2) asking how many individuals having *Education* = 5 earn 10K. The first group of Table 4 needs to be retrieved to answer q_2, but since values in *Education* are generalised to [0-9], one cannot be certain about how many individuals have exactly 5 years of education. Thus, the answer to q_2 may contain an error.

This suggests that query answering accuracy may depend on which QID is used. None of the measures discussed in Section 3 capture the impact of different QIDs on query answering accuracy. DM measures group size, which is the same for all QIDs. UM measures value ranges in a group, but does not consider how these ranges may be queried. For example, the *qd* scores (see Definition 2) for *Age* and *Education* for the first group in Table 4 are the same, i.e. $\frac{23-20}{27-20} = \frac{9-0}{21-0} = \frac{3}{7}$. Finally, RE derives an average score for the whole table [8,11] without examining specifically how different attributes used in queries may affect accuracy.

Table 4. A 2-anonymised table

Age	Education	Income
[20-23]	[0-9]	10K
[20-23]	[0-9]	10K
[25-27]	[13-21]	25K
[25-27]	[13-21]	30K

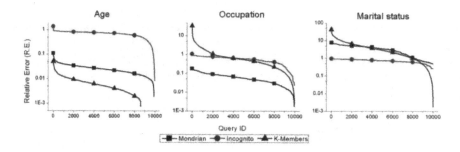

Fig. 3. The impact of attribute selection on query answering accuracy

In order to show the impact of QID selection on query answering accuracy, we report RE values for each query included in our workload. Figure 3 reports the result for queries asking the number of individuals that have a certain value in *Income* and whose *Age, Occupation* or *Marital status* falls in a randomly selected range [2]. For *Age*, a range refers to an interval covering 19% of its domain, while for other QIDs, a generalised value appearing on the first level of hierarchy (i.e. a generalised value closest to the original vales) was used [11].

As can be seen, query answering accuracy is heavily dependent on the selected QID. For instance, K-Members outperformed the other two methods by an order of magnitude when *Age* was used, but it did derive some groups with very poor utility when using *Occupation* or *Marital Status* in the queries. Interestingly, these groups were produced during the later iterations of K-Members algorithm, a result of its greedy strategy attempting to cluster the "good" tuples for utility in earlier iterations. In contrast, Mondrian outperformed others for queries involving *Occupation*. This is attributed to its partitioning strategy. The more often data is partitioned on a QID, the more useful data is w.r.t. this QID [14]. Furthermore, Incognito performed substantially better than the other two when *Marital Status* was used. This algorithm examines whether anonymity and (c, l)-diversity [4] hold for increasingly larger subsets of QIDs, and generates all possible generalisations that satisfy these requirements and are consistent with a type of single-dimensional global recoding called full-domain recoding. However, the choice of which of these generalisations should be released is left to the anonymiser. In our example, we chose the anonymisation with the best UM score, in which original values in *Marital status* were retained. Thus, this method performed well when queries involved this QID.

So, anonymisers should avoid "over" generalising QIDs that are more likely to be queried in applications. This may be achieved by using unsupervised feature selection. One approach is to specify *utility constraints* on QIDs before data grouping. For example, user preferences on utility of specific QIDs (e.g. based on RE scores) may be specified as constraints and solved using a skyline operator [15] before anonymisation. Alternatively, feature selection can be

---

[2] Due to space limitation, we do not report the results for *Education* and *Gender* here, which were qualitatively similar.

performed by anonymisers using *attribute weighting* or *split attribute selection*. For example, weights can be assigned to each QID when clustering data using K-Members, so that close values w.r.t. these attributes are preferred when forming clusters [9]. Similarly, anonymisers may specify how QIDs should be chosen for partitioning by Mondrian, thereby maximising the utility of more significant QIDs in anonymisation.

4.2   QID Value Selection

We first discuss how QID values used in query answering may influence the utility of anonymised data, by considering two different anonymisations of the same dataset, as shown in Figure 4, and a workload of 10 COUNT(*) queries, also shown in Figure 4. We also assume that the answer to every query when applied on the original dataset (not shown here) is 1. We now show how an answer can be estimated from anonymised data. Since all the values of *Income* in the anonymised tables satisfy the queries, the number of tuples satisfying *Education* $= r$, where r is a uniformly selected random value in [0-7], will determine the answers to the queries. Computing the RE score for Table A (see Section 2), we have $RE = \frac{|1-\frac{1}{3}|}{1} + \frac{|1-\frac{1}{5}|}{1} = \frac{22}{15}$. Similarly, we can compute the RE score for Table B, which is $\frac{22}{15}$ as well. Furthermore, Tables A and B have the same *DM* and *UM* scores, since the sum of squared size and average range for all groups are the same for these tables. Thus, these tables would be considered as equally useful when these measures are used.

Now assume that a user is interested in individuals having an *Education* level of 0, 1 or 2, i.e. $r \in [0,2]$. It is easy to calculate that RE scores for Tables A and B are now $\frac{2}{3}$ and $\frac{4}{5}$ respectively, implying that Table A is more useful for this user's task. Similarly, if another user is interested in $r \in [5-7]$, the RE scores for Tables A and B will be $\frac{4}{5}$ and $\frac{2}{3}$ respectively and Table B becomes more useful in this case.

To test the effect of querying different QID values on utility, we considered a workload containing two types of query. The first involves queries that retrieve any value in the domain of a QID and SA. These queries were generated by

Educ.	Income
[0-2]	10
[0-2]	10
[0-2]	12
[3-7]	15
[3-7]	20
[3-7]	17
[3-7]	40
[3-7]	30

Table A

Educ.	Income
[0-4]	10
[0-4]	10
[0-4]	12
[0-4]	15
[0-4]	20
[5-7]	17
[5-7]	40
[5-7]	30

Table B

select COUNT(*)
from anonymised table
where *Education* $= r$ and
Income between 10 and 40

COUNT(*) query

Fig. 4. Example anonymisations and query

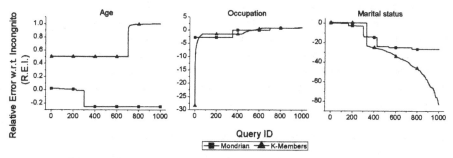

Fig. 5. The impact of value selection on query answering

randomly selected queries from the workload considered in Section 4.1. Queries of the second type retrieve some "rare" cases, i.e. a pair of QID and SA values having a very low occurrence frequency in the table. Our workload contained 30% and 70% of each type of query respectively.

We configured all the methods as in Section 3. Since Incognito is less affected by which values are queried (due to its full domain single dimensional global recoding [5]), we treat it as a baseline method and measure the RE of the other two methods relative to Incognito's. That is, we derive R.E.I. (Relative Error to Incognito) by replacing p (the probability of finding a tuple that satisfies q using the original data) by p_I (the corresponding probability using the data anonymised by Incognito) in Definition 3 and normalising it by p_I, i.e. $REI = \frac{|\sum_{t' \in T'} p_I - \sum_{t' \in T'} p'|}{\sum_{t' \in T'} p_I}$. Figure 5 reports the R.E.I. scores for queries constructed according to the form given in Figure 2, which involved *Age*, *Occupation* or *Marital status* as a QID and *Income*. Queries of the first type have IDs in [0,300) in Figure 2, while those of the second type have IDs in [300-1000).

Comparing Figures 5 and 3, it is clear that the utility of anonymisations produced by these algorithms may vary according to value selection in queries. Mondrian was worse than Incognito (i.e. the R.E.I. scores for Mondrian were negative) for queries of the second type. This is because Mondrian splits data along the median of QIDs, and thus the utility of anonymised data is substantially affected by outliers [14]. In contrast, the relative performance of K-Members w.r.t. Incognito was not significantly affected by the type of query used, since the negative R.E.I. scores for K-Members shown in Figure 5 correspond to queries for which K-Members performed poorly in the experiment of Section 4.1. This is attributed to the furthest-first seed selection strategy employed by K-Members, which makes this algorithm relatively insensitive to outliers [14].

In general, users will want to obtain QID values from anonymised data as accurately as possible. Neither DM or UM measures takes this requirement into account. Some collaboration between users and anonymisers may help address this issue. That is, a user can provide anonymisers with a sample of the queries he intends to use. This will enable anonymisers to know which QID values are more important and tune anonymisation methods to minimally generalise them. LeFevre et al. have considered this approach for simple selection queries [16].

However, it may not be feasible for users to disclose their queries due to privacy concerns. For instance, an advertising company using a location-based service may be unwilling to reveal its queries to the company providing the service. In this case, knowledge about how QID values will be queried can be incorporated in anonymisation by constructing "optimal" generalisation hierarchies. Such hierarchies can be constructed by anonymisers, either manually or automatically [17], or given by users.

4.3   The Impact of Dimensionality on Query Answering

So far we have studied queries that involve one QID and one SA. However, queries involving more QIDs are common in many applications, for example, building datacubes for OLAP tasks. Therefore, we examined how the number of QIDs involved in queries (QID dimensionality) can affect query answering accuracy. Aggarwal [18] has already shown that k-anonymisation is difficult to achieve without fully generalising data in high-dimensional datasets (i.e. when there are more than 10 QIDs). We show that even when k-anonymisation is achieved, anonymised data may not allow accurate aggregate query answering due to a large amount of information loss incurred.

We first note that DM is insensitive to changes in QID dimensionality, since it is based on group size. UM refers to the average group range across QIDs (see Definition 2), thus it takes QID dimensionality into account. Figure 6 confirms that UM scores can vary with various dimensionalities. For this experiment, we used the same settings as in Section 4.1.

We first formally show that query answering accuracy as captured by RE measure may improve when QID dimensionality increases when certain conditions are met, as explained in Theorem 1.

Theorem 1. *Given a table T, a k-anonymisation T' of T and two workloads $W = \{q_1, \ldots, q_l\}$ and $W' = \{q'_1, \ldots, q'_l\}$ comprised of l COUNT(*) queries s.t. $q'_i \in W'$ has the same predicates as $q_i \in W$ and an additional QID predicate, we have that $ARE(W') \leq ARE(W)$ when i) q'_i and q_i retrieve exactly the*

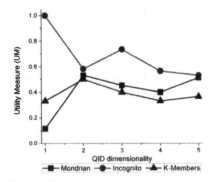

Fig. 6. UM scores w.r.t. dimensionality

same tuples and ii) q_i' retrieves less tuples when applied on T than on T', where $ARE(W')$ and $ARE(W)$ denote the average RE scores for T' and all queries in W' and W respectively.

Proof. The proof has been omitted for space reasons.

The result in Figure 6 w.r.t. UM may not confirm Theorem 1, as when QID dimensionality increases from 1 to 2 in Figure 6 for Mondrian, for example. The reason is that an increase in QID dimensionality often results in a decrease in query selectivity. Consequently, queries retrieve a large number of tuples with fairly small probabilities when applied on anonymised data. This makes it hard to answer such queries accurately from anonymised data, thereby resulting in relatively large ARE scores.

To investigate the behaviour of RE w.r.t. dimensionality, we computed RE statistics for a workload of 10000 queries, involving an increasingly larger subset of QIDs. Figure 7 illustrates the results for this experiment, using the same anonymisations as those in Section 4.1.

As can be seen, an increase in QID dimensionality does not necessarily decrease utility, although the general trend is that RE scores increase. In fact, the average RE score was five times larger when QID dimensionality increased from 1 to 5, while the increase in maximum and the standard deviation of RE scores was even larger. This is because increasing QID dimensionality in a query tends to decrease selectivity, making it hard to answer queries accurately using anonymised data.

This experiment suggests that it may be difficult to answer queries involving multiple QIDs and detailed values from anonymised data accurately. In response, Xiao and Tao [13] and Koudas et al. [19] proposed techniques which work by retaining original values in all QIDs, while achieving protection by limiting the way SA values are grouped. Since QID values are not generalised, these techniques are not affected by QID dimensionality. However, releasing original QID values helps an attacker in learning whether an individual is present in an anonymised dataset [13]. Thus, such techniques are only applicable when this type of inference does not constitute a privacy threat. An alternative is to develop methods

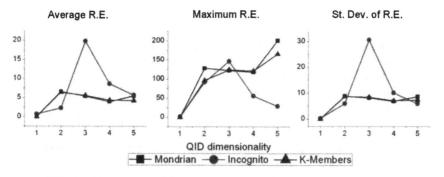

Fig. 7. The impact of QID dimensionality on query answering

that control the amount of information loss to be incurred by generalisation on each QID, as discussed in Section 4.1. For example, dimensionality reduction techniques can be used to ensure that the utility of the most "informative" QIDs is sufficiently preserved in anonymised data.

5   Conclusion

An increasing number of applications need to use microdata which for privacy concerns must be anonymised. While it is crucial to preserve privacy in anonymised data, ensuring that data is still useful for intended applications is equally important. Several measures have been proposed to capture utility of anonymised data produced k-anonymisation methods. In this paper, we have shown through extensive experiments that commonly used measures fail to capture utility consistently when specific workloads are considered. Based on our analysis, we suggested how to increase data utility by taking additional steps in anonymisation. We are currently working towards specific anonymisation techniques that take user requirements into account.

References

1. Gedik, B., Liu, L.: Location privacy in mobile systems: A personalized anonymization model. In: ICDCS 2005, pp. 620–629 (2005)
2. Sweeney, L.: k-anonymity: a model for protecting privacy. International Journal on Uncertainty, Fuzziness and Knowledge-based Systems 10, 557–570 (2002)
3. Zhang, N., Zhao, W.: Privacy-preserving data-mining systems. IEEE Computer 40, 52–58 (2007)
4. Machanavajjhala, A., Gehrke, J., Kifer, D., Venkitasubramaniam, M.: l-diversity: Privacy beyond k-anonymity. In: ICDE 2006, p. 24 (2006)
5. LeFevre, K., DeWitt, D., Ramakrishnan, R.: Incognito: efficient full-domain k-anonymity. In: SIGMOD 2005, pp. 49–60 (2005)
6. Bayardo, R., Agrawal, R.: Data privacy through optimal k-anonymization. In: ICDE 2005, pp. 217–228 (2005)
7. Loukides, G., Shao, J.: Capturing data usefulness and privacy protection in k-anonymisation. In: SAC 2007, pp. 370–374 (2007)
8. LeFevre, K., DeWitt, D., Ramakrishnan, R.: Mondrian multidimensional k-anonymity. In: ICDE 2006, p. 25 (2006)
9. Xu, J., Wang, W., Pei, J., Wang, X., Shi, B., Fu, A.W.C.: Utility-based anonymization using local recoding. In: KDD 2006, pp. 785–790 (2006)
10. Byun, J., Kamra, A., Bertino, E., Li, N.: Efficient k-anonymity using clustering technique. In: Kotagiri, R., Radha Krishna, P., Mohania, M., Nantajeewarawat, E. (eds.) DASFAA 2007. LNCS, vol. 4443, pp. 188–200. Springer, Heidelberg (2007)
11. Xiao, X., Tao, Y.: Personalized privacy preservation. In: SIGMOD 2006, pp. 229–240 (2006)
12. Fung, B.C.M., Wang, K., Yu, P.S.: Top-down specialization for information and privacy preservation. In: ICDE 2005, pp. 205–216 (2005)
13. Xiao, X., Tao, Y.: Anatomy: simple and effective privacy preservation. In: VLDB 2006, pp. 139–150 (2006)

14. Loukides, G., Shao, J.: Clustering-based k-anonymisation algorithms. In: Wagner, R., Revell, N., Pernul, G. (eds.) DEXA 2007. LNCS, vol. 4653, pp. 761–771. Springer, Heidelberg (2007)
15. Börzsönyi, S., Kossmann, D., Stocker, K.: The skyline operator. In: ICDE 2001, pp. 421–430 (2001)
16. LeFevre, K., DeWitt, D., Ramakrishnan, R.: Workload-aware anonymization. In: KDD 2006, pp. 277–286 (2006)
17. Tang, L., Zhang, J., Liu, H.: Acclimatizing taxonomic semantics for hierarchical content classification from semantics to data-driven taxonomy. In: KDD 2006, pp. 384–393 (2006)
18. Aggarwal, C.C.: On k-anonymity and the curse of dimensionality. In: VLDB 2005, pp. 901–909 (2005)
19. Koudas, N., Zhang, Q., Srivastava, D., Yu, T.: Aggregate query answering on anonymized tables. In: ICDE 2007, pp. 116–125 (2007)

HLS: Tunable Mining of Approximate Functional Dependencies

Jeremy T. Engle and Edward L. Robertson

Department of Computer Science, Indiana University, Bloomington, IN 47405 USA
{jtengle,edrbtsn}@cs.indiana.edu

Abstract. This paper examines algorithmic aspects of searching for approximate functional dependencies in a database relation. The goal is to avoid exploration of large parts of the space of potential rules. This is accomplished by leveraging found rules to make finding other rules more efficient. The overall strategy is an attribute-at-a-time iteration which uses local breadth first searches on lattices that increase in width and height in each iteration. The resulting algorithm provides many opportunities to apply heuristics to tune the search for particular data-sets and/or search objectives. The search can be tuned at both the global iteration level and the local search level. A number of heuristics are developed and compared experimentally.

1 Introduction

There has been a growing range of applications of Approximate Functional Dependencies (AFDs)[1] and thus there is a growing need for an AFD-mining framework that can be tailored for different applications. Such tailoring should take into account information about a dataset in order to tune search performance and should also tune search in terms of the nature of the rules mined. These two considerations led to the development of the Heuristic Lozenge Search (HLS) framework, presented in this paper. This framework is not itself heuristic but it enables incorporation of heuristics to provide the suggested tunings.

Algorithms for mining AFDs face two dominant costs: the combinatoric cost of searching the rule space and the cost of visiting the data to calculate the approximate value of rules. This paper will focus on the first of these; the second will be reported on in a later paper, as this cost is very sensitive to the way approximateness is measured.

The first dominant cost factor, which many mining problems share, is the combinatoric complexity of searching a space related to the power set lattice of some underlying set, the set of attributes in the case of AFDs [11]. Frameworks use a variety of tools from constraint pruning to sampling in an effort to reduce the combinatoric cost. At the core of most frameworks are traditional algorithms like

---

[1] As its name suggests, an AFD is a rule similar to a traditional Functional Dependency (FD) except that the universal requirement of the FD is relaxed. The details of this relaxation will be covered when measures of approximation are introduced.

A. Gray, K. Jeffery, and J. Shao (Eds.): BNCOD 2008, LNCS 5071, pp. 28–39, 2008.

Breadth First Search (BFS) or Depth First Search (DFS). We instead propose an attribute-at-a-time iterative algorithm which provides efficiency and tunability.

Section 3 discusses other AFD mining algorithms and AFD applications. Section 2 explains the conventions and definitions used in the paper. Section 4 defines a lozenge, motivates Lozenge Search, and gives the generalized Lozenge Search algorithm. Section 5 discusses how heuristics are used to make decisions in HLS. Section 6 discusses the experimental results, comparing the performance of HLS to two variations of BFS.

2   Definitions and Conventions

Through out the paper we will use the following conventions.

- R is a relation schema and r is an instance of R.
- $A, B, C, \cdots$ are individual attributes of R.
- $X, Y, Z, \cdots$ are sets of attributes.
- XY means $X \cup Y$.
- $X \rightarrow Y$ is a rule, a pair of subsets of R.

Definition 1. $X \rightarrow A$ *is a* parent *of* $W \rightarrow A$ *when* $W \subset X$ *and* $|X| = |W|+1$. *Additionally* child, descendant, *and* ancestor *have their usual interpretation with respect to* parent.

Historically, an FD has more often been a declarative constraint applied to R, in that an r that did not satisfy the constraint condition was considered, in some sense, invalid. However, we are concerned with the situation where FD's and their approximations are to be discovered in a particular instance r.

The definition of FD's is absolute, in that $X \rightarrow Y$ fails to hold in an instance of r if there are two tuples in r that violate the condition. Real datasets, however, often have situations where an FD "almost holds", in that only a few violators exist, and discovering such situations has substantial value. This leads to the notion of *Approximate Functional Dependency* (AFD) and the question "How approximate?" Answering this question requires an *approximation measure*.

Definition 2. *An* approximation measure *is a function from two attribute sets,* X *and* Y, *to* $[0, 1]$, *written* $\varphi(X \rightarrow Y)$, *such that*

(a) $\varphi(X \rightarrow Y) = 0$ *iff the FD* $X \rightarrow Y$ *holds,*
(b) $\varphi(X \rightarrow Y) = 1$ *iff* X *has a single value and* Y *is a key for the dataset,*
(c) $Y \subset Z \Rightarrow \varphi(X \rightarrow Y) \leq \varphi(X \rightarrow Z)$,
(d) $X \subset W \Rightarrow \varphi(X \rightarrow Y) \geq \varphi(W \rightarrow Z)$, *and*
(e) $\varphi(X)$ *is defined as* $\varphi(C \rightarrow X)$ *where* C *has a single value.*

For the rest of this paper, we will use the information dependency measure InD [3]. InD is defined so that $InD(X \rightarrow Y) = \mathcal{H}_{XY} - \mathcal{H}_X$ [3], where $\mathcal{H}$ is Shannon's entropy [14] measure as manifest in a database relation. As defined, InD is unnormalized; normalization is achieved so that $\varphi(X \rightarrow Y) = \frac{\mathcal{H}_{XY} - \mathcal{H}_X}{\mathcal{H}_r}$.

Armstrong's Axioms [13], imply that $X \to Y$ and $X \to Z$ iff $X \to YZ$ and hence it is sufficient to consider only single attribute RHSs when dealing with FDs. This same property does not hold when dealing with AFDs [3]. None the less, we limit our interest in the remainder of this paper to RHS's with single attributes. Additionally, transitivity only holds with respect to bounds that are known for a specific φ. As a result we search for all *minP* rules instead of a minimal cover. The search is then not for FDs, but AFDs that are "close enough" according to a threshold, ϵ, and an instance r which is an implicit parameter.

Definition 3. $X \to C$ *is a* minimal pass rule *(written minP) provided that* $\varphi(X \to C) \leq \epsilon$ *and for all* Y, $Y \subset X$, $\varphi(Y \to C) \leq \epsilon$ *does not hold.*

Definition 4. $X \to C$ *is a* maximal fail rule *with respect to* Z *(maxF(Z)) provided that* $\varphi(X \to C) > \epsilon$ *and for no* Y, $X \subset Y \subseteq Z$, $\varphi(Y \to C) > \epsilon$. *The context* Z *is omitted if it is in fact all attributes.*

The terms lattice and sublattice imply that all rules share the same RHS attribute and there is some rule $X \to A$, $X \subseteq \boldsymbol{R} - A$ which is the ultimate ancestor of all rules in the lattice/sublattice. A ragged sublattice[2] is a space defined by a set of sub-maximal rules (boundary point rules) and all of their descendants. The pruning of *minP* rule ancestors requires that the approximation measure be monotone. How close an AFD is to perfect generally relies on the interaction between the rule's LHS and RHS. The closer a LHS or RHS grows to an approximate key or constant the greater it alone can impact the rule's entropy.

Observation 1. *In an arbitrary* r, *there are the following tendencies[3]:*

- *The closer a LHS is to a key, the better its ability to predict any RHS.*
- *The closer a RHS is to a constant, the better any LHS will predict it.*
- *The closer a RHS is to a key, the harder it is for a LHS to predict it.*
- *When augmenting a LHS with an attribute, the closer that attribute is to a constant the less it will improve the LHS's ability to predict the RHS.*
- *With keys on the LHS or constants on the RHS, rules have shorter LHSs.*
- *With keys on the RHS or constants on the LHS, rules have longer LHSs.*

3   Related Work

AFD work can loosely be categorized as analysis of measures, algorithms for AFD mining, and use of AFD's to facilitate some task. HLS does not analyze measures as it is independent of a specific choice. Measures applicable for AFD mining come from a wide range of domains [6,10,7].

While there has been significant work on AFD mining frameworks, there have been few unique algorithms. The CORDS framework [9] was developed for the

---

[2] Not a true sublattice because join may not be defined.

[3] These tendencies are based on probability theory, however without knowing the behavior of a specific φ, they can not be expressed more precisely.

specific purpose of using rules in query optimization. Because of this, the CORDS system only mines rules with a single attribute on the LHS and RHS. Additionally, it uses techniques such as sampling and is not concerned with the soundness or completeness of its search because rules are merely a means not an end. There is also work with frameworks developed in SQL to take advantage of the pervasiveness of SQL. This approach was originally proposed by Bell *et al.* [1] for FDs and then adapted for AFDs [12]. A unique aspect was that Bell recognized the advantage of creating a lattice for each attribute on the RHS. We refer to this lattice approach as *fixed RHS*. The most popular algorithm is the TANE [8] algorithm, whose primary focus is efficiency both in the algorithm and the measure it uses, G_3. TANE groups all lattices into a single space irrespective of what attribute is on the RHS, which we refer to as a *single space* approach. These algorithms differ slightly in motivations, but all share the same bottom-up BFS search approach and address efficiency by adding constraints and using techniques such as sampling.

The frameworks above leave a void in the field for an efficiency approach as in TANE, which also addresses a domain task as in CORDS. By approaching efficiency through a new algorithm, we can add savings to a base algorithm which combines constraints, heuristics, and efficiency techniques; to reach new levels of efficiency. Additionally, HLS's iterative approach allows techniques otherwise requiring pre/post processing to be incorporated into the algorithm itself. The use of AFDs has been growing and diversifying. As novel uses for AFDs are developed a mining framework's flexibility must also grow. Similar to CORDS, Horizontal-Vertical Decomposition [5] uses AFDs for query optimization, though how AFDs are found is not discussed. One of the new uses is for data cleaning [2]. Another usage of AFDs is for query answering as in the the QPIAD [15] system. Wolfe *et al.* when discussing QPIAD specifically mentions pruning AFDs which have dataset keys on the LHS as a post processing step to their use of TANE. No other system has the flexibility of HLS to address the needs of different domains for which AFDs are used without having to alter their algorithms or add pre/post processing steps.

4   Searching Lozenges

The use of learned information to improve performance is a common technique in machine learning. HLS uses statistical information to guide search, but also leverages *minP* rules as an information source. The main iteration of HLS is over a sequence of lozenges. The iteration order may be fixed or dynamically determined during execution.

4.1   Characteristics of Lozenge Search

A variety of factors are woven into HLS. Some of these may be explicitly implemented, others only suggest heuristics. In no particular order:

- The global order in which attributes are considered can impact how the search is done, to improve performance, produce interesting rules first, and facilitate top-k search.
- The ordering and pruning of attributes can be determined dynamically.
- Decisions about search strategies can be made per lozenge or per lattice.
- `searchStrategy` as a pluggable component allows new search algorithms to be developed without altering the framework.
- As the size of lattices grow, so does the information for making decisions.
- *minP* rules are used to seed later lattices, thus pruning their ancestors.
- Searching a lozenge is sound and complete with respect to the attributes defining that lozenge.

4.2   Composition of a Lozenge

HLS works on the premise that more decisions on a smaller scale are preferable, lessening the impact of incorrect decisions. A lozenge is best thought of as a space which includes multiple lattices that are all related but separate.

A lozenge is characterized by the set of all attributes seen, `act`, and an individual attribute, `new`. The *active lozenge* or *lozenge* is composed of two categories of lattices.

(1) The lattice with `act` $\rightarrow$ `new` as the maximal rule
(2) Lattices with maximal rules $(\texttt{act} - A)\texttt{new} \rightarrow A$ where $A \in \texttt{act}$

These points describe the space for each lozenge, but in reality varying portions of the lattices with `new` on the LHS will be pruned by *minP* rules found in previous lozenges. Also, only rules where `new` $\in$ LHS are searched in the lattices defined by (2) above.

4.3   Seeding Search with *maxF* Rules

The boundary formed by *minP* and *maxF* rules provides starting points in searching for further rules. In order to do this, the `carryForward` list stores *maxF* rules. Because each lozenge adds an attribute to the space, the Z used in the definition of *maxF* grows with each iteration. This means that newly found *maxF* rules can potentially supersede rules on the `carryForward`. The lattices with `new` on the LHS are seeded by augmenting each rule on `carryForward` with `new`. We refer to these augmented rules as boundary point rules. The space searched in a lattice is a ragged sublattice which consists of the descendants of the set of boundary point rules. The hope is that by using Observation 1 we can minimize the space between boundary point rules and *minP* rules.

5   Implementation

HLS is independent of how decisions are made. In this section we will discuss how decisions are incorporated in HLS, and potential heuristics for these decisions.

5.1 Pseudocode

```
1   pick attribute as new for each in R
2       for ''X → A'' in carryForward
3           add ''X∪ new → A'' to queue
4       add ''act → new '' to queue
5       evaluateLozenge(queue)
6       add new to act

7   evaluateLozenge(queue)
8       pop first rule on queue until empty
9           if rule is minP, write to result set
10          else if rule is maxF, place on carryForward
11          else add new rules to queue using searchStrategy
```

5.2 Lozenge Ordering

The order in which lozenges are evaluated determines much about the behavior of an HLS search. This is the outer iteration and is governed by the order in which new is chosen seen in Line 1. Possible orderings include Coreness, which selects the next attribute A with the minimal value for $|median\{\varphi(B) : B \in \mathbf{R}\} - \varphi(A)|$, and Keyness, which selects an A with maximal $\varphi(A)$. The Coreness order generalizes pruning keys and constants by pushing them to the end of the search. Keyness uses Observation 1 to minimize the space between boundary point rules and $minP$ rules. Note that when φ is based on InD, Keyness chooses attributes in order of decreasing entropy. A future ordering, Differentness, would pick the next attribute which is "most different" from some standard. Orderings can be determined dynamically on a lozenge by lozenge basis. Further, dynamic decisions can entail attribute pruning and accomplishing top-k search (more work is required to characterize how the framework communicates the state of the search to such a dynamic order evaluator).

5.3 Lozenge Search Strategies

Like the global picking of attributes, HLS does not specify the mechanism for searching a lattice. The queue is a priority queue, so that the choice of a priority function determines how a lattice is evaluated (for example, prioritizing by RHS would yeild search by lattice). The enqueing operation (lines 3, 4, and 11) also adds certain state information which can be used in priority functions, can be used by the searchStrategy to determine whether parent or children rules should be generated, and is used to prevent re-evaluation of rules. As long as a searchStrategy ultimately explores all children or parents, either explicitly or by inference, the overall HLS search is sound and complete.

Deciding how to search entails picking a search strategy – say BFS, which could be done either top-down or bottom-up. To implement top-down BFS, line 11 would enqueue all children of the current rule. To implement bottom-up BFS, line 11 would distinguish rules placed on `queue` in lines 3 and 4, in that case jumping to the bottom of the lattice to enqueue new rules `new` $\rightarrow$ A in the case of line 3 and $B \rightarrow$ `new`, $B \in$ `act` in the case of line 4. This means that the effective starting point for a search is at the bottom of the lattice. Line 11 would than enqueue parents of the current rule. Note that distinct lattices could use distinct strategies. More sophisticated search strategies could jump around a sublattice, doing more inference and less explicit evaluation; we are evaluating some such strategies and will develop others in the future. Experimental results for top-down versus bottom-up are explored in Section 6.5.

6   Experimentation

Experiments were run on four datasets from the Illinois Semantic Integration archive [4] and one artificial dataset (LowInfo). Specifically, the four university course datasets from Reed, UWM, Washington, and WSU were used. The attributes in all four datasets are fairly evenly distributed over the zero to one entropy range. WSU is slightly larger with 16 attributes while Reed, UMW, Washington, and LowInfo all have eleven or twelve attributes. The LowInfo dataset has one strong approximate key attribute and all others are strong approximate constants. The *single space*, *fixed RHS*, and HLS algorithms were run and each was done with top-down and bottom-up variants. The lozenge orderings used were Coreness, Keyness, and a Random ordering developed as a control.

6.1   Statistics

We use five statistics to discuss the results:

1. The maximum number of rules in `queue` at any one time (`maxQueueSize`)
2. The number of rules that the search visits (`numRulesVisited`)
3. The number of attribute sets evaluated (`numSetsEval`, specific to InD)
4. The average length of the LHS for $minP$ rules (`avgLHS`)
5. A improves B is the percentage for a statistic that A improves B

As stated in Section 2, InD allows reuse of known attribute set entropies, which means that even when the `numRulesVisited` differ dramatically between search variants the `numSetsEval` may not. If the measure used does not reuse entropies or we did not cache attribute set entropies, the `numRulesVisited` would represent the cost of the search. Though caching does save evaluations, there is an obvious space/time trade off.

6.2   Memory Usage

The size of `queue` is the dominant cost in the space complexity. We assume that each item on `queue` is a fixed size in memory and then analyze `maxQueueSize` values to look at the "bulge".

The experimental results in general followed the expected results. *Fixed RHS* was considerable better than *single space*. However, HLS not only compares but

Table 1. maxQueueSize values for bottom-up variant

Dataset	*single space*	*fixed RHS*	HLS Keyness	HLS Keyness improves *fixed RHS*
Reed	1383	388	147	62.1%
UWM	1484	358	191	46.6%
Washington	786	225	102	54.7%
WSU	13116	5245	1137	78.3%
LowInfo	2772	336	1128	-236.7%

improves over *fixed RHS*, except in the case of LowInfo which is discussed in the next section.

The LowInfo dataset displayed an aberration from these results. It showed similar improvement for *single space* to *fixed RHS*, but actually worsened from *fixed RHS* to HLS. The first factor to consider is that LowInfo was artificially created so that a large number of attributes would be needed on the LHS for a *minP* rule to occur. Thus less pruning will occur and in later lozenges the widest levels of lattices are potentially being search. The combined width of these lattices could approach the width of *single space*. The second but dominant factor is related to the discussion in Section 5.3. HLS as tested prioritizes rules by cardinality of a LHS and then the RHS. This means that we explore levels with the same cardinality across all lattices. Searching a lattice at a time would avoid this problem.

6.3 Computational Efficiency: *fixed RHS* Vs. HLS

Single space and *fixed RHS* have the same computation costs so we limit the discussion to experiments for *fixed RHS* and HLS. For all HLS results, Keyness and bottom-up search were used unless otherwise stated.

Table 2 shows that HLS Keyness compares favorably with *fixed RHS* in terms of numRulesVisited. Though in the Reed and Washington datasets, HLS performed worse, the difference was minimal. All three datasets which showed improvement also had a larger avgLHS. It is only once rules reach a cardinality of 3 that entering a ragged sublattice could provide a savings over bottom-up search. UWM's avgLHS increases slightly over Reed and Washington and we see UWM performing slightly better over *fixed RHS*, while Reed and Washington performed slightly worse than *fixed RHS*. Both WSU and LowInfo have higher

Table 2. Number of Rules Visited with Bottom-up Search

Dataset	avgLHS	*fixed RHS*	HLS			HLS Keyness
			Keyness	Random	Coreness	improves *fixed RHS*
Reed	2.51	1178	1260	1858	2770	-7.0%
UWM	2.71	1275	1155	2369	3421	9.4%
Washington	2.49	664	704	1275	3901	-6.0%
WSU	3.6	14074	8457	24890	27581	39.9%
LowInfo	5.98	5682	3796	3792	8408	33.2%

Table 3. Number of Rules Visited with Top-down Search

Dataset	fixed RHS	HLS Keyness	HLS Keyness improves fixed RHS
Reed	27391	6633	75.8%
UWM	27691	5272	81.0%
Washington	12813	2829	77.9%
WSU	558882	74282	86.7%
LowInfo	12396	5191	58.1%

avgLHS values and we see marked savings between HLS Keyness and *fixed RHS*. This supports the hypothesis that using starting point to find later rules can improve efficiency.

The comparative results between datasets for numSetsEval are similar to those for numRulesVisited. The fact that HLS is evaluating fewer attribute sets means that those attribute sets and the rules that use them are never visited in any part of HLS. This indicates that HLS finds a different and more efficient path to *minP* rules compared to *fixed RHS*.

Though top-down searches cost more than bottom-up ones, comparing top-down *fixed RHS* and top-down HLS is interesting because they are both doing pure top-down searches, whereas a bottom-up HLS is forced to do some ragged sublattices as top-down. We see in Table 3 that the numRulesVisited with top-down search is significantly better using HLS Keyness compared to *fixed RHS*. The numRulesVisited is explained by the fact that using carryForward allows the search to enter lattices some place other than the top, which provides the improved performance over *fixed RHS*. Though we do not show the numSetsEval results for sake of brevity, there is little savings between *fixed RHS* and HLS Keyness. This is because the lattices with new as the RHS are searched almost completely, meaning that most attribute sets are evaluated.

6.4   Impact of Lozenge Ordering

It is clear that ordering affects efficiency as can be seen in Table 2. We only discuss the numRulesVisited for the different heuristics, because numSetsEval results are similar. The differences in numRulesVisited can be explained by how well the heuristics minimize the space between boundary point and *minP* rules and how closely new adheres to the second tendency in Observation 1. Keyness incorporates both of these techniques, which is why it performs significantly better than the Coreness and Random heuristics. These results show how the order of attributes can effect search efficiency and that even simple heuristics can provide significant savings. It also makes clear that in order for semantic-oriented heuristics to be efficient good decision heuristics and the ability to do bottom-up searches on lattices initialized from carryForward are needed.

6.5   Top-Down vs. Bottom-Up

Though datasets exist where a top-down search would be more efficient, bottom-up predominantly is more efficient. Below we present a portion of the results from

Table 4. Top-down vs Bottom-up comparison on LowInfo using HLS Coreness

Attribute		3		8		10		11	
Entropy		.1137		.1137		.1137		.6662	
Side of rules with **new**		LHS	RHS	LHS	RHS	LHS	RHS	LHS	RHS
`numSetsEval`	Top-down	63	1	147	16	252	130	847	55
	Bottom-up	63	64	154	93	336	130	847	228
`numRulesVisited`	Top-down	189	36	616	121	1638	340	3820	66
	Bottom-up	189	127	616	247	1638	466	3820	1023

the LowInfo dataset. LowInfo is an artificial dataset specifically created to test what happens when the `avgLHS` $\approx \frac{|R|}{2}$. The LHS and RHS columns correspond to lattices where **new** is on the LHS or RHS. We separate them because as stated the effects of an attribute are different depending on the side of the rule on which it appears.

Though LowInfo is an artificial case, its attributes' distributions are conceivable in real datasets. Additionally, since semantic orderings might come up with any ordering, an inefficient ordering is also conceivable. The results shown in Table 4 are the last four lozenges for the dataset. Having an approximate key as **new** for the last lozenge is potentially a worst case scenario in HLS with bottom-up search. We see this with attribute 11. With bottom-up HLS search the lattice with **new** on the RHS is searched bottom-up, and ragged sublattices with **new** on the LHS are searched in a top-down manner. Guided by Observation 1, we see an approximate key emphisizes the tendencies which push *minP* rules farther away from these starting points. Added to this is that in the last lozenge the space is the largest of any lozenge. In the case of attribute 11, the `avgLHS` when it is on the RHS is 9, which explains why top-down searching proves more efficient. We see that results for the approximate constants do not as closely follow what would be expected given Observation 1. Specifically, top-down searching out performs bottom-up even with an approximate constant on the RHS. This is explained by the fact that every attribute on the LHS is also an approximate constant, and that LowInfo was specifically designed so that the approximate constants would not easily determine each other. It is important to recall that the LHS portion of a lozenge potentially contains a lattice for each attribute in **act**, whereas the RHS portion is only a single lattice, which accounts for the differences in scale. Though in this example always picking top-down would lead to the optimal efficiency in terms of decisions, it is more likely in real datasets that some combination of top-down and bottom-up searches will lead to the optimal set of decisions.

7   Conclusion

HLS shows that search can be improved by using information about a dataset. We also showed how HLS could incorporate techniques like attribute analysis, typically done with preprocessing, as a search feature and allow decisions to be dynamic. Additionally, searching the top-k lozenges is done in a sound and complete way, where k can result from a decision process instead of a predetermined constant. Designed to move away from the idea that search is uniform, HLS provides a framework into which domain specific modules can be plugged, in order to adapt search to meet user requirements. Even with simple heuristics HLS showed strong comparative performance.

A number of variations to HLS will potentially improve efficiency and make that efficiency more robust, but reaching this potential will require further work. In particular, a better search strategy has potential for greatly improving performance when semantic-oriented orderings such as Coreness are used. We demonstrated how HLS can improve space complexity even over *fixed RHS*, but scenarios remain which must be addressed. HLS also allows new optimizations for evaluating approximation measures based on using act instead of R. We demonstrated how Keyness could make HLS competitive, and we saw that when using semantic oriented heuristics efficiency was a concern. To improve search we can develop starting point decision heuristics, the ability to make starting point decisions for ragged sublattices, and continue to explore orderings which could maximize efficiency. Lastly, constraints and efficiency techniques from other AFD mining systems could be adapted for HLS.

Acknowledgement

We would like to thank Catharine Wyss for discussions concerning the pruning of key or constant attributes and the need for a generalized approach.

References

1. Bell, S., Brockhausen, P.: Discovery of constraints and data dependencies in databases (extended abstract). In: European Conference on Machine Learning, pp. 267–270 (1995)
2. Bohannon, P., Fan, W., Geerts, F., Jia, X., Kementsietsidis, A.: Conditional functional dependencies for data cleaning. In: ICDE, pp. 746–755. IEEE, Los Alamitos (2007)
3. Dalkilic, M.M., Robertson, E.L.: Information dependencies. In: PODS, pp. 245–253 (2000)
4. Doan, A.: Illinois semantic integration archive, http://pages.cs.wisc.edu/~anhai/wisc-si-archive/
5. Giannella, C., Dalkilic, M., Groth, D., Robertson, E.: Improving query evaluation with approximate functional dependency based decompositions. In: Eaglestone, B., North, S.C., Poulovassilis, A. (eds.) BNCOD 2002. LNCS, vol. 2405, pp. 26–41. Springer, Heidelberg (2002)
6. Giannella, C., Robertson, E.: On approximation measures for functional dependencies. Inf. Syst. 29(6), 483–507 (2004)
7. Hilderman, R., Hamilton, H.: Knowledge discovery and interestingness measures: A survey. Technical Report 99-04, University of Regina (1999)

8. Huhtala, Y., Kärkkäinen, J., Porkka, P., Toivonen, H.: TANE: An efficient algorithm for discovering functional and approximate dependencies. The Computer Journal 42(2), 100–111 (1999)
9. Ilyas, I.F., Markl, V., Haas, P., Brown, P., Aboulnaga, A.: Cords: automatic discovery of correlations and soft functional dependencies. In: SIGMOD Proceedings, pp. 647–658. ACM Press, New York (2004)
10. Kivinen, J., Mannila, H.: Approximate inference of functional dependencies from relations. In: ICDT, pp. 129–149. Elsevier Science Publishers, Amsterdam (1995)
11. Mannila, H., Räihä, K.-J.: On the complexity of inferring functional dependencies. Discrete Applied Mathematics 40(2), 237–243 (1992)
12. Matos, V., Grasser, B.: Sql-based discovery of exact and approximate functional dependencies. In: ITiCSE Working Group Reports, pp. 58–63. Association for Computing Machinery, New York (2004)
13. Ramakrishnan, R., Gehrke, J.: Database Management Systems. McGraw-Hill Higher Education, New York (2002)
14. Shannon, C.E.: A mathematical theory of communication. Bell System Tech. J. 27, 379–423, 623–656 (1948)
15. Wolf, G., Khatri, H., Chokshi, B., Fan, J., Chen, Y., Kambhampati, S.: Query processing over incomplete autonomous databases. In: VLDB Proceedings. VLDB Endowment, pp. 651–662 (2007)

Sentence Ordering for Coherent Multi-document Summary Generation

C.R. Chowdary and P. Sreenivasa Kumar

Department of Computer Science and Engineering
Indian Institute of Technology Madras
Chennai 600 036, India
{chowdary,psk}@cse.iitm.ac.in

Abstract. Web queries often give rise to a lot of documents and the user
is overwhelmed by the information. Query-specific extractive summarization of a selected set of retrieved documents helps the user to get a gist
of the information. The current extractive summary generation systems
focus on extracting query-relevant sentences from the documents. However, the selected sentences are presented either in the order in which the
documents were considered or in the order in which they were selected.
This approach does not guarantee a coherent summary. In this paper,
we propose incremental integrated graph to represent the sentences in a
collection of documents. Sentences from the documents are merged into
a master sequence to improve coherence and flow. The same ordering is
used for sequencing the sentences in the extracted summary. User evaluations indicate that the proposed technique markedly improves the user
satisfaction with regard to coherence in the summary.

Keywords: Summarization, Coherent, Incremental Integrated Graph,
Ordering of Sentences.

1 Introduction

Currently, the World Wide Web is the largest source of information. Huge
amount of data is being added to the Web every second. Search engines retrieve
a set of web pages which are relevant to the topic of interest. Often the information related to the topic will be distributed across the web pages. To get the
complete information on a topic we may have to go through several web pages.
It is a tedious task for the user to study huge amount of data present across
the web pages. Most of the times user's need does not demand the complete
reading of each web page. If the information which is of user's interest, present
across multiple web pages is retrieved and arranged in appropriate manner then
it would be of great help to the user. "Multiple web page summarization", is one
such useful method which saves lot of time of the user. There are two ways in
which summarization systems can be classified - Abstractive and Extractive.

In abstractive summary generation[17,7,15], the input will be a set of documents, which can be obtained from the web for the query given by the user. The

A. Gray, K. Jeffery, and J. Shao (Eds.): BNCOD 2008, LNCS 5071, pp. 40–50, 2008.

output would be the abstract of the documents, generated with the aid of natural language processing (NLP) algorithms. In extractive summary generation[14,5], the input is same but the output is obtained by extracting the sentences from the documents and arranging them in a meaningful way to make a readable summary. Query specific multiple document summary takes us one step further by generating summaries which are biased towards the given query. Statistical measures are used by the systems that generate extractive based summaries. Recently graph based models[16] are used in extraction based summarization.

In graph based models each sentence of the document is considered as a node in the graph and the edges are present between sentences, if the sentences are related. To find the degree of relatedness, measures like *cosine similarity* are used. In a graph the neighbouring nodes(nodes which are adjacent) are highly related to each other and it is highly probable that these nodes contain the content which is very much similar and coherent. A node will be given importance based on the content it contains and the content that its neighboring nodes contain.

In this paper we deal with the problem of arranging the extracted nodes from the graph in a way that makes the summary coherent and meaningful. To achieve this task we construct an Incremental Integrated Graph(IIG) and the nodes selected for the summary are arranged in the IIG order. In Section 2 we discuss the related work. Framework is discussed in Section 3. We discuss the algorithm to construct the Incremental Integrated Graph in Section 4 . In Section 5 we discuss the MEAD system, with which we compare our results and the corpus used for our experimentation and we discuss the performance of our system. Conclusions are given in Section 6.

2   Related Work

MEAD[14] introduced centroid based summarization. It deals with both single and multi document summarization. Centroid is calculated by calculating the average of tf*idf, of all the words across the documents in a cluster. A sentence is said to be important if its similarity is close to the centroid. In the generated summary, sentences are arranged in the document order and the documents are arranged chronologically. CLASSY[5] uses HMM(Hidden Markov Model) for giving score to sentences. Pivoted QR algorithm is used to form a summary. In the graph based models like[12] each sentence is considered as a node and the score is given to a sentence based on the lines similar to PageRank[13] or HITS[6]. Edge weight is given by considering the degree of overlap between the two sentences.

In [11] both single and multi-document summary are discussed. For single document summary it uses DR-LINK[9] to select MRS(most relevant section) and is presented to the user. In multi-document summary it uses DR-LINK[9] to select MRP(Most Relevant Paragraph) from the MRS. [4] uses cosine similarity measure to give importance to the sentence in the document based on the query. MMR re-ranking is used to select the sentences into the summary. While generating summary, sentences are arranged in document order or MMR-reranking order. In [10] important units of text are identified and the relationship among them is exploited for summarizing similarities and differences in a pair of related documents using a graph representation for text.

In [8] both event-based summary (to select and organize the sentences in a summary with respect to the events or the sub-events that the sentences describe) and extractive summary are integrated. In [2] sentence ordering is addressed but is highly oriented towards news articles and the ordering of sentences is based on the number of times it is preceding or following the other sentences in the documents(a sentence s_i precedes sentence s_j if in majority documents s_i precedes sentence s_j). All the approaches mainly concentrate on retrieving relevant sentences from the documents and very less attention is given to the meaningful arrangement of the sentences within the selected sentences. Though [2] specifically addresses this problem, it mainly focuses on news documents. In our approach we arrange the nodes of documents by taking the context into consideration, due to which coherence is preserved.

3   Framework

Each document is considered as a graph. Sentences are considered as nodes and edges in the document reflect the degree of similarity between nodes. We use *cosine similarity* to measure the similarity between nodes. An edge weight $w(e_{ij})$ quantifies contextual similarity between sentences s_i and s_j. It is computed using the Equation 1[3]. Stop words(e.g. a, an, the etc.) are removed while calculating similarity.

$$w(e_{ij}) = sim(\overrightarrow{s_i}, \overrightarrow{s_j}) = \frac{\overrightarrow{s_i}.\overrightarrow{s_j}}{|\overrightarrow{s_i}||\overrightarrow{s_j}|} \tag{1}$$

where $\overrightarrow{s_i}$ and $\overrightarrow{s_j}$ are term vectors for sentences s_i and s_j respectively. The weight of each term t is calculated using $tf_t * isf_t$ where tf_t is the term frequency and isf_t is inverse sentential frequency i.e., $log(\frac{n}{n_t})$ where n is the total number of sentences and n_t is number of sentences containing the term t in the graph under consideration. Stop words are removed and remaining words are stemmed before computing these weights. A low similarity value reflects a weak contextual relationship(i.e. sentences that are not related).

4   Incremental Integrated Graph Construction

In this section we explain the algorithms for the construction of the IIG (Incremental Integrated Graph). Input to Algorithm 1 is a set of documents in the decreasing order of the number of sentences and the output is the IIG. The document with the maximum number of nodes(D_0)[1] is taken as the base graph.

---

[1] D_i represents i^{th} document, d_j represents j^{th} sentence in a given document and n_k represents k^{th} sentence in the Incremental Integrated Graph.

Each node of the base graph is assumed to form a context. We arrange the base graph nodes in a manner by which the ith node of the base graph will be arranged in the position $i * gap$ i.e., position$(n_i) = i * gap$. Here, the parameter gap is used to control the number of positions available between a pair of base graph nodes for placing new nodes. A node is said to be a *context node* if it is positioned at integral multiples of gap. Each node from the other documents is added in the neighbourhood of one of the context nodes. Adding a node y in the neighbourhood of a context node x indicates that y has maximum similarity with x and it is above $\alpha(0.1)$. We then denote x as *contextOf(y)*. We call the collection of nodes whose position lies between $position(x)$ and $position(x) + gap$ as the neighbourhood of x. If we consider gap as 100 and 0 100 101 102 200 201 202 300 as nodes in IIG then 0,100,200,300 are context nodes. 201 and 202 are in the context of 200, 101 and 102 are in the context of 100. 101 to 199 are the neighbourhood of 100 and 201 to 299 are the neighbourhood of 200. In this case, $position(y)$ will be greater then the $position(x)$ and less then the $position(x) + gap$, as explained in Algorithm 2. If the *similarity* is below α, then the node is added as a new context node as explained in Algorithm 3.

Algorithm 1. Incremental Integrated Graph Construction

1: **Input**: Set of documents in the decreasing order of their size(number of sentences)
2: **Output**: Incremental Integrated graph IIG
3: Incremental Integrated Graph $IIG = D_0$ {//base graph}
4: Set *position* of each node in IIG as position$(n_k) = k * gap$ $(0 \le k \le |D_0|)$
5: $i = 1$
6: **while** $i \le$ number of *Documents* **do**
7:    **for** each node $d \in D_i$ considered in the document order find the context node, called *MaxSimilarContextNode*, with which it is having maximum similarity **do**
8:        **if** $sim(d, MaxSimilarContextNode) \ge \alpha$ **then**
9:            Insert d in the context of *MaxSimilarContextNode* as explained in Algo 2
10:        **else**
11:            Set d as the new context in IIG as explained in Algo 3
12:        **end if**
13:    **end for**
14:    $i + +$
15: **end while**

Though it can be argued that *gap* should be large enough to accommodate *all* the nodes from all other documents between a pair of base graph nodes(worst-case scenario), in practice it is highly unlikely to be so. From our empirical studies, we observe that *gap* value of twice the number of documents in the corpus is sufficient. In any case, it can be set to an appropriate value after experimenting with the corpus of interest.

In Algorithm 3 we deal with two cases - first one is when the node to be added as a context is the first node of a document and the second one is when the node to be added is not the first node of a document. In the first case, we add the node

---

Algorithm 2. Insertion of a node in the neighbourhood of a context node

---

1: **Input:** Partially constructed IIG, context node(c) and the node to be inserted(d)
2: **Output:** IIG with the node inserted in the Context
3: $i = \text{position}(c)$
4: **while** (There is a node at position i) AND (sim($c, NodeAtPosition(i)$) $\geq$ sim(c, d)) **do**
5:    $i + +$
6: **end while**
7: Increment the position of all the neighbouring nodes of c which are having position numbers greater than or equal to i by one
8: Place d at position i

---

as a context node, following the current last context node of the IIG and position it as given in Line 4 of algorithm. All the non-context nodes are re-arranged, if necessary. If the non-context node x is more similar to the newly added context node c than to its current context, then x is shifted to the neighbourhood of c. In the second case we add the node as a context immediately following its parent node. x is *parent* of y if y follows x in the document. All the non-context nodes are re-arranged, if necessary.

The parameter *gap* is the difference of the positions of two consecutive context nodes in IIG. The context nodes will be positioned at $0, 1 * gap, 2 * gap, 3 * gap$ etc. in IIG. *gap* is chosen in such a way that it is large enough to accommodate the nodes falling in a context. Figure 1 illustrates the working of the algorithm

---

Algorithm 3. Adding a context to the partially constructed IIG

1: **Input:** Partially constructed IIG and the node(d) to be inserted as the context
2: **Output:** IIG with d included
3: **if** d is the first node in the document **then**
4:    ADD d as a new context node to IIG following the current last context node and Set position(d) = position($CurrentLastContextNodeOfIIG$) + gap
5: **else**
6:    $i = \lfloor position(parent(d))/gap \rfloor *gap + gap$ {//for gap = 100, if parent(d) is at 213 then i will be assigned 300 }
7:    **for** each node n starting from position i **do**
8:       position(n) = position(n) + gap
9:    **end for**
10:    Insert d as a context node and Set position(d) = i
11: **end if**
12: **for** each non context node n **do**
13:    **if** $sim(n, d) > sim(n, CurrentContext)$ **then**
14:       Delete n and place it in the context of d using Algo 2
15:       Re-arrange the nodes following the non context node till the next context node {//decrease the position value by 1}
16:    **end if**
17: **end for**

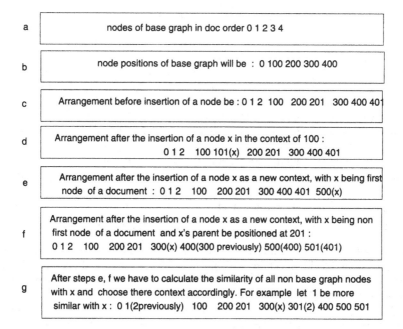

a   nodes of base graph in doc order 0 1 2 3 4

b   node positions of base graph will be : 0 100 200 300 400

c   Arrangement before insertion of a node be : 0 1 2 100   200 201   300 400 401

d   Arrangement after the insertion of a node x in the context of 100 :
                0 1 2   100 101(x)   200 201   300 400 401

e   Arrangement after the insertion of a node x as a new context, with x being first
        node of a document : 0 1 2   100   200 201   300 400 401 500(x)

f   Arrangement after the insertion of a node x as a new context, with x being non
        first node of a document and x's parent be positioned at 201 :
        0 1 2   100   200 201   300(x) 400(300 previously) 500(400) 501(401)

g   After steps e, f we have to calculate the similarity of all non base graph nodes
        with x and choose there context accordingly. For example let 1 be more
        similar with x : 0 1(2previously)   100   200 201   300(x) 301(2) 400 500 501

Fig. 1. Illustration of algorithm with *gap* as 100

through an example. A base graph is taken with 5 nodes(0,..,4) as shown in Figure 1(a). We have Figure 1(b) after positioning the base graph nodes as explained in Algorithm 1. In Figure 1(c) 1, 2, 201 and 401 are non base graph nodes. Figure 1(d) illustrates the arrangement after the insertion of x in the context of 100. Figure 1(e) and 1(f) illustrates the insertion of node x as a new context. Figure 1(g) illustrates the re-arrangement(based on similarity measures) of the non base graph nodes after the insertion of the new context as explained in Algorithm 3.

The extractive summarizer MEAD is used to extract sentences on the given cluster of documents. IIG is constructed on the same set of documents. The position numbers of extracted sentences in IIG are determined. These sentences are arranged in the increasing order of their position numbers to generate the summary as per the proposed approach. For e.g., if MEAD extracts s_1, s_2, s_3, s_4 and s_5 sentences as part of the summary, if the corresponding positions are 101,2,300,4 and 10 respectively then the summary given by IIG approach would be s_2, s_4, s_5, s_1 and s_3.

5   Experimental Setup and Results

We have implemented IIG construction in Java. We took α value as 0.1 and *gap* as 100 for our experiments. We compared our system with MEAD[14]. MEAD computes a score for each sentence from the given cluster of related documents

Table 1. Query: "Beckham moving to Barcelona"

MEAD
[1] Beckham appeared resigned to being sold.
[2] BARCELONA, Spain, June AFP - Joan Laporta, the man who wants to bring England skipper David Beckham to Barcelona in a 50-million-dollar deal, became the president of the Spanish giants on Sunday and insisted that he will continue his campaign to sign the Manchester United star.
[3] However Eriksson added that wherever Beckham played would make no difference to his role for England.
[4] ROME, May AFP - Champions League winners AC Milan want to sign Manchester United midfielder David Beckham for next season, according to Friday's Gazzetta dello Sport.
[5] But just weeks ago, Beckham issued a statement saying he wanted to remain at Old Trafford.

IIG
[2] BARCELONA, Spain, June AFP - Joan Laporta, the man who wants to bring England skipper David Beckham to Barcelona in a 50-million-dollar deal, became the president of the Spanish giants on Sunday and insisted that he will continue his campaign to sign the Manchester United star.
[4] ROME, May AFP - Champions League winners AC Milan want to sign Manchester United midfielder David Beckham for next season, according to Friday's Gazzetta dello Sport.
[3] However Eriksson added that wherever Beckham played would make no difference to his role for England.
[5] But just weeks ago, Beckham issued a statement saying he wanted to remain at Old Trafford.
[1] Beckham appeared resigned to being sold.

by considering a linear combination of several features. We have used centroid score, position and cosine similarity with query as features with 1,1,10 as their weights respectively. MMR(Maximum Marginal Relevance) re-ranker, which is provided by MEAD is used for redundancy removal with a similarity threshold of 0.6.

Our focus in this paper is on arranging the extracted sentences from the documents in a way that makes it more readable. MEAD was used to extract the sentences from the documents for the given query. The passage so obtained is compared to the passage generated by rearranging the same sentences as per our algorithm. Table 1 shows the summaries generated by MEAD and IIG for the query "Beckham moving to Barcelona". Table 2 shows the summaries generated for the query "Jackson ruling on Microsoft".

We used the publicly available database provided by University of Michigan[1]. We experimented on *eight* different topics. Each topic was described in 10 to 14 documents. The nature of the documents is that they discuss particular topic like global warming, water on mars etc. If we consider any two documents(within the cluster), most of the time it so happens that at least 30% of one document will be having same information as the other.

Table 2. Query: "Jackson ruling on Microsoft"

MEAD
[1] "This ruling turns on its head the reality that consumers know," he said.
[2] However, a ruling on sanctions, the last stage of the trial, is not likely before October.
[3] In fact, he said, Jackson's approach could make the ruling "bulletproof" on appeal.
[4] "Microsoft placed an oppressive thumb on the scale of competitive fortune, thereby effectively guaranteeing its continued dominance," U.S.
[5] District Judge Thomas Penfield Jackson wrote in a sweeping decision that said Microsoft violated the Sherman Act, the same law used to break up monopolies from Standard Oil to AT& T.
[6] The judge issued his ruling Monday after the stock market closed, but word that it was coming caused Microsoft stock to drop by more than 15 a share to 90.87, costing Gates about 12.1 billion in paper losses.
IIG
[5] District Judge Thomas Penfield Jackson wrote in a sweeping decision that said Microsoft violated the Sherman Act, the same law used to break up monopolies from Standard Oil to AT&T.
[2] However, a ruling on sanctions, the last stage of the trial, is not likely before October.
[4] "Microsoft placed an oppressive thumb on the scale of competitive fortune, thereby effectively guaranteeing its continued dominance," U.S.
[1] "This ruling turns on its head the reality that consumers know," he said.
[6] The judge issued his ruling Monday after the stock market closed, but word that it was coming caused Microsoft stock to drop by more than 15 a share to 90.87, costing Gates about 12.1 billion in paper losses.
[3] In fact, he said, Jackson's approach could make the ruling "bulletproof" on appeal.

We have given the summaries generated on the eight topics to 51 volunteers(under graduate and graduate students) for evaluation. While giving the summary document, we randomized the arrangement of the order in which the summary generated by MEAD and IIG are placed in the file. This precaution is essential as the user selects one of the two summaries as the answer and the one which he reads first may not be satisfactory to him, but at this point we have to remember that after going through the first summary, he will get an idea of the subject and then while going through the second one that impact will be there definitely. So for half of the summary pairs MEAD preceded IIG and for the remaining half IIG preceded MEAD.

Table 3. Choice for each query

System/Query	Q1	Q2	Q3	Q4	Q5	Q6	Q7	Q8
MEAD	5	8	37	23	23	21	22	15
IIG	46	43	14	28	28	30	29	36

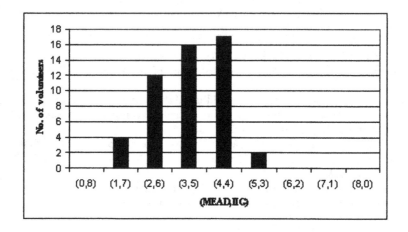

Fig. 2. Number of volunteers who voted for (MEAD,IIG)

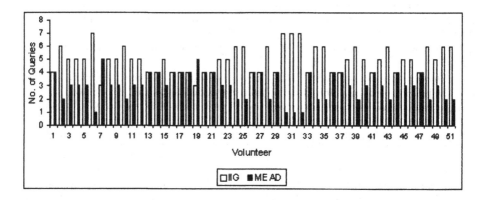

Fig. 3. Graph showing the volunteers choice

For each topic, the volunteers were asked to select the summary that is more coherent than the other. Table 3 shows for each query, the number of volunteers that have chosen MEAD/IIG as the satisfactory system. For example, five volunteers have chosen MEAD system for query one(Q1) and the rest forty six has selected IIG. Figure 2 shows a graph in which (a, b) on X-axis indicates that for "a" of 8 queries, MEAD was chosen and for remaining $(8 - a)$ i.e., "b" IIG was chosen as satisfactory. The Y-axis indicates the number of volunteers corresponding to each (a, b). From the Figure 2 it is clear that only two out of fifty one volunteers feel that MEAD is giving better coherence than IIG. Figure 3 shows the volunteers choice for both MEAD and IIG. Figure 3 shows for each individual volunteer, for how many queries the IIG(white bar) and the MEAD(black bar) was chosen as a system that gives better summary.

6 Conclusions

In this paper, we have proposed Incremental Integrated Graph as a structure to order the sentences in a cluster of documents. IIG is constructed incrementally with the document containing largest number of nodes taken as a base graph. Each node in base graph is considered as a context. All the nodes of other documents are added to the context if they have similarity with context otherwise a new context is formed with the new node as a context. Sentences selected by the extractive query-specific summarizer are then ordered according to their position in IIG. Experimental results show that our approach has improved the quality of the extracted summary in terms of coherence.

References

1. CSTBank Corpus Available at,
   http://tangra.si.umich.edu/clair/CSTBank/phase1.htm
2. Barzilay, R., Elhadad, N., McKeown, K.R.: Sentence ordering in multidocument summarization. In: HLT 2001: Proceedings of the first international conference on Human language technology research, pp. 1–7. Association for Computational Linguistics, Morristown, NJ, USA (2001)
3. Frakes, W.B., Baeza-Yates, R.A. (eds.): Information Retrieval: Data Structures & Algorithms. Prentice-Hall, Englewood Cliffs (1992)
4. Goldstein, J., Carbonell, J.: Summarization (1) using mmr for diversity - based reranking and (2) evaluating summaries. In: Proceedings of a workshop, Baltimore, Maryland, pp. 181–195. Association for Computational Linguistics, Morristown, NJ, USA (1996)
5. Schlesinger, J.D., Conroy, J.M., Stewart, J.G.: CLASSY query-based multidocument summarization. In: Proceedings of the Document Understanding Conference (DUC) (2005)
6. Kleinberg, J.M.: Authoritative sources in a hyperlinked environment. J. ACM 46(5), 604–632 (1999)
7. Knight, K., Marcu, D.: Statistics-based summarization - step one: Sentence compression. In: Proceedings of the Seventeenth National Conference on Artificial Intelligence and Twelfth Conference on Innovative Applications of Artificial Intelligence, pp. 703–710. AAAI Press / The MIT Press (2000)
8. Li, W., Wu, M., Lu, Q., Xu, W., Yuan, C.: Extractive summarization using inter- and intra- event relevance. In: ACL 2006: Proceedings of the 21st International Conference on Computational Linguistics and the 44th annual meeting of the ACL, pp. 369–376. Association for Computational Linguistics, Morristown, NJ, USA (2006)
9. Liddy, E.D., Paik, W., Yu, E.S., McVearry, K.A.: An overview of dr-link and its approach to document filtering. In: HLT 1993: Proceedings of the workshop on Human Language Technology, pp. 358–362. Association for Computational Linguistics, Morristown, NJ, USA (1993)
10. Mani, I., Bloedorn, E.: Multi-document summarization by graph search and matching. In: Proceedings of the Fifteenth National Conference on Artificial Intelligence (AAAI 1997), pp. 622–628. AAAI/IAAI (1997)

11. McKenna, M., Liddy, E.: Multiple & single document summarization using dr-link. In: Proceedings of a workshop, Baltimore, Maryland, pp. 215–221. Association for Computational Linguistics, Morristown, NJ, USA (1996)
12. Mihalcea, R., Tarau, P.: Multi-Document Summarization with Iterative Graph-based Algorithms. In: Proceedings of the First International Conference on Intelligent Analysis Methods and Tools (IA 2005), McLean, VA (May 2005)
13. Page, L., Brin, S., Motwani, R., Winograd, T.: The pagerank citation ranking: Bringing order to the web. In: Proceedings of the 7th International World Wide Web Conference, Brisbane, Australia, pp. 161–172 (1998)
14. Radev, D.R., Jing, H., Budzikowska, M.: Centroid-based summarization of multiple documents: sentence extraction, utility-based evaluation, and user studies. In: NAACL-ANLP 2000 Workshop on Automatic summarization, pp. 21–30. Association for Computational Linguistics, Morristown, NJ, USA (2000)
15. Radev, D.R., McKeown, K.R.: Generating natural language summaries from multiple on-line sources. Comput. Linguist. 24(3), 470–500 (1998)
16. Varadarajan, R., Hristidis, V.: A system for query-specific document summarization. In: CIKM 2006: Proceedings of the 15th ACM international conference on Information and knowledge management, pp. 622–631. ACM Press, New York (2006)
17. Witbrock, M.J., Mittal, V.O.: Ultra-summarization (poster abstract): a statistical approach to generating highly condensed non-extractive summaries. In: SIGIR 1999: Proceedings of the 22nd annual international ACM SIGIR conference on Research and development in information retrieval, pp. 315–316. ACM, New York (1999)

Schema Matching across Query Interfaces on the Deep Web

Zhongtian He, Jun Hong, and David Bell

School of Electronics, Electrical Engineering and Computer Science,
Queen's University Belfast, Belfast, BT7 1NN, UK
{zhe01,j.hong,da.bell}@qub.ac.uk

Abstract. Schema matching is a crucial step in data integration. Many approaches to schema matching have been proposed so far. Different types of information about schemas, including structures, linguistic features and data types, etc have been used to match attributes between schemas. Relying on a single aspect of information about schemas for schema matching is not sufficient. Approaches have been proposed to combine multiple matchers taking into account different aspects of information about schemas. Weights are usually assigned to individual matchers so that their match results can be combined taking into account their different levels of importance. However, these weights have to be manually generated and are domain-dependent. We propose a new approach to combining multiple matchers using the Dempster-Shafer theory of evidence, which finds the top-k attribute correspondences of each source attribute from the target schema. We then make use of some heuristics to resolve any conflicts between the attribute correspondences of different source attributes. Our experimental results show that our approach is highly effective.

1 Introduction

There are now many searchable databases on the Web. These databases are accessed through queries formulated on their query interfaces only which are usually query forms. The query results from these databases are dynamically generated Web pages in response to form-based queries. The number of such dynamically generated Web pages is estimated around 500 times the number of static Web pages on the surface Web [1]. In many domains, users are interested in obtaining information from multiple sources. Thus, they have to access different Web databases individually via their query interfaces. For large-scale data integration over the Deep Web, it is not practical to manually model and integrate these Web databases. We aim to provide a uniform query interface that allows users to have uniform access to multiple sources [2]. Users can submit their queries to the uniform query interface and be responded with a set of combined results from multiple sources automatically.

Schema matching across query interfaces is a critical step in Web data integration, which finds attribute correspondences between the uniform query interface

A. Gray, K. Jeffery, and J. Shao (Eds.): BNCOD 2008, LNCS 5071, pp. 51–62, 2008.

and the query interface for a local database. In general, schema matching takes two schemas as input and produces a set of attribute correspondences between the two schemas [3, 4]. The problem of schema matching has been extensively studied [4,5,6,7,8,9,10,11,12,13,14,15,16]. Some of these methods [9,10,12,13,14] make use of information about schemas, including structures, linguistic features, data types, value ranges, etc to match attributes between schemas.

Match results from individual matchers are not accurate and certain, because they rely on individual aspects of information about schemas only, which are not sufficient for finding attribute correspondences between schemas. Individual matchers, however can generate some degree of belief on the validity of possible attribute correspondences.

In addition, sometimes given a source attribute, there might be two or more attribute correspondences that are not clearly distinguishable from each other by an individual matcher. For example, a data type matcher may not be able to distinguish some attribute correspondences for the same source attribute if they all have the same data type as the source attribute.

Recent research efforts have been focused on combining multiple matchers. However, how to combine different measures is a difficult issue. In the example shown in Figure 1, when we use a string similarity-based matcher, the similarity value between "Published Date" and "Publisher" is greater than the one between "Published Date" and "Release Date", while when a semantic similarity-based matcher is used, the similarity values are the other way around. Current approaches use different strategies to combine matcher-specific similarity values [12].

However, these strategies sometimes do not truly reflect how well two attributes match. Given a pair of attributes, the Max strategy selects the maximal similarity value among all the similarity values from different matchers as their similarity value. For example, if one of our matchers is data type-based matcher, and the attributes, "Publisher" and "Author", have the same data type, then the similarity value is 1 which will be chosen as their final similarity value. But obviously they do not match. On the other hand, the Min strategy selects the

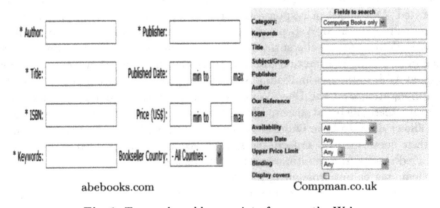

abebooks.com   Compman.co.uk

Fig. 1. Two real-world query interfaces on the Web

lowest similarity value. For example, if a string similarity-based matcher is one of the matchers, the similarity value of "Published Date" and "Release Date" is very low, but actually they are a right match. The third strategy, Average, treats all the matchers equally. For instance, if two matchers are string similarity-based matcher and semantic similarity-based matcher respectively, the average similarity value between "Published Date" and "Publisher" is higher than the one between "Published Date" and "Release Date", but we all know that "Published Date" and "Release Date" is the correct match. It appears that the semantic similarity-based matcher should have a higher level of importance. The Weighted strategy is the most popular strategy that calculates a weighted sum of the similarity values of all the individual matchers, where weights correspond to different levels of importance of the individual matchers. However, assigning weights to different matchers now becomes an issue. Weights have to be manually generated and are domain dependent.

To address these issues, we propose a new strategy for combining multiple matchers. We use four individual matchers to measure the similarity between attributes, and make use of Dempster-Shafer (DS) theory of evidence to combine the results from these matchers.

Finally, sometimes two or more different source attributes may have the same attribute correspondence. In our approach, we keep the top-k matches of each source attribute. We then use some heuristics to resolve any conflicts between the matches of different source attributes.

The rest of this paper is organized as follow. Section 2 introduces the Dempster-Shafer (DS) theory of evidence. Section 3 describes how to use DS theory in our approach. Section 4 describes how to resolve conflicts of different source attributes. In Section 5, we report our experiments on our prototype using a dataset which contains the schemas of real-world query interfaces. Section 6 compares our work with related work. Section 7 concludes the paper.

2   Dempster-Shafer Theory of Evidence (DS)

The DS theory of evidence, sometimes called evidential reasoning [17] or belief function theory, is a mechanism formalized by Shafer [18] for representing and reasoning with uncertain, imprecise and incomplete information. It is based on the modeling of uncertainty in terms of upper and lower probabilities that are induced by a multi-valued mapping rather than as a single probability value.

Definition 1. *Frames of Discernment. A frame of discernment (or simply a frame), usually denoted as Θ, contains mutually exclusive and exhaustive possible answers to a question, one and only one of which is true.*

In DS theory, a frame of discernment is used to represent a set of possible answers to a question. For example, a patient has been observed having two symptoms: "coughing" and "sniveling" and only three types of illness could have caused these symptoms: "flu" (F), "cold" (C) and "pneumonia" (P). We use a frame $\Theta = \{F, C, P\}$ to represent these types of illness.

Definition 2. Mass functions. *A function, $m: 2^{\Theta} \rightarrow [0,1]$, is called a mass function on a frame Θ if it satisfies the following two conditions:*

$$m(\phi) = 0 \tag{1}$$

$$\sum_{A \subseteq \Theta} m(A) = 1 \tag{2}$$

where ϕ is an empty set and A is any subset of Θ.

Given a frame of discernment, Θ, for each source of evidence, a mass function assigns a mass to every subset of Θ, which represents the degree of belief that one of the answers in the subset is true, given the source of evidence. For example, when the patient has been observed having the symptom "coughing", the degree of belief that the patient has "flu" or "cold" is 0.6 and the degree of belief that the patient has "pneumonia" is 0.4, that is $m_1(\{C, F\}) = 0.6$ and $m_1(\{P\}) = 0.4$. Similarly, with the symptom of "sniveling", we have another mass function: $m_2(\{F\}) = 0.7$, $m_2(\{C\}) = 0.2$ and $m_2(\{P\}) = 0.1$.

When more than one mass function is given on the same frame of discernment, the theory also provides us with Dempster's combination rule. If m_1 and m_2 are two mass functions on frame Θ, then $m = m_1 \oplus m_2$ is the combined mass function, where $\oplus$ means using Dempster's combination rule, defined as follows:

$$m(C) = \frac{\sum_{A \cap B = C} m_1(A) m_2(B)}{1 - \sum_{A \cap B = \phi} m_1(A) m_2(B)} \tag{3}$$

In the above example, we combine two mass functions, m_1 and m_2, to get m($\{C\}$)=0.207, m($\{F\}$)=0.724 and m($\{P\}$)=0.069. Therefore given the two symptoms the patient has, it is more likely that he is having "flu".

3   Combining Multiple Matchers Using DS Theory

Given a source schema and a target schema, our approach combines a set of individual matchers using the Dempster-Shafter theory of evidence to produce a set of attribute correspondences between the two schemas. Our approach consists of a number of steps: 1. Applies each of the individual matchers to the two given schemas; 2. Interprets the results from the individual matchers using the DS theory; 3. Combines the results from the individual matchers using the Dempster's combination rule to produce the top k attribute correspondences of each source attribute; 4. Decides on the attribute correspondence of each source attribute and resolves conflicts between attribute correspondences of two or more source attributes.

3.1   Individual Matchers

We use four individual matchers, the first three matchers are based on the linguistic features of attribute names and the last matcher uses the data types of attributes.

Semantic Similarity: We use WordNet[1], an ontology database to compute the semantic similarity between two words. We use the traditional edge counting approach to measuring word similarity. We define similarity between two words as $S(w_1, w_2) = 1/L$, where L is the shortest path in WordNet between these two words. Suppose that two attribute names have two sets of words $S_1 = \{w_1, w_2, ..., w_m\}$ and $S_2 = \{w'_1, w'_2, ..., w'_n\}$. We compare the similarity values between each word in S_1 with every word in S_2 and find the highest semantic similarity value. We then get a similarity value set for S_1: $Sim_1 = \{s_1, s_2, ..., s_m\}$. Using the same method we get a similarity value set for S_2: $Sim_2 = \{s'_1, s'_2, ..., s'_n\}$. From these two similarity value sets we calculate the similarity value between two attribute names S_1 and S_2 as:

$$Sim(S_1, S_2) = \frac{\sum_{i=1}^{m} s_i + \sum_{i=1}^{n} s'_i}{m + n} \tag{4}$$

where m is the number of the words in S_1, n is the number of the words in S_2.

Edit Distance-Based Matcher: Edit distance is the number of edit operations necessary to transform one string to another [19]. We define the edit distance-based string similarity as follows:

$$sim_{ed}(w_1, w_2) = \frac{1}{1 + ed(w_1, w_2)} \tag{5}$$

where w_1 and w_2 are two words, $ed(w_1, w_2)$ is the edit distance between these two words. Similar to the semantic similarity matcher, we get two similarity value sets for two attribute names first and then calculate the similarity value between two attribute names based on the two similarity value sets using the formula defined in (4).

Jaro Distance: Similar to the edit distance matcher, we use the formula in (4) to calculate the similarity value between two attribute names, where the similarity value between two words is calculated using the Jaro distance instead. The Jaro distance measures the similarity of two strings based on the number and order of the common characters between them. Given two strings $s = a_1 \cdots a_k$ and $t = b_1 \cdots b_l$, a character a_i in s is in common with t, if there is a $b_j = a_i$ in t such that $i - H \leq j \leq i + H$, where $H = \frac{min(|s|,|t|)}{2}$. Let $s' = a'_1 \cdots a'_{k'}$, be the characters in s which are in common with t (in the same order they appear in s) and $t' = b'_1 \cdots b'_{l'}$ similarly. We define a *transposition* for s' and t' to be a position i such that $a'_i \neq b'_i$. Let $T_{s,t}$ be half the number of transpositions of s' and t'. The Jaro similarity metric for s and t is defined as follows [21]:

$$Jaro(s, t) = \frac{1}{3} \cdot \left(\frac{|s'|}{|s|} + \frac{|t'|}{|t|} + \frac{|s'| - T_{s',t'}}{|s'|} \right) \tag{6}$$

Data Types: As discussed in [8], we define that two data types are compatible if they are the same or one subsumes another (is-a relationship). Currently we focus

---

[1] http://wordnet.princeton.edu/

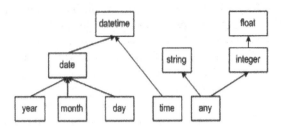

Fig. 2. Data types and their relationships

only on the data types that are shown in Figure 2. For example, in Figure 2, an
"integer" is a "float". So we say that their data types are the same or compatible
(incidentally, "null" is compatible to any data type). The similarity value between
two attribute names is 1, if their data types are the same. Otherwise it is 0.

3.2 Interpreting Results from Individual Matchers

Assume that we have a source schema, $S = \{a_1, a_2, ..., a_m\}$, where a_i, for $i =$
$1, 2, ..., m$, is a source attribute, and a target schema, $T = \{b_1, b_2, ..., b_n\}$, where
b_j, for $j = 1, 2, ..., n$, is a target attribute. For each source attribute, a_i, we have a
set of possible correspondences in the target schema $\{< a_i, b_1 >, < a_i, b_2 >, ..., <$
$a_i, b_l >\}$. It is also possible that a_i, may have no correspondence in the target
schema at all. We therefore have a frame of discernment for a_i, $\Theta = \{< a_i, b_1 >$
$, < a_i, b_2 >, ..., < a_i, b_l >, < a_i, null >\}$, where $< a_i, null >$ represents that there
is no correspondence for a_i in the target schema. This frame of discernment
contains an exclusive, exhaustive set of answers (see Definition 1) to the question
of finding an attribute correspondence for a_i, in the target schema. One and only
one of these answers is true.

Generating Indistinguishable Subsets of Attribute Correspondences.
For some matchers we cluster Θ into a set of indistinguishable subsets, because
some attribute correspondences may not be distinguishable. For example, if a
source attribute has the same data type with two target attributes, then the two
correspondences cannot be distinguished from each other, so we cluster these
indistinguishable correspondences into a subset.

Generating Mass Distributions on Indistinguishable Subsets. We now
describe how to generate a mass distribution that assigns a mass to an indistinguishable subset of Θ, on the basis of the similarity measures on the attribute
correspondences in the subset.

Given an indistinguishable subset of attribute correspondences, we have a
similarity value for each correspondence, which represents how well the two
attributes in the correspondence match according to the criterion used by the
matcher. Suppose the subset is $\{< a_i, b_{i1} >, < a_i, b_{i2} >, ..., < a_i, b_{il} >\}$, a mass

assigned to the subset is calculated based on the similarity values for all the attribute correspondences in the subset as follows:

$$m'(A) = 1 - \Pi_{j=1}^{l}(1 - Sim(a_i, b_{ij})) \tag{7}$$

where $Sim(a_i, b_{ij})$ is the similarity value for one of the correspondences in the subset. For the special singleton subset, $\{< a_i, null >\}$, since we do not have a similarity value for it by any matcher, the mass assigned to the subset is calculated as follows:

$$m'(\{< a_i, null >\}) = \Pi_{j=1}^{l}(1 - Sim(a_i, b_{ij})) \tag{8}$$

The mass distributed to $\{< a_i, null >\}$, therefore, represents the degree of belief that none of the target attributes is the attribute correspondence of source attribute, a_i.

DS theory requires that the sum of all masses assigned to every indistinguishable subset equals to 1. We scale the mass distribution, m', by the following formula:

$$m(A) = \frac{m'(A)}{\sum_{B \subseteq \Theta} m'(B)} \tag{9}$$

where A and B are subsets of Θ. The mass distribution produced by (9) assigns a mass to every indistinguishable subset of Θ, which represents the degree of belief by the matcher that the attribute correspondence of the source attribute, a_i, belongs to the subset.

3.3   Combining Mass Distributions from Multiple Matchers

We now have a mass distribution by each of the individual matchers, which assigns a mass to every indistinguishable subset of Θ. A mass distribution can be seen as an opinion expressed by a matcher on the degree of belief that the attribute correspondence of the source attribute belongs to an indistinguishable subset. Using Dempster's combination rule, we can take into account different opinions by different matchers by combining the mass distributions by these matchers. The mass distribution produced after this is used to select the top k attribute correspondences of each source attribute.

4   Resolving Conflicts between Attribute Correspondences

We have now the top k attribute correspondences of each source attribute. However, these attribute correspondences have so far been selected for an individual source attribute only. There might be conflicts between attribute correspondences of two or more source attributes (ie. the best correspondences of two different source attributes are the same target attribute). To resolve any conflicts that may arise between attribute correspondences, the attribute correspondences of source attributes are collectively selected to maximize the sum of all the masses on the attribute correspondence of every source attribute. The algorithm is given in Algorithm 1.

For example, suppose that both source and target schemas have three attributes, the source attributes are {*Author, Publisher, Published Date*}, and the target attributes are {*Author, Keywords, Release Date*}. We have the top k ($k = 3$) correspondences of each source attribute: { m($<Author,Author>$) = 0.88, m($<Author,null>$) = 0.11, m($<Author,Keywords>$) = 0.01 }, { m($<Publisher,Author>$) = 0.47, m($<Publisher,null>$) = 0.40, m($<Publisher, Keywords>$) = 0.13}, { m($<Published Date,Release Date>$) = 0.87, m($<Published Date,null>$) = 0.13, m($<Published Date, Author>$) = 0.0 }. The top attribute correspondence of "Author", $<Author,Author>$, is in conflict with the top correspondence of "Publisher", $<Publisher,Author>$. By using our algorithm, { $<Author,Author>$,$<Publisher,null>$,$<Published Date,Release Date>$ } has the maximum sum of mass function values.

Algorithm 1. Resolving Conflicts

Input: A set of all the possible combinations of attribute correspondences $\Omega = \{C|C = \{< a_1, b_1' >, < a_2, b_2' > ... < a_m, b_m' >\}\}$,where $< a_i, b_i' > \in \{< a_i, b_{i1} >, < a_i, b_{i2} >, ..., < a_i, b_{ik} >\}$ (the top $k$only correspondences of a_i)

Output: A collection of correspondences with the maximum sum of the mass values of the correspondences for every source attribute

1: $Max \leftarrow 0$; $Best \leftarrow null$.
2: **for** each $C \in \Omega$ **do**
3:   $Sum = \Sigma_{i=1}^{m} m(< a_i, b_i' >)$, where $m(< a_i, b_i' >)$ is the mass function value of $< a_i, b_i' >$
4:   **if** $Sum > Max$ **then**
5:     $Max \leftarrow Sum$; $Best \leftarrow C$;
6:   **end if**
7: **end for**
8: **return** Best

---

5   Experimental Results

5.1   Dataset

To evaluate our approach, we have selected a set of query interfaces on the real-world websites from the ICQ Query Interfaces dataset at UIUC, which contains manually extracted schemas of 100 interfaces in 5 different domains: Airfares, Automobiles, Books, Jobs, and Real Estates. In this paper we have focused on 1:1 matching only, so only 88 interfaces are chosen from the dataset. In each domain we choose an interface as the source interface, and use others as the target ones.

5.2   Performance Metrics

We use three metrics: precision, recall, and F-measure [20, 10, 22]. Precision is the percentage of correct matches over all matches identified by a matcher.

Table 1. The precisions of different matchers

	Edit distance	Jaro distance	Semantic similarity	Our matcher
Airfares	83.3%	56.8%	86.4%	92.0%
Automobiles	84.4%	48.1%	93.1%	96.3%
Books	87.0%	48.8%	92.0%	94.4%
Jobs	68.5%	50.0%	71.0%	91.9%
Real Estates	86.8%	52.9%	81.6%	93.8%
Average	82.1%	51.3%	84.8%	93.7%

Recall is the percentage of correct matches by a matcher over all the matches by domain experts. F-measure is the incorporation of precision and recall. In our approach the "no match" ("null") is also an answer to the source attribute. So it is always possible to find a correspondence to each source attribute, that is, the number of matches by our approach equals to the number of matches identified by experts. So in our approach, precision and recall are both the same, and we use precision only.

5.3 Discussion on Experimental Results

First, for each domain we perform four experiments, we use three individual matchers: edit distance, Jaro distance and semantic similarity (the data type matcher cannot be used alone) separately to find matches between the source and target schemas, and compare their results with our new approach. In Table 1, we can see that the precisions of individual matchers and our approach. Our matcher gets an average precision of "93.7%" which is much higher than individual matchers.

Second, we compare our results with the work in [9], which also uses the same dataset for their experiments. However, in [9], they not only focus on 1:1 matching but also handle 1:m matching. In their experiments, a 1:m match is counted as m 1:1 matches. So we can only roughly compare our approach with their work.

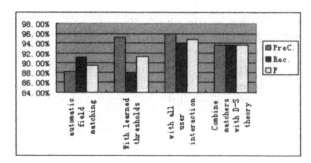

Fig. 3. Precision, recall and K measure of different matchers

As we discussed in section 5.2, precision is the same as recall in our experiments. According to the definition of F-measure in [9], $F = \frac{2PR}{P+R}$, where P is precision and R is Recall, the F-measure is also the same as precision. In [9] they did three experiments, the first one is on automatic matching which used a weighted strategy to combine multiple matchers and a 0 threshold is used to select the combined match results. The second experiment is almost the same as the first one but the threshold is obtained by training. The last one allowed user interaction. As shown in Figure 3, we can see that without training (learned threshold), the results of our approach are better. When they use the learned threshold, their precision is better than ours, but we have higher recall and F-measure. Finally, when user interactions are allowed in their approach, their results are better than ours. So we can see, our approach is effective and accurate for an automatic schema matching across query interfaces without training and user interaction.

6   Related Work

Many approaches have been proposed for automatic schema matching [9, 10, 12, 13, 14, 15, 16]. We relate our work to the existing works in two kinds of matching methods.

First, like in our approach, strategies have also been proposed in some approaches [10, 12] to combine multiple matchers. Cupid [10] considers linguistic similarity and structural similarity between elements and uses a weighted formula to combine these two similarities together. The weighted strategy is the most popular strategy used in combining individual matchers. However, weights have to be manually generated and are domain dependent.

COMA [12] also does 1:1 matching, and combines individual matchers in a flexible way. It allows users to tailor match strategies by selecting the match algorithms and their combination for a given match problem. It also allows users to provide feedback which can help improve match results. In this system, several aggregation strategies have been provided for users to choose. They are Max, Min, Average and Weighted strategies. As we discussed in Section 1, these strategies are effective in some situations while sometimes they cannot combine results well, and choosing strategies by users involves human efforts.

In [9], they also used weights to combine multiple matchers. However, they used clustering to find attribute correspondences across multiple interfaces. A threshold is required for the combined match results, which needs to be manually generated and is domain dependent. So this approach also involves human effort.

Second, some approaches [6, 8] do not combine multiple matches. MGS [6] and DCM [8] depend on the distribution of attributes rather than linguistic or domain information. Superior to other schema matching approaches, these approaches can discover synonyms by analyzing the distribution of attributes in the given schemas. However, they work well only when a large training dataset is available, and this is not always the case.

7   Conclusions and Future Work

In this paper we proposed a new approach to combining multiple matchers by using the Dempster-Shafer theory of evidence and presented an algorithm for resolving the conflicts among the correspondences of different source attributes. In our approach, different matches are viewed as different sources of evidence, and mass distributions are defined on the basis of the match results from these matchers. We use Dempster's combination rule to combine these mass dustributions, and choose the top k correspondences of each source attribute. Conflicts between the correspondences of different source attributes are finally resolved. We have implemented a prototype and tested it using a large dataset that contains real-world query interfaces in five different domains. The experimental results demonstrate the feasibility and accuracy of our approach.

We have focused on one-to-one matching between schemas in this paper. In the near future we will extend our approach to complex matching. There are more issues on uncertainty in complex matching, such as how many groups the attributes in a schema should be divided into, and which group should contain a specific attribute. Using uncertainty theory to address these issues could be feasible and effective.

References

1. Bergman, M.K.: The deep web: Surfacing hidden value. BrightPlanet (2001)
2. Dragut, E.C., Yu, C.T., Meng, W.: Meaningful labeling of integrated query interfaces. In: Proceedings of the 32th International Conference on Very Large Data Bases (VLDB 2006), pp. 679–690 (2006)
3. Shvaiko, P., Euzenat, J.: A survey of schema-based matching approaches. Journal of Data Semantics, 146–171 (2005)
4. Rahm, E., Bernstein, P.A.: A survey of approaches to automatic schema matching. VLDB Journal 10(4), 334–350 (2001)
5. He, B., Tao, T., Chang, K.C.C.: Clustering structured web sources: A schema-based, model-differentiation approach. In: Proceedings of the joint of the 20th International Conference on Data Engineering and 9th International Conference on Extending Database Technology (ICDE/EDBT) Ph.D. Workshop, pp. 536–546 (2004)
6. He, B., Chang, K.C.C.: Statistical schema matching across web query interfaces. In: Proceedings of the 22th ACM International Conference on Management of Data (SIGMOD 2003), pp. 217–228 (2003)
7. Melnik, S., Garcia-Molina, H., Rahm, E.: Similarity flooding: A versatile graph matching algorithm and its application to schema matching. In: Proceedings of the 18th International Conference on Data Engineering (ICDE 2002), pp. 117–128 (2002)
8. He, B., Chang, K.C.C., Han, J.: Discovering complex matchings across web query interfaces: a correlation mining approach. In: Proceedings of the 10th ACM SIGKDD International Conference on Knowledge Discovery and Data Mining (KDD 2004), pp. 148–157 (2004)

9. Wu, W., Yu, C.T., Doan, A., Meng, W.: An interactive clustering-based approach to integrating source query interfaces on the deep web. In: Proceedings of the 23th ACM International Conference on Management of Data (SIGMOD 2004), pp. 95–106 (2004)
10. Madhavan, J., Bernstein, P.A., Rahm, E.: Generic schema matching with cupid. In: Proceedings of the 27th International Conference on Very Large Data Bases (VLDB 2001), pp. 49–58 (2001)
11. Wang, J., Wen, J.R., Lochovsky, F.H., Ma, W.Y.: Instance-based schema matching for web databases by domain-specific query probing. In: Proceedings of the 30th International Conference on Very Large Data Bases (VLDB 2004), pp. 408–419 (2004)
12. Do, H.H., Rahm, E.: Coma - a system for flexible combination of schema matching approaches. In: Proceedings of the 28th International Conference on Very Large Data Bases (VLDB 2002), pp. 610–621 (2002)
13. Beneventano, D., Bergamaschi, S., Castano, S., Corni, A., Guidetti, R., Malvezzi, G., Melchiori, M., Vincini, M.: Information integration: The momis project demonstration. In: Proceedings of the 26th International Conference on Very Large Data Bases (VLDB 2000), pp. 611–614 (2000)
14. Castano, S., Antonellis, V.D., di Vimercati, S.D.C.: Global viewing of heterogeneous data sources. IEEE Transactions on Knowledge and Data Engineering 13(2), 277–297 (2001)
15. Doan, A., Domingos, P., Levy, A.Y.: Learning source description for data integration. In: Proceedings of the 3rd International Workshop on the Web and Databases (WebDB 2000) (Informal Proceedings), pp. 81–86 (2000)
16. Doan, A., Domingos, P., Halevy, A.Y.: Reconciling schemas of disparate data sources: A machine-learning approach. In: Proceedings of the 20th ACM International Conference on Management of Data (SIGMOD 2001), pp. 509–520 (2001)
17. Lowrance, J.D., Garvey, T.D.: Evidential reasoning: An developing concept. In: Proceedings of the IEEE International Conference on Cybernetics and Society (ICCS 1981), pp. 6–9 (1981)
18. Shafer, G.: A Mathematical Theory of Evidence. Princeton University Press, Princeton (1976)
19. Hall, P., Dowling, G.: Approximate string matching. Computing Surveys, 381–402 (1980)
20. Halevy, A.Y., Madhavan, J.: Corpus-Based Knowledge Representation. In: Proceedings of the 18th International Joint Conference on Artificial Intelligence (IJCAI 2003), pp. 1567–1572 (2003)
21. Cohen, W.W., Ravikumar, P., Fienberg, S.E.: A comparison of string distance metrics for name-matching tasks. In: Proceedings of the 18th International Joint Conference on Artificial Intelligence Workshop on Information Integration on the Web (IIWeb 2003), pp. 73–78 (2003)
22. van Rijsbergen, C.J.: Information Retrieval. Butterworths (1979)
23. Doan, A., Madhavan, J., Dhamankar, R., Domingos, P., Halevy, A.Y.: Learning to match ontologies on the semantic web. VLDB Journal 12(4), 303–319 (2003)

A Generic Data Level Implementation of ModelGen

Andrew Smith and Peter McBrien

Dept. of Computing, Imperial College London,
Exhibition Road, London SW7 2AZ

Abstract. The model management operator ModelGen translates a schema expressed in one modelling language into an equivalent schema expressed in another modelling language, and in addition produces a mapping between those two schemas. This paper presents an implementation of ModelGen which in addition allows for the translation of data instances from the source to the target schema, and *vice versa*. The translation mechanism is distinctive from others in that it takes a generic approach that can be applied to any modelling language.

1 Introduction

ModelGen is a model management [1] operator that translates a schema from one **data modelling language** (**DML**) into an equivalent schema in another DML and also produces a mapping between the schemas. To date, no implementation of ModelGen completely meets these criteria [2].

In this paper we describe a generic implementation of ModelGen that creates data level translations between schemas by the composition of generic transformations, as well as a bidirectional mapping from the source to the target schema. A distinguishing feature of this work is that the choice of transformations does not rely on knowledge of the source DML. An implementation of ModelGen such as this is useful in a number of circumstances. For example, an e-business may wish to move data between its back end SQL database and its XML based web pages without having to re-engineer the mappings every time the database schema or web pages are changed.

There are two specific prerequisites to translating schemas between DMLs automatically. Firstly we need an accurate and generic UMM capable of describing the schemas and the constructs of both the source and the target DML, so the system can recognise when a given schema matches those constructs. In this paper we make use of the **hypergraph data model** (**HDM**) [3] to accurately describe constructs and schemas. The constructs of a number of DMLs, including XML, UML class diagrams, ER and SQL, have already been defined in terms of the HDM [3,4]. Secondly we need an information preserving [5] way of *transforming* the resulting HDM schema such that the structure of its constructs match those of the target DML. We use the **Both-As-View** (**BAV**) data integration technique [6] to transform schemas.

Figure 1 gives an overview of our approach. In step 1 the source schema S_s is translated into an equivalent HDM schema, S_{hdm-s}. Next, a series of transformations are applied to S_{hdm-s} to transform it to S_{hdm-t} that is equivalent to a schema in the target DML. In step 3 the constructs in S_{hdm-t} are translated into their equivalents in the target DML to create S_t.

A. Gray, K. Jeffery, and J. Shao (Eds.): BNCOD 2008, LNCS 5071, pp. 63–74, 2008.

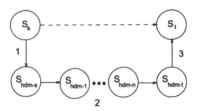

Fig. 1. Overview of the approach taken

Step one of this process depends on existing definitions of high level DML constructs in the HDM. The contribution we make in this paper is to show how steps 2 and 3 can be automated without having to know the DML used to create S_s. Firstly we present an algorithm for identifying schema objects within the HDM schema that match constructs in the target DML and secondly we present an automatic way of choosing the transformation rules at run time that transform a schema expressed in the HDM and its data into an equivalent schema that matches the constructs of the target DML.

The remainder of this paper is structured as follows: Section 2 gives a brief overview of the HDM and the BAV data integration technique and introduces an example schema. We also describe BAV composite transformations and introduce a new one. In Section 3 we present our algorithm for matching HDM schema objects with constructs in a target DML. Section 4 introduces the algorithm we use to select appropriate composite transformations for the translation. Section 5 gives an example translation. In Section 6 we present some experimental results and some analysis. Section 7 describes other proposals for **ModelGen** as well as some specific model to model translators. Finally Section 8 offers some conclusions.

2 HDM and BAV

The HDM uses a set of three simple constructs: nodes, edges and constraints, to model high level constructs in a given DML. HDM nodes and edges can have associated data values or extents. Each element in the XML instance document is assigned a unique object identifier (OID) shown next to the element. If the node representing the element is not a leaf node and does not have any key nodes associated with it then this OID becomes the extent of the node. For example, Figure 3 shows how HDM represents the XML Schema and accompanying XML instance document in Figure 2. The extent of HDM node $\langle\langle \text{dept} \rangle\rangle$ is $\{01,04,07\}$. If there is a key associated with the element then the extent of the element node is that of the key. For example the extent of $\langle\langle \text{person} \rangle\rangle$ is $\{1,2\}$. The extent of an edge is a tuple made up of values from the nodes or edges it joins. For example the extent of HDM edge $\langle\langle \_,\text{person,name} \rangle\rangle$ is $\{\langle 1,\text{'John Smith'} \rangle, \langle 2,\text{'Peter Green'} \rangle\}$.

When defining the constructs of high level DMLs in the HDM each construct falls into one of four categories [3], the following three of which we use in this paper when describing the XML Schema and SQL data models:

- **Nodal** constructs can exist on their own and are represented by a node. The root node of an XML Schema and an SQL table are examples of a nodal constructs.

- **Link-Nodal** constructs are associated with a parent construct and are represented by a node and an edge linking the node to the parent. XML attributes and elements are link-nodal constructs, as are SQL columns.
- **Constraint** constructs have no extent but rather constrain the values that can occur in the constructs they are associated with. They are represented in HDM by one or more of the HDM constraint operators [3]. Those used in this paper are: inclusion ($\subseteq$), mandatory ($\triangleright$), unique ($\triangleleft$) and reflexive ($\xrightarrow{id}$). A SQL foreign key is an example of a constraint construct that is represented in the HDM by an inclusion constraint between two HDM nodes representing SQL columns.

The variants of a high level construct can be modelled using different combinations of constraints. For example, the fact that the XML attribute, id, in Figure 2 is a `required` attribute is modelled in HDM by adding a $\triangleright$ operator between $\langle\langle person\rangle\rangle$ and $\langle\langle \_,person,id\rangle\rangle$. This means that every value in $\langle\langle person\rangle\rangle$ must also appear in the edge *i.e.* there can be no value of the parent element without an associated attribute value. An attribute that does not have the `required` flag set would not generate this extra constraint.

We use the BAV data integration technique [6] to transform our schemas. A BAV **transformation pathway** is made up of a sequence of transformations which either add, delete or rename a single schema object thereby generating a new schema. The extent of the new schema object or of the one removed is defined as a query on the extents of the existing schema objects. In this way the information preserving transformation

```
<xsd:complexType name = "person_type">
 <xsd:sequence>
  <xsd:element name = "name" type = "xsd:string" />
 </xsd:sequence>
 <xsd:attribute name = "id" type = "xsd:int" use = "required"/>
</xsd:complexType>
<xsd:element name = "staff">
 <xsd:complexType>
  <xsd:sequence>
   <xsd:element name = "dept" maxOccurs = "unbounded">
    <xsd:complexType>
     <xsd:sequence>
      <xsd:element name = "person" type = "person_type"
        minOccurs = "0" maxOccurs = "unbounded" />
     </xsd:sequence>
     <xsd:attribute name = "dname" type = "xsd:string"/>
    </xsd:complexType>
   </xsd:element>
  </xsd:sequence>
 </xsd:complexType>
 <xsd:key name = "personkey">
  <xsd:selector xpath = "./dept/person" />
  <xsd:field xpath = "@id" />
 </xsd:key>
</xsd:element>

<staff> 00
<dept dname = 'Finance'> 01
     <person id = "1"> 02
         <name>John Smith</name> 03
     </person>
</dept>
<dept dname='HR'> 04
     <person id = "2"> 05
         <name>Peter Green</name> 06
     </person>
</dept>
<dept dname='IT'> 07
</dept>
</staff>
```

Fig. 2. S_{xml} **Fig. 3.** $S_{hdm-xml}$

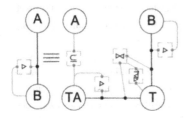 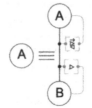 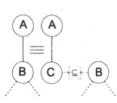

Fig. 4. expand_mv   **Fig. 5.**   **Fig. 6.** inc_expand
id_node_expand

pathway made up of schemas and transformation operations is created that shows in detail how a source schema is transformed into a target schema. This transformation pathway forms a mapping between the schemas.

2.1 Composite Transformations

BAV transformations are fine grained and allow for accurate translations, but since each step only changes one schema object a large number of transformations are needed for most operations. To avoid the need to programme each transformation step separately, information preserving **composite transformations** (**CT**s) can be defined that are templates, describing common patterns of transformation steps.

Three such CTs are used when we translate between schemas in the XML Schema and SQL modelling languages. Two of those used, namely id_node_expand and inc-_expand, have been previously defined [3] and are shown graphically in Figures 5 and 6, respectively. The third CT, expand_mv, is defined by the pseudo code in Algorithm 1 and illustrated in Figure 4. It is useful when translating from a DML that supports multivalued attributes (such as XML Schema) into to a target DML that does not (such as SQL). In the figure, the $\bowtie$ symbol represents a join operation between $\langle\!\langle\_,T,B\rangle\!\rangle$ and $\langle\!\langle\_,T,TA\rangle\!\rangle$ *i.e.* the constraints linked to the join apply to both edges. The *contains* predicate [3] in the algorithm holds when its first argument appears as a construct in the formula that is in the second argument. We will see in Section 5 how these three CTs can be used to translate the XML schema in Figure 2 to SQL.

3 AutoMatch

The detailed constraint language used in the HDM allows us to accurately identify groups of HDM constructs that correspond to an equivalent high level DML construct. Table 3 shows the constraints associated with the various constructs in SQL. $\langle\!\langle T\rangle\!\rangle$ is an HDM node representing an SQL table, $\langle\!\langle C\rangle\!\rangle$ represents a column in that table and $\langle\!\langle\_,T,C\rangle\!\rangle$ links the two nodes. In the final line of the table $\langle\!\langle C\rangle\!\rangle$ represents a foreign key column and $\langle\!\langle T\rangle\!\rangle$ the table the foreign key links to.

In Figure 3, the constraints associated with $\langle\!\langle\_,person,name\rangle\!\rangle$ match those of a not null SQL column as shown in Table 3, where $\langle\!\langle person\rangle\!\rangle$ acts as the table node and

---

Algorithm 1. expand_mv($\langle\langle B \rangle\rangle, \langle\langle \_,A,B \rangle\rangle$)

if $\langle\langle A \rangle\rangle \lhd \langle\langle \_,A,B \rangle\rangle$ **then**
  └ Exception
addNode($\langle\langle T \rangle\rangle, \langle\langle \_,A,B \rangle\rangle$)
addNode($\langle\langle TA \rangle\rangle, [\{x\} \mid \{x,y\} \leftarrow \langle\langle \_,A,B \rangle\rangle]$)
addEdge($\langle\langle \_,T,TA \rangle\rangle, [\{\{x,y\},x\} \mid \{x,y\} \leftarrow \langle\langle \_,A,B \rangle\rangle]$)
addEdge($\langle\langle \_,T,B \rangle\rangle, [\{\{x,y\},y\} \mid \{x,y\} \leftarrow \langle\langle \_,A,B \rangle\rangle]$)
addCons($\langle\langle TA \rangle\rangle \subseteq \langle\langle A \rangle\rangle$)
addCons($\langle\langle T \rangle\rangle \lhd \langle\langle \_,T,TA \rangle\rangle \bowtie \langle\langle \_,T,TA \rangle\rangle$)
addCons($\langle\langle T \rangle\rangle \rhd \langle\langle \_,T,B \rangle\rangle \bowtie \langle\langle \_,T,B \rangle\rangle$)
addCons($\langle\langle T \rangle\rangle \xrightarrow{\text{id}} \langle\langle \_,T,TA \rangle\rangle \bowtie \langle\langle \_,T,B \rangle\rangle$)
addCons($\langle\langle TA \rangle\rangle \rhd \langle\langle \_,T,TA \rangle\rangle$)
addCons($\langle\langle B \rangle\rangle \rhd \langle\langle \_,T,B \rangle\rangle$)
foreach $c \in Cons$ forwhich contains($\langle\langle \_,A,B \rangle\rangle, c$) **do**
  └ deleteCons(c)
deleteEdge($\langle\langle \_,A,B \rangle\rangle, \langle\langle T \rangle\rangle$)

Table 1. SQL constructs and the associated constraints

SQL Construct	Variant	HDM Constraints
Column	null	$\langle\langle T \rangle\rangle \rhd \langle\langle \_,T,C \rangle\rangle, \langle\langle T \rangle\rangle \lhd \langle\langle \_,T,C \rangle\rangle$
Column	not null	$\langle\langle C \rangle\rangle \rhd \langle\langle \_,T,C \rangle\rangle, \langle\langle T \rangle\rangle \lhd \langle\langle \_,T,C \rangle\rangle, \langle\langle T \rangle\rangle \rhd \langle\langle \_,T,C \rangle\rangle$
Primary Key		$\langle\langle T \rangle\rangle \xrightarrow{\text{id}} \langle\langle \_,T,C \rangle\rangle, \langle\langle C \rangle\rangle \rhd \langle\langle \_,T,C \rangle\rangle, \langle\langle T \rangle\rangle \lhd \langle\langle \_,T,C \rangle\rangle$
		$\langle\langle T \rangle\rangle \rhd \langle\langle \_,T,C \rangle\rangle$
Foreign Key		$\langle\langle C \rangle\rangle \subseteq \langle\langle T \rangle\rangle$

$\langle\langle name \rangle\rangle$ the column node. Conversely the constraints on $\langle\langle \_,staff,dept \rangle\rangle$ do not match any of the SQL constructs.

AutoMatch as shown in Algorithm 2, loops through all the edges in S, $edges(S)$, comparing the associated constraints with those generated when a construct from the target DML is expressed in the HDM. Each edge in $edges(S)$ has a target model construct label attached to it that is initially set to null. We use this label to identify the target DML construct that the HDM schema object has been matched to. A similar algorithm is used to identify matches between HDM constraint constructs in S, and constructs in the target DML.

get_constraints(S, e) returns the list of constraint operators in S that are attached to e. get_target_constraint_constraints returns the constraint list for ts. For example, if ts was a SQL column, the function would return the first and second lines from Table 3. match(dc, tc) returns true if dc matches any of the variants of ts. label_dependent_schema_objects(e, ts) sets the label of e in $edges(S)$ to ts. If the HDM representation of ts includes constructs other than e these are also labelled with the appropriate target DML construct.

Consider $\langle\langle \_,person,name \rangle\rangle$ in Figure 3. If our target model was SQL then the algorithm would identify this edge as part of a SQL column. $\langle\langle person \rangle\rangle$.label would be set to `table` and $\langle\langle \_,person,name \rangle\rangle$.label and $\langle\langle name \rangle\rangle$.label would be set to `column`.

Algorithm 2. AutoMatch(S,TM)

Input: S:an HDM schema, TM:the list of target DML constructs
return *true if all edges have been labelled, otherwise false*
all_labelled := true;
foreach *e in edges(S)* **do**
    dc := get_constraints(S, e);
    foreach *ts in TM* **do**
        if *e.label = null* **then**
            tc := get_target_construct_constraints(ts);
            if match(dc, tc) **then**
                label_dependent_schema_objects(e, ts);

    if *e.label = null* **then**
        all_labelled := false;
return *all_labelled*;

In contrast $\langle\!\langle\_,dept,person\rangle\!\rangle$ cannot be matched to any target DML structures and so $\langle\!\langle\_,dept,person\rangle\!\rangle$.label remains null.

4   AutoTransform

AutoTransform transforms the unidentified HDM constructs of our source schema into equivalent groups of HDM constructs that match those representing a construct in the target DML. It is based on a search of the set of possible schemas that can be created by applying CTs to unidentified schema elements. This set is called the **world space** [7] of the problem. It can be represented as a graph whose nodes are the individual HDM schemas and whose edges are the CTs needed to get from one HDM schema to the next. The world space graph for the example in Section 5 is shown in Figure 7. The algorithm performs a depth first search on the world space starting from the initial state and executing CTs until a solution or a dead end is reached.

To limit the number of possible actions that may be performed at each node of the world space graph, each action must satisfy certain preconditions before it can be

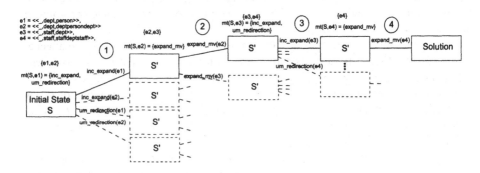

Fig. 7. The world space graph for the example

Table 2. The preconditions of the CTs used in the example

Transformation	edge	leaf	reflexive	join
inc_expand	Y	N	N	N
um_redirection	Y	N	DNC	N
expand_mv	Y	Y	N	N
id_node_expand	N	Y	N	N

executed. In our algorithm the preconditions rely on the structure of the graph surrounding the schema object the CT is to be applied to. Some of the CTs and their preconditions are shown in Table 2. In addition to those mentioned in Section 2.1 we include um_redirection [3]. The DNC in the table means we Do Not Care (DNC) whether the precondition is met or not. If we assume *so* is the current schema object the preconditions are:

edge is *so* an edge
leaf is *so* a leaf node or connected to a leaf node
reflexive is there a reflexive constraint attached to *so*
join does *so* take part in a join

As an example consider the inc_expand transformation. It can only be applied to an edge, the edge must not be attached to leaf node, there must not be a reflexive constraint on the edge and the edge must not take part in a join. As we saw in the previous section, AutoMatch was unable to match $\langle\langle\_,\text{dept,person}\rangle\rangle$ in Figure 3 to any target DML construct. We see, however, that this edge matches all the preconditions for inc_expand. These preconditions provide a heuristic method of selecting the CTs to execute. Those CTs that match the preconditions for a given node in the world space graph are put into a list and those have the fewest DNCs, *i.e.* that match the preconditions most closely, are put at the top of the list.

AutoTransform works as follows, first AutoMatch is run to label $edges(S)$. If AutoMatch is able to label all the edges in $edges(S)$ the transformation has been a success, the current schema is added to the result pathway and the algorithm returns the pathway. Otherwise, the algorithm loops through all the edges in $edges(S)$ looking for those with null labels. When one is found the matching_cts function is called to create an ordered list of CTs whose preconditions match the structure of the graph surrounding the edge. The hashmap, CT_tried, is checked to make sure the CT at the top of the list has not been tried on the current edge in the current schema. If it has the next CT is tried. If not the CT is applied to the edge to create schema S'. The current schema, S, is then added to the result pathway and CT_tried is updated with the current edge and schema. The algorithm is then called again with the transformed schema and the tail of the pathway.

If no suitable transformation can be found for any of the unidentified schema elements then the head function is used to remove the most recent schema from the result pathway to allow backtracking. For example, in Figure 7 if we came to a dead end after step 1 we could backtrack to schema S and try the inc_expand transformation on e2. If the result path is empty then we have failed to transform the schema. If it does not fail the algorithm is run again on S' with the updated result pathway.

Algorithm 3. AutoTransform(S, TM, CT, pathway)

Input: S: an HDM schema, TM: the list of target DML constructs,
CT: the set of possible CTs, $pathway$: the transformation pathway, initially []
return *a transformation pathway describing how to transform the source schema into one*
that matches the constructs of the target DML
CT_tried = new HashMap;
if AutoMatch(S, TM) **then**
    $pathway$:= Concatenate($S, pathway$);
    return *pathway*;
else
    S' := null;
    foreach *e in edges(S)* **do**
        if *e.label = null* **then**
            $mt[]$:= matching_cts(S, e);
            foreach *t in mt[]* **do**
                if *!CT_tried.(t) contains (S,e)* **then**
                    S' := the result of applying t to e;
                    $pathway$:= Concatenate($S, pathway$);
                    $CT\_tried.put((S, e), t)$;
                    AutoTransform($S', TM, CT, pathway$);

    if *S' = null* **then**
        S' := head($pathway$);
        if *S' = null* **then**
            Exception;
        else
            AutoTransform(S', TM, CT, tail($pathway$));

---

5   Example Transformation from XML to SQL

In this section, we show how AutoTransform is used to transform the schema shown in
Figure 3 into one that matches the structure of an SQL schema represented in the HDM.
The world space for the example is shown in Figure 7 and the list of CTs selected by
the algorithm is shown below.

1. inc_expand($\langle\!\langle$person$\rangle\!\rangle, \langle\!\langle$_,dept,person$\rangle\!\rangle$)
2. expand_mv($\langle\!\langle$deptpersondept$\rangle\!\rangle, \langle\!\langle$_,dept,deptpersondept$\rangle\!\rangle$)
3. inc_expand($\langle\!\langle$dept$\rangle\!\rangle, \langle\!\langle$_,staff,dept$\rangle\!\rangle$)
4. expand_mv($\langle\!\langle$staffdeptstaff$\rangle\!\rangle, \langle\!\langle$_,staff,staffdeptstaff$\rangle\!\rangle$)

In the first iteration AutoMatch returns $\langle\!\langle$_,dept,person$\rangle\!\rangle$ and $\langle\!\langle$_,staff,dept$\rangle\!\rangle$ with null
labels. If we consider $\langle\!\langle$_,dept,person$\rangle\!\rangle$ first, and compare the structure of the surrounding schema with the preconditions in Table 2, we see that two CTs match. inc_expand
matches with one DNC, whereas um_redirection has two DNCs, so inc_expand is exe-
cuted. The resulting schema is shown in Figure 8. In the second iteration $\langle\!\langle$_,staff,dept$\rangle\!\rangle$

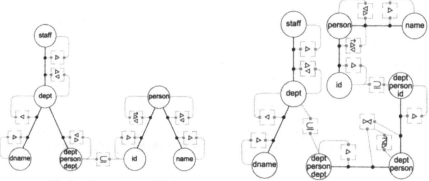

Fig. 8. After applying CT 1   **Fig. 9.** After applying CT 2

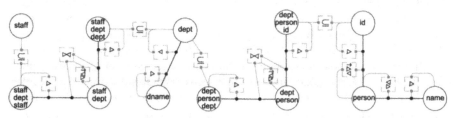

Fig. 10. Final HDM Schema

and the newly created edge $\langle\!\langle$ _,dept,deptpersondept$\rangle\!\rangle$ will be returned with null labels by **AutoMatch**. The only CT whose preconditions are met by $\langle\!\langle$ _,dept,deptpersondept$\rangle\!\rangle$ is **expand_mv**. The resulting schema is shown in Figure 9. Two similar iterations that execute CTs 3 and 4, transform $\langle\!\langle$ _,staff,dept$\rangle\!\rangle$ to create the schema shown in Figure 10, where all the HDM constructs match those of the SQL model. The $\langle\!\langle$ person$\rangle\!\rangle$, $\langle\!\langle$ deptperson$\rangle\!\rangle$, $\langle\!\langle$ dept$\rangle\!\rangle$, and $\langle\!\langle$ staffdept$\rangle\!\rangle$ nodes become tables, the nodes linked to them become columns in those tables. The remaining $\subseteq$ constraints become foreign keys.

The final HDM schema is, however, not equivalent to a well designed SQL schema. The algorithm has identified $\langle\!\langle$ dept$\rangle\!\rangle$ and $\langle\!\langle$ staff$\rangle\!\rangle$ as tables but there is no key column for either table. As part of Step 3 from Figure 1 a number of target DML specific rules to overcome cases such as this are defined. Here **id_node_expand**($\langle\!\langle$ dept$\rangle\!\rangle$) can be applied to $\langle\!\langle$ dept$\rangle\!\rangle$ and $\langle\!\langle$ staff$\rangle\!\rangle$ to create $\langle\!\langle$ dept_pk$\rangle\!\rangle$ and an edge linking it to $\langle\!\langle$ dept$\rangle\!\rangle$, along with $\langle\!\langle$ staff_pk$\rangle\!\rangle$ and an edge linking it to $\langle\!\langle$ staff$\rangle\!\rangle$ that represent key columns for the tables.

6   Analysis and Experimental Results

In analysing **AutoMatch**, we count the number of checks for equality between the source graph structures and those of the target DML. If we let the number of objects in the graph be num_o and the number of constructs, including all variants, in the target

dept
staff_pk
00
00
00

staffdept	
staffdeptstaff	staffdeptdept
00	01
00	06
00	09

dept	
dept_pk	dname
01	Finance
06	HR
09	

person	
id	name
1	John Smith
2	Peter Green

deptperson	
deptpersondept	deptpersonid
01	1
06	2

deptperson.deptpersondept → dept.dept_pk, deptperson.deptpersonid → person.id
staffdept.staffdeptstaff → staff.staff_pk, staffdept.staffdeptdept → dept.dept_pk

Fig. 11. Translated SQL Schema

DML be num_s, then the total number of checks is $num_o \times num_s$. This is $O(num_o)$ in the number of objects in the schema, since num_s is a constant. In the example num_s is four since there are four different constructs in the SQL model that we represent in the HDM.

We can analyse AutoTransform by counting the number of times we need to run AutoMatch. In the worst case, no structures in the source graph are identified as matching target structures by AutoMatch, and we will need to iterate num_o times. If we further assume we have num_t different composite transformations to choose from, and a world space graph of depth x, in a worst case scenario we will need to visit $(num_o \times num_t)^x$ nodes in the world space graph. Within each node of the world space graph we will need to perform the checks in AutoMatch.

It is clearly vital to limit both the size of $num_e \times num_t$ and x. There is a trade off here though. The more CTs we use the more likely we are to reach our goal in fewer steps, but each extra one will increase the size of the world space graph exponentially. To get around this, the CTs we use have stringent preconditions so that in practice the number that can be chosen at each iteration of the algorithm is limited. We also want to limit the chances of costly backtracking in the algorithm. The preconditions also help here in that they ensure as far as possible that CTs are only chosen in the correct circumstances. In our experiments so far we have found that very little backtracking is necessary and in most cases the most useful transformation is chosen first. We have successfully translated a number of different ER, SQL and XML schemas using the six existing CTs [3] and the new CT defined in Algorithm 1.

Figure 12 shows the number of match operations verses the number of schema objects required to translate various subsets of an XML Schema representation of DBLP into SQL. The gradient is steepest when schema objects from the source DML that have not direct equivalent in the target DML are added to the source schema, in this case nested XML Schema complex types. Where the graph is flatter constructs that could be matched directly with the target model, like XML Schema attributes, were added. Figure 13 shows matches vs schema objects for the translation of a SQL database to ER. Again the graph is steeper when tables with foreign keys are added.

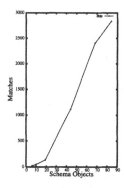

Fig. 12. DBLP XML Schema to SQL

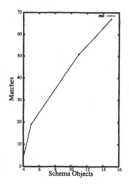

Fig. 13. SQL database to ER

The experimental results described here were produced using the AUTOMED [8] inter model data integration tool. AUTOMED implements the BAV schema transformation approach and uses the HDM as its UMM.

7   Related Work

The work most closely related to ours is that done by Atzeni et al in their MIDST system [9,10]. They also generate data-level translations by composition of elementary transformations to translate schemas and data between a number of different DMLs. Each DML, however, is defined with a number of variants. This is not necessary with our approach. In contrast to our schema level approach the rules they use are applied across an entire pair of data models and must be predefined for each pair of models in the system. Our rules are chosen at run time independently of the source DML.

The design of our UMM also differs from that used in MIDST. They create a complex, high-level model that includes abstractions of all the constructs of the models the UMM is to represent. We, on the other hand, use a set of simple UMM constructs and use combinations of these to create any complex structures needed. This is a more flexible approach and is the one most commonly adopted, Batini et al., in their survey of a data integration methods [11], suggest that a simpler UMM has advantages over more complex models.

Schema only implementations of **ModelGen** include Rondo [12] and AutoGen [13]. Numerous examples of systems for translating between specific models exist in the literature. XML and relational schemas [14] as well as ER and relational [15] and ER and XML schemas [16]. More recent work on object relational to SQL translation has been done by Mork and Bernstein [17].

8   Conclusion

This paper has presented a generic data level implementation of the **ModelGen** model management operator that returns the translated schema along with its data instances as well as a mapping from the source to the target schema. We have shown how a schema and its associated data instances can be translated from one DML to another by the application of information preserving CTs. We have described an algorithm for choosing the most suitable CT at each stage of the translation process and a mechanism for determining when a given schema matches the constructs of the target DML. Finally we presented some experimental results. Our on going work in this area includes investigating the translation of OWL schemas into the other DMLs we currently support.

References

1. Bernstein, P.A., Halevy, A.Y., Pottinger, R.: A vision of management of complex models. SIGMOD Record 29(4), 55–63 (2000)
2. Bernstein, P.A., Melnik, S.: Model management 2.0: manipulating richer mappings. In: SIGMOD Conference, pp. 1–12 (2007)
3. Boyd, M., McBrien, P.: Comparing and transforming between data models via an intermediate hypergraph data model. J. Data Semantics IV, 69–109 (2005)
4. McBrien, P., Poulovassilis, A.: A semantic approach to integrating XML and structured data sources. In: Dittrich, K.R., Geppert, A., Norrie, M.C. (eds.) CAiSE 2001. LNCS, vol. 2068, pp. 330–345. Springer, Heidelberg (2001)
5. Hull, R.: Relative information capacity of simple relational database schemata. SIAM J. Comput. 15(3), 856–886 (1986)
6. McBrien, P., Poulovassilis, A.: Data integration by bi-directional schema transformation rules. In: ICDE, pp. 227–238 (2003)
7. Weld, D.S.: An introduction to least commitment planning. AI Magazine 15(4), 27–61 (1994)
8. Boyd, M., Kittivoravitkul, S., Lazanitis, C., McBrien, P.J., Rizopoulos, N.: AutoMed: A BAV Data Integration System for Heterogeneous Data Sources. In: Persson, A., Stirna, J. (eds.) CAiSE 2004. LNCS, vol. 3084, pp. 82–97. Springer, Heidelberg (2004)
9. Atzeni, P., Cappellari, P., Bernstein, P.A.: Modelgen: Model independent schema translation. In: ICDE, pp. 1111–1112 (2005)
10. Atzeni, P., Cappellari, P., Bernstein, P.A.: Model-Independent Schema and Data Translation. In: Ioannidis, Y., Scholl, M.H., Schmidt, J.W., Matthes, F., Hatzopoulos, M., Böhm, K., Kemper, A., Grust, T., Böhm, C. (eds.) EDBT 2006. LNCS, vol. 3896, pp. 368–385. Springer, Heidelberg (2006)
11. Batini, C., Lenzerini, M., Navathe, S.B.: A comparative analysis of methodologies for database schema integration. ACM Comput. Surv. 18(4), 323–364 (1986)
12. Melnik, S., Rahm, E., Bernstein, P.A.: Rondo: A programming platform for generic model management. In: SIGMOD Conference, pp. 193–204 (2003)
13. Song, G.L., Kong, J., Zhang, K.: Autogen: Easing model management through two levels of abstraction. J. Vis. Lang. Comput. 17(6), 508–527 (2006)
14. Shanmugasundaram, J., et al.: Efficiently publishing relational data as XML documents. VLDB Journal: Very Large Data Bases 10(2–3), 133–154 (2001)
15. Premerlani, W.J., Blaha, M.R.: An approach for reverse engineering of relational databases. Commun. ACM 37(5), 42–49, 134 (1994)
16. Arijit Sengupta, S.M., Doshi, R.: XER - Extensible Entity Relationship Modeling. In: Harnad, J., et al. (eds.) Proceedings of the XML 2003 Conference, Philadelphia, PA, USA (2003)
17. Mork, P., Bernstein, P.A., Melnik, S.: Teaching a schema translator to produce o/r views. In: Parent, C., Schewe, K.-D., Storey, V.C., Thalheim, B. (eds.) ER 2007. LNCS, vol. 4801, pp. 102–119. Springer, Heidelberg (2007)

Reconciling Inconsistent Data in Probabilistic XML Data Integration

Tadeusz Pankowski[1,2]

[1] Institute of Control and Information Engineering,
Poznań University of Technology, Poland
[2] Faculty of Mathematics and Computer Science,
Adam Mickiewicz University, Poznań, Poland
tadeusz.pankowski@put.poznan.pl

Abstract. The problem of dealing with inconsistent data while integrating XML data from different sources is an important task, necessary to improve data integration quality. Typically, in order to remove inconsistencies, i.e. conflicts between data, data cleaning (or repairing) procedures are applied. In this paper, we present a probabilistic XML data integration setting. A probability is assigned to each data source and its probability models the *reliability level* of the data source. In this way, an answer (a tuple of values of XML trees) has a probability assigned to it. The problem is how to compute such probability, especially when the same answer is produced by many sources. We consider three semantics for computing such probabilistic answers: *by-peer*, *by-sequence*, and *by-subtree* semantics. The probabilistic answers can be used for resolving a class of inconsistencies violating XML functional dependencies defined over the target schema. Having a probability distribution over a set of conflicting answers, we can choose the one for which the probability of being correct is the highest.

1 Introduction

In general, in data integration systems (especially in P2P data management [12,13]) violations of consistency constraints cannot be avoided [10,15]. Data could violate consistency constraints defined over the target schema, although it satisfies constraints defined over source schemas considered in separation. In the paper we focus on XML functional dependencies as constraints over XML schemas. From a set of inconsistent values violating the functional dependency we choose one which is most likely to be correct. The choice is based on probabilities of data. We propose a model of calculating such probabilities using the reliability levels assigned to data sources.

Related Work. Dealing with inconsistent data is the subject of many work known as data cleaning [14] and consistent query answering in inconsistent databases [2]. There are two general approaches to resolve conflicts in inconsistent databases [4,8,9]: (1) the user provides a procedure deciding how the conflicts should be resolved; (2) some automatic procedures may be used – the

A. Gray, K. Jeffery, and J. Shao (Eds.): BNCOD 2008, LNCS 5071, pp. 75–86, 2008.
© Springer-Verlag Berlin Heidelberg 2008

procedures can be based on timestamps (outdated data may be removed from consideration) or reliability of data (each conflicting data has a probability of being correct assigned to it). A model based on reliabilities of data sources was discussed in [16] and was used for reconciling inconsistent updates in collaborative data sharing. In [6], authors develop a model of probabilistic relational schema mappings. Because of the uncertainty about which mapping is correct, all the mappings are considered in query answering, each with its own probability. Two semantics for probabilistic data are proposed in [6]: *by-table* and *by-sequence* semantics. Probabilities associated to data are then used to rank answers and to obtain top-k answers to queries in such a setting.

In this paper, we discuss a probabilistic XML data integration setting, where the probability models *reliability levels* of data sources. Based on these we calculate probabilities associated with answers (probabilistic answers) to queries over the target schema. We propose three semantics for producing probabilistic answers: *by-peer*, *by-sequence* (of peers), and *by-subtree* semantics. Two first of them are based on *by-table* and *by-sequence* semantics proposed in [6], but the interpretation of probabilistic mappings as well as data integration settings are quite different.

The main novel contribution of this paper is the introduction of the *by-subtree* semantics. This semantics takes into account not only sources where the answer comes from, but also contexts in which it occurs in data sources. Thanks to this, the method has the advantage over other methods because the computation of the probability is more sensitive to contexts of data in interest.

In Section 2 we introduce a motivating example and illustrate basic ideas of reconciling inconsistent data in a data integration scenario. We show the role of XML functional dependencies and probabilistic answers in reconciliation of inconsistent data. In Section 3 we discuss XML schemas and XML data (XML trees). Schema mappings and queries for XML data integration are described in Section 4 and Section 5, respectively. In Section 6, schema mappings are generalized to *probabilistic* schema mapping. They are used to define probabilistic answers to queries. Section 7 concludes the paper.

2   Reconciliation of Inconsistent Data

To illustrate our approach, let us consider Figure 1, where there are three peers P_1, P_2, and P_3 along with schema trees, S_1, S_2, S_3, and schema instances I_1, I_2, and I_3, respectively.

Over S_3 the following XML functional dependency (XFD) [1] can be defined

$$/authors/author/book/title \rightarrow$$
$$/authors/author/book/year, \qquad (1)$$

meaning that a text value (a tuple of text values) of the left-hand path (tuple of paths) uniquely determines the text value of the right-hand path. Let J be an instance of S_3. If in J there are two subtrees of type */authors/author/book*

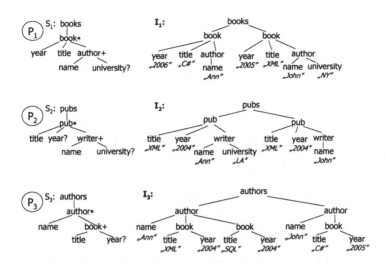

Fig. 1. XML schema trees S_1, S_2, S_3, and their instances I_1, I_2 and I_3, located in peers P_1, P_2, and P_3

which have equal values of *title*, say t, and different values of *year*, say y_1 and y_2, then we say that the set C_t

$$C_t = \{(/authors/author/book/title : t, /authors/author/book/year : y_1),$$
$$(/authors/author/book/title : t, /authors/author/book/year : y_2)\}$$

is inconsistent with respect to the XFD (1). Further on, the paths labeling values will be omitted, so we will write $C_t = \{(t, y_1), (t, y_2)\}$.

Our aim is to choose such a tuple $(t, y) \in C_t$, that can be treated as the most reliable of all tuples belonging to the inconsistent set C_t. The process of selecting such a tuple is called *reconciliation of inconsistent data*. To this order we will consider three different ways for computing probabilities for any tuple belonging to C_t, where the probability reflects trustworthiness of being correct for the corresponding tuple. Finally, a tuple with the highest probability will be selected.

To build a *probabilistic XML data integration setting*, it will be assumed that a numeric *reliability level* [16] is assigned to every peer's partner and the following *trust policy* is applied:

1. A vector $r_1, ..., r_n$ of reliability levels is assigned to source schemas $S_1, ..., S_n$, with respect to the target schema T, $\Sigma_{i=1}^n r_i = 1$. A value r_i is treated as the trustworthiness of data obtained from the source S_i.
2. Reliability level will be understood as *probability* which will be assigned to the mapping m_i from a source schema S_i to the target schema T. In this way we can say about *probabilistic schema mappings*.

Now, assume that we are interested in all pairs $(title, year)$ and that the appropriate query q has been issued against the schema S_3 on the peer P_3.

Table 1. Answers to the query q

S_1 (0.5)	$(C\#, 2006), (XML, 2005)$
S_2 (0.2)	$(XML, 2004), (XML, 2004)$
S_3 (0.3)	$(XML, 2004), (SQL, 2004), (C\#, 2005)$

Assume that reliability levels of sources S_1, S_2, and S_3 are 0.5, 0.2, and 0.3, respectively. In Table 1 there are answers returned from the three sources.

We have seven answers, where some of them are duplicated. The answers can be clustered into the following sets:

$$C_{XML} = \{(XML, 2005), (XML, 2004)\},$$
$$C_{C\#} = \{(C\#, 2006), (C\#, 2005)\},$$
$$C_{SQL} = \{(SQL, 2004)\},$$

where C_{XML} and $C_{C\#}$ are inconsistent. Thus, we have to decide which of two answers $(XML, 2005)$ or $(XML, 2004)$ is more *certain*, similarly for $(C\#, 2006)$ and $(C\#, 2005)$. As the measure of uncertainty we assign probabilities to answers, where probabilities are calculated using *reliability levels* of data sources.

To calculate probability of data in the target instance, the following three semantics will be discussed: *by-peer*, *by-sequence*, and *by-subtree* semantics.

By-peer semantics.

Any mapping is considered as a separate event in the space of elementary events. Then probability of data depends only on the peer (data source) where the data comes from. If the same data comes from many sources then its probability is the sum of probabilities of these sources. In [6] this way of creating probabilistic data is referred to as *by-table* semantics.

In Table 3 we can find probabilities of answers according to the *by-peer* semantics. Note that the fact that the tuple $(XML, 2004)$ is returned two times from S_2, has no impact on the final probability of this tuple.

By-sequence semantics.

In this approach, any sequence of mappings (of a given length) is considered as a separate event in the space of elementary events. Then probability of data depends not only on the mapping creating the data but also on the *context in which it is created*. In [6], this way of creating probabilistic data is called *by-sequence* semantics.

In Table 2 there are sequences of mappings of length 2, where a sequence (m_i, m_j) maps an instance, (I_i, I_j) of the pair of schemas (S_i, S_j) into an instance J of the schema S_3, $1 \leq i, j \leq 3$. The probability of each sequence is the multiplication of probabilities of composing mappings, e.g. $Prob(m_1, m_3) = Prob(m_1) * Prob(m_3) = 0.15$. Using probabilities of sequences, we can determine probabilities of answers to q. The probability of an answer is the sum of

Table 2. Calculation of probabilities for $(XML, 2004)$ and $(XML, 2005)$ in the *by-sequence* and *by-subtree* semantics

Seq	Prob	$(XML, 2004)$ by-sequence	$(XML, 2004)$ by-subtree	$(XML, 2005)$ by-sequence	$(XML, 2005)$ by-subtree
(m_1, m_1)	0.25	N	N	Y	Y
(m_1, m_2)	0.10	Y	Y	Y	N
(m_1, m_3)	0.15	Y	N	Y	N
(m_2, m_1)	0.10	Y	Y	Y	Y
(m_2, m_2)	0.04	Y	Y	N	N
(m_2, m_3)	0.06	Y	Y	N	N
(m_3, m_1)	0.15	Y	Y	Y	Y
(m_3, m_2)	0.06	Y	Y	N	N
(m_3, m_3)	0.09	Y	Y	N	N

Table 3. Probabilities of answers to q in three semantics

Tuple	By-peer	By-sequence	By-subtree
$(C\#, 2006)$	0.5	0.75	0.5
$(XML, 2005)$	0.5	0.75	0.5
$(XML, 2004)$	0.5	0.75	0.6
$(SQL, 2004)$	0.3	0.51	0.3
$(C\#, 2005)$	0.3	0.51	0.3

probabilities of these sequences which return the answer (denoted in the relevant columns in Table 2 by Y). Observe that, like in the case of *by-peer* semantics, the probability of an answer does not depend on the number of occurrences of the answer in the source.

By-subtree semantics.

In this method we also consider sequences of mappings, but probabilities of answers are computed in a different way. Our aim is to make the probability of an answer dependent *on the number of contexts* in which the answer occurs. For example, $(XML, 2004)$ occurs in two contexts within I_2 (and also in the target instance $J = I_1 \cup I_2 \cup I_3$), i.e. in the context of "*Ann*" and the context of "*John*". A context will be understood as a subtree (a highest-level subtree) in the target instance J. The subtree is identified by a key value. There are two subtrees in our running example, the *Ann-subtree*, and the *John-subtree*, corresponding to key values "*Ann*" and "*John*", respectively. The subtrees are ordered in the document order.

Let $(a_1, ..., a_s)$ be a tuple of key values determining subtrees in the target instance J. Let $(m_1, ..., m_s)$ be a sequence of mappings from source instances to J. The probability of the sequence $(m_1, ..., m_s)$ is taken into account while computing probability of an answer *ans*, if *ans* is inserted into the a_i-*subtree* by the mapping m_i, for some $1 \leq i \leq s$.

For example, the sequence (m_1, m_3) returns $(XML, 2004)$. However, it is re-turned by the *second* mapping, i.e. m_3, and inserted into the *first* subtree, i.e. the *Ann-subtree*. Thus, the probability of (m_1, m_3) is not taken into account while computing the probability of $(XML, 2004)$ (see Table 2) according to the *by-subtree* semantics – denoted by N in the *by-subtree* column. However, it is taken into account by the *by-sequence* semantics.

In comparison to the *by-peer* and *by-sequence* semantics, the *by-subtree* better assess trustworthiness of answers. It takes into account the number of contexts in which the answer occurs. For example, since $(XML, 2004)$ occurs in two contexts in the source I_2, the *by-subtree* semantics takes it into account and in the result its probability is higher than this of $(XML, 2005)$.

3   XML Schemas and Instances

In this paper, XML schemas will be specified by *tree-pattern formulas* [3,13]. It means that we will restrict ourselves to a subset of XML schemas – namely, to schemas without recursions and alternatives.

Definition 1. *A schema over a set L of labels conforms to the syntax:*

$$\begin{aligned} S &::= /l[E] \\ E &::= l = x \mid l[E] \mid E \wedge ... \wedge E, \end{aligned} \tag{2}$$

where $l \in L$, and x is a variable. If variable names are significant, we will write $S(\mathbf{x})$, where $\mathbf{x}$ is a vector of text-valued variables.

Example 1. The schema S_3 in Figure 1 has the following specification:
$S_3(x_1, x_2, x_3) := /authors[author[name = x_1 \wedge book[title = x_2 \wedge year = x_3]]]$.

An XML database consists of a set of XML data. We define XML data as an unordered rooted node-labeled tree (XML tree) over a set L of labels, and a set $Str \cup \{\perp\}$ of strings and the distinguished null value $\perp$ (both strings and the null value, $\perp$, are used as values of text nodes).

Definition 2. *An XML tree I is a tuple $(r, N^e, N^t, child, \lambda, \nu)$, where:*

- *r is a distinguished root node, N^e is a finite set of element nodes, and N^t is a finite set of text nodes;*
- *$child \subseteq (\{r\} \cup N^e) \times (N^e \cup N^t)$ – a relation introducing tree structure into the set $\{r\} \cup N^e \cup N^t$, where r is the root, each element node has at least one child (which is an element or text node), text nodes are leaves;*
- *$\lambda : N^e \to L$ – a function labeling element nodes with names (labels);*
- *$\nu : N^t \to Str \cup \{\perp\}$ – a function labeling text nodes with text values from Str or with the null value $\perp$.*

It will be useful to perceive an XML tree I with schema S over variables $\mathbf{x}$, as a pair (S, Ω) (called a *description*), where S is the schema, and Ω is a set of valuations of variables in $\mathbf{x}$. A valuation $\omega \in \Omega$ is a function assigning values from $Str \cup \{\perp\}$ to variables in $\mathbf{x}$, i.e. $\omega : \mathbf{x} \to Str \cup \{\perp\}$.

Example 2. The instance I_3 in Figure 1 can be represented by the following description:
$I_3 := (S_3(x_1, x_2, x_3), \{(Ann, XML, 2004), (Ann, SQL, 2004), (John, C\#, 2005)\}).$

An XML tree I satisfies a description (S, Ω), denoted $I \models (S, \Omega)$, if I satisfies (S, ω) for every $\omega \in \Omega$, where this satisfaction is defined as follows:

Definition 3. *Let S be a schema over $\mathbf{x}$, and ω be a valuation for variables in $\mathbf{x}$. An XML tree I satisfies S by valuation ω, denoted $I \models (S, \omega)$, if the root r of I satisfies S by valuation ω, denoted $(I, r) \models (S, \omega)$, where:*

1. $(I, r) \models (/l[E], \omega)$, *iff* $\exists n \in N^e \ child(r, n) \wedge (I, n) \models (l[E], \omega)$;
2. $(I, n) \models (l[E], \omega)$, *iff* $\lambda(n) = l$ *and* $\exists n' \in N^e(child(n, n') \wedge (I, n') \models (E, \omega))$;
3. $(I, n) \models (l = x, \omega)$, *iff* $\lambda(n) = l$ *and* $\exists n' \in N^t(child(n, n') \wedge \nu(n') = \omega(x))$;
4. $(I, n) \models (E_1 \wedge ... \wedge E_k, \omega)$, *iff* $(I, n) \models (E_1, \omega) \wedge \cdots \wedge (I, n) \models (E_k, \omega)$.

A description (S, Ω) represents a class of S instances with the same set of values (the same Ω), since elements in instance trees can be grouped and nested in different ways. By a *canonical instance* we will understand the instance with the maximal width, i.e. the instance where subtrees corresponding to valuations are pair-wise disjoint. For example, I_1 and I_2 in Figure 1 are canonical, whereas I_3 is not since two books are nested under one author. A canonical instance may be transformed into a required form using specification of keys [13].

4 Schema Mappings

A schema mapping specifies the semantic relationship between a source schema and a target schema. We define it as a *source-to-target dependency* [3,7,13].

Definition 4. *A mapping from a source schema S to a target schema T is an expression of the form*

$$m := \forall \mathbf{x}(S(\mathbf{x}) \Rightarrow \exists \mathbf{y} T(\mathbf{x}', \mathbf{y})), \tag{3}$$

where $\mathbf{x}' \subseteq \mathbf{x}$, and $\mathbf{y} \cap \mathbf{x} = \emptyset$.

A mapping defines one-to-one correspondence between source and target paths. Variable names are used to indicate correspondences between paths bound to variables. In practice, a correspondence also involves a function that transforms values of source and target variables. Using such functions we can express many-to-one and many-to-many correspondences. However, in this paper these functions are irrelevant to our discussion, so they will be omitted.

Example 3. The mapping from S_3 to S_2 is:
$\forall x_1, x_2, x_3(/authors[author[name = x_1 \wedge book[title = x_2 \wedge year = x_3]]] \Rightarrow \exists x_4/pubs[pub[title = x_2 \wedge year = x_3 \wedge writer[name = x_1 \wedge university = x_4]]]).$

In the following mappings we will omit quantifications.

Example 4. m_1, m_2, and m_3 are mappings from S_1 to S_3, S_2 to S_3, and S_3 to S_3, respectively:

$$m_1 := /books[book[year = x_1 \wedge title = x_2 \wedge author[name = x_3 \wedge university = x_4]$$
$$\Rightarrow /authors[author[name = x_3 \wedge book[title = x_2 \wedge year = x_1]]]$$
$$m_2 := /pubs[pub[title = x_1 \wedge year = x_2 \wedge writer[name = x_3 \wedge university = x_4]]]$$
$$\Rightarrow /authors[author[name = x_3 \wedge book[title = x_1 \wedge year = x_2]]]$$
$$m_3 := /authors[author[name = x_1 \wedge book[title = x_2 \wedge year = x_3]]]$$
$$\Rightarrow /authors[author[name = x_1 \wedge book[title = x_2 \wedge year = x_3]]]$$

A schema mapping m from a source schema S to a target schema T expresses a *constraint*, which is or is not satisfied by a pair (I, J) of XML trees, where I and J are instances of S and T, respectively.

Definition 5. *A pair (I, J) of XML trees satisfies a mapping m, $(I, J) \models m$, if for any valuation ω of variables in $\mathbf{x}$ there is a valuation σ of variables in $\mathbf{y}$ such that:*

$$I \models (S, \omega) \Rightarrow J \models (T, (\omega', \sigma)),$$

where ω' is the restriction of ω to the set $\mathbf{x}'$, denoted $\omega' = \omega[\mathbf{x}']$. Then we say that J is consistent with I and m.

In general, there may be zero or many different target instances J consistent with a given source instance I and a given mapping m [7,3].

Definition 6. *An XML data integration setting (XDI) is a triple $(\mathbf{S}, T, \mathbf{M}_{\mathbf{S}T})$, where:*

- $\mathbf{S} = (S_1, ..., S_n)$ – *an ordered set of source schemas;*
- T – *a target schema,*
- $\mathbf{M}_{\mathbf{S}T} = (m_1, ..., m_n)$ – *a set of mappings; m_i is a mapping from S_i to T.*

The following definition specifies the notion of consistency between a target instance J, a set of source instances $(I_1, ..., I_n)$ (called a *complex* source instance $\mathbf{I}$), and a given set of mappings $(m_1, ..., m_n)$.

Definition 7. *Let $\mathbf{M}_{\mathbf{S}T} = (m_1, ..., m_n)$ be a set of mappings, where m_i is a mapping from S_i to T. Let $\mathbf{I} = (I_1, ..., I_n)$ be an instance of $(S_1, ..., S_n)$. We say that a pair $(\mathbf{I}, J)$ satisfies $\mathbf{M}_{\mathbf{S}T}$, denoted $(\mathbf{I}, J) \models \mathbf{M}_{\mathbf{S}T}$, if for each m_i, J is consistent with I_i and m_i. Then J is said to be consistent with $\mathbf{I}$ and $\mathbf{M}_{\mathbf{S}T}$.*

5   Queries and Answers

In this paper we consider queries which return tuples of values (valuations) as opposed to arbitrary trees (like in [3]).

Definition 8. *A query over a target schema $T(\mathbf{x}')$, is an expression of the form*

$$q := \{\mathbf{x} \mid \exists \mathbf{x}'' T(\mathbf{x}')\}, \tag{4}$$

where $\mathbf{x}, \mathbf{x}'' \subseteq \mathbf{x}'$, $\mathbf{x} \cap \mathbf{x}'' = \emptyset$.

Example 5. *"Get all pairs (title,year)"*, can be expressed by the following query over the schema S_3:

$$\{(x_2, x_3) \mid \exists x_1(/authors[author[name = x_1 \wedge book[title = x_2 \wedge year = x_3]]])\}$$

Definition 9. *Let $q(\mathbf{x})$ be a query over a schema $T(\mathbf{x}')$ and J be an instance of T. A valuation ω of $\mathbf{x}$ is an answer to q against J, denoted $\omega \in q(J)$, if there is a valuation ω' of $\mathbf{x}'$ such that $J \models (T, \omega')$ and $\omega = \omega'[\mathbf{x}]$, i.e. ω is the restriction of ω' on $\mathbf{x}$.*

Now, let us consider an answer to a query in an XML data integration setting. Such answers in data integration settings are referred to as *certain answers* [11].

Definition 10. *Let $q(\mathbf{x})$ be a query over the target schema T in an XDI $(\mathbf{S}, T, \mathbf{M_{ST}})$. Let $\mathbf{I}$ be an instance of $\mathbf{S}$. A valuation ω of $\mathbf{x}$ is an answer (a certain answer) to q against $\mathbf{I}$, if ω is an answer to q against every J, where J is the target instance consistent with $\mathbf{I}$ and $\mathbf{M_{ST}}$, denoted $\omega \in q(\mathbf{M_{ST}}(\mathbf{I}))$.*

6   Probabilistic XML Data Integration Setting

Probabilistic schema mapping describes a probability distribution of a set of (ordinary) schema mappings. As we mentioned in Section 2, the probability of a mapping is equal to the probability (modeling the reliability) of the data source (peer) that is the domain of the mapping. In this way we define a *probabilistic XML data integration setting*.

Definition 11. *A probabilistic XML data integration setting (pXDI) is a quadruple $(\mathbf{S}, T, \mathbf{M_{ST}}, Prob)$, where $(\mathbf{S}, T, \mathbf{M_{ST}})$ is an ordinary XDI, and $Prob$ is a probability function over $\mathbf{M_{ST}}$ such that for each $m \in \mathbf{M_{ST}}$:*

- *$Prob(m) \in [0, 1]$, and*
- *$\Sigma_{m \in \mathbf{M_{ST}}} Prob(m) = 1$.*

An answer to a query q in a $pXDI$ is a pair (ω, p), where ω is an answer to q in ordinary XDI and p is a probability assigned to ω. The probability models uncertainty about haw reliable is data provided by ω. Three methods can be used to compute this probability: *by-peer* and *by-sequence* semantics, which are based on the *by-table* and *by-sequence* semantics proposed in [6], and *by-subtree* a new semantics proposed in this paper. These semantics were informally discussed in Section 2.

6.1   By-Peer Semantics

Let $(\mathbf{S}, T, \mathbf{M_{ST}}, Prob)$ be a $pXDI$ and $\mathbf{I}$ be a source instance of $\mathbf{S}$. In the *by-peer* interpretation, all the data from one source has the probability determined by the probability of the mapping defined on this data source. The probability of an answer $\omega \in q(\mathbf{M_{ST}}(\mathbf{I}))$ is the sum of the probabilities of all mappings producing this answer.

For example, answers in Table 1 are produced by mappings m_1, m_2, and m_3 with probabilities 0.5, 0.2, and 0.3, respectively. The probabilities of answers, i.e. of tuples $(title, year)$, are given in Table 3.

Definition 12. *Let q be a query over T in $(\mathbf{S}, T, \mathbf{M}_{\mathbf{S}T}, Prob)$. Let $\mathbf{I}$ be an instance of $\mathbf{S}$. Let $\mathbf{m}(\omega)$ be the subset of $\mathbf{M}_{\mathbf{S}T}$, such that for each $m \in \mathbf{m}(\omega)$, $\omega \in q(m(\mathbf{I}))$ (if m is a mapping from S_i to T, then $m(\mathbf{I}) = m(I_i)$).*

Let $p = \Sigma_{m \in \mathbf{m}(\omega)} Prob(m)$. Then we say that the pair (ω, p) is a by-peer answer to q with respect to $\mathbf{I}$ and $(\mathbf{S}, T, \mathbf{M}_{\mathbf{S}T}, Prob)$.

6.2 By-Sequence Semantics

In contrast to the *by-peer* semantics, where all the mappings were considered in separation, in the *by-sequence* model we will consider sequences of mappings. Thus, if there are n mappings (and also n peers and n data sources), we can analyze sequences with length s of (not necessarily distinct) mappings, $s \geq 1$.

In general, if we have n mappings, then there are n^s sequences of length s. Let $(\mathbf{M}_{\mathbf{S}T}, Prob)$ be a probabilistic mapping. By $\mathbf{seq}^s(\mathbf{M}_{\mathbf{S}T})$ will be denoted the set of all sequences of lengths s created from mappings in $\mathbf{M}_{\mathbf{S}T}$. Then we can think of every sequence $seq \in \mathbf{seq}^s(\mathbf{M}_{\mathbf{S}T})$ as a separate event. Probabilities assigned to sequences satisfy the following formulas:

$$Prob(seq) = \Pi_{m \in seq} Prob(m),$$
$$\Sigma_{seq \in \mathbf{seq}^s(\mathbf{M}_{\mathbf{S}T})} Prob(seq) = 1.$$

Each sequence $seq \in \mathbf{seq}^s(\mathbf{M}_{\mathbf{S}T})$ creates an instance of the target schema T. This instance will be denoted by $J_{seq} = seq(\mathbf{I}) = \bigcup_{m \in seq} m(\mathbf{I})$ and it is consistent with $\mathbf{I}$ and seq, i.e.:

- for each $m_k \in seq$, J_{seq} is consistent with I_k and m_k,
- for each ω, if $J_{seq} \models (T, \omega)$ then there is $m_k \in seq$ such that $I_k \models (S_k, \omega)$.

In our running example, we consider sequences of length 2. There are 9 such sequences (see Table 2). According to the above considerations, an answer in the *by-sequence* semantics is defined as follows:

Definition 13. *Let q be a query over T in $(\mathbf{S}, T, \mathbf{M}_{\mathbf{S}T}, Prob)$. Let $\mathbf{I}$ be an instance of $\mathbf{S}$. Let $\mathbf{seq}(\omega)$ be the subset of $\mathbf{seq}^s(\mathbf{M}_{\mathbf{S}T})$, such that for each $seq \in \mathbf{seq}(\omega)$, $\omega \in q(seq(\mathbf{I}))$.*

Let $p = \Sigma_{seq \in \mathbf{seq}(\omega)} Prob(seq)$. Then we say that the pair (ω, p) is a by-sequence answer to q with respect to $\mathbf{I}$ and $(\mathbf{S}, T, \mathbf{M}_{\mathbf{S}T}, Prob)$.

In Table 3 there are also probabilistic answers according to the *by-sequence* semantics in our running example.

6.3 By-Subtree Semantics

While computing a probabilistic answer in the *by-subtree* semantics we take into account that the answer may occur in many *contexts* in the target instance. The more contexts in which the answer occurs the highest is the probability of the answer (i.e. the answer is more likely to be correct). Note that the *by-peer* and *by-sequence* semantics are not sensitive to the number of contexts containing the considered answer.

As the contexts we assume the highest-level subtrees in the target instance. The subtree is identified by an absolute XML key [5] or a key functional dependency [1,13]. For example, for the schema S_3 we can define the key functional dependence $/authors/author/name \rightarrow /authors/author$. In our approach this key functional dependency can be equivalently expressed by the following path formula [13]:

$$\kappa(x_1) := /authors/author[name = x_1] \tag{5}$$

meaning that for a given value of x_1, the value of $\kappa(x_1)$ contains at most one node (the root of the subtree of type $/authors/author$ determined by x_1). Then an instance of S_3 contains as many subtrees, of type $/authors/author$, as there are different text values of the path $/authors/author/name$.

In our running example we have two subtrees determined by "*Ann*" and "*John*", respectively. Thus, we can consider sequences of length 2 of mappings as in the *by-sequence* semantics. However, we will use another semantics to compute probabilities of answers (as was informally discussed in Section 2).

Similarly as in *by-sequence* semantics, let q be a query over a target schema T, $\mathbf{I} = (I_1, ..., I_n)$ be an instance of $(S_1, ..., S_n)$, and $(\mathbf{M_{ST}}, Prob)$ be a probabilistic mapping. Let J be an instance of T with s subtrees, and let J be by-sequence consistent with $\mathbf{I}$ and $\mathbf{M_{ST}}$. Let $\kappa(\mathbf{z})$ be the key definition over S, where $\mathbf{z}$ is a vector of text variables. Then there are s different values of $\mathbf{z}$, say $\mathbf{a_1}, ..., \mathbf{a_s}$.

In the *by-subtree* semantics, probabilistic answers of q are defined as follows:

Definition 14. *Let* **subtree**(ω) *be the subset of* **seq**$^s(\mathbf{M_{ST}})$, *such that for each* $seq = (m^1, ..., m^s) \in \mathbf{subtree}(\omega)$

$$\omega \in q[\mathbf{z} \mapsto \mathbf{a_1}](m^1(\mathbf{I}))) \cup \cdots \cup q[\mathbf{z} \mapsto \mathbf{a_s}](m^s(\mathbf{I}))),$$

where $q[\mathbf{z} \mapsto \mathbf{a_i}]$ *is a query created from* q *by substituting variables in* $\mathbf{z}$ *(the key variables) by text values from the vector* $\mathbf{a_i}$.

Let $p = \Sigma_{seq \in \mathbf{subtree}(\omega)} Prob(seq)$. *Then we say that* ω *is a by-sebtree answer to* q *with probability* p, *with respect to* $\mathbf{I}$ *and* $(\mathbf{M_{ST}}, Prob)$.

Example 6. For the sequence (m_1, m_2) of mappings (Example 4), the query q (Example 5), and the key (5), we have (compare Table 2):

$$q[x_1 \mapsto "Ann"](m_1(I_1)) = \{(C\#, 2006)\},$$
$$q[x_1 \mapsto "John"](m_2(I_2)) = \{(XML, 2004)\}.$$

7   Conclusion

In this paper we discussed an approach to probabilistic XML data integration systems. We use probabilities to model reliabilities of data sources and use them to compute probabilistic answers. We discuss three ways to determine probabilistic answers: *by-peer*, *by-sequence*, and *by-subtree* semantics. We claim that the *by-subtree* semantics has the advantage over two others, since it more precisely computes probabilistic answers. This is significant contribution of this paper. Probabilities associated to inconsistent answers can be used to select these which are more likely to be correct and can be used to resolve inconsistencies violating XML functional dependencies.

Acknowledgement. The work was supported in part by the Polish Ministry of Science and Higher Education under Grant N516 015 31/1553.

References

1. Arenas, M.: Normalization theory for XML. SIGMOD Record 35(4), 57–64 (2006)
2. Arenas, M., Bertossi, L.E., Chomicki, J.: Consistent Query Answers in Inconsistent Databases. In: PODS, pp. 68–79 (1999)
3. Arenas, M., Libkin, L.: XML Data Exchange: Consistency and Query Answering. In: PODS Conference, pp. 13–24 (2005)
4. Bohannon, P., Flaster, M., Fan, W., Rastogi, R.: A Cost-Based Model and Effective Heuristic for Repairing Constraints by Value Modification. In: SIGMOD Conference, pp. 143–154 (2005)
5. Buneman, P., Davidson, S.B., Fan, W., Hara, C.S., Tan, W.C.: Reasoning about keys for XML. Information Systems 28(8), 1037–1063 (2003)
6. Dong, X.L., Halevy, A.Y., Yu, C.: Data Integration with Uncertainty. In: VLDB, pp. 687–698. ACM, New York (2007)
7. Fagin, R., Kolaitis, P.G., Popa, L., Tan, W.C.: Composing Schema Mappings: Second-Order Dependencies to the Rescue. In: PODS, pp. 83–94 (2004)
8. Fuxman, A., Fazli, E., Miller, R.J.: ConQuer: Efficient Management of Inconsistent Databases. In: SIGMOD Conference, pp. 155–166 (2005)
9. Greco, G., Lembo, D.: Data Integration with Preferences Among Sources. In: Atzeni, P., Chu, W., Lu, H., Zhou, S., Ling, T.-W. (eds.) ER 2004. LNCS, vol. 3288, pp. 231–244. Springer, Heidelberg (2004)
10. Greco, S., Sirangelo, C., Trubitsyna, I., Zumpano, E.: Preferred Repairs for Inconsistent Databases. In: IDEAS 2003, pp. 202–211. IEEE Computer Society, Los Alamitos (2003)
11. Lenzerini, M.: Data Integration: A Theoretical Perspective. In: Popa, L. (ed.) PODS, pp. 233–246. ACM, New York (2002)
12. Madhavan, J., Halevy, A.Y.: Composing Mappings Among Data Sources. In: VLDB, pp. 572–583 (2003)
13. Pankowski, T.: XML data integration in SixP2P – a theoretical framework. In: EDBT 2008 Workshop on Data Management in P2P Systems, ACM Digital Library (2008)
14. Rahm, E., Do, H.H.: Data Cleaning: Problems and Current Approaches. IEEE Data Eng. Bull. 23(4), 3–13 (2000)
15. Staworko, S., Chomicki, J., Marcinkowski, J.: Preference-Driven Querying of Inconsistent Relational Databases. In: Grust, T., Höpfner, H., Illarramendi, A., Jablonski, S., Mesiti, M., Müller, S., Patranjan, P.-L., Sattler, K.-U., Spiliopoulou, M., Wijsen, J. (eds.) EDBT 2006. LNCS, vol. 4254, pp. 318–335. Springer, Heidelberg (2006)
16. Taylor, N.E., Ives, Z.G.: Reconciling while tolerating disagreement in collaborative data sharing. In: SIGMOD Conference, pp. 13–24. ACM, New York (2006)

A Semantics for a Query Language over Sensors, Streams and Relations

Christian Y.A. Brenninkmeijer, Ixent Galpin,
Alvaro A.A. Fernandes, and Norman W. Paton

School of Computer Science, University of Manchester,
Manchester M13 9PL, United Kingdom
{brenninkmeijer,ixent,alvaro,norm}@cs.man.ac.uk

Abstract. We introduce a query language over sensors, streams and relations and formally describe its semantics. Although the language was
specifically designed for sensor network querying, where data is pulled
into streams, the semantics contributed in the paper also encompasses
the case in which data is pushed onto streams or else lies stored in classical relations. The approach taken is that continuous queries over streams
are an extension of classical queries over stored extents. Apart from the
fact that query evaluation over streams is reactive, or periodic, the main
difference is the conception of windows as an additional collection type
with the consequent use of type converter operations to and from streams
and windows (which, as bounded collections of tuples, can be operated
on in a relational-algebraic setting). The language and the semantics we
provide for it advance on previous work in being more comprehensive
with respect to the collection types allowed and in being more flexible as
to the number and content of the windows contributing to the result at
each evaluation event of a continuous query. The formalization advances
on previous work in clarifying the implementation onus.

Keywords: Stream/Sensor Network Data, Query Language Semantics.

1 Introduction

Data streams [4,9] have become an important information resource in both commercial and scientific contexts. In the last ten years, many query languages and
stream data management systems have been designed and implemented [1, 2, 5,
6, 7, 13]. This burst of activity stems, at least in part, from the fact that certain
characteristics of data streams challenge some foundational assumptions under-
pinning classical database management systems. Among the many issues raised
in [4], this paper focusses on the issue of assigning a semantics to continuous
queries over extents with unbounded size in the presence of blocking operators. One of the issues arising is that blocking operations such as cross-product
(and hence, in general, joins) and group-by aggregation are not well-defined over
unbounded extents.

A. Gray, K. Jeffery, and J. Shao (Eds.): BNCOD 2008, LNCS 5071, pp. 87–99, 2008.

While systems and languages that constrain themselves to operating on unbounded extents exist (e.g., [7]), most rely on one or more mechanisms to cope with the unbounded cardinality of data streams. Broadly, one may resort to data reduction techniques (e.g., filtering, data merging and data dropping, synopses and sketches) or one may characterize bounded subsets of the stream that one can operate upon using either punctuation (thereby relying on stream semantics) or sliding windows. A variation on the latter relies on materializing bounded subsets of the stream as views. A survey of most of these techniques is given in [12]. We focus on windows as the mechanism to cope with unbounded cardinality.

The remainder of the paper is structured as follows. Sec. 2 briefly describes the background for the paper, its motivation and the contributions reported, which centre on a query language over sensors, streams and relations called SNEEql. Sec. 3 describes the SNEEql data model; Sec. 4, its syntax; Sec. 5, its translation to a logical algebra; and Sec. 6, the formal definition of the algebraic operators. Sec. 7 draws contrasts with related work, Sec. 8 concludes the paper.

2   Background, Motivation, Contributions

Two of the questions raised in [4] as providing directions for future work implicitly touch on the issue of the semantic relationship between streams and classical relations as they impact on the data modelling and query language traditions. Semantic issues have been explored informally by most system-description papers [1, 2, 5, 6, 7, 13], but formal accounts [1, 3, 11] are comparatively fewer, often not exhaustive, and not as informative as could be wished by an implementer.

We explore the relationship of window-based continuous query semantics over streams and relations. In particular, our treatment encompasses push-based streams (which have been predominant in the literature so far) and pull-based streams (as arise in sensor network query processing [10, 14]). Our treatment assigns a semantics to queries over unbounded streams and over bounded subsets of unbounded streams. While this paper does not provide a detailed account of it, the semantics for continuous queries we describe can accommodate classical queries as the special case of one-off queries over stored extents only. In this way, the paper contributes a wide-ranging account that is distinctive in encompassing (1) streams and relations, (2) push- and pull-based streams, and (3) blocking and non-blocking operators, and that clarifies the relationship with classical relational-algebraic semantics. Our approach is inspired by CQL [2] in that we also view windows as a collection type resulting from a conversion operation that maps from unbounded extents (i.e., streams) to bounded ones (i.e., relations, as bags of tuples), thereby allowing both non-blocking and blocking operators to be supported. The account given here advances on previous work in providing a formal, unified account for more expressive queries than previously done. Thus, the reactive, or periodic, nature of result production is explained in terms of tuples that either simply arrive in push-based streams, or are acquired from sensors, or are scanned from stored tables. If windows are used, slide events may be triggered by new inputs and evaluation may produce new results.

Secs. 3-6 describe (briefly, due to the space constraints) the underlying data model used in SNEEql and the syntax and semantics of the language. Discussion of related work then follows.

3   SNEEql Data Model

The *primitive types* are integer, float, string and time. The *compound types* are tuple and tagged tuple. A tuple type consists of a set of typed attributes, $a_1 : t_1, \ldots, a_n : t_n$, where each a_i is an attribute name and each t_i is a primitive type. A tagged tuple type is a tuple type including two distinguished attributes: one, named tick, of type integer, and another, named index, of type integer. Values of type tick are drawn from a system-wide ordinal domain, those of type index are ordered inside the collection in which they appear. A tick value denotes the *timestamp* in which a tagged tuple was created, an index value denotes its *position* in a sequence where it was placed. The *collection types* are window and stream. A window type is a pair whose first element is a distinguished attribute, named tick, of type integer, denoting the *timestamp* in which the window was created, and whose second element is of type bag of tuples of the same tuple type. A stream is a potentially infinite, append-only sequence of values of the same tagged tuple or window type.

As an example SNEEql schema, consider a system with access to (1) road sensors that detect temperature and vibration levels every minute at four sites (named 1,2,3, and 4); (2) a push stream that reports, at a frequency of its choosing, the weight and class of passing traffic; and (3) a table of temperature classes. The schema could be expressed as follows:

road: sensed (site:integer, time:integer, temp:integer, vibration:integer)
traffic: pushed (site:integer, time:integer, weight:integer, vehicle:integer)
tempClass: stored (temp:integer, category:string)

Sensed extents are pull-based, i.e., associated with a declared acquisition rate (one tuple per minute per site, in this example), and for this reason can also be referred to as *acquisitional*. Streamed extents are push-based, i.e., associated with an unknown, presumed variable, arrival rate. From the viewpoint of continuous SNEEql queries, both sensed and pushed extents, like road and traffic, are streams of tagged tuples, whereas stored extents, like tempClass, are streams of windows, as described further below. Note that tick and index are implicitly-defined attributes of tagged tuples, as is tick for windows.

4   SNEEql Syntax

This section introduces the kinds of SNEEql queries whose semantics is described in later sections, viz., stream queries and windows queries. **Stream queries** are of the form SELECT $a_1 \ldots a_n$ FROM s WHERE p where $a_1 \ldots a_n$ is a project list, s denotes a stream of tagged tuples (i.e., either the name of a sensed or pushed extent, or a subquery of type stream), and p is a predicate. Restrictions on stream queries that are relaxed for window queries (described below) include: the FROM clause must reference a single stream because cross product is not well defined over infinite collections; and the projection list elements a_i cannot apply aggregate operations over values from s. Evaluating a stream query yields a stream of tagged tuples. Let **Q1** be the following acquisitional stream query:

```
SELECT  road.time, road.site, road.vibration
FROM    road
WHERE   road.temp < 50 AND road.vibration > 20
```

Window queries are of the form:

SELECT $a_1 \ldots a_n$ FROM $w_1 \ldots w_m$ WHERE p

where $a_1 \ldots a_n$ is a project list, $w_1 \ldots w_m$ is a list of window definitions, and p is a predicate. Window queries can be extended with GROUP BY and HAVING clauses: these are not described here due to space constraints. Evaluating a window query yields a stream of windows. Each w_i in the FROM clause refers to either a streamed (sensed or pushed) or a stored extent, as follows.

A window on a stream is of the form s[FROM t_1 TO t_2 SLIDE int $unit$], where s denotes a stream of tagged tuples (i.e., either the name of a sensed or pushed extent, or a subquery of type stream), and both t_i are either of the form NOW or NOW $- int$, where NOW denotes the current tick or index, int is a positive integer, and $unit \in \{SEC, MIN, HOUR, ROWS\}$. The FROM and TO parameters define a window that selects all tuples in s in the range relative to when the window is created, while the SLIDE parameter determines how often a new window is created.

A window on a table is of the form t[SCAN int $timeUnit$], where t is a table, int is a positive integer, and $timeUnit \in \{SEC, MIN, HOUR\}$. The SCAN parameter indicates how often the table t is scanned and a window created that contains the result of the scan.

Let **Q2** be a window query in SNEEql that requests the minimum temperature and maximum vibration from the road sensors over the last 10 minutes, but only for sites and times where the traffic stream reported a vehicle passing. **Q2** returns a stream of windows and can be written as follows:

```
SELECT   MIN(temp), MAX(vibration)
FROM     road     [FROM NOW-10 TO NOW SLIDE 1 MIN],
         traffic  [FROM NOW-10 TO NOW SLIDE 1 ROW]
WHERE    road.site=traffic.site AND road.time=traffic.time
```

The result of a SNEEql window query can be converted into a stream using the CQL [2] type-conversion functions RSTREAM, ISTREAM and DSTREAM (see Section 6.3). The next query, **Q3**, shows how SNEEql allows data acquired from sensors to be combined with stored data scanned from a table. **Q3** returns a stream of tuples and can be written as follows:

```
ISTREAM( SELECT    road.site, tempClass.category
         FROM      road       [FROM NOW-5 TO NOW SLIDE 5 MIN],
                   tempClass  [SCAN 10 MIN]
         WHERE     tempClass.temp = road.temp)
```

5   SNEEql Translation to a Logical Algebra

The SNEEql semantics contributed in this paper is defined in terms of a mapping to a logical algebra, whose operators are defined using Haskell[1]. This section both introduces the algebra and describes the mapping from SNEEql. Stream queries are mapped to the algebra as follows:

SELECT $a_1 \ldots a_n$ FROM s WHERE p
$\Rightarrow$ evaluateStream (StreamProject $[a_1 \ldots a_n]$ (
      StreamSelect (p) (
         StreamAcquire $(s,\ s.acquisitionInterval,\ s.sites)$)))

where, given an instance of an operator on streams, **evaluateStream** returns the stream that results from evaluating that operator. The operators are further described in Sec. 6, but their arguments are now briefly explained. **StreamProject** takes a list of projection expressions and the stream from which their values are obtained. **StreamSelect** takes a predicate expression and the stream over which it is applied as a filter. **StreamAcquire** takes the name, the acquisition interval and the sensing sites from which the desired stream of data is obtained. For example, **Q1** from Sec. 4 maps to the following algebraic expression:

evaluateStream (
  StreamProject [Attr "road.time", Attr "road.site", Attr "road.vibration"] (
    StreamSelect (Predicate "road.temp>50 and road.vibration>20") (
      StreamAcquire "road" (Tick 60) [1,2,3,4])))

Window queries are mapped to the algebra as follows:

SELECT $a_1 \ldots a_n$ FROM $w_1 \ldots w_m$ WHERE p
$\Rightarrow$ evaluateWindow (WindowProject $[a_1 \ldots a_n]$ (
      WindowSelect (p) (
         WindowCrossProduct $(w_1), \ldots, (w_m)$)))

where, given an instance of an operator on streams of windows, **evaluateWindow** returns the stream of windows that results from evaluating that operator. The operators are further described in Sec. 6, but their arguments are now briefly explained. **WindowProject** takes a list of projection expressions and the stream from which their values are obtained. **WindowSelect** takes a predicate expression and the stream over which it is applied as a filter. **WindowCrossProduct** takes the operators that yield the windows to which the cross product is applied. The translation of a window operator, whose argument is a window definition, depends on the form of the latter. For example, a time window definition over an acquisitional stream is mapped to the algebra as follows:

s[FROM t_1 TO t_2 SLIDE int $timeUnit$]
$\Rightarrow$ evaluateWindow (TimeWindow (TimeScope($t_1.offset,t_2.offset$), $slide$) (
      evaluateStream (StreamAcquire $(s,\ s.acquisitionInterval,\ s.sites)$))))

---

[1] In the Haskell notations used, lower case is used to name variables and functions; upper case is used to name types and constructors.

where TimeWindow takes two offsets relative to NOW, which define the endpoints of the window on s; the slide value, which indicates how frequently windows are created; and the stream from which tuples are obtained for creating the window. For example, **Q3** from Sec. 4 maps to the following algebraic expression:

```
evaluateStream(IStream (
   WindowProject [Attr "road.site", Attr "tempClass.category"] (
      WindowSelect (Predicate "tempClass.temp=road.temp") (
         WindowCrossProduct (
            TimeWindow (TimeScope ((Tick (-300)) (Tick 0)) (Tick 300)) (
               StreamAcquire "road" (Tick 60) [1,2,3,4])) (
            Scan (Tick 600) "tempClass")))))
```

where most of the operators have been introduced except IStream, which returns an output stream of tagged tuples containing the tuples most recently added to its input; and Scan, which, given the name of a stored extent and a time interval, returns the stream of windows that results from scanning the given table with a frequency governed by the scanning interval.

6   Semantics of the SNEEqI Logical Algebra

The semantics of the algebra introduced in Sec. 5 is defined in this section using Haskell. Because Haskell is a lazy, pure functional programming language, the computation of a value is deferred until it is needed. This allows us to represent streams as unbounded lists and operators as functions which take as input and return unbounded lists. The Haskell definitions of the operators aim at clarity, not space- and time-efficiency. Note that even though SNEEqI was designed to run over sensor networks as a distributed query evaluation system [8], the semantics does not take distributed execution into account because, in practice, in-network query evaluation is carried out through the translation of the logical algebra into a parallel algebra, in which the semantics of operators in the logical algebra is preserved. The semantics is organized as follows: Sec. 6.1 defines operators that return streams of tuples, and which together support **stream queries**; Sec. 6.2 defines operators that return streams of windows, and which together with the operators from Sec. 6.1 support **window queries**; and Sec. 6.3 describes operators for converting from windows to tuple streams.

In the Haskell notations, a declaration e :: t asserts the expression e to be of type t. For example, the increment function may be declared as inc :: Integer -> Integer. The expression h:t denotes the list with head h and tail t. List concatenation is denoted by ++, list difference by \\. The expression e == ee is true iff e and ee are equal. The expression id = e binds the expression e to the name id. If h = 1 and t = 2:3:[], then h:t == [1,2,3] is true. Local definitions use let e in ee blocks. Given a function f and a list L, map returns the list that results from applying f to each $l \in L$. Given a function f from type a to type Bool and a list L of elements of type a, filter returns $l \in L$ such that f is true of l.

```
evaluateStream  :: StreamOp->[TaggedTuple]
evaluateStream  (StreamAcquire sourceName tick sites) =
  acquire sourceName tick sites (Tick 0) (Index 1)
evaluateStream  (StreamReceive source) = receive source
evaluateStream  (StreamSelect predicate streamOp) =
  filter (predicateOnTaggedTuple predicate) (evaluateStream streamOp)
evaluateStream  (StreamProject projectList streamOp) =
  map (projectOnTaggedTuple projectList) (evaluateStream streamOp)
evaluateStream (RStream windowOp) =
  rStream (Index 1) (evaluateWindow windowOp)
evaluateStream  (IStream windowOp) =
  iStream (Index 1) [] (evaluateWindow windowOp)
evaluateStream  (DStream windowOp) =
  dStream (Index 1) [] (evaluateWindow windowOp)
```

Fig. 1. Definition of `evaluateStream`

6.1 Tuple Stream Operators

A tuple stream is represented as a lazily evaluated list of tagged tuples. Operations that return tuple streams fall into the following groups: *input operators*, which obtain data from sensors and from pushed streams; *filtering operators*, which select or project tuples, and *conversion operators*, which generate a tuple stream from a stream of windows (and whose definition is postponed to Sec. 6.3). The definition of `evaluateStream` is in Fig. 1.

Input. The leaf operators in tuple stream queries either acquire data from sensors or receive data from pushed streams. `StreamAcquire` is defined using `acquire` (in Fig. 2). Given the name of a sensed extent, the acquisition interval, the list of associated sites, the tick at which to take a reading and the index of the next value to be read, `acquire` returns a potentially infinite list of tagged tuples. The function `lookupAttributes` returns the list of attribute names for a sensed extent. The function `getData` abstracts away from low-level calls to physical sensors. In Haskell, this can be simulated by generating readings of individual tuples at the specified points in time. `StreamReceive` is defined using `receive::String -> [TaggedTuple]`. Given the name of a pushed extent, `receive` returns a potentially infinite list of tagged tuples. Unless a tuple arrives timestamped, it is tagged with the current tick at its arrival, and assigned an index. The function abstracts away from a port onto which an external source can write. In Haskell, this can be simulated by generating a variable number of tuples at variable intervals. The semantics of other operators accommodates multiple tuples with the same timestamp, as well as timestamps for which there are no tuples.

Filtering. Filtering operators are applied to each tuple independently. `Stream-Project` is defined using `map` (see Fig. 1) to apply `projectOnTaggedTuple` (in Fig. 3) to each tuple in the stream. Given an attribute list and a tagged tuple,

```
acquire::String->Tick->[Int]->Tick->Index->[TaggedTuple]
acquire sourceName acquisitionInterval sites now index =
        let attributeNames = lookupAttributes sourceName
  in let tuples = acquireTuples attributeNames now index sites
  in let nextTick = (now + acquisitionInterval)
  in let nextIndex = index + Index (length sites)
  in tuples ++ acquire sourceName
                acquisourceNamerval sites nextTick nextIndex


acquireTuples::[AttributeName]->Tick->Index->[Int]->[TaggedTuple]
acquireTuples _ _ _ [] = []
acquireTuples attributeNames tick index, (site:sites) =
  let tupleData = map (getData tick site) attributeNames
  in [TaggedTuple tick index (Tuple attributeNames tupleData)]
    ++ acquireTuples attributeNames tick (inc index) (sites)
```

Fig. 2. Definition of acquire

```
projectOnTaggedTuple :: [AttributeName]->TaggedTuple->TaggedTuple
projectOnTaggedTuple attributeNames(TaggedTuple tick index tuple)=
  TaggedTuple tick index (projectOnTuple attributeNames tuple)

projectOnTuple :: [AttributeName]->Tuple->Tuple
projectOnTuple attributeNames tuple =
  Tuple attributeNames (map (getAttribute tuple) attributeNames)
```

Fig. 3. Definition of projectOnTaggedTuple

projectOnTaggedTuple returns a tagged tuple that retains from the input tuple the tick, the index and the attributes named in the list. StreamSelect is directly defined using filter (see Fig. 1).

6.2   Window Stream Operators

A window stream is represented as a lazily evaluated list of windows. Operations that return window streams fall into the following groups: *input operators* that obtain windows from stored tables, *creation operators* that generate windows from streams, *single-window operators* that are applied to the individual windows in a stream independently, and *multiple-window operators* that act on windows from more than one stream. The definition of evaluateWindow is in Fig. 4.

Input. Most window streams are obtained from tuple streams, as described below. However, tables can be scanned at regular intervals, thereby allowing SNEEql queries to access stored data (e.g., in normal databases, or in persistent memory or in data loggers in sensor networks). Scan is defined using the function scan (see Fig. 5) which, given the name of a stored extent, the scanning interval specified in the query, and the current tick, returns the stream of windows that results from scanning the table. The function scanTable abstracts away from

```
evaluateWindow :: WindowOp->[Window]
evaluateWindow (Scan tick tableName) = scan tableName tick (Tick 0)
evaluateWindow (TimeWindow windowScope tick streamOp) =
  createTimeWindow windowScope tick (Tick 0) (evaluateStream streamOp)
evaluateWindow (RowWindow windowScope index streamOp) =
  createRowWindow windowScope index index (evaluateStream streamOp)
evaluateWindow (WindowSelect predicate windowOp) =
  map (selectOverWindow predicate) (evaluateWindow windowOp)
evaluateWindow (WindowProject attributeNames windowOp) =
  map (projectOnWindow attributeNames) (evaluateWindow windowOp)
evaluateWindow (WindowAggregation attributeNames windowOp) =
  map (aggregateOverWindow attributeNames) (evaluateWindow windowOp)
evaluateWindow (WindowCrossProduct leftWindowOp rightWindowOp) =
  crossProduct (evaluateWindow leftWindowOp)
               (evaluateWindow rightWindowOp)
```

Fig. 4. Definition of `evaluateWindow`

```
scan :: String->Tick->Tick->[Window]
scan tableName scanInterval now =
  let window = Window now (scanTable now tableName)
  in [window] ++ scan tableName scanInterval (now+scanInterval)
```

Fig. 5. Definition of `scan`

the access to an external table. In Haskell, this can be simulated by generating bags of tuples at the specified points in time.

Creation. Window creation operators take as input a stream of tuples and output a stream of windows. Window creation involves determining when to create a new window and which tuples to include in the window. `RowWindow` is defined using `createRowWindow` (see Fig. 6), which, given the offsets, the slide, the current index and the input tuple stream, returns a window stream in which windows are created containing tuples from the tuple stream with a frequency that respects the slide and a size that reflects the number of tuples that satisfy the offsets. As the offsets that characterize window membership are expressed relative to the current index, `getWindowTuples` simply drops tuples whose index is less than `currentIndex` adjusted by the `FROM` offset or greater than `currentIndex` adjusted by the `TO` offset. Note that since SNEEql was designed to query sensor networks, windows are not created at every tick as in [2]. Instead, windows are created at the frequency requested, through the specified slide. There can be zero, one or many windows created at each tick. `TimeWindow` differs from `RowWindow` only in that the window membership test is applied to timestamps rather than to indexes, so the definitions are omitted due to space constraints.

Single- and Multiple-Window Operators. The operators `WindowSelect`, `WindowProject` and `WindowAggregation` are evaluated over each window in a

```
createRowWindow :: WindowScope->Index->Index->[TaggedTuple]->[Window]
createRowWindow windowScope slide index taggedTuples =
  let tuples = takeWhile (lessEqualsIndex index) taggedTuples
  in let(TaggedTuple now lastIndex lastTuple) = last tuples
  in [Window now (getWindowTuples windowScope now index tuples)]
  ++ createRowWindow windowScope slide (index+slide) taggedTuples

getWindowTuples::WindowScope->Tick->Index->[TaggedTuple]->[Tuple]
getWindowTuples _ _ _ [] = []
getWindowTuples windowScope@(RowScope from to)now currentIndex input =
  let passedFrom=dropWhile (lessThanIndex (currentIndex + from))input
  in let window=filter (lessEqualsIndex(currentIndex + to))passedFrom
  in map getTuple window
```

Fig. 6. Definition of `createRowWindow`

```
crossProduct :: [Window]->[Window]->[Window]
crossProduct left right =
  let ticks = getTickUnion left right
  in tickCrossProduct ticks left right

tickCrossProduct :: [Tick]->[Window]->[Window]->[Window]
tickCrossProduct (tick:ticks) left right =
  let leftTick = findLastTick tick left
  in let rightTick = findLastTick tick right
  in let leftWindows = getWindowsAtTick leftTick left
  in let rightWindows = getWindowsAtTick rightTick right
  in let windowPairs = mapMap windowCrossProduct leftWindows rightWindows
  in windowPairs ++ tickCrossProduct ticks left right

windowCrossProduct :: Window->Window->Window
windowCrossProduct (Window leftTick leftTuples)
         (Window rightTick rightTuples) =
  let windowTick = maxTick leftTick rightTick
  in let tuples = mapMap concatTuples leftTuples rightTuples
  in Window windowTick tuples
```

Fig. 7. Definition of `windowCrossProduct`

stream of windows individually, as if each were a relation (see Fig. 4). The `tick` of a window is not changed by the application of a single-window operator.

Multiple-window operators relate windows from more than one stream. Only `WindowCrossProduct` is considered here (see Fig. 7), but, in our sensor network implementation [8], we rely on the optimizer to rewrite selections over cross products into joins. Many stream systems, such as CQL, map one window per stream to every tick, so that the cross product of two streams of windows is the cross product of the two windows mapped to each tick. Because in SNEEql, there may be zero, one or many windows at each tick, the cross product operator has been extended to deal with ticks for which there is not necessarily exactly one window in each stream. To avoid unnecessary work, cross product only occurs at ticks where at least one of the streams contains a window. Given two window streams, `crossProduct` identifies these ticks and executes a cross product at each such tick. At each identified tick, the most recent window(s) in each stream at or before this tick are identified. Every such window identified in each stream is combined with those from the other stream, thereby creating a new window for each pair. The `windowCrossProduct` function takes two windows as input, removes their `tick`, concatenates every tuple from one window with every tuple from the other window, and uses the most recent timestamp found as the `tick` of the new window. A `mapMap` function (i.e., a map on a list of lists) applies `windowCrossProduct` to every pair of windows identified in `tickCrossProduct` as having timestamps that should be matched.

6.3   Window-to-Stream Converters

A SNEEql query can specify that a stream of windows is to be converted into a stream of tuples using the keywords RSTREAM, ISTREAM and DSTREAM from CQL [2]. In combination with the TimeWindow and RowWindow operators, the corresponding conversion operators enable window queries to be nested within the FROM clauses of stream queries, and *vice versa*. RStream is defined using the function rStream (see Fig. 8), which, given the index of the next tuple to be returned and the window stream from which tuples are obtained, appends to the output stream all the tuples in each window. In common with the other window to stream operators, each tuple in the output stream receives its `tick` from its source window and a running `index` unique to the stream. IStream is defined using iStream (see Fig. 8), which, given the index of the next tuple to be returned, the tuples in the previous window, and the window stream from which tuples are obtained, appends tuples into the output stream that were not in the

```
rStream :: Index->[Window]->[TaggedTuple]
rStream index ((Window tick tuples):windows) =
 (append  tuples tick index) ++
    rStream (index + Index (length tuples)) windows

append :: [Tuple]->Tick->Index->[TaggedTuple]
append [] _ _ = []
append (tuple:tuples) tick index =
  [TaggedTuple tick index tuple]++(append tuples tick (inc index))

iStream :: Index->[Tuple]->[Window]->[TaggedTuple]
iStream index previousTuples ((Window tick tuples):windows) =
  let insertTuples = tuples \\ previousTuples
  in (append  insertTuples tick index) ++
      iStream (index + Index (length insertTuples)) tuples windows
```

Fig. 8. Definition of rStream and iStream

previous window. `DStream`, which returns the tuples deleted from the window is similar to `IStream` except for the swapped arguments in the list difference line.

7   Related Work

The literature on stream data management is quite large: we focus on window-based accounts. With respect to sensor network query languages, no formal description of either TinyDB [10] or Cougar [14] has been published. The TinyDB query language uses materialization points to offer limited support for blocking operators, does not allow window specifications (other then for aggregates) and is, therefore, less expressive than SNEEql in these respects. The Cougar query language has not been sufficiently described to allow a meaningful contrast to be drawn. With respect to query languages on pushed streams, CQL [2] was given a denotational semantics [3]. While being the major inspiration behind it, CQL is less expressive than SNEEql. For example, in assuming that there is exactly one window associated with every tick (whereas in SNEEql, there can be zero, one or many), and in not supporting bag of tuples (i.e., relations) as a primitive collection type. While the denotational semantics given to CQL is exemplary, it is, by its nature, less informative from an implementer's viewpoint than the one contributed in this paper, in that query language implementation tends to build on algebras. The other previous formal treatments fail to be as exhaustive and systematic as the one given here, in that the account in [11] only applies to pushed, punctuated streams, while the account in [1] only applies to pushed streams and to a significantly more constrained notion of window.

8   Conclusions

This paper has shown that a query language over streams and relations can be given a formal semantics that clarifies the relationship between stream query processing and classical query processing. Building on the pioneering work on CQL [2], the paper shows that taking windows as a collection type obtained by type-conversion operations on streams suffices to encompass more cases of interest in the same semantic account than previously done. Thus, the paper has shown how streams and relations, as well as push- and pull-based streams, relate to one another in the presence of both non-blocking and blocking operators. As shown, SNEEql advances on previous work in supporting windows without the requirement to do so in every query. By defining a window stream as a stream of zero, one or even many windows per tick, rather than exactly one for each tick, SNEEql avoids having to drop windows if too many tuples arrive at once and having to contend with repeated evaluations that produce repeated results

The semantics of SNEEql, as described in this paper, has been implemented in Haskell, with the resulting code, using simulated inputs, acting as a SNEEql interpreter. The subset of SNEEql that pertains to sensed extents has been fully implemented (as was TinyDB) over a nesC/TinyOS software environment, as described in [8]. Work is in progress to accommodate, as informed by the semantics contributed in this paper, pushed streams and stored extents.

Acknowledgements. This work was funded by UK EPSRC WINES EP/C014774/1 DIAS-MC project. We are grateful for this support and to our collaborators in the project. C.Y.A. Brenninkmeijer thanks the School of Computer Science.

References

1. Abadi, D.J., Carney, D., Çetintemel, U., Cherniack, M., et al.: Aurora: A new Model and Architecture for Data Stream Management. VLDB J. 12(2), 120–139 (2003)
2. Arasu, A., Babu, S., Widom, J.: The CQL continuous query language: semantic foundations and query execution. VLDB J 15(2), 121–142 (2006)
3. Arasu, A., Widom, J.: A Denotational Semantics for Continuous Queries over Streams and Relations. SIGMOD Record 33(3), 6–12 (2004)
4. Babcock, B., Babu, S., Datar, M., Motwani, R., Widom, J.: Models and Issues in Data Stream Systems. In: PODS, pp. 1–16 (2002)
5. Chandrasekaran, S., Cooper, O., Deshpande, A., Franklin, M.J., et al.: TelegraphCQ: Continuous Dataflow Processing for an Uncertain World. In: CIDR (2003)
6. Chen, J., DeWitt, D.J., Tian, F., Wang, Y.: NiagaraCQ: A Scalable Continuous Query System for Internet Databases. In: SIGMOD, pp. 379–390 (2000)
7. Cranor, C.D., Johnson, T., Spatscheck, O., Shkapenyuk, V.: Gigascope: A Stream Database for Network Applications. In: SIGMOD, pp. 647–651 (2003)
8. Galpin, I., Brenninkmeijer, C.Y.A., Jabeen, F., Fernandes, A.A.A., Paton, N.W.: An Architecture for Query Optimization in Sensor Networks. In: Proc. ICDE (2008)
9. Golab, L., Özsu, M.T.: Issues in data stream management. SIGMOD Record 32(2), 5–14 (2003)
10. Madden, S., Franklin, M.J., Hellerstein, J.M., Hong, W.: TinyDB: An Acquisitional Query Processing System for Sensor Networks. ACM Trans. Database Syst. 30(1), 122–173 (2005)
11. Maier, D., Li, J., Tucker, P.A., Tufte, K., Papadimos, V.: Semantics of Data Streams and Operators. In: Eiter, T., Libkin, L. (eds.) ICDT 2005. LNCS, vol. 3363, pp. 37–52. Springer, Heidelberg (2004)
12. Maier, D., Tucker, P.A., Garofalakis, M.: Filtering, Punctuation, Windows and Synopses. In: Chaudhury, N.A., et al. (eds.) StreamDataManagement, ch. 3, Springer, Heidelberg (2005)
13. Rundensteiner, E.A., Ding, L., Sutherland, T.M., Zhu, Y., et al.: CAPE: Continuous Query Engine with Heterogeneous-Grained Adaptivity. In: VLDB (2004)
14. Yao, Y., Gehrke, J.: Query Processing in Sensor Networks. In: CIDR (2003)

Load Shedding in MavStream: Analysis, Implementation, and Evaluation*

Balakumar Kendai and Sharma Chakravarthy

IT Laboratory and Department of Computer Science & Engineering,
The University of Texas at Arlington, Arlington, TX 76019
sharma@cse.uta.edu

Abstract. In data stream management systems (DSMSs), Quality of Service (or QoS) requirements, as specified by users, are extremely important. To satisfy QoS requirements throughout the life of a data stream, result characteristics need to be monitored at runtime and adjustments made continuously. It has been shown that in a DSMS, switching scheduling strategies at runtime can change tuple latency requirements. DSMSs also experience significant fluctuations in input rates (termed bursty inputs). In order to meet the QoS requirements in the presence of bursty inputs, a load shedding strategy is critical. This also entails monitoring of QoS measures at run-time to meet expected QoS requirements.

This paper addresses load shedding issues for MavStream, a DSMS being developed at UT Arlington. To cope with situations where the arrival rates of input streams exceed the processing capacity of the system, we have incorporated load shedders into the query processing model. The runtime optimizer continually monitors the output and decides when to turn on the shedders and how much to shed. Choice of shedders is done to minimize the error in the output. Shedders have been incorporated as part of the buffers to minimize the overhead for load shedding. Finally, load shedders are activated and deactivated dynamically by the runtime optimizer. Both random and semantic load shedding techniques are supported to match application semantics.

1 Introduction

The wide-scale deployment of pervasive devices (sensors, RFID's, and hand held devices) have created sources that produce data continuously at unreliable and unpredictable rates. Furthermore, the size of this data is unbounded and can be considered as a relation with infinite tuples (not stored on a secondary device as in DBMSs). These data sequences coming in continuously are called data streams [1, 2, 3] Examples of applications [1] that have streaming input are network monitoring, stock tickers and variable tolling in highways.

Many stream based applications require real-time (or near real-time) results to be useful and this is measured in terms of tuple latency – the amount of time (on the average) it takes for a system to from input to output. This and other requirements (memory usage and throughput) are collectively known as Quality of Service (QoS), necessitate

---

* The work done in this paper is currently supported by NSF IIS - 0534611, NSF IIS - 0326505 and NSF EIA - 0216500.

A. Gray, K. Jeffery, and J. Shao (Eds.): BNCOD 2008, LNCS 5071, pp. 100–112, 2008.

that the data be processed on the fly as they arrive. The large amount of time required for secondary storage access and lack of QoS support in DBMSs rule out the possibility of storing the data in secondary storages and processing them. Though main memory databases process data without storing them on secondary storage, they assume the data to be readily available which is not the case with data streams. These characteristics of data streams have necessitated the development of specialized applications for handling them and are termed Data Stream Management Systems [1, 3].

As the data rate of a stream is unpredictable, operators may not always have the data to perform computation when scheduled. There can also be periods where data arrives at a very high rate. This necessitates buffering [4] as there may not be enough capacity in a DSMS to process all incoming data without buffering. Since main memory is always limited in a system, there is a possibility of memory overflow. Research in this field has proposed techniques such as storing excess tuples into secondary storage [1] and scheduling strategies [5]aimed at reducing the amount of tuples that reside in the memory. Mechanisms have also been developed to reduce the memory requirement of join and aggregate operators which operate on windows by using histograms, timeout, slack, and discarding tuples to reduce window sizes [6].

The utility of results produced by a DSMS often depends on the delay with which it is produced. This requirement is generally specified as QoS requirements for a query. The three QoS measures that are mainly used in a DSMS are: tuple latency, memory utilization and throughput. Tuple latency is specified as the difference in arrival and departure time of a tuple in the system. Memory utilization is the total memory usage of the tuples that reside in the queues of operators. This generally does not include the tuples stored in the internal queues (synopsis) of window-based operators. Throughput is defined as the rate at which output is produced by the system. Various scheduling strategies have been proposed to improve the performance of a particular QoS measure given the unpredictable nature of data. Also load shedding [2, 7] and other approximation techniques have been proposed to deal with situations when the system is unable to meet the QoS requirements. An additional complication is that a continuous query issued to a DSMS may have multiple QoS constraints associated with it.

Any DSMS is ultimately limited by the physical resources available to the system. There may arise situations where the system may not be able to meet the QoS requirements because of periods of extremely high arrival rates. As many of the stream-based applications can tolerate approximate answers, tuples can be dropped from the system in order to meet the QoS requirements. This process of gracefully dropping tuples from the system is known as load shedding. Load shedding [2, 7, 8] is a well researched problem and various groups have proposed different mechanisms. In this paper, we have proposed a load shedding mechanism that incurs the minimal overhead among all proposed load shedding mechanisms. This is achieved by making load shedding a function of the input queues of operators. The load shedding strategy proposed in this paper is a feedback based approach, where QoS measures are monitored and tuples are dropped either randomly or based on the semantics specified as part of the continuous query. The proposed mechanism also activates load shedders at specific locations which maximizes the gain in processing time while minimizing the error it introduces. The load shedding component has been implemented as part of the runtime optimizer.

The runtime optimizer monitors QoS measures for each continuous query in the system and chooses an appropriate scheduling strategy, and beyond that load shedding to meet QoS requirements. Our approach also tries to ensure that none of the QoS measures that are currently satisfied do not get violated by switching to a new strategy. Moreover the runtime optimizer also tries to minimize the number of switches between strategies based on heuristics.

2 Related Work

In this section we present some of the work that has been carried out on load shedding in data stream processing systems.

Stream: Stream [2] is a prototype implementation of a DSMS developed at Stanford. Load shedding techniques [2] proposed in Stream focus only on aggregation queries over sliding windows. The algorithm for load shedding tries to determine the most effective sampling rate for each query so that the error is distributed uniformly among all queries and optimal location of load shedder that increases the throughput without violating the load equation. For JOIN operations, a memory usage reduction [9] method has been introduced using maximum subset and sampling techniques, for a novel age-based model and frequency-based model. Two algorithms B-Int and L-Int have been developed for sharing resources among aggregate sliding window operators. These algorithms assume that a stream can be split into sub streams which is used to compute multiple aggregates. B-Int algorithm pre-computes aggregates for intervals such that any interval can be expressed as union of base intervals.

Aurora: Aurora [1] is a data flow system that uses a primitive box and arrow representation of queries. Tuples flow from source to destination through the operational boxes. It can support continuous queries, ad-hoc queries and views at the same time. The QoS evaluator in Aurora continually monitors system performance and activates the load shedder, which sheds load until the performance of the system matches user-specified values. It is specified in terms of a two-dimensional graph that specifies the output in terms of several performance-related and quality-related services. It is the QoS that determines how resources are allocated to the processing elements along the path of query operation.

Aurora handles high load situations by dropping load using a drop operator. Load shedding [7] is treated as an optimization problem and consists of determining when and where to shed load and how much to shed. The QoS requirements are specified as value utility graphs and loss tolerance graphs. The load shedding algorithm consists of a load evaluation step where system load is determined using load coefficients. Load coefficient, which is statically computed, represents the number of processor cycles required to push a single input tuple through the network to the outputs. The next step creates a load shedding road map which consists of an ordered sequence of entries. Each entry in the road map has a drop insertion plan which guarantees that number of cycles saved is maximized without sacrificing the utility of the result. At times of overload, the road map is searched for the right amount of cycle savings to find a drop insertion plan. The load shedding mechanism proposed in Aurora uses static information for deciding

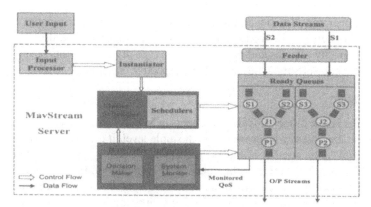

Fig. 1. MavStream Architecture

dropping strategies. The dropping mechanism proposed in Aurora is independent of the scheduling mechanism. However, it makes the assumption that cycles gained by dropping tuples will utilized by scheduler effectively.

In addition to the above, there are several systems that address stream processing (such as Telegraph [10], TinyDB [11]) but they do not address load shedding explicitly.

3   MavStream Architecture

MavStream is a DSMS being developed at UTA for processing continuous queries over data streams. MavStream is modeled as a client-server architecture. The various components of MavStream are shown in Fig. 1. The MavStream server, upon receiving a query from the client, transforms the input to create the query plan object. A query plan object is a tree of objects that contain information about the operators of a query. The input processor uses the instantiator module to instantiate all the operators, paths and segments [12]. The instantiated objects are put in to the appropriate ready queue based on the chosen scheduling strategy. The operators are scheduled using a scheduling strategy and output of the query is given back to the client. The following sections provide a brief overview of some of the modules in the MavStream system:

3.1   MavStream Server

MavStream server is a TCP Server which provides integration and interaction of various modules such as input processor, instantiator, operators, buffer manager and scheduler for efficiently producing correct output.

3.2   Input Processor

The input processor processes text input to generate a query plan object. This module extracts the information of operators and query tree from the input. The query plan object is a sequence of operator nodes where every node describes an operator completely. The operator hierarchy defines the direction of data flow starting from leaves to the root. On visiting each node, input processor calls the instantiator module to instantiate the operators. The query tree is traversed in a bottom-up manner to ensure that required child operators are instantiated prior to parent operators. It also computes the processing capacity of paths and memory release capacity of segments (a subpath of an operator path) and sorts them based on their respective capacities.

3.3 Scheduler

The scheduler is one of the critical components in MavStream. In MavStream, scheduling is done at the operator level and not at the tuple level. It is not desirable to schedule at a tuple level as the number of tuples entering the system is very large (unbounded). On the other hand, scheduling at the query level loses flexibility of scheduling, as the granularity offered by the scheduler may not be acceptable. MavStream schedules operators based on their state and priority. The scheduler maintains a ready queue, which decides the order in which operators are scheduled. This queue is initially populated by the server. The operators must be in a ready state in order to get scheduled. Several scheduling policies [12]– round-robin (RR), weighted RR, path capacity strategy (PCS), segment scheduling (SS), and simplified segment scheduling (SSS) – are supported by MavStream. The execution of all schedulers is controlled by the master scheduler. The master scheduler allocates a time quantum to each scheduler to execute. At any instance of time only one scheduler is allowed to run by the master scheduler.

3.4 Operators and Buffer

The operators of DSMSs are designed to handle long running queries producing results continuously and incrementally. Blocking operators (an operator that cannot produce output unless all the input is present) like Aggregates and Join may block forever on their input as streams are potentially unbounded. Stream operators are executed using the *window* concept so as to overcome the blocking nature of operators. MavStream supports the following operators - split, select, project , join (hash and nested versions), group by and various aggregate operators (sum, average, max, min, count).

The objective of buffer management is to provide a mechanism to handle the mismatch between input rates and the processing capacity by using available memory. But when we have limited main memory, there is an upper limit on the number of tuples that can be stored in the main memory. If tuples exceed this limit, they have to be either discarded or stored in secondary storage. The option of storing excess tuples onto a disk is a hindrance for meeting QoS requirements such as throughput and latency. Load shedding functions have been incorporated into the buffer to deal with situations of high load. The load shedders are controlled (activated and deactivated) entirely by the runtime optimizer without involving the operators.

4   Design of the Load Shedder

The resources available to any DSMS are limited. It is possible that the arrival rate of input streams can exceed far beyond the processing capabilities of the system. These situations lead to the system being overwhelmed with a large number of tuples, increasing tuple latency and memory utilization. As some of the stream processing applications can tolerate approximate answer but not delay in results, dropping some tuples can provide better results for QoS measures. This process, known as *Load shedding*, is formally defined as the process of gracefully discarding unprocessed or partially processed tuples improving the QoS constraints of continuous queries. If a sufficient number of tuples are discarded, the processing capacity will match the load and satisfy QoS measures. Due to dropping of tuples, errors may be introduced in the output values. Load shedding is an optimization problem and consists of the following subproblems: (i) When and How much to shed load, (ii) Where to shed, and (iii) How to shed.

Load shedding is a trade off between tuple latency and accuracy and various techniques for load shedding have been proposed. In this paper we have proposed a feedback based load shedding approach that adds the least overhead to the system. The predefined QoS requirements considered also include the most-tolerable relative error (MTRE) of a continuous query in its final query results.

4.1   Location of Shedders

Most of the current load shedding mechanisms have proposed special purpose operators [2, 7] to drop load. This requires the insertion of new operators in to a query plan when the system is loaded. In addition to being a special operator, load shedding can be either part of the operator or the queues. Among the possible options – as a special operator, function of an operator, and as part of the queue/buffer, the option of adding a load shedder using a special operator incurs the highest overhead as it needs to be inserted into a query plan and requires scheduling. Also, the load shedding operator has an input queue which buffers tuples before the operator decides to drop a tuple or not. The option of adding load shedding as a function of an operator costs less than the first option as the load shedder need not be scheduled separately. But it still buffers tuples that are likely to dropped. This makes the last option of adding load shedders as part of the queues most viable. By making load shedding a function of input queues, decision to drop tuples is made when a tuple is enqueued thereby reducing latency. In addition to saving CPU cycles this option reduces the memory requirement as well by dropping tuples as early as possible.

4.2   The Runtime Optimizer

The runtime optimizer determines the measures violated by comparing monitored values to expected values. If the runtime optimizer does not find better strategies to meet QoS it can invoke the load shedders (already built into the buffers and are inactive by default) to save computational time. Load can continue to be shed as long as the error introduced is within the tolerable limits specified by MTRE. As soon as QoS measures start meeting the expected values, load shedding can be deactivated. The use of feedback from the system monitor provides a reliable metric on the actual performance of a query in the system . Hence, this feedback can be used to control the operation of load shedders without adding any overhead.

The load shedding approach proposed in [13] is used in this implementation. Briefly, it estimates the load of the system based on the current arrival rates and tries to prevent an overloaded state from occurring. Since these techniques require the estimation of system load which is based on the system characteristics, they may not be accurate.

Since load shedding mechanisms work to achieve the QoS requirements of a query the feedback on their performance can be used to determine whether to shed load or not.

4.3 Where to Shed

Load shedders are incorporated into the buffers to minimize the overhead. As each active load shedder needs some CPU cycles to decide whether to keep or drop a tuple, it adds some overhead to the system. To reduce this overhead, the number of active load shedders should be minimized. Towards this goal, for each operator path (a path from leaf to root for a query plan), we activate at most one load shedder in its path. This requires finding an optimal position for the load shedder. We use the concept of place weight of shedders developed in [13] which is some what similar to the loss/gain [7] ratio used in Aurora.

The placement of load shedders has a significant impact on the accuracy of the final results, and on the amount of time (or computation units) it releases. Placing a load shedder earlier in the query plan is most effective in saving computational time units but its effect on the accuracy is most pronounced. On the other hand, placing a load shedder after the operator which has biggest output rate in the query plan has the lowest impact on accuracy when a tuple is dropped, but the amount of computation time units released and the storage saved may not be the largest. Therefore, the best candidate location for a load shedder along an operator path is the place where the shedder is capable of releasing maximal computational time (and possible storage) units while introducing minimal relative errors in final query results by dropping one tuple. The formula for calculating place weight described in [13] is reproduced below 4.3.

Calculation of Place Weight. In a simple operator path $\mathcal{X}$ with k operators there are k locations to place a load shedder. Let $x_1, x_2, \ldots, x_k$ be its path label string, and v be the input rate of the data stream for this operator path. Let $b_1, b_2, \cdots, b_k$ be its k candidate places, where $b_i, 1 \leq i \leq k$ is the place right before the operator x_i. The place weight W of a candidate place is the ratio of the amount of saved percentage of computation time units α to the relative error ϵ in its final results introduced by a load shedder at that place by discarding one tuple. The place weight W of a shedder at a particular location of an operator path with its Most Tolerable Relative Error ($MTRE = E_i$) is defined as:

$$W = \frac{\alpha}{\epsilon} \tag{1}$$

$$\alpha = \frac{v(d)}{C^S} - \frac{v_{shedder}}{C^O_{shedder}}$$

$$\epsilon = \begin{cases} \dfrac{v(d)}{v_{shedder}} & \text{for a random shedder;} \\ f\left(\dfrac{v(d)}{v_{shedder}}\right) & \text{for a semantic shedder;} \end{cases}$$

$$v(d) = \begin{cases} E_i * v_{shedder} & \text{for a random shedder;} \\ E_i * f\left(\dfrac{1}{v_{shedder}}\right) & \text{for a semantic shedder;} \end{cases}$$

$$v_{shedder} = v \prod_{i=x_1}^{x_n} (\sigma_i), x_1 \text{ to } x_n \text{ are operators before the shedder}$$

where C^S is the processing capacity of the segment starting from the operator right after the load shedder until the root node (excluding the root node) along the operator path.

If there is no operator after the shedder, $\mathcal{C}^S$ is defined as infinity and ($\frac{v(d)}{\mathcal{C}^S} = 0$). The computational units that can be saved is therefore zero and the shedder itself introduces extra overhead by $\frac{v_{shedder}}{\mathcal{C}^O_{shedder}}$. $v(d)$ is the maximal drop rate at which shedder can drop tuples at this location without violating the MTRE E_i defined for that operator path. $\frac{v(d)}{\mathcal{C}^S}$ is the total computation time units it saves by dropping tuples at a rate of $v(d)$. However, a shedder also introduces additional overhead, which is $\frac{v_{shedder}}{\mathcal{C}^O_{shedder}}$, to the system as it needs to determine whether a tuple should be dropped or not. $v_{shedder}$ is the input rate of the load shedder, and x_1 to x_n are the operators before the load shedder starting from leaf operator, and σ_i is the selectivity of the operator x_i. If an operator is a leaf node, then $v_{shedder} = v$ and v is the input rate of the stream for the operator path $\mathcal{X}$. $\mathcal{C}^O_{shedder}$ is the processing capacity of the load shedder. If the load shedder is a semantic one, $f(.)$ is a function from selectivity of the shedder to the relative error in final query results.

In equation (1), the input rate of stream is the only parameter that changes over time. All other items do not change until we revise the query plan. We compute the place weight for each of the k candidate places. The partial order of load shedders in a path do not change with the input rate as all of them have the same input at any time instant. Hence, the place where the load shedder has the biggest place weight is the most effective one. The arrival rates of input streams can be monitored and the mean rate of arrival can be used for calculating place weight. The processing capacity of operators and shedders can be determined by collecting statistics for the system. The processing capacities can be determined from the average service time required to process a single tuple. The drop rate is assumed to be the maximum that is allowed without violating MTRE. This can be determined by using mean arrival rate and selectivity of operators as mentioned in the above equation (1).

4.4   How to Shed Load

The location of shedders are determined before the query starts executing. Since the number of active shedders has to be kept to a minimum to minimize the overhead, we have to ensure that maximum savings are achieved by activating any shedder. Hence, the shedders are initialized at positions having the highest place weight. We can obtain the maximum gains by activating the shedders with the highest place weight. Therefore when the runtime optimizer detects that queries are likely to violate QoS requirements, it takes a greedy approach and activates the shedder with the highest place weight in the list of non active shedders.

To achieve highest gains, the list of load shedders are kept sorted by their place weights. The list is kept sorted when location of shedders are determined and hence does not involve any overhead. When activated, the load shedder starts dropping tuples at the maximum allowed drop rate. The runtime optimizer keeps the load shedder active until either the QoS requirements are met or when it finds a better strategy for the query after dropping some tuples. The load shedders are deactivated when a new strategy is found so that the results produced by the query is closer to the actual. Furthermore, the availability of a new strategy can denote potential availability of resources to meet QoS requirements without dropping load.

5 Implementation

The load shedders are implemented as part of the input queues of operators as they incur the least overhead and drop tuples earliest. Load shedding is implemented as a function in the *Buffer* class. The initial approach was to create a load shedder object and to place it inside the *Buffer* object when it needs to be activated. As this involves the overhead of creating an object and then performing the checks for drop, the simpler approach of making load shedding a function of the buffer was taken. The state of shedders is inactive initially in all the buffers. The state of the load shedder is checked when every tuple is enqueued. If the shedder is inactive tuples are enqueued into the buffer, else the functions to determine whether a tuple has to be dropped are called. The *QoSData* object maintains a list of buffers where load shedders have the highest place weight. When QoS requirements begin to get violated, the Decision Maker starts activating load shedders using *activateShedder* in *QoSData* object . The activation of shedders only involve setting the state of load shedders inside the input queues to true. Once activated every tuple enqueued into the buffer is subject to additional checks for determining whether it needs to be dropped using the *checkDropCondition* function. This function determines the type of load shedder and calls the appropriate function.

5.1 Random Load Shedder

The random load shedder drops tuples at random based on a set probability. The runtime optimizer has the option of setting the drop probability, with an upper limit that is determined by maximum probability. The maximum drop probability is computed while the location of load shedders is computed using the arrival rates and maximum tolerant relative error. The maximum drop probability specifies the highest probability at which tuples can be dropped without violating the tolerable error limits. This value is set by the Input Processor module using *initializeRandomLoadShedder* function. On activation of random load shedder, *checkRandomDropCondition* is called. A random value is generated for each tuple enqueued. If the value generated is greater than the drop probability of the shedder tuple is enqueued else it is dropped.

5.2 Semantic Load Shedder

Semantic load shedders drop tuples based on the semantics specified along with query and work similar to *select* operators . The Input Processor performs the additional check of adding a buffer to the list of load shedder only if the input stream of that path contains the attribute that will be used for load shedding. Once the semantic shedder is initialized by the Input Processor using *initializeSemanticLoadShedder* function , the *monitorSemanticShedderRange* function is called every time a tuple is enqueued into the buffer. This function keeps track of the highest and lowest values for the attribute specified. On activation by the runtime optimizer, the semantic shedder uses the values seen so far and uses them to drop the tuples based on the range specified. For example, the center first shedder will drop all the tuples that fall with in a fixed percentage around the mean. The percentage of tuples to be dropped around the range of interest can be specified optionally. The *checkSemanticDropCondition, checkCondition* functions of the *Buffer* class performs the check for semantic shedder.

6 Experimental Evaluations

To validate the implementation of load shedding effectiveness, experiments were performed using the MavStream system described above. Below, we describe some of the experiments and analyze the results obtained. MavStream is implemented in Java and experiments were run using synthetically generated data streams.

Effect of Load Shedding on QoS Measures: These experiments were conducted to observe the effect of load shedding on QoS measures. The performance of QoS measures without shedding was compared to the performance of QoS measures with various error tolerance limits for shedding. The higher error tolerance limits translate to higher drop probability for the random load shedders. This will lead to more tuples being dropped from the system decreasing the tuple latency and memory utilization. The query used for these experiments consisted of eight operators with two Hash Joins and three input streams, each stream containing 2 Million tuples.

For the first experiment, a tuple based join of 1000 tuples/window was used. The streams were fed using poisson distribution with a mean rate of 1000, 750 and 500 tuples/ second. The mean for the poisson distribution was doubled at different points in time to simulate bursty nature of streams. The QoS measure considered was tuple latency and a single value was specified with start and end values of 1 second. Memory utilization was set to "Don't Care" and hence did not affect the decisions made by runtime optimizer. The error tolerance in the results of the query was varied from 10 to 30 percent. The decision table-based runtime optimizer chose PCS, the optimal strategy for tuple latency. The runtime optimizer, after changing the scheduling strategy of the query to PCS, determines that the latency is still being violated and hence starts activating load shedders. As seen from the Fig.2, the higher the error tolerance limit, the lower the tuple latency. This is as expected. As the load shedders are part of the input queues of operators, tuples are dropped immediately and hence they provide lower memory utilization which can be seen from Fig.3. In the figures LSn corresponds to load shedding of n% of tuples.

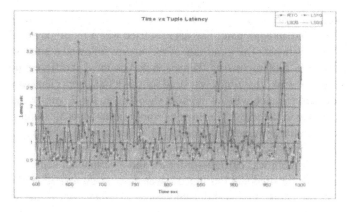

Fig. 2. Effect of Load Shedding on Tuple Latency

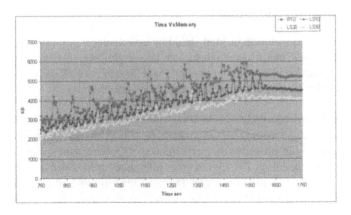

Fig. 3. Effect of Load Shedding on Memory Utilization

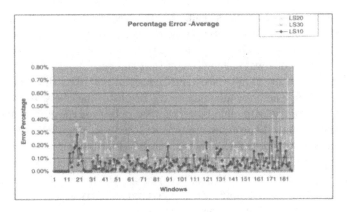

Fig. 4. Random Shedders: Error in Average

Effect of Load Shedding on Error in Results: This experiment was conducted to observe the error introduced by load shedders in the results. The query consisted of two operators: select and an aggregate. The data set used was a modified version of Linear Road Benchmark data set. The input rate of the stream followed a poisson distribution with the mean set to 2000 tuples/sec. The mean was doubled at different points in time. A time based window of 20 seconds was used for this experiment. The average speed of cars was calculated for each window without shedding and with various error tolerance levels for random load shedding. The error tolerance limits translate to the maximum allowed drop probability for random shedders. The error introduced in the average speed of car was much lower than the tolerant limits as indicated in Fig.4.

The same experiment was carried out for the three variants of semantic shedder. As expected the semantic shedders introduce lower error as compared to that of random load shedders. The center first shedder introduces a higher error as the values at center affect the results most by dropping more tuples near the mean. The lowest and the highest first shedder introduce very small errors as shown in Fig.5 and Fig.6. As the

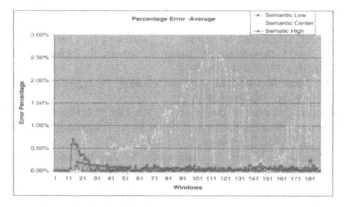

Fig. 5. Semantic Shedders: Error in Average

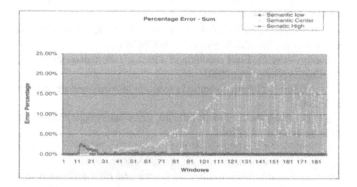

Fig. 6. Semantic Shedders: Error in Sum

query used in semantic shedders calculate the average and sum, the impact of highest and lowest first shedders are minimal due to outliers in the data. The center first shedder drops tuples around the mean and therefore has the highest impact on the results. As most of the tuples fall in the range of the mean more tuples are dropped. The results emphasize the importance of knowledge about the distribution of data while using semantic shedders.

7   Conclusions

In this paper, we have described the implementation and evaluation of the load shedding component of the MavStream system. The runtime optimizer not only monitors QoS measures for load shedding purposes, it also dynamically changes scheduling strategies to satisfy QoS requirements before load shedding is attempted. Currently, the system is being integrated with complex event processing to provide an end-to-end solution for monitoring applications.

References

[1] Balakrishnan, H., Balazinska, M., Carney, D., Çetintemel, U., Cherniack, M., Convey, C., Galvez, E.F., Salz, J., Stonebraker, M., Tatbul, N., Tibbetts, R., Zdonik, S.B.: Retrospective on aurora. VLDB J. 13(4), 370–383 (2004)

[2] Babcock, B., Datar, M., Motwani, R.: Load shedding for aggregation queries over data streams. In: ICDE, pp. 350–361 (2004)

[3] Chandrasekaran, S., Cooper, O., Deshpande, A., Franklin, M.J., Hellerstein, J.M., Hong, W., Krishnamurthy, S., Madden, S., Reiss, F., Shah, M.A.: Telegraphcq: Continuous dataflow processing. In: SIGMOD Conference, p. 668 (2003)

[4] Gilani, A., Sonune, S., Kendai, B., Chakravarthy, S.: The Anatomy of a Stream Processing System. In: Bell, D.A., Hong, J. (eds.) BNCOD 2006. LNCS, vol. 4042, pp. 232–239. Springer, Heidelberg (2006)

[5] Jiang, Q., Chakravarthy, S.: Scheduling strategies for processing continuous queries over streams. In: Williams, H., MacKinnon, L.M. (eds.) BNCOD 2004. LNCS, vol. 3112, pp. 16–30. Springer, Heidelberg (2004)

[6] Arasu, A., Widom, J.: Resource sharing in continuous sliding-window aggregates. In: VLDB, pp. 336–347 (2004)

[7] Tatbul, N., Çetintemel, U., Zdonik, S.B., Cherniack, M., Stonebraker, M.: Load shedding in a data stream manager. In: VLDB, pp. 309–320 (2003)

[8] Jiang, Q., Chakravarthy, S.: Load shedding in a data stream management system. TR CSE-2003, UT Arlington (November 2003)

[9] Srivastava, U., Widom, J.: Memory-limited execution of windowed stream joins. In: VLDB, pp. 324–335 (2004)

[10] Shah, M.A., Chandrasekaran, S.: Fault-tolerant, Load-balancing Queries in Telegraph. In: SIGMOD Conference, p. 611 (2001)

[11] Madden, S., Franklin, M.J., Hellerstein, J.M., Hong, W.: TinyDB: an acquisitional query processing system for sensor networks. ACM TODS 30(1), 122–173 (2005)

[12] Chakravarthy, S., Pajjuri, V.: Scheduling strategies and their evaluation in a data stream management system. In: Bell, D.A., Hong, J. (eds.) BNCOD 2006. LNCS, vol. 4042, pp. 220–231. Springer, Heidelberg (2006)

[13] Qingchun, J.: A framework for supporting quality of service requirements in a data stream management system. Ph.D. dissertation, University of Texas at Arlington, Arlington (2005)

Event-Driven Database Information Sharing

Luis Vargas, Jean Bacon, and Ken Moody

University of Cambridge, Computer Laboratory
{firstname.lastname}@cl.cam.ac.uk

Abstract. Database systems have been designed to manage business critical information and provide this information on request to connected clients, a passive model. Increasingly, applications need to share information actively with clients and/or external systems, so that they can react to relevant information as soon as it becomes available. Event-driven architecture (EDA) is a software architectural pattern that models these requirements based on the production of, consumption of, and reaction to events. Publish/subscribe provides a loosely-coupled communication paradigm between the components of a system, through many-to-many, push-based event delivery. In this paper, we describe our work integrating distributed content-based publish/subscribe functionality into a database system. We have extended existing database technology with new capabilities to realise EDA in a reliable, scalable, and secure manner. We discuss the design, architecture, and implementation of PostgreSQL-PS, a prototype built on the PostgreSQL open-source database system.

1 Introduction

Organisations invest in information technology to realise benefits through lower business costs, better information and better communication. Through the years, they have moved most of their critical data into databases, and automated many business processes using a variety of applications. Database systems and applications have been deployed incrementally to satisfy the needs of some particular area or *domain* of the business (e.g. a company branch). Domains are autonomous; each administers its own resources independently of others. With the passage of time, the number of databases, applications, and domains has multiplied. What once were closely controlled environments have evolved into large-scale information spaces that are both highly distributed and dynamic. Within such a domain-structured environment, the active sharing of information has become vital for the organisation's success. This applies not only within a domain, but also between different domains of the same organisation (and increasingly others).

To meet the need for active information sharing, domains often implement a large set of targeted tools. Different types of information are captured at different places (e.g. databases and applications), with different tools, each using its own propagation mechanism, and implementing its own method of consumption at the destination. Developers and database administrators must become proficient in all these tools, and the system must be able to support them all at runtime. Adding more applications to such an environment becomes a major ordeal.

A. Gray, K. Jeffery, and J. Shao (Eds.): BNCOD 2008, LNCS 5071, pp. 113–125, 2008.

Databases are an obvious point to implement active information sharing, since they maintain most of a business's critical information and reflect its current state. For example, an application may cause a change in a database, which can signal an event that is of interest to other applications within the same domain, or in other domains. Similarly, the receipt of an event by an application often results in a change in database state within its domain to record the event persistently. Such a style of interaction is best modelled by an event-driven architecture (EDA) [1]. In EDA, all interactions between components in a distributed system build on the production of, consumption of, and reaction to events. In parallel with the emergence of EDA, publish/subscribe middleware [2] has been designed and deployed, providing a popular communication paradigm for event-driven distributed systems. Publish/subscribe realises many-to-many, push-based delivery of events between loosely-coupled components. In this paper, we describe our work integrating distributed content-based publish/subscribe functionality into a database system to realise EDA in a reliable, scalable, and secure manner.

We complete this Section with a motivating scenario. Section 2 sets up the background in EDA, the publish/subscribe paradigm, and the PostgreSQL database system [3]. Section 3 discusses the design of PostgreSQL-PS, a database system enhanced with publish/subscribe functionality. The architecture of the system is described in Section 4. Section 5 discusses how events are distributed between multiple connected databases. The system's programming interface is presented in Section 6 and its implementation is discussed in Section 7. Section 8 outlines related work, and Section 9 concludes the paper.

1.1   Motivating Scenario

Consider a large-scale financial services firm. The firm has offices in different cities across America and Europe, see Figure 1. Each office (domain) is autonomous, and maintains a database system that stores its critical data and a set of applications, e.g. for automated trade processing. In such a scenario, most interaction lies within a domain, but there is also a need for inter-domain communication. For example, while some data feeds used to publish the latest stock

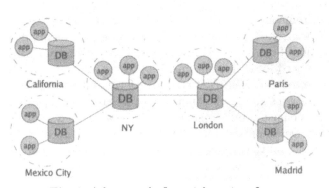

Fig. 1. A large-scale financial services firm

prices are made available only locally, others are also sent to external offices. Trading applications are specialised and thus expect different subsets of the available data feeds, e.g. based on the stock symbol, price, risk level, or combinations. Besides general stock processing, many other processes continuously keep track of specific situations, e.g. when a stock's minimum price-earnings ratio (PER) falls below a threshold. There will be a number of systems, both within and outside the local office, that require to be notified of such events, e.g. for real-time risk analysis.

Notice that information sharing in the scenario is inherently event based. To remain competitive, the firm requires an event-driven infrastructure to integrate the applications distributed across the various offices, and to support the active sharing of information. We believe that such infrastructure can be built efficiently on the database system. Firstly, database changes frequently trigger events. Secondly, for scalability, security, or simplicity purposes, business logic associated with event processing is often moved to the database (as stored procedures or triggers). Lastly, events must be logged in the database for reporting and audit.

2 Background

In this Section we establish the background on event-driven architecture (EDA), the publish/subscribe paradigm, and the PostgreSQL database system.

2.1 Event-Driven Architecture (EDA) and Publish/Subscribe

EDA [1] is an architectural pattern built on the production, detection, consumption of, and reaction to events. An event is defined as a happening of interest in the system. Events are generated by *event producers*. Based on its characteristics, an event is delivered to one or more *event consumers*. Consumers process the event and optionally execute an action. The architecture is loosely-coupled as producers and consumers do not require any knowledge about each other.

Publish/subscribe [2] is an asynchronous many-to-many event-based communication paradigm. In publish/subscribe, an *event client* may be an event producer (publisher), an event consumer (subscriber), or both. Event producers advertise the event types they will publish, and publish events, needing no knowledge of the subscribers. An event consumer specifies a set of subscriptions on events of interest. The event communication substrate, comprising one or more *event brokers*, accepts events from publishers and notifies them to subscribers whose subscriptions match. In a large-scale environment an event broker may serve a subset of the clients in the environment, for example, being associated with an administrative domain. Event brokers cooperatively distribute (route) events, while attempting to exploit locality and contain system complexity. A number of strategies for distributed event dissemination are discussed in [4].

Publish/subscribe comes in two flavours: *topic-based* and *content-based*. In topic-based publish/subscribe, events are published under a topic and consumers subscribe to that topic. In content-based publish/subscribe, event types are defined as comprising typed attributes. A subscription includes a filter expression indicating attribute values of interest. Events with content that matches the filter expression are delivered to the appropriate consumers.

2.2 PostgreSQL

PostgreSQL [3] is an open-source object-relational database system written in C. Domain, referential, and transactional integrity, as well as multi-version concurrency control, are offered as some of its features. Active functionality is provided in the form of triggers and active rules. Because its operation is catalogue-driven, PostgreSQL can be extended, for example by adding new data types and functions. Functions can be written in C, Python, or procedural SQL (PgSQL).

3 PostgreSQL-PS Design

In this section we discuss the design of PostgreSQL-PS, a database system enhanced by distributed content-based publish/subscribe functionality. We describe the EDA aspects to be supported and establish requirements for the system.

3.1 EDA Aspects

The design of the PostgreSQL-PS system covers the four aspects of EDA: event publication, subscription, consumption and distribution. The first three relate to the role of the database system as a publish/subscribe event client. The fourth delegates to the database system the role of event broker.

Event Production: to define events and specify conditions for their generation.

Event Subscription: to define an interest in receiving specific event instances.

Event Consumption: to define local actions to be executed when events matching a subscription are notified.

Event Distribution: to receive events from external parties, e.g. applications and other database systems. Events (either received or generated at the database system) should be delivered to the relevant subscribers. Multiple interconnected database systems should cooperate to route events between locally-connected applications and applications connected to remote database systems.

3.2 Requirements

In the design of PostgreSQL-PS we have considered the following requirements: expressiveness, reliability, scalability, access control and operational simplicity.

Expressiveness. The event model must support fine-grained subscriptions.

Reliability. The system must provide guarantees regarding its operation. We focus on two aspects: transactional semantics and guaranteed event delivery.

Transactional Semantics

Event production. We must ensure that events are produced only by committed operations to avoid *dirty reads* by event consumers. We therefore need to defer the publication of an event until its triggering transaction has committed. Further, we must guarantee the production of events from committed transactions.

Event consumption. We must guarantee the *ACID* consumption of events. In particular, the execution of event-processing actions must be transactional.

Guaranteed Event Delivery. In general, the delivery of an event must be guaranteed despite failures between producer and consumer. Specifically, a consumer must (eventually) receive each event exactly once. Events from the same producer must be delivered to a consumer in the same order in which they were published.

Scalability. System performance must degrade gracefully with the number of clients, subscriptions, and events. For a single database system this requires an efficient mechanism for matching events against subscriptions. For multiple connected database systems, it also entails efficient event distribution.

Access Control. Each database system must be able to control which clients can publish and subscribe to each event type.

Operational Simplicity. The database system must provide an integrated view of database and publish/subscribe operations through a simple interface.

4 PostgreSQL-PS Architecture

In this Section we describe the different components of the PostgreSQL-PS system architecture. All these components are defined in the context of a database. Multiple databases, each having different instances of these components, can be hosted within the same distributed database environment.

4.1 Event Types

Event types are used to structure the event space, each event being an instance of an event type. An event type has a system-wide unique name [5] and a schema that describes it. The schema is a set of attribute-name, data-type pairs. Valid data types are the native types defined by the SQL92 specification [6] (e.g. varchar, int, datetime). Event types are stored in the database system catalogue. They are used to verify that a) an event instance conforms to its type schema, b) a subscription filter refers to existing attributes, and c) functions and operators in the filter are valid for the attribute types.

4.2 Events

An event is a set of attribute name/value pairs conforming to an event type schema. In the database it is represented as a tuple structure. Events generated at the database have two properties: *visibility* and *reliability*. The visibility of an event determines when the event is published with regard to the transaction triggering the event. It can be either *immediate* or *deferred*. In the former, the event is published as soon as it is generated. In the latter, the publication of the event is deferred until its triggering transaction has committed. The reliability of an event determines whether its delivery is *non-guaranteed* or *guaranteed*. In the former, events are delivered at-most-once. In the latter, events are delivered exactly-once, ordered with respect to each producer.

4.3   Subscriptions

A subscription expresses interest in consuming (a subset of) events of some type. Subscriptions are named and specify an event type, an optional filter, and a source. The filter is a SQL predicate over the event type's attributes and, possibly, stored data. A large number of built-in operators and functions can be specified as part of the filter. The source of a subscription can be *external* or *internal*. An external subscription is issued by a client application or received from another database. An internal subscription is defined at the database to process local events. Subscriptions have a *local* or *global* scope. A local subscription only applies to events known to the local database. A global subscription also expresses interest in events known to other databases (directly or indirectly) connected to the database. Subscriptions are persistently stored in the database system catalogue, in order to survive system failures and client disconnections.

4.4   Queues

Queues contain events. For each event type there are three queues: *in*, *out*, and *exception*. Events locally produced or received from external parties are enqueued in their corresponding *in-queue*. Events that have been matched against subscriptions are enqueued in their *out-queue* for their delivery (external subscriptions) or local processing (internal subscriptions). Events for which processing fails are enqueued in their *exception queue*. Each in- and out- queue has two instances, *non-persistent* and *persistent*. Non-persistent queues are volatile data structures that hold non-guaranteed events in memory. Persistent queues use database storage to store guaranteed events reliably on disk. They are implemented as special tables with no INSERT, UPDATE, DELETE, or trigger statements. Events stored in a queue can be consulted via SELECT queries on the event schema and additional system information (e.g. enqueue time). Persistent queues can be *non-auditable* or *auditable*. In the first (default) case, an event is deleted from a queue when it is no longer required (e.g. it has been successfully delivered to a consumer). In the second, the event is retained in the queue for auditing purposes.

4.5   Advertisements

Advertisements are either directly created at a database or introduced by a local application. A database must advertise an event type before it can produce or distribute events of that type. Advertisements are stored persistently in the database system catalogue.

4.6   Links

A link represents a connection to a remote database. It specifies contact information and associated authentication data. On startup, a database connects to all its defined links. Advertisements, global subscriptions, and events are propagated through these links. A connected set of databases forms a distributed system that actively shares information as described in the next Section.

5   PostgreSQL-PS Cooperative Event Distribution

In this Section we describe the mechanism used to distribute events cooperatively between connected databases. In the current prototype, we consider a peer-to-peer interconnection model in which databases communicate symmetrically in an acyclic topology. In practice databases can be connected in any way, provided that we identify a spanning tree for routing purposes. Factors to consider when connecting two databases include: administrative constraints, knowledge about the locality of consumers (or producers) of events of interest, and network latency.

Events are cooperatively distributed using an *advertisement-based* filtering scheme [7]. In this scheme, databases build event dissemination trees by propagating advertisements and subscriptions as follows:

1. An advertisement for an event type is propagated by following every database link. Each database stores advertisements received from the previous database. This builds, for the event type, a dissemination tree from the advertising database to every other database.
2. A subscription is propagated by reversing the links of databases with stored advertisements for that type. Each database stores the subscription received from the previous database. This builds, for the event type, a dissemination tree from the subscribing database to every database that produces events of that type.

Events are distributed by following the links of databases with stored subscriptions that match their type and content. After receiving an event, a database evaluates 1) the set of internal subscriptions and external subscriptions issued by local client applications, and 2) the external subscriptions received by linked databases. If no subscription matches the event, it is discarded.

We illustrate event distribution in Figure 2. For clarity we consider a single event type t. We show six connected databases DB_{1-6} and a set of applications App_{1-6}. App_1 and DB_2 produce events of t, and App_3 and DB_6 are event consumers.

First, App_1 advertises t with a_1, via its local database DB_1. a_1 is propagated to, and stored by DB_{2-6}. Then DB_2 creates the advertisement a_2 which is propagated to, and stored by DB_3, the only DB with a new source of events for t.

Next, DB_6 creates the global subscription s_6, which by reversing the paths of a_1 and a_2, is propagated to, and stored by DB_4, DB_3, DB_1, and DB_2. On request of App_3, DB_3 creates the global subscription s_3, which is propagated to, and stored by DB_1 and DB_2, extending the dissemination route for t. When DB_1 receives the event e_1 from App_1, it is propagated to App_3 and DB_6.

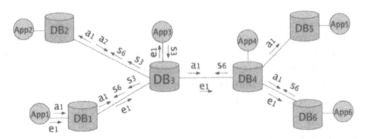

Fig. 2. Cooperative Event Distribution

6   PostgreSQL-PS Programming Interface

PostgreSQL-PS provides two interfaces to programmers. A *database program-ming interface* supports system administration and database-side event process-ing. An *application programming interface* is available to client applications.

6.1   Database Programming Interface

This interface, see Table 1, extends SQL with a number of publish/subscribe re-lated statements. It is accessible from the database system console (Psql), as well as from client-level interface implementations such as JDBC.

An event type is created using the CREATE EVENT TYPE statement. This state-ment also creates in, out, and exception queues for the event type. ALTER QUEUE sets the auditable behaviour of a queue. An event type must be advertised be-fore events of that type can be published or subscribed to. This is done using ADVERTISE. Events are generated at the database using PUBLISH; the statement is parametrised with the event *visibility* and *reliability*. PUBLISH can be used as a separate statement or within a transaction. It can also be set as the *action* of an active rule. This automates the production of events after data manipulation commands, possibly referring to the transition tables NEW and OLD. A database

Table 1. Database Programming Interface

CREATE EVENT TYPE *event_type* AS (*att1 datatype, att2 datatype, ..*)
ALTER QUEUE *queue_name* SET [NON-AUDITABLE|AUDITABLE]
ADVERTISE *event_type*
PUBLISH [IMMEDIATE|DEFERRED] [NON-GUARANTEED|GUARANTEED] *event_type* (*attvalue1, attvalue2, ..*)
CREATE RULE *rule_name* AS ON {INSERT|UPDATE|DELETE} TO *table* [WHERE *filter*] PUBLISH *event_type*(*attvalue1, attvalue2, ..*)
CREATE [LOCAL|GLOBAL] SUBSCRIPTION *sub_name* ON *event_type* [WHERE *filter*] EXECUTE *func_name*(*args*) [WITH *priority*]
CREATE LINK *link_name* TO *address port* USING *user password*
GRANT [PUBLISH|SUBSCRIBE] ON EVENT TYPE *event_type* TO {*user*|*role*}

subscribes to events of some type using CREATE SUBSCRIPTION; the statement is parametrised with the subscription scope. As an optional filter, an SQL predicate can be specified via a WHERE clause on attributes of the event type, as well as on stored data. Subscriptions created at the database are always *internal*, and must specify a function to process received events. Functions can be written in any of the languages supported by the database, allowing developers to focus on the most suitable for a given task (e.g. PgSQL for data-centric operations or C for computationally intensive logic). The way in which a function is passed an event depends on its implementation language, e.g. as a pointer to an Event structure in C, or a top-level RECORD variable in PgSQL. An optional priority can be assigned to the subscription, an absolute value that determines the order of evaluation for subscriptions to a given event type. A link is defined using CREATE LINK, which specifies the address and port on which a remote database services publish/subscribe connections, and an authorised user and password in that database. There are DROP statements for EVENT TYPE, RULE, SUBSCRIPTION, and LINK, as well as an UNADVERTISE statement. Privileges on each of these statements can be assigned and removed from database users and roles using GRANT and REVOKE. Information about existing publish/subscribe-related objects (e.g. event types, subscriptions, and links) is made available through restricted catalogue views.

6.2   Application Programming Interface (API)

This interface, depicted in Table 2, allows applications to access the database system publish/subscribe functionality. We provide a Java implementation of the API. In this, functions are supported via a Client object as described next.

An application connects to the database system using the Client connect method. This requires the address and port where the database services publish/subscribe clients. A valid user and password are needed to authorise the client, and to associate any stored subscriptions to the connection. Event types are created by instantiating the EventType class. This class contains a name, and a *Map* of two attributes: name and type. Valid types are *String*, *Date*, and all subclasses of *Number*. The API translates these types to SQL92 data types when an application requests the database to advertise an event type using the advertise method. Events are created by instantiating the Event class. This class has an associated event type and a *Map* of two attributes: name and value. The value is an object of the corresponding attribute type. Events are published, with the requested reliability, via publish. A subscription is issued, with the specified scope, via subscribe. An optional filter can be defined via

Table 2. Application Programming Interface

| Client.connect(*address, port, user, password*) |
| Client.advertise(*EventType*) |
| Client.publish(*reliability, Event*) |
| Client.subscribe(*sub_name, EventType, scope, filter, Callback*) |

an SQL predicate. Finally, a class implementing the `Callback` interface must be specified to process any events received. The API keeps a persistent *Map* of subscriptions and callbacks. Events from the database are piggybacked with the matched subscription name. Based on the SQL92 data types of attributes in events received, the programming interface builds an `Event` Java object that is passed to the callback class.

7 PostgreSQL-PS Implementation

We have implemented PostgreSQL-PS by extending the PostgreSQL [3] 8.0.3 code base. We chose PostgreSQL for its rich set of features and the ability to analyze and extend its source code. We now describe the PostgreSQL-PS process architecture and discuss how we fulfil the requirements established in Section 3.2.

7.1 Process Architecture

Figure 3 shows the PostgreSQL-PS process architecture. The various PostgreSQL components that are reused are shown on the left.

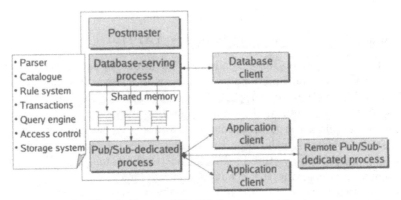

Fig. 3. PostgreSQL-PS Process Architecture

As in PostgreSQL, a Postmaster listens on a well-known port and forks a new database-serving process for each database client TCP connection. These clients, usually Psql or JDBC-based, are served using synchronous request-reply. The PostgreSQL parser was extended to provide clients with the database publish/subscribe programming interface. A process dedicated to publish/subscribe handles TCP connections from publish/subscribe clients and remote databases. The Postmaster forks this process on startup. Communication with publish/subscribe clients is message-oriented and asynchronous, via non-blocking sockets. We notify the publish/subscribe process of relevant operations (e.g. events and subscriptions) issued from a database-serving process; for this we use a set of control queues in a shared memory segment. Database-serving processes enqueue notifications that are dequeued and analysed by the publish/subscribe process.

7.2   Transactional Event Production and Consumption

We currently implement two event visibility and reliability combinations, *immediate non-guaranteed* and *deferred guaranteed*, as we expect them to cover most application scenarios. For the former, a published event is enqueued in its non-persistent in-queue. There is no dependency between the transaction producing the event and the publish operation. When the event is dequeued from its in-queue, it is matched against subscriptions and immediately sent to its consumers, via its non-persistent out-queue. For the latter, a publish operation enqueues the event in its persistent in-queue. This is done within the running transaction to ensure the atomicity of publish with other operations. If enqueuing fails, the transaction rolls-back and the user is notified of the error. Otherwise the event, together with the ID of its producing transaction, is stored in the queue. When the transaction commits, a notification containing the transaction ID is enqueued in a control queue. On-commit hooks [8] have been incorporated for this purpose. When the publish/subscribe process dequeues the notification, it matches events with the notified transaction ID against subscriptions. For each matched consumer, one instance of the event is enqueued in the event's persistent out-queue for processing or delivery. Once matching is completed, the event is removed from its persistent in-queue. The insertion of the event instances in the out-queue and the removal of events from the in-queue are executed within the same transaction.

On consumption, the dequeue of an event from its persistent out-queue and the execution of its processing function take place within a transaction. The execution of multiple functions for the same event is serial. Functions are executed in turn, in separate transactions, according to subscription priority. This ensures atomicity of function execution and isolation of execution for independent functions. If processing an event fails (e.g. due to a violated constraint), the event is removed from its out-queue and enqueued in its exception-queue with a description of the error. These two operations are executed in a single transaction.

7.3   Guaranteed Event Delivery

We ensure exactly-once ordered delivery of events between a sender and a receiver on a direct connection using an acknowledgement-based protocol with unbounded sequence numbers [9]. At the application side, the protocol is handled automatically by the API. Sender S keeps a sequence number s that is incremented for each event e to be sent to receiver R. Before sending $e[s]$, i.e. event e with sequence number s, S persistently stores it with an associated timestamp. We denote as $S.e[s]$ the event e with sequence number s sent by S. To enforce ordering, a receiver keeps an array N of sequence numbers, one for each sender. $N[S]$ denotes the sequence number associated with sender S. N is stored persistently so it survives receiver failures. On receipt of an event $S.e[n]$: if $n < N[S]$, R acknowledges n to S and discards the event. If $n = N[S]$, R processes the event, increments $N[S]$, and acknowledges n to S. If $n > N[S]$, R acknowledges $N[S]$ to S and discards the event. The sender can delete $e[s]$ when it receives an acknowledgement for s. If S does not receive an acknowledgement for $e[s]$ within a predefined timeout, it resends using an *exponential backoff*. In this, the timeout starts at 4 seconds and doubles at each retry up to a maximum of 64 seconds.

7.4 Scalability

Publish/Subscribe-related data indexing: At a database we need to quickly retrieve 1) the event type schema used to validate an event, 2) the in, out, or exception queue where an event must be stored, and 3) the set of subscriptions to be evaluated against the event. Fetching this data from disk every time would damage database performance. Therefore, we cache and index publish/subscribe-related data in main memory. A hash table indexes event types by name: each bucket stores the schema of the event type, its associated queues, and a pointer to a dynamic array of subscriptions. Because of sequential locality, this structure allows efficient iteration over the set of subscriptions for a given event type.

Execution Plan Caching for Subscription Filters: When the database receives a subscription, its filter is parsed and translated into an *execution plan*. When the subscription is evaluated, the database query engine needs only to execute this plan. Parsing and planning is thus performed only once, instead of at each evaluation. The performance gain is more significant if the subscription filter refers to stored data, as planning of queries on tables takes more time.

Logical Event Deletes: An event in an in-queue is deleted after it has been processed locally and matched against subscriptions. An event in an out-queue is deleted after it has been acknowledged. In PostgreSQL a DELETE operation is logical, i.e. it does not physically remove a tuple from disk. To reclaim the space of deleted tuples, a separate VACUUM operation is used. This approach reduces the time to delete an event from a queue, at a cost in disk space utilisation. We expect that all queues in the database are vacuumed periodically (e.g. once a day at a low-usage time), with more frequent vacuuming of heavily updated queues.

8 Related Work

"Queues are databases" was stated more than ten years ago [10]. Accordingly, some vendors have incorporated message queuing into their database systems. SQL Server Service Broker [11] provides asynchronous and reliable dialogues between databases to support distributed applications. Communication is bi-directional between two databases; publish/subscribe is not supported. Oracle Streams [12] supports one-to-many asynchronous replication via multi-consumer queues. Replicas can specify content-based rules to propagate only a subset of data changes from the master database. Rules are not global (they must specify a source and a destination queue) so that a replica cannot express interest in data beyond its master, unlike PostgreSQL-PS's global subscriptions.

9   Conclusions

Maintaining most of a business's critical information and reflecting the state of its daily processes, database systems are in a cardinal position to support active information sharing. EDA provides an appropriate model for active data sharing based on the production and consumption of events. Publish/subscribe is a suitable loosely-coupled communication paradigm. Integrating distributed content-based publish/subscribe functionality into the database system is therefore a promising approach to active information sharing. On one hand, databases already provide many features that an event-driven architecture can exploit, such as persistent storage, transactions, and active rules. On the other hand, integrating publish/subscribe into the database system leads to information-sharing systems that are simpler to deploy and maintain. We are currently evaluating PostgreSQL-PS against a decoupled database - publish/subscribe system. Preliminary experimental results show that the execution of functions that require to access the database frequently, e.g. logging events or evaluating subscriptions that refer to tables, is faster in PostgreSQL-PS. However, the evaluation of subscriptions that refer only to event content is, on average, slower, as the query engine incurs an additional overhead. We are thus planning to incorporate an event/subscriptions matching algorithm that pre-filters subscriptions based on event content and employs the query engine only as needed.

References

1. Luckham, D.: The Power of Events: An Introduction to Complex Event Processing in Distributed Enterprise Systems. Addison-Wesley Professional, Reading (2002)
2. Eugster, P., Felber, P., Guerraoui, R., Kermarrec, A.: The Many Faces of Publish/Subscribe. ACM Computing Surveys 35(2), 114–131 (2003)
3. The PostgreSQL Global Development Group (2008), www.postgresql.org
4. Mühl, G., Fiege, L., Pietzuch, P.: Distributed Event-Based Systems. Springer, Heidelberg (2006)
5. Pesonen, L.I.W., Bacon, J.: Secure Event Types in Content-Based, Multi-domain Publish/Subscribe Systems. In: Proc.of the 5th International Workshop on Software Engineering and Middleware, pp. 98–105 (2005)
6. American National Standards Institute: Standard x3.135-1992 (1992)
7. Carzaniga, A., Rosenblum, D., Wolf, A.: Design and Evaluation of a Wide-Area Event Notification Service. ACM Tran. on Computer Systems 19(3), 332–383 (2001)
8. Paton, N.W., Díaz, O.: Active Database Systems. ACM Computing Surveys 31(1), 63–103 (1999)
9. Comer, D.E.: Internetworking with TCP/IP vol II. ANSI C Version: Design, Implementation, and Internals. Prentice-Hall, Englewood Cliffs (1998)
10. Gray, J.: Queues are Databases. In: Proc. of the 7th High Performance Transaction Processing Workshop (1995)
11. Aschenbrenner, K.: SQL Server 2005 Service Broker. Apress (2007)
12. Oracle: 11g Streams Replication Administrator's Guide (2007)

Smooth Interpolating Histograms
with Error Guarantees

Thomas Neumann[1] and Sebastian Michel[2]

[1] Max-Planck-Institut Informatik, Saarbrücken, Germany
neumann@mpi-inf.mpg.de
[2] École Polytechnique Fédérale de Lausanne, Lausanne, Switzerland
sebastian.michel@epfl.ch

Abstract. Accurate selectivity estimations are essential for query optimization decisions where they are typically derived from various kinds of histograms which condense value distributions into compact representations. The estimation accuracy of existing approaches typically varies across the domain, with some estimations being very accurate and some quite inaccurate. This is in particular unfortunate when performing a parametric search using these estimations, as the estimation artifacts can dominate the search results. We propose the usage of linear splines to construct histograms with known error guarantees across the whole continuous domain. These histograms are particularly well suited for using the estimates in parameter optimization. We show by a comprehensive performance evaluation using both synthetic and real world data that our approach clearly outperforms existing techniques.

1 Introduction

Query optimization is largely based on selectivity (and thus cardinality) estimations. Typically, these cardinalities are the most significant parameters of cost estimations. The selectivity estimates are derived from precomputed statistical information, usually in the form of histograms. A histogram contains a condensed representation of the value distribution of one attribute (or multiple attributes for multidimensional histograms). When a query contains a predicate on that attribute, the corresponding histogram can be used for selectivity estimation. For these estimations, the histograms are probed with values derived from the query itself. These are only a few constants for most of the queries, but in some situations the query optimizer itself will generate new constants.

As a showcase application for these kind of query optimization problems we briefly discuss a typical issue in the area of top-k query processing. Among the ample work on top-k query processing, the family of threshold algorithms (cf, e.g., [1,2,3]) stands out as an extremely efficient and highly versatile method. However, none of these algorithms can be directly applied in a widely distributed setting, as they still incur an unbounded number of message rounds. In contrast, state-of-the-art algorithms for distributed top-k aggregation use a fixed number of communication rounds to bound latency. The first algorithm in this family

A. Gray, K. Jeffery, and J. Shao (Eds.): BNCOD 2008, LNCS 5071, pp. 126–138, 2008.

was the TPUT (Three-Phase Uniform Threshold) algorithm [4], in which the top-k query is translated into a range scan with appropriate postprocessing. Yu et al [5] present a modification of TPUT where the range bounds are adapted to the specifics of the value distributions. Along these lines stands our own work [6] on distributed top-k query optimization. The basic idea behind the algorithms presented in [4,5,7] is the transformation of a top-k query into the union of range queries where the range is determined by an initial retrieval phase. In a simple example of a top-k query that involves two index lists with a given range of 0.9, i.e., all documents with an aggregated score of at least 0.9 are potential candiates, for summation the second retrieval phase can be written as

(**select** id **from** list1 **where** score$\geq$0.5)
union all
(**select** id **from** list2 **where** score$\geq$0.4)

Although this query requires some post processing, as it produces a super set of the original top-k query, it can be executed more efficiently. As for normal range queries, histograms can be used to estimate the number of qualifying data items. Note however that the constants 0.5 and 0.4 in this query do not occur in the original top-k query and that they were chosen somewhat arbitrarily. In general any pair (a, b) of score thresholds would be suitable as long as $a+b \leq 0.9$. During query optimization, histograms are probed for many different (generated) values that will often not occur in the actual data.

This has consequences for the requirements on histograms. The two main requirements for constant optimization are:

1. Smooth estimations, i.e., the estimations do not create artificial extrema. Formally, $\forall_{[a,b]\supseteq[a',b']}H([a,b]) \geq H([a',b'])$, where $H([.,.])$ is the estimator for a range query.
2. Interpolating estimations, i.e., the estimation works well for any value in the potential domain.

The smoothness requirement implies that numerical methods can be used on the histogram. This is sometimes violated by more complex histograms (e.g., [8]) when modeling the CDF. As this is to some extent application specific, we do not elaborate on this in the paper, although our histograms satisfy the requirement. As we will see in Section 5, the interpolation requirement is not satisfied by many existing approaches as they usually concentrate on creating histograms to accurately represent the actual data while rarely occurring or non-occurring attribute values cause large errors.

In this paper, we propose the usage of continuous linear splines to model data distributions and present algorithms to efficiently construct interpolating splines that have a low error guarantee across the whole domain, and that allow smooth selectivity estimations. These spline histograms have some further nice properties for top-k processing, in particular, they are reversible and allow for determining the range bounds when the cardinality is known. Moreover, the spline histograms are not limited to information retrieval settings, the experimental results show that they are superior to existing approaches even if the additional properties are not required. The rest of this paper is organized as follows: Section 2 discusses related work. Section 3 reasons about the usage of splines for interpolation. Subsequently, Section 4 presents an optimal and a greedy algorithm to construct spline histograms. Section 5 presents the experimental evaluation.

2   Related Work

Histograms are a well studied field in database research. In fact, there are so many different kinds of histograms that we can only highlight closely related work here, and refer to [9] for a comprehensive overview. In our work, we concentrate on histograms that can be used for selectivity estimations of range queries. More general histograms exist, for example for multidimensional data [10], but this is beyond the scope of this work.

Spline based histograms have been mentioned in the literature before [11], but there the knot placement problem is considered as too difficult. The paper mentions that heuristic spline construction is possible, but the results shown in [11] indicate that these heuristic splines are not relevant (the paper explicitly classifies them as "poor histograms"). Another spline based histogram approach has been proposed in [8], that in contrast to our work, disregards spline features like smoothness and continuity. It partitions the value domain into buckets, computes the frequencies inside each bucket, and fits a linear function to the frequencies using least squares fitting. As we will see in Section 5, this bucket-wise fitting can cause huge errors near the bucket boundaries.

A very well known histogram construction technique are V-Optimal histograms [12]. The algorithm minimizes the frequency variance inside the buckets, which results in a good accuracy in general. It is not well suited for continuous data, where the frequencies are usually all equal to 1 (see Section 5). Recently histogram approaches have been suggested that deviate further from the classical view of histograms. Two examples are [13,14], that construct a wavelet representation of the original data and then discards coefficients to reduce the space consumption. This is very similar to lossy compression techniques. One difficulty is that the data has to be discretized first, and that the accuracy is sensitive to the chosen approximation, as we will see in Section 5.

3   Spline Interpolation

The goal of histogram construction is to find a compressed representation of the raw data that still allows for accurate estimations. We propose the usage of splines; partially because they can represent distributions efficiently, and partially because we can construct them in way that provides smooth estimations with error guarantees. In this section we discuss the general approach of using spline histograms, the concrete algorithms are shown in Section 4.

3.1   Data Representation

The raw data itself consists of a multiset of values, potentially from a continuous domain. For query optimization, the histogram is typically queried in two different ways. Either it should determine how many occurrences of an attribute that have a certain value are in the data (*point query*) or how many occurrences of an attribute are within a given range (*range queries*). We concentrate on range queries here, as point queries on a continuous domain are not meaningful in general since the expected number of occurrences is zero. On a discrete domain, range queries can be used to approximate point queries.

The best representation for our purpose is the *cumulative distribution function* (CDF). For each point in the domain it gives the number of values less or equal to this point, which can easily be used to answer range queries. Additionally, it is reasonably easy to interpolate, as it grows monotonically and has a contiguous support (in contrast to the density function). Note that for multisets of values the CDF describes a step function. While the algorithms presented in this paper could directly interpolate this, we simplify the representation by disregarding the lower point of each step (i.e. connecting the upper points linearly). Disregarding the lower points of each step reduces the number of data points relevant for the interpolation, which speeds up the histogram construction, and already constructs a linear spline. Thus the goal of spline construction in this paper is to reduce a linear spline with n data points (n being the number of values in the original data) to a linear spline with k data points (k being the allowed histogram size) such that approximation is as good as possible.

3.2   Approximation Criterion

When approximating one function with another, it is necessary to define an approximation criterion to decide which approximation to choose. A commonly used measure is the mean squared error, like, for instance, used in [8] during the histogram construction. The mean squared error is very popular, but primarily because analytic solutions for minimizing it are known, the value itself is hard to interpret. Further, as only the average is minimized, the quality of the approximation can vary arbitrarily over the domain. As we want a smooth approximation, mean squared error is not a good choice.

A more robust error is the maximum error [13], which has a well defined meaning even for continuous domains. If we construct an approximation function with a maximum error of ϵ, we know that this maximum deviation of ϵ is guaranteed for all queries, regardless of the concrete value and without outliers. Of course this error measure is only helpful if we can achieve a reasonably low ϵ, we will see detailed algorithms for this in Section 4. For the spline interpolation, a maximum error ϵ defines an error corridor around the original function such that the resulting spline is guaranteed to stay within the error corridor. As a consequence, the maximum error is known over the whole domain. A slight variation of this is the maximum of the relative error, where the corridor size is defined relative to the real value. As we will later see, our algorithms can handle both relative and absolute errors. In our experiments we used the maximum relative error, as it is more critical in practice since.

3.3 Formalization

Using these observations, we can formalize the problem as follows: Given a linear spline S and a line segment $\overline{S_1 S_2}$, we define the maximum error induced by this line segment as the maximum deviation of knot points from the line segment. This is

$$\delta(S, \overline{S_1 S_2}) = \max_{p \in S \wedge p.x \in [S_1.x, S_2.x]} |p.y - \overline{S_1 S_2}[p.x]|$$

when using the absolute error, and

$$\delta(S, \overline{S_1 S_2}) = \max_{p \in S \wedge p.x \in [S_1.x, S_2.x]} \frac{|p.y - \overline{S_1 S_2}[p.x]|}{p.y}$$

when using the relative error. Note that it is sufficient to calculate the difference at the knot points, as the spline knots are connected linearly.

Using the maximum error induced by a single line segment, we can define the maximum error for interpolating a linear spline S by a linear spline S' as maximum of all errors induced by the line segments of S'.

$$\Delta(S, S') = \max_{1 \leq i < |S'|} \delta(S, \overline{S'[i] S'[i + 1]})$$

Now the interpolation problem can be written as: Given a linear spline S and a natural number k, $k \geq 2$. Construct a linear spline S' such that $|S'| \leq k$, $S'[1] = S[1]$, $S'[|S'|] = S[|S|]$ and $\Delta(S, S')$ is minimal. Note that the requirement that the first and the last points of the splines must be identical prevents approximating splines that only cover part of the original spline.

4   Spline Construction

The goal of the spline construction algorithms is to construct a spline with a given size that approximates the cumulative frequency distribution with the minimal (or at least a low) maximum error. By using the spline interpretation of the original data as discussed in Section 3, the algorithms reduce a spline with n points (the original data) to a spline with k points. The key difficulty here is that n can be very large, potentially even larger than main memory, whereas k is relatively small (e.g. for $k = 100$ the histograms consume 1.6KB). Note that the spline representing the original data can be constructed trivially when the values are sorted and is therefore not an issue. We now present two algorithms for spline construction, first a greedy heuristic that can handle arbitrarily large inputs and then a DP based algorithm that constructs the optimal spline. For large inputs the two can be combined to produce good results, as we will see below.

4.1 Greedy Construction

Minimizing the maximum error with a greedy algorithm is difficult, as the effect of knot placement on later knots is hard to predict. Instead, we solve the dual problem (constructing the smallest spline with a given maximum error), and use its solution to solve the original approximation problem. The greedy spline construction is therefore split into two parts. The first part (*GreedySplineCorridor*) constructs a linear spline approximation for a given error corridor, and the second part (*GreedySpline*) minimizes the size of the error corridor using the first part.

The pseudo code of the spline construction with a given error corridor is shown in Figure 1. It starts constructing the result spline R by choosing the first point in S as first point of R. During the algorithm, the last point in R is called B (base point). It then performs a linear scan over the spline and checks if the line segment between B and the current point C is still within the error corridor. If not, the maximum error constraint would be violated if connecting B and C, i.e., $\delta(S, \overline{BC}) > \epsilon$. The last point before C allows for interpolation within the error boundaries, therefore it is chosen as new base point and added to R.

If a point is not chosen as a new base point, it still affects the error corridor. An important observation is that it is not required to keep track of the real error corridor, it is sufficient to remember the most limiting points. In the algorithm these are U for the the upper bound and L for the lower bound, that denote the most narrowing points of the error corridor relative to B. For each point C, the individual upper and lower bounds U' and L' are calculated by adding ϵ to the y value (or for relative errors by multiplying y with $1 + \epsilon$ and $1 - \epsilon$). If a new bound is more restrictive, it replaces the old bound. An illustration of this

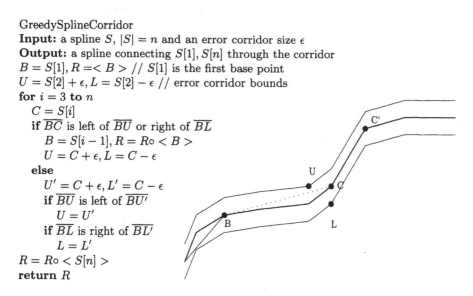

GreedySplineCorridor
Input: a spline S, $|S| = n$ and an error corridor size ϵ
Output: a spline connecting $S[1], S[n]$ through the corridor
$B = S[1], R = < B >$ // $S[1]$ is the first base point
$U = S[2] + \epsilon, L = S[2] - \epsilon$ // error corridor bounds
for $i = 3$ **to** n
  $C = S[i]$
  if $\overline{BC}$ is left of $\overline{BU}$ or right of $\overline{BL}$
    $B = S[i-1], R = R \circ < B >$
    $U = C + \epsilon, L = C - \epsilon$
  else
     $U' = C + \epsilon, L' = C - \epsilon$
    if $\overline{BU}$ is left of $\overline{BU'}$
     $U = U'$
    if $\overline{BL}$ is right of $\overline{BL'}$
     $L = L'$
$R = R \circ < S[n] >$
return R

Fig. 1. Greedy Spline Approximation with a Given Error Corridor

GreedySpline
Input: a spline S, $|S| = n$, and a desired spline size k
Output: a spline connecting $S[1], S[n]$ with $\leq k$ knots
$R = \emptyset, \epsilon_R = \infty$
$\epsilon_L = 0, \epsilon_U =$ error when approximating S with 0
while $\epsilon_U - \epsilon_L > \Delta$
$\quad \epsilon = \frac{\epsilon_L + \epsilon_U}{2}$
$\quad S_\epsilon =$ GreedySplineCorridor(S,ϵ)
$\quad$ **if** $|S_\epsilon| > k$
$\quad\quad \epsilon_L = \epsilon$
$\quad$ **else**
$\quad\quad$ **if** $\epsilon < \epsilon_R$
$\quad\quad\quad R = S_\epsilon, \epsilon_R = \epsilon$
$\quad\quad \epsilon_U = \epsilon$
return R

Fig. 2. Greedy Spline Approximation Algorithm

approach is included in Figure 1. The point B has been chosen as a base point (i.e. the second point in the output spline), and now the scan continues to point C. C is still reachable from B, thus it is skipped for now. The lower bound L is updated to the new lower bound derived from C, whereas the previous upper bound U is tighter than the bound derived from C and is thus unchanged. The next scan point C' is no longer reachable from B, therefore C will be added as new base point when scanning to C'.

The scan continues until the last point of S is reachable within the error corridor, after which it is added to R as the final point. The spline R now consists of the smallest spline (regarding the greedy selection method) that satisfies the maximum error ϵ across the domain. The whole algorithm performs a single scan over the original data and requires only constant memory in addition to the result itself. Thus, it has a runtime complexity of $O(n)$ and a space complexity of $O(k)$.

This spline construction logic can now be used to find splines with a low maximum error. The pseudo code is shown in Figure 2: It performs a binary search over the maximum error until the desired accuracy is reached (which can be derived from the data). For each error bound ϵ, *GreedySplineCorridor* is used to construct a spline. If the spline is too large, the error bound has to be increased, otherwise it can be decreased. After the binary search is done, the algorithm returns the best spline found that consists of at most k points. In an implementation, the spline construction can stop if the spline candidate gets larger than k points, therefore the overall algorithm runs in $O(n \log n)$ time and $O(k)$ space. The algorithm is very fast, which makes it attractive as a pre-filter for slower algorithms (reducing a huge n to a more manageable n'). Due to its sequential access pattern it could even be used if the original spline does not fit into main memory.

4.2 Optimal Construction

Disregarding memory restrictions, there is no need to use an approximate solution, at least from a theoretical point of view. In his seminal work, Goodrich [15] showed that the optimal linear spline can be constructed in $O(n \log n)$, i.e., with the same asymptotic complexity as our greedy heuristic. Unfortunately these are primarily theoretical results. Several steps of the algorithm are very involved, and [15] already mentions that a potential implementation would have very large constants. To our knowledge, no implementation of the algorithm exists.

Instead, we use a dynamic programming algorithm that constructs the spline in $O(n^2 k)$ time and $O(nk)$ space. The resulting spline is optimal when solely considering the original data points as potential spline knots, which is reasonable here (as $k \ll n$), but not necessarily optimal in some cases [15]. We ignore this possibility, as n is very large and offers enough potential knot points.

The pseudo code for the DP algorithm is shown in Figure 3. It constructs a DP table that for each data point j $(1 \leq j \leq n)$ and each value l $(1 \leq l \leq k)$ gives the minimum error ($dpError$) of reaching this point with a spline of size l, and the previous point ($dpPrevious$) in the spline. The table is filled as follows: For the first point $S[1]$, the interpolation is perfect as we start with it, resulting in an error of zero for all spline sizes. Then, the algorithm considers all potential starting points of spline segments i and all potential ending points for each segment j. For each of these segment candidates it computes the maximum error ϵ_{ij} caused by choosing a spline segment $\overline{S[i]S[j]}$. Note that as the error corridor for the greedy algorithm, ϵ_{ij} can be maintained incrementally. If $i = 1$, i.e., the spline segment starts with the first point, we can construct a spline of size 1, setting $dpError[j, 1] = \epsilon_{ij}$. Otherwise, the spline must consist of at least one other spline segment that reached i. The algorithm tries out all possible spline

DPSpline
Input: a spline S, $|S| = n$ and a desired spline size k
Output: a spline connecting $S[1], S[n]$ with $\leq k$ knots

```
dpPrevious = map ([1, n], [1, k]) → [1, n]
dpError = map ([1, n], [1, k]) → ℝ⁺
for l = 1 to k
    dpError[1, l] = 0, dpPrevious[1, l] = 1
for i = 1 to n − 1
    for j = i + 1 to n
        εij = δ(S, S[i]S[j])
        if i = 1
            dpError[j, 1] = εij, dpPrevious[j, 1] = 1
        for l = 2 to k
            ε = max(εij, dpError[i, l − 1])
            if i = 1 or ε < dpError[j, l]
                dpError[j, l] = ε, dpPrevious[j, l] = i
R = <>, r = n
for l = k to 1
    R =< S[r] > ∘R
    r = dpPrevious[r, l]
return R
```

Fig. 3. Dynamic Programming Spline Construction Algorithm

sizes l, using the maximum of ϵ_{ij} and the error of the preceding, smaller spline ($dpError[i, l-1]$) as total error ϵ. If ϵ is smaller than the best known error for this end point and this spline size, the error bounds are updated and the starting point stored in $dpPrevious$. After all segments were considered, $dpError[n, k]$ contains the maximum error of the best spline, and $dpPrevious[n, k]$ the previous to last point of this spline. Walking backwards over $dpPrevious$, the algorithm reconstructs the best spline R from the DP table.

4.3 Large Inputs

As the runtime complexity of the DP algorithm is $O(n^2 k)$, it cannot be used for arbitrarily large problems. Our implementation could solve $n = 5,000$ and $k = 100$ in less than two seconds on a standard PC, but the runtime increases quadratically with n. And n can be very large in practice. We therefore use the greedy algorithm as a reduction step. The greedy algorithm itself is very fast even for large inputs ($n = 1,000,000$ in less than a second), and constructs approximating splines with known maximum errors. Thus, when solving large problems with the DP algorithm, we use the greedy algorithm to reduce the input to a spline with 5,000 knots and then use the DP algorithm on the reduced spline. Due to the geometric interpretation of the error corridors, the errors of the two algorithms at most add up, and the error for $k = 5,000$ is very low. As we will see in Section 5, this allows us to efficiently handle very large inputs, while still maintaining hard error boundaries across the whole domain.

5 Experimental Results

In this section we study the prediction quality of our spline histograms in comparison with existing approaches. We first discuss the general setup, then we present the particular approaches that we consider in our evaluation, and finally we present the experimental results for real-world IR data.

5.1 General Setup

To evaluate the accuracy of the different approaches, we construct histograms of varying size for each approach. As the approaches differ in the information stored per bucket, we measure the size in bytes instead of buckets. For each histogram size, we construct 1 million range queries of the form $attr \geq x$, where x is varied uniformly between the minimum and the maximum attribute value. For each of these range queries, we compute the actual number of tuples in this range and the prediction made by each histogram. The difference between the two, the absolute error, is reduced by one to eliminate rounding issues (the predictions are reals while the actual number of tuples is an integer) and then divided by the actual number of tuples to get the relative error. We show three measures: the maximum relative error over all queries, as this was our optimization criterion and shows the worst case for each approach. The average relative error, as this show the "expected" error for an arbitrary query. And the mean squared error, as this is a standard measure in statistics.

Note that we (intentionally) use queries whose boundaries do not necessarily correspond to values occurring in the data. This mimics our original motivation, where the query compiler tries out potential constants, and in fact shows a major problem: Most approaches perform significantly better when only using range queries whose parameters occur in the data. Or in other words, most approaches fail when using arbitrary constants as range boundaries. This is often caused by a kind of overfitting, where the algorithms model the existing values very well at the expense of the general approximation. We include results when only considering existing values as comparison.

5.2 Considered Approaches

We compare our spline histograms with a number other approaches in the experiments. Our spline histograms, as described in Section 4, and are called *Greedy Spline* and *DP Spline* in the experiments. For the DP base spline construction, we first reduce the input to a spline with 5000 knots using the greedy construction and then run the DP algorithm to get the final spline. The *Sampling* strategy derives its estimation from a sample of the original data [16]. The *Koenig* histograms are described in [8], and construct a linear spline approximation within each histogram bucket. Unfortunately, they are only defined for integer domains in [8], and a generalization to real numbers is not straightforward (e.g., Formula 10 relies on the integer domain). As point queries are well defined even for real numbers, we used a CFG representation for range queries. The *V-Optimal* histograms described in [12] minimize the frequency variance in one bucket. This causes problems with continuous data, as most frequencies are 1. We therefore discretize the input into 2^{12} buckets. This number was derived empirically, changing the exponent reduced the accuracy. We also considered *Equi-Width* and *Equi-Depth* histograms, but omit the result here, as they are clearly dominated by *V-Optimal* histograms. The *Wavelet* histograms are described in [14]. They require a discrete domain, therefore we discretize the values into 2^{10} buckets (again, empirically determined). The *Wavelet RelErr* histograms described in [13] use a different coefficient selection algorithm to minimize the relative error, we therefore include them in our experiments.

5.3 Real Data

As a data set we use the GOV collection from the TREC-12 Web Track benchmark (http://trec.nist.gov/), which consists of roughly 1.25 million documents crawled from the .gov domain. We compute the inverted lists for the terms occurring in the Web Track's topic distillation task, scoring each document with normalized TF*IDF*PageRank scores (real values in $[0,1]$). We show here the results of the inverted list for term *public*, which is the largest inverted list (the other terms show similar results). The inverted lists contains of $427,940$ entries with $359,505$ distinct score values. The scores themselves are heavily skewed towards low values, even though there are relatively few duplicates.

Figure 4 a shows the maximum relative error of the different approaches with varying histogram size. As the maximum is sensitive to outliers, the maximum

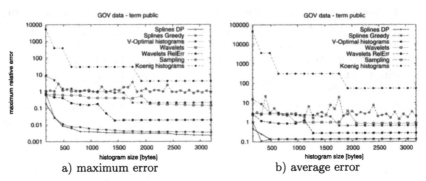

Fig. 4. Maximum and average relative error for the GOV term list *public*

error is quite high for most approaches. The spline histograms guarantee a maximum error of ≈ 13% for all queries. Interestingly even this number is a kind of outlier, as it is caused by ignoring the steps in the distribution function in our data model. A more forgiving error measure is the average relative error, as this shows the expected error for an arbitrary query. The results are shown in Figure 4 b. Again, the spline histograms perform very well, with an average error of ≈ 0.3% for *Greedy Splines*. The *DP Splines* perform a bit better (≈ 0.2%), but the overall performance is similar.

A very popular error measure in statistics is the mean squared error, which we show in Figure 5 a. The interpretation of the absolute values is somewhat difficult, as the impact on queries is unclear, but low values are most likely good. Again, the spline histograms perform very well, only Koenig histograms which explicitly minimize the mean squared error perform better. Note though that Koenig histograms performed quite poorly for the more insightful relative error. Some of approaches, in particular Koenig histograms, perform surprisingly badly in the experiments seen so far. This is due to the fact that the query boundaries are chosen from all over the domain, regardless of whether a data

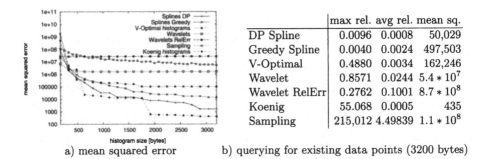

	max rel.	avg rel.	mean sq.
DP Spline	0.0096	0.0008	50,029
Greedy Spline	0.0040	0.0024	497,503
V-Optimal	0.4880	0.0034	162,246
Wavelet	0.8571	0.0244	$5.4 * 10^7$
Wavelet RelErr	0.2762	0.1001	$8.7 * 10^8$
Koenig	55.068	0.0005	435
Sampling	215,012	4.49839	$1.1 * 10^8$

a) mean squared error   b) querying for existing data points (3200 bytes)

Fig. 5. Mean squared error and querying for existing data for the GOV term list *public*

item with this exact value exists or not. If we instead chose all existing values as query boundaries once, the results are much better (Figure 5 b), which suggests overfitting to the data. Koenig histograms for example perform very well when only queried for existing values, but perform quite poor overall. The DP strategy has a slightly higher maximum error than the Greedy strategy. This is caused by the pre-filtering steps, which removes data points from its input, causing an underestimation of the maximum error.

5.4   Effect on Queries

While the accuracy results above compare histograms using different error metrics, we measure the effect on real queries in this section. We use the optimization framework described in [6], as the experiments in the paper operate on the same data set, using the official GOV benchmark queries. For the comparison, we optimize the queries using different cardinality estimators, execute them, and then compare the resulting runtime and network traffic. Due to space constraints, we only show the average results for the *Spline* histograms (Greedy and DP produced the same plans), *V-Optimal* histograms, and *Wavelet RelErr* histograms, as these were by far the most accurate:

	Splines	V-Optimal	Wavelet
runtime [ms]	585	649	618
net [bytes]	23,918	39,660	26,715

Here, even the relatively simple GOV queries can be improved just by using splines instead of the other histograms. Note that using the *WaveLet RelErr* histograms increased the optimization time to > 10 min and the memory consumption to $> 2.5GB$, as the optimization framework constructs histograms over intermediate result approximations and the wavelet construction is very expensive. Optimization with the other histograms took < 20 ms.

In conclusion, our spline histograms offer smooth predictions for arbitrary values, and guarantee a known maximum error over the whole domain.

References

1. Fagin, R., Lotem, A., Naor, M.: Optimal aggregation algorithms for middleware. J. Comput. Syst. Sci. 66(4), 614–656 (2003)
2. Güntzer, U., Balke, W.T., Kießling, W.: Optimizing multi-feature queries for image databases. In: VLDB, pp. 419–428 (2000)
3. Nepal, S., Ramakrishna, M.V.: Query processing issues in image (multimedia) databases. In: ICDE, pp. 22–29 (1999)
4. Cao, P., Wang, Z.: Efficient top-k query calculation in distributed networks. In: PODC, pp. 206–215 (2004)
5. Yu, H., Li, H.G., Wu, P., Agrawal, D., Abbadi, A.E.: Efficient processing of distributed top-k queries. In: Andersen, K.V., Debenham, J., Wagner, R. (eds.) DEXA 2005. LNCS, vol. 3588, pp. 65–74. Springer, Heidelberg (2005)
6. Neumann, T., Michel, S.: Algebraic query optimization for distributed top-k queries. In: BTW, pp. 324–343 (2007)

7. Michel, S., Triantafillou, P., Weikum, G.: Klee: A framework for distributed top-k query algorithms. In: VLDB, pp. 637–648 (2005)
8. König, A.C., Weikum, G.: Combining histograms and parametric curve fitting for feedback-driven query result-size estimation. In: VLDB, pp. 423–434 (1999)
9. Ioannidis, Y.E.: The history of histograms (abridged). In: VLDB, pp. 19–30 (2003)
10. Deshpande, A., Garofalakis, M.N., Rastogi, R.: Independence is good: Dependency-based histogram synopses for high-dimensional data. In: SIGMOD, pp. 199–210 (2001)
11. Poosala, V., Ioannidis, Y.E., Haas, P.J., Shekita, E.J.: Improved histograms for selectivity estimation of range predicates. In: SIGMOD, pp. 294–305 (1996)
12. Jagadish, H.V., Koudas, N., Muthukrishnan, S., Poosala, V., Sevcik, K.C., Suel, T.: Optimal histograms with quality guarantees. In: VLDB, pp. 275–286 (1998)
13. Garofalakis, M.N., Kumar, A.: Wavelet synopses for general error metrics. ACM Trans. Database Syst. 30(4), 888–928 (2005)
14. Matias, Y., Vitter, J.S., Wang, M.: Wavelet-based histograms for selectivity estimation. In: SIGMOD, pp. 448–459 (1998)
15. Goodrich, M.T.: Efficient piecewise-linear function approximation using the uniform metric. Discrete & Computational Geometry 14(4), 445–462 (1995)
16. Scott, D.W.: Multivariate Density Estimation: Theory, practice, and visualization. Wiley, Chichester (1992)

Virtual Forced Splitting, Demotion and the BV-Tree

Alan P. Sexton and Richard Swinbank

School of Computer Science, University of Birmingham
Edgbaston, Birmingham, B15 2TT, UK
{A.P.Sexton,R.J.Swinbank}@cs.bham.ac.uk

Abstract. In external multi-dimensional access methods, *Forced Splitting* is an approach used to ensure that, when a page splits, no sub-tree of the page belongs under both halves, thereby guaranteeing that only one path from the root need be searched to find any point in the tree. This reduces occupancy of forcibly split pages, possibly down to single entries in pathological cases. Freeston introduced a novel approach to obtaining the benefits of forced splitting while avoiding the negative consequences for a class of access methods he called BV-Trees. Perhaps because of its rather abstract presentation and the lack of complete algorithm descriptions, we believe that this idea has not achieved the recognition it deserves. We present a different view of the BV-Tree concept in terms of what we call Virtual Forced Splitting (VFS), show how the semantics of a VFS tree can be understood by its relationship to a much simpler Forced Split tree obtained by reduction from the VFS tree. This allows an explanation of the complex issue of demotion; a requirement for correct implementation that is acknowledged but not discussed in the literature before now. We show how various multi-dimensional algorithms such as *k*-Nearest Neighbour and Range Search can be effectively implemented on such trees, and, finally, discuss our own implementation of a BV-Tree, and report performance results in comparison to the R*-Tree.

1   Introduction

External hierarchical multidimensional access methods can be divided into those that partition data into groups described by regions that may overlap, e.g. the R-tree family [1,7], and those that partition the space directly, for example the K-D-B tree [9] and the BANG-file [6]. The latter class has the property that partition regions do not overlap, and therefore exact match search algorithms on these structures do not need to backtrack. Providing this property, together with other desirable properties of height balance and guaranteed minimum fanout, is a research objective of long standing. The BV-tree [3] offers a promising approach to meeting this objective, but one that has received little attention, partly, we believe, because it is rather poorly understood.

In this paper we examine the BV-tree in the wider context of access methods that employ what we call *virtual forced splitting* to achieve efficient representation on disk while providing the properties described above during processing. In

A. Gray, K. Jeffery, and J. Shao (Eds.): BNCOD 2008, LNCS 5071, pp. 139–152, 2008.

section 2 we introduce the general concept of virtual forced splitting and describe the BV-tree in this context, and in section 3 describe transformation between on-disk and runtime representations of such structures that enables implementation of standard tree operations. Some experimental results from our BV-tree implementation are given in section 4 followed by our conclusions in section 5.

2   Virtual Forced Splitting and the BV-Tree

2.1   Forced Splitting

The K-D-B tree [9] uses a *kd*-tree [2] based spatial decomposition to partition points and regions of space, and as such does not permit overlap between partitions. This means that it is possible to decompose a space in such a way that the subregions produced can not be split in a balanced ratio. The K-D-B tree solution to this problem is to employ *forced splitting*: when splitting a node, entries are allocated to one or the other of a pair of parent regions in the usual way, but if a region is partially enclosed in both parents, it is split into two regions, each of which is enclosed solely by one parent region. The effect of this is to produce a well-balanced split locally, but, as the split plane must then be enforced throughout the entire subtree of the affected entry, it leads to breaking minimal occupancy guarantees in portions of the two resulting subtrees.

Other structures, for example variants of the BANG file [5], have used forced-splitting for the same reason and with the same results. We refer to structures using forced splitting as forced-split trees (FS-trees).

2.2   Virtual Forced Splitting and the VFS-Tree

The use of forced splits in FS-trees is a sacrifice made to achieve *region disjointness*. Given a query point and a collection of disjoint regions, a maximum of one region may contain the point; a search tree describing only disjoint spatial regions in each internal node therefore exhibits (at most) a single, deterministic path from the root of the tree to a leaf node for any given point in the space. We refer to this as the *single path property*, or SPP. Maintenance of the SPP in FS-trees comes at a cost of possible disk page under-occupancy and, consequently, low fanout, something that adversely affects tree search efficiency, but enables exact match searching without backtracking.

We examine, as an alternative to forced-splitting, an idea first presented by Freeston in the BV-tree [3]. For simplicity, we discuss it in the context of the K-D-B tree. When splitting a K-D-B node along a plane, we may find entries that lie directly across the plane. Figure 1(a) shows such a spatial decomposition in which the only direct planar partitioning possible is in the ratio 1:4 ({A}, {B,C,D,E}); a better ratio is provided by {B,C}, {D,E}, but if either group of entries is forced to include A, the bounding boxes of the two groups will overlap, thereby breaking the SPP. The K-D-B approach is to split entry A and its subtree. Figure 1(b) shows the overflowing node M and Figure 1(c) the effect of executing a forced split of A.

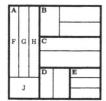

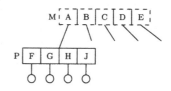

(a) Five index partitions and their subregions.

(b) Node M is overflowing; no disjoint balanced split is available.

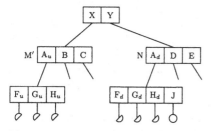

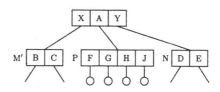

(c) FS-tree split of node M (into M' and N) splits A and its subtree forcibly.

(d) VFS-tree split of node M elevates entry A into the new root.

Fig. 1. Forced vs virtually forced splitting (leaf pages indicated by whole or half circles)

The alternative is to *elevate* the entry into the level above while promoting the parent entries of the two new nodes, as in Figure 1(d). We refer to this as elevation to distinguish it from the usual post-and-grow promotion of new node parents (Freeston refers to elevated entries as *guards*). The effect of this on node occupancy is strictly local; that of the parent node has increased further than would normally be the case, but (unless the parent node then overflows) no further reorganisation is required. In general, further splitting can cause nodes to be elevated more than once, and, indeed, elevations can occur within subtrees underneath an elevated node.

We are left with the issue of how to execute a search in a tree with elevated entries. It is not correct to simply treat an elevated entry as a normal unelevated one (we shall refer to such unelevated entries as *"primary"* entries), as the region it describes is not disjoint from the regions described by the primary entries in the node in which it finds itself and, in fact its contents really belong distributed in the subtrees under at least two different entries in this node. In practice, an elevated entry can only be correctly interpreted in the level it was elevated from, i.e. its *"natural"* level. For this reason, during a search down the tree, an elevated entry must not be considered as a potential branch in the search path in the level at which it occurs. Instead it is merely picked up and carried down as the search progresses down the tree until the search arrives at the elevated entry's natural level. At this point it is considered as if it had never been elevated in the first place. In Figure 1(d), this means carrying entry A into the subtree of either entry X or Y pending its consideration as required. We therefore refer to a set of elevated entries carried down the tree in this way as a *pending set*. This reconstructs the semantics of the forced split of entry A on-the-fly, and so we also refer to A as being *virtually-split* and call trees of this kind *virtual forced split trees* (VFS-trees). There are a number of concerns that must be addressed to make this work:

Elevation Export Upperbound: A split might cause more than one entry to be elevated. If too many entries are elevated, then one or both of the split nodes they are elevated from may become under-occupied. Therefore a practical scheme must limit the number of entries that can be elevated from a node.

Elevation Import Upperbound: Elevated entries in a node occupy space that could otherwise be occupied by primary entries, thus reducing the fan-out of the node. In extreme cases, if there were not enough space for at least one primary entry, the tree would fail. A practical scheme must provide an upperbound guarantee on the number of entries that can be elevated into a node, lest the structure deteriorate from log-based search and update cost behaviour, and ensure that the node's page size is large enough to accommodate the required number of elevated entries. While the upperbound guarantee is specific to the concrete VFS-tree scheme, we solve the page size concern by implementing nodes as buckets consisting of one primary and zero or more secondary disk pages. Primary entries are permitted to occupy primary pages only and the node is considered full when the primary page is full of primary entries. Elevated entries fill up remaining space in the primary page before overflowing into the secondary node pages, which are allocated as required. This scheme is slightly different to that suggested by Freeston [3] and Samet [10], which has pages of increasing size at higher levels in the tree (although of fixed size in any given level).

Over-Elevation: If an elevated entry is split, both resulting entries are just as elevated as the orignal entry was, but, as the regions described are smaller, one or both of them may no longer need to be virtually split at all. Accumulation of unnecessarily elevated entries causes nodes to become excessively large and, in the case of the BV-Tree, would cause the critical guarantee on the upperbound of the number of elevated entries in a node to be broken. Such entries must therefore be demoted. A similar source of over-elevated entries arises during deletion, when two primary entries are merged, causing elevated entries that were virtually split to now be demotable into the new merged sub-tree.

2.3   The BV-Tree

The BV-tree [3] is a practical VFS-Tree. The key to how it provides the guarantees required lies in its approach to region decomposition based on the removal of *holes* from regions, with a containment relationship between resulting regions: namely any two regions in a BV-Tree decomposition must either be disjoint or one must contain the other.

When a BV-node overflows, a subregion of the node's region is identified which contains between 1/3 and 2/3 of the node's primary entries. Separation of the

(a) Holey region decomposition.   (b) Exploded to show true region extent.

Fig. 2. Meaning of regions described by a collection of boundaries

entries that fall within this subregion from those outside it corresponds to the formation of a hole in the outer region. As the nodes undergo further insertions and node splits, a spatial decomposition of holey regions develops, as shown in Figure 2.

The containment requirement means that, when a node is split, the split boundary, S, divides the region, P, of at most one primary entry. Every other primary region in the node is either contained by S, in which case it will go into the split node corresponding to the hole defined by S, or either contains P or is disjoint from S, in which case it will go into the split node corresponding to the remnant region without the hole. The only problem is the entry corresponding to P itself, part of which belongs in the split node corresponding to the hole, whereas the remainder belongs in the remnant node. This entry, then, is the only primary entry that must be elevated from a single node split, thus providing the required elevation export upperbound.

Note that elevated entries in a splitting node may, just like primary entries, lie across the split boundary and require further virtual splitting. Given a number of elevated entries of a single natural level, at most one of those entries will require elevation by virtue of the containment property. In general, therefore, the split of a node of level L may require as many as $L+1$ entries to be elevated into the level above: one of each natural level from 0 to L.

In a BV-tree with no over-elevated entries, there can not be more than one elevated entry per level per primary entry. The proof is too long to include here in detail, but the basic insight is that every elevated entry in a node must be virtually split across at least two primary entries. We say that an elevated entry E *dominates* a primary entry P if E contains P and there is no other elevated entry E' of the same natural level as E which is contained by E and which contains P. Any such E' would describe a hole in E and, since P is contained in E', no part of E could then belong inside P, i.e. E could not then be virtually split across P. Hence any elevated entry is only virtually split across primary entries that it dominates and, possibly, the least (in containment order) primary entry that contains it. If the set dominated by an elevated entry is empty, then it is over-elevated and can be demoted. Alternatively, if the dominated set of E is a singleton, $\{P\}$, and if P also contains E (i.e. their boundaries coincide), then E can be demoted into P. Since the maximum number of distinct dominated sets is the number of primary entries in the node, we get the required result and satisfy the elevated import upperbound requirement.

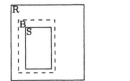

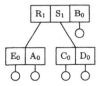

Fig. 3. Parent regions R and S   **Fig. 4.** Position of split between R and S   **Fig. 5.** BV-tree

The holey regions that entries represent in a BV-Tree could be arbitrarily complex, which leads to a problem in representing them in a node. Freeston's solution is to record only the outer boundary of the region with the entry, allowing its holey structure to be inferred from other outer boundaries recorded in other entries in the node. If an entry is separated from its holes by elevation, this may mean that the entry is included unnecessarily in a pending set, which Freeston refers to as a *guard set*. However the hole will be discovered on descent into the appropriate subtree, allowing the inferred holey structure to be discerned and the entry discarded. For example, consider a search for point q in the tree of Figure 4. On examination of the root node, the point is found to be contained in regions S and B; descent into the subtree of S accompanied by B in the pending set reunites B with holes C and D, indicating that the point is, in fact, to be found in the child of entry C.

3   Reduction and the RVFS-Tree

We introduce the concept of reduction of VFS-Trees to provide a conceptual framework to address the above issues. We suggest that the key to understanding and designing algorithms on VFS-Trees in general and the BV-Tree in particular is to recognise that a VFS-Tree is merely a compact storage representation for a simpler balanced forced split tree, a reduced VFS-Tree (RVFS-Tree), derived from the VFS-Tree, which is never materialised on disk but, rather, is generated lazily in memory on demand.

We introduce a **reduce** operation that converts a full VFS-Tree into the associated RVFS-Tree. RVFS-Trees contain no elevated entries and are fully balanced, although nodes may suffer from under-occupancy or over-occupancy (i.e. more entries than can fit in a normal node). Reduction consists essentially of the execution of the hitherto avoided forced splits. However an RVFS-tree is not a conventional FS-tree, because a full RVFS-node does not split when an elevated entry is reduced into it — it merely becomes 'overfull'. The RVFS-tree is not a practical access method, but generalises the conversion required to search a VFS-tree fragment, and hence underlies every VFS-tree operation.

When we carry an elevated entry, in a pending set, down a path in a tree as part of a search or a reduction operation, it is important to remember that although the entry describes a whole sub-tree, we should really only be carrying that part of the sub-tree that belongs down that path. That is, if an elevated entry, e, is virtually split across two primary entries, p and q, then some of the contents of the node pointed to by e belong under p, and some under q. If we descend the tree into p, carrying e in the pending set for this descent, we should exclude any contents of the e node which belong under the q branch from consideration. Since we are proceeding lazily, we do not eagerly forcibly split the e subtree at the first opportunity, but annotate it with the branching entry, in this case p, and write it as e_p. This annotation is inherited by the children of e, and, when accessing the contents of an annotated node, we simply discard any child whose region does not intersect that of the child's annotations.

Reduction of a VFS-Tree is a recursive process operating on a node, N, which is of level L, and a pending set P. It begins with the root node and an empty pending set. A new RVFS node has to be constructed from N. It will also be of level L. Let Q be the set of primary entries in N together with the subset of (possibly annotated) entries in the pending set P, whose natural level is L. These will form the basis of the entries of the new node. The remaining elements of the pending set, i.e. those whose natural level is less than L, plus all the elevated elements in N, form a new master pending set M. From these will be extracted the pending sets used to produce the subtrees for the new node. The entries of the new node are then $\{\texttt{reduce}(q, M_q) \mid q \in Q\}$ where $M_q = \{m_q \mid m \in M \wedge m \cap q \neq \emptyset\}$, where $m \cap q$ means the intersection of the regions defined by the outer region boundary of the entries m and q.

Figure 6 shows a BV-tree and Figure 7 the RVFS-tree it yields under **reduce**. The entries in the VFS-tree have their natural levels shown as subscripts. The

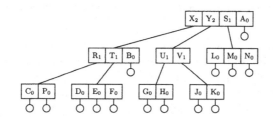

Fig. 6. VFS (BV) tree

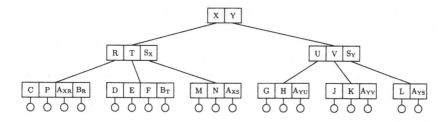

Fig. 7. Reduced VFS (BV) tree

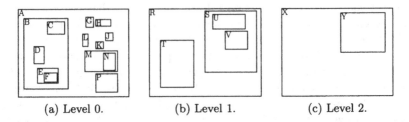

| (a) Level 0. | (b) Level 1. | (c) Level 2. |

Fig. 8. Region components of entries of different level in the BV-tree of Figure 6

associated spatial decomposition is given in Figure 8. In the RVFS-tree of Figure 7, entry S now appears in the children of both entries X and Y. Note, however, that the children of the two S entries differ; as entry L falls outside region X, it does not appear in the subtree rooted on entry X, likewise neither do entries M and N appear in Y's subtree. The contents of leaf nodes are similarly restricted; entry B appears straightforwardly as a child of entries R and T, but the contents of leaf nodes B_R and B_T consist of the set of points from the original leaf rooted on B that are contained in (inferred) regions R and S respectively. Finally, although entry A_0 appears in the root of the BV-tree in Figure 6, note that it does not appear in every super-leaf level node; as region T is contained by region B, T falls into a hole in A and contains no space also contained by A.

3.1 Algorithm Design for VFS-Trees

The sole published algorithm for the BV-tree is that of exact-match (insert is described only by example). The key problem in implementing other algorithms is twofold.

1. For non-updating algorithms (i.e., searches), how can we choose which elevated entries should be carried down in the pending sets in every step?
2. For updating algorithms such as insert and delete, and subordinate algorithms such as demotion of over-elevated entries and splitting of nodes, what is the correct semantics of such operations in the face of complex arrangements of elevated entries of differing levels within the underlying tree?

For example, if insertion of a point into the BV-Tree of Figure 6 results in descending into Y_2, carrying the pending set $\{S_1, A_0\}$, then descends into S_1, carrying the pending set $\{A_0\}$, inserts the point there, causing A_0 to split, then we need to post into the parent of A_0. But which node is the parent of A_0? The root node is certainly a candidate, for A_0 physically hangs from it, but we actually descended two levels before reaching A_0, so the root appears to be only a grandparent of A_0. This suggests S_1 is the parent, as the last node descended into before descending into A_0. However, when one considers that not all the contents of the node A_0 belongs under S_1, nor even under Y_2, it seems questionable to post to S_1.

To resolve this and more convoluted cases, we need a guiding principle. We offer the following: To understand what an operation should do on a VFS-Tree, consider what effect that operation should have on the corresponding, and much simpler, RVFS-Tree, and design the operation on the VFS-Tree accordingly. In the example above, consider the reduced tree in Figure 7. Here we immediately see our confusion was caused by a misinterpretation of A_0. What we actually inserted into was not A_0, but A_{YS}; that part of A_0 that belongs in that leaf position. However, what has to be split is not A_{YS}, but the whole A_0. This can only be split at the root, although one or both of the split parts might then be demotable down X_2 or Y_2, depending on the split boundary chosen.

Range Query: A multidimensional range query on an RVFS-Tree must descend all branches of the tree whose regions intersect the range query, pruning any sub-trees which do not intersect the query region as we proceed. In the VFS-Tree case we do the same, but now we need to decide which elevated entries to carry in the pending sets as we descend. In fact, any elevated entry that does not intersect the query region will eventually be merged, by **reduce**, into a branch of the RVFS-tree that will be pruned. Hence we need to carry down all and only the elevated entries that intersect the query region.

Exact Match Query: This is a special case of the range query above where the query region is a single point, and, as expected, the algorithm collapses to precisely that described by Freeston in the BV-Tree case.

*k***-Nearest Neighbour:** Hjaltason and Samet's priority-queue implementation of k-Nearest Neighbour searching [8] allows a tree to be searched 'best-first' rather than depth- or breadth-first, enqueueing tree entries in order of their distance from the query point. This has an obvious and simple implementation in an RVFS-Tree. The algorithm on the VFS-Tree is almost exactly the same, except that the tree entries that are enqueued must be sufficient to (lazily) construct the corresponding RVFS-Tree branch when it is dequeued and explored. The necessary information that must be enqueued is given by the parameters to the recursive **reduce** operation: namely a pair consisting of a VFS-Tree entry (possibly annotated) and the pending set of (again possibly annotated) elevated entries being carried down with that entry.

Insert: Here the published description, while correct as far as it goes, does not quite give the full story. It describes using the exact match algorithm to identify the correct leaf page to insert the item into, and, if the leaf page overflows, the usual post and grow scenario follows. What is not entirely clear is that post and grow can lead to situations where one or more elevated entries need to be demoted and, if in the original descent of the tree the pending sets were restricted to those necessary for the exact match phase only, there may be insufficient information available even to identify that a demotion is necessary or to carry it out correctly. We discuss this in more detail in Section 3.2.

We observe that searching a 'virtual' RVFS-tree while traversing the physical VFS-tree creates the possibility of multiple visits to the same page during a query. In the example of Figure 6, a region query of region A based strictly on **reduce** would be required to visit the associated physical page five times; once

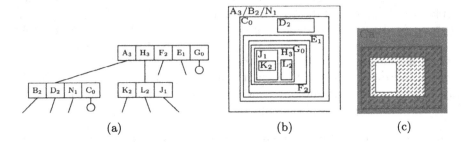

Fig. 9. VFS-tree fragment and associated regions

for each of the A subregions in each subtree, represented by the children of A_{XR}, A_{XS}, A_{YU}, A_{YV} and A_{YS}. We rely on the practical fact that each subsequent visit is likely to find the page still in the buffer pool. The obvious optimisation of inspecting A only once, on its first visit, and considering all its contents rather than just those contents specific to the current branch of the search, is certainly possible, but requires careful reasoning in the general case to ensure correctness.

3.2 Demotion

When descending into a VFS-Tree node as part of an insert operation, it is critical that the pending set at that point contains all elevated entries whose regions intersect with that of the node rather than, as suggested in [3], merely those elevated entries that intersect with the insertion point. An example demonstrates the problem; Figure 9(a) shows a VFS-tree fragment; the region boundaries corresponding to entries in the tree are given in Figure 9(b). From the set of boundaries given, part of the holey structure of entries E_1 and C_0 can be inferred and, as can be seen in Figure 9(c), entry C_0 is not only virtually split across entries B_2 and D_2 but also across E_1 and N_1. Suppose now that the point q (see Figure 9(c)) is inserted into the leaf child of entry C_0, causing it to overflow and post a new level 0 entry, say M_0, into the node containing entry C_0. If M_0, a hole in C_0, is also contained in E_1, then it is into the latter that it should be demoted (via B_2). If, however, E_1 is not available for examination in a pending set when M_0 is posted, this can not be determined; M_0 may be demoted erroneously into N_1 (via B_2), and lost. Similarly, if M_0 contains E_1, but E_1 can not be examined, M_0 may be considered demotable into N_1, despite the fact that it remains virtually split across E_1 and N_1.

The approach in [3] is essentially to construct only the part of the RVFS-tree that indexes the 'space' of the insertion point. If, however, an entry becomes available for demotion, a larger part of the RVFS-tree is required. At each node on the path from the root to the insertion point, the RVFS subtree corresponding to that node must be constructable via the **reduce** operation. That is, the pending set for that node must be not just the elevated entries whose regions intersect the query point, but the those whose regions intersect the region of the node itself.

Demotion causes another problem: it can trigger a chain of demotions that update the VFS-Tree, causing problems in the lazy interpretation of the corresponding RVFS-Tree. Consider again the overflow of the child of C_0 in Figure 9, but assume that M_0 is coincident with D_2. Neither C_0' (the amended C_0) nor M_0 is now virtually-split at level 2 and so can be demoted into B_2 and D_2 respectively, however C_0' remains virtually-split at level 1, across entries E_1 and N_1. Note that entry C_0' is now physically resident in the child of entry B_2, but that the entries across which it is virtually-split are elevated to higher positions in the tree. If the child of C_0' now overflows and splits into two along the boundary of region E_1, the two entries resulting, say $C_0'^E$ and $C_0'^N$ must now be demoted into E_1 and N_1 respectively. Suppose that we demote $C_0'^E$ first, and in doing so cause the child of entry E_1 to overflow. This posts a new level 1 entry into the root, and either E_1 or the new entry is now likely to require demotion. This leaves us in rather a difficult position — it is not clear whether we should first perform this newly-required demotion or return to that of $C_0'^N$; in either case we would require some mechanism to record the requirement for the second demotion while we perform the first, and what if that first demotion triggers yet another set of demotions? Even if we decide to demote $C_0'^N$ first, we must recognise that the RVFS-tree we have constructed now no longer matches that which would be produced by reduce on the amended VFS-tree on disk; we must either take action to amend the RVFS-tree or begin again, and construct the RVFS-tree from the root to enable demotion of $C_0'^N$.

The change to the RVFS-tree caused by the first demote is the real problem here; we wish to demote two entries into an RVFS-tree, but in demoting the first, we alter the underlying VFS-tree and thus the RVFS-tree into which the second demotion is to take place. Because of the risk of changes being made to the RVFS-tree by a demotion, we have taken the approach of explicitly restarting the construction of the pending set corresponding to a demotable entry from the root for *every* demotion: this involves simply descending the single path from the root of the tree to the demotable entry in the usual way, collecting the pending set as we proceed. In order to record the entries to be demoted we use a *demote queue*. When, during insertion, an entry is found to be demotable, it is added to the demote queue but no further action is taken. When the initial insertion is complete, the first demotee in the demote queue is inserted into the VFS-tree from the root; if this demotion itself necessitates further demotions, these are scheduled using the queue in the same way. Insertion of the original point is only complete once the demote queue is empty.

The requirement for demotion obviously increases the cost of inserting a point; indeed Freeston [4] suggests that demotions might be postponed until a subsequent insertion passes through the node containing the prospective demotee(s), allowing the cost to be amortized over future insertions. However, this strategy suffers from a number of problems. First, delaying demotions in this way breaks the BV-Tree guarantee on the number of elevated entries in a node. In particular one can then have more than one elevated entry of the same natural level for each primary entry in the node, this can cause the structure to fail if fixed size pages are used, even if these sizes are greater at higher levels in the tree. Second, because demotion modifies the VFS-Tree, the insertion passing through the node with the demotable entry can not continue until the local view of the RVFS tree has been *"refreshed"*, from the modified VFS-tree. Hence it essentially has to be restarted and can not be done on the fly.

From the description above it may not be clear that a cascade of demotions will terminate, however it is certain to do so for a simple reason: demotion of an entry of level n can only ever trigger a demotion of at most two entries of level $n+1$. If every insertion and demotion caused a further pair of demotions, in the worst case a single insertion into a tree of height h can cause 2^{h-2} demotions.

4   Experimental Results

For experimental evaluation, the performance of our BV-tree implementation was compared against that of the R*-tree [1]. Both structures were implemented in a common framework with a fixed page size, using the same core code to provide primitive functions like reading entries from a node, and to handle instrumentation. Trees were constructed using artificially clustered datasets of 50,000 points in 2–16 dimensions. In all cases, cost of operations is measured in disk IOs and assumes sufficient buffers available to ensure that a page need only be read from disk once during execution of a single operation.

Figure 10(a) illustrates the average IO-cost to insert an entry into the tree. Both trees demonstrate little variation with dimensionality since both select a single path for insertion. The R*-tree insertion cost exceeds that of the BV-tree by around 40%, suggesting that the amount of reorganisation due to reinsertion in the former is greater than that caused by demotion in the latter.

Exact-match query cost was evaluated by querying every point known to be in the tree and computing the average IO cost across all queries. The results are given in Figure 10(b) and illustrate, as expected, that while the performance of the R*-tree deteriorates in higher numbers of dimensions, that of the BV-tree does not — simply because the BV-tree has the single path property and each tree was of the same height in each dimensionality case.

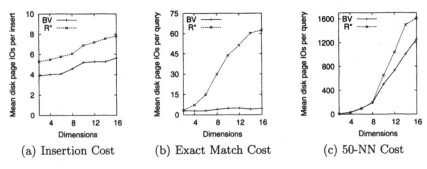

(a) Insertion Cost   (b) Exact Match Cost   (c) 50-NN Cost

Fig. 10. Performance results

Figure 10(c) shows the average cost of retrieving the 50 nearest neighbours of a selected query point. In each case, the cost is the average over 19 query points, spaced equally along the diagonal of the space (irrespective of the dimensionality). In as many as 8 dimensions the performance of the two structures is comparable, but at higher dimensionality the R*-tree reads up to 40% more pages from disk than does the BV-tree.

5   Conclusions and Further Work

We have presented a new view of the BV-Tree, and its generalisation into a class of Virtually Forced Split trees. Further we have presented a reduction operation that transforms VFS-Trees into a simpler Reduced VFS-Tree. This approach has provided us with the tools to reason about subtle algorithmic issues in the BV-Tree and to refine a number of aspects of the structure that have not heretofore been published in the literature. Using this framework, we were not only able to design and implement correct insertion and exact match algorithms for the structure, including correct treatment of the complex demotion problem, but implement multidimensional range query and k-Nearest Neighbour algorithms as well. As a result, we have been able to present the first, to our knowledge, experimental performance results for the BV-Tree. These results show that the BV-Tree is, in general, very well behaved and, on a multidimensional clustered dataset, it outperforms the R*-Tree on insertion costs and exact match costs in all numbers of dimensions, and k-Nearest Neighbour costs in all numbers of dimensions except dimensionality 2 (in which it requires approximately 1.5 times the number of IOs as in the R*-Tree).

The above results, along with more detailed explanations and performance analyses, can be found in [11]. We are currently working on formal proofs of correctness of the algorithms, based on the framework described here, using separation logic.

References

1. Beckmann, N., Kriegel, H.-P., Schneider, R., Seeger, B.: The R*-tree: An efficient and robust access method for points and rectangles. In: Proc. ACM SIGMOD, pp. 322–331 (1990)
2. Bentley, J.L.: Multidimensional binary search trees used for associative searching. Comm. ACM 18(9), 509–517 (1985)
3. Freeston, M.: A general solution of the n-dimensional B-tree problem. In: Proc. ACM SIGMOD, San Jose, California, May 1995, pp. 80–91 (1995)
4. Freeston, M.: On the complexity of BV-tree updates. In: Proc. 2nd Int. Workshop on Constraint Database Systems, Delphi, Greece, pp. 282–293 (1997)
5. Freeston, M.: Advances in the design of the BANG file. In: Proc. 3rd Int. Conf. on Foundations of Data Organization and Algorithms, June 1989, pp. 322–338 (1989)
6. Freeston, M.: The BANG file: A new kind of grid file. In: Proc. ACM SIGMOD, San Francisco, May 1987, pp. 260–269 (1987)

7. Guttman, A.: R-trees: A dynamic index structure for spatial searching. SIGMOD Record 14(2), 47–57 (1984)
8. Hjaltason, G.R., Samet, H.: Ranking in spatial databases. In: Proc. 4th Int. Symp. on Large Spatial Databases, pp. 83–95 (1995)
9. Robinson, J.T.: The K-D-B-tree: A search structure for large multidimensional dynamic indexes. In: Proc. ACM SIGMOD, pp. 10–18 (1981)
10. Samet, H.: Decoupling partitioning and grouping: Overcoming shortcomings of spatial indexing with bucketing. ACM Trans. Database Syst. 29(4), 789–830 (2004)
11. Swinbank, R.: Virtual Forced Splitting in Multidimensional Access Methods. PhD thesis, School of Computer Science, University of Birmingham, UK (2008) (due for completion, May 2008)

A Functional Data Model Approach to Querying RDF/RDFS Data

João Martins, Rui Nunes, Merja Karjalainen, and Graham J.L. Kemp

Department of Computer Science and Engineering,
Chalmers University of Technology, SE-412 96 Göteborg, Sweden

Abstract. We are developing a multi-database architecture to provide integrated access to heterogeneous, distributed databases. The work described here is motivated by the desire to have RDF/RDFS collections as component data resources in this system, along with relational and other databases. To achieve this, the RDF/RDFS collection, like all other component resources in the system, is mapped to the functional data model, and a query translator is implemented that can translate queries originally expressed in Daplex (the query language associated with the functional data model) into SPARQL. SPARQL is the prominent query language for RDF and it is used here to bridge between the functional data model and the Semantic Web.

1 Introduction

In earlier work a federated system was built in which queries that require data values from distributed heterogeneous data resources were processed by a prototype program called the P/FDM Mediator [11,4]. Tasks performed by the P/FDM Mediator include determining which external databases are relevant in answering users' queries, dividing queries into parts that will be sent to different external databases, translating these sub-queries into the language(s) of the external databases, and combining the results for presentation. A new implementation of the P/FDM Mediator, with a more modular architecture, has been undertaken recently [9]. Resource Description Framework (RDF) collections described in RDF Schema (RDFS) are being used increasingly with biological data, and in order to make these RDF/RDFS collections accessible as part of a database federation we have implemented a mapping between Daplex (the query language used in the P/FDM Mediator) and the SPARQL Protocol And RDF Query Language (SPARQL).

In this paper we focus on the code generator that carries out query translation from Daplex to SPARQL. In Section 2 we describe the functional data model, which is central to our work, and how this can be mapped onto RDF/RDFS. In Section 3 we show how queries expressed in Daplex against an FDM schema can be translated automatically to SPARQL. Some of the design issues that arose in this work are discussed in Section 4, and we outline directions for future research. The contributions of this work are summarised in Section 5.

A. Gray, K. Jeffery, and J. Shao (Eds.): BNCOD 2008, LNCS 5071, pp. 153–164, 2008.

```
declare project ->> entity               declare student ->> person
  declare code(project) -> string          declare year(student) -> integer
  declare title(project) -> string
  declare duration(project) -> integer   declare researcher ->> member_of_staff
  key_of project is title                  declare employed_on(researcher) -> project

declare course ->> entity                declare teacher ->> member_of_staff
  declare level(course) -> integer         declare supervises(teacher) ->> project
  declare units(course) -> integer
  declare code(course) -> string         declare undergrad ->> student
  key_of course is code                    declare takes(undergrad) ->> course

declare person ->> entity                declare postgrad ->> student
  declare forename(person) -> string       declare works_on(postgrad) -> project
  declare surname(person) -> string
  key_of person is surname, forename     declare section ->> entity
                                           declare section_name(section) -> string
declare member_of_staff ->> person         declare has_course(section) -> course
  declare position(member_of_staff) -> string    declare has_lecturer(section) -> teacher
  declare room(member_of_staff) -> string  key_of section is key_of(has_lecturer),
                                                           key_of(has_course)
```

Fig. 1. FDM schema for a university database in Daplex syntax

2   Data Models

2.1   The Functional Data Model and P/FDM

The P/FDM Mediator is implemented as an extension of the P/FDM database management system [8], which is an object database management system that is based on a semantic data model — the functional data model (FDM) [14]. The basic concepts in the P/FDM database are entities and functions. Entities are used to represent conceptual objects, while functions represent the properties of an object. Functions are used to model both scalar attributes and relationships. Functions may be single-valued or multi-valued, and their values can either be stored or computed on demand. Entity classes can be arranged in subtype hierarchies, with subclasses inheriting the properties of their superclass, as well as having their own specialised properties. As an example, the Daplex schema for a university database is given in Figure 1.

2.2   Mapping FDM onto RDF/RDFS

Statements in RDF are expressed as triples. When mapping between a P/FDM schema and RDFS the following rules [6] were used:

- a P/FDM class c defined as an entity (declared as c ->> entity) maps to an RDF resource of type rdfs:Class, where rdfs is the namespace prefix for the RDF Schema descriptions;
- a P/FDM class c declared to be a subtype of another class s (declared as c ->> s) maps to an RDF resource of type rdfs:Class, with an rdfs:subClassOf property the value of which is the class named s;
- a P/FDM function f declared on entities of class c, with result type r (declared as $f(c)$ -> r) maps to an RDF resource of type rdfs:Property with an rdfs:domain of c and a rdfs:range of r.

```
<rdfs:Class rdf:about="&unidb;person"/>
<rdf:Property rdf:about="&unidb;#forename">
    <rdfs:domain rdf:resource="&unidb;#person"/>
    <rdfs:range rdf:resource="&rdfs;Literal"/>
</rdf:Property>
</rdfs:Class>
<rdf:Property rdf:about="&unidb;#surname">
    <rdfs:domain rdf:resource="&unidb;#person"/>
    <rdfs:range rdf:resource="&rdfs;Literal"/>
</rdf:Property>
<rdfs:Class rdf:about="&unidb;member_of_staff">
    <rdfs:subClassOf rdf:resource="&unidb;person"/>
</rdfs:Class>
<rdfs:Class rdf:about="&unidb;researcher">
    <rdfs:subClassOf rdf:resource="&unidb;member_of_staff"/>
</rdfs:Class>
<rdfs:Class rdf:about="&unidb;teacher">
    <rdfs:subClassOf rdf:resource="&unidb;member_of_staff"/>
</rdfs:Class>
<rdf:Property rdf:about="&unidb;employed_on">
    <rdfs:domain rdf:resource="&unidb;researcher"/>
    <rdfs:range rdf:resource="&unidb;project"/>
</rdf:Property>
```

Fig. 2. An extract from the RDFS describing the university database

Figure 2 shows part of the class hierarchy involving *person* and some subclasses, and a representation of function *employed_on* in RDFS.

Some of the information that is present in the FDM version of the schema is absent in the RDFS version. In the FDM schema, the cardinality of functions must be declared, for example the relationship function *employed_on* is declared to be single-valued (denoted by ->), whereas the relationship function *supervises* is multi-valued (denoted by ->>). There is no possibility to make this distinction in the RDFS version. Another difference is that the key of each entity class must be specified in the FDM schema, whereas the keys are not enforced in RDFS.

Relationships between instances can be expressed as RDF triples where a *subject* represents an entity identifier, a *predicate* will stand for a relationship name and the *object* identifies another entity. It is also possible to add a class/subclass hierarchy making use of the RDFS data model which, in common with the FDM, follows the principle of data independence, allowing an abstraction over the data storage system [7].

2.3 RDF/RDFS Data Representation

In the RDF/RDFS data representation used here, a URI identifying a resource consists of key information. Thus each resource has a unique identifier. In the case of composite keys, a dot is used as a separator between the parts of a key. However, using key information in this way is not important for the SPARQL code generation task that is the focus of this paper — in practice, no information about keys is needed in order to query RDF data since joins are implicit. In RDF, an object of a foreign key relationship is an RDF URI reference, and not a data value used to identify the object. Within an RDF graph a node can serve as both the object and subject of relationships.

```
<unidb:researcher rdf:about="&unidb;Doe.John">
  <unidb:position rdf:datatype="&xsd;string">RA</unidb:position>
  <unidb:surname rdf:datatype="&xsd;string">Doe</unidb:surname>
  <unidb:forename rdf:datatype="&xsd;string">John</unidb:forename>
  <unidb:room rdf:datatype="&xsd;string">S36</unidb:room>
  <unidb:employed_on rdf:resource="&unidb;PFDM_Project"/>
</unidb:researcher>
```

Fig. 3. XML serialisation of RDF data: instance of researcher

Figure 3 illustrates some aspects of the mapping between FDM data and RDF/RDFS. It represents an instance of *researcher* which is a subclass of *member_of_staff*. The first statement starts with *unidb:researcher* meaning that an instance of researcher is being declared, and is identified by "&unidb;Doe.John" (using `rdf:about`) which is a URI reference representing a *subject* that is itself a resource. Next, the properties of this instance are declared, and typed literals (`rdf:datatype`) are used to define the properties and their values (*unidb:position, unidb:surname, unidb:forename, unidb:room*). Finally, a function *employed_on* is declared. This function is a property having a domain *researcher* and a range *project* (cf. Figure 2). Thus, it is a property of *researcher* and is identified by "&unidb;PFDM_Project", a URI reference identifying a *project* (`rdf:resource`).

3   Query Processing

In the P/FDM Mediator, Daplex queries expressed against a federated schema are first compiled into an internal Intermediate Code ("ICode") [5] which is a Prolog term structure that resembles a list comprehension. ICode can be analysed and manipulated conveniently using Prolog [2], and plays an important role in query processing within the mediator. Various transformation steps are performed before fragments of ICode that refer to the same component database are grouped together into sub-queries. ICode representing a sub-query is passed to a wrapper, which invokes a code generator to translate the ICode for the sub-query into the query language of the component database (e.g. SQL if the component resource is a relational database) [9].

In this paper we focus on the code generation task in the case of an RDF/RDFS component database. Here, the ICode form of the query is translated into a SPARQL query by a code generator, so that the query can be executed. There are several RDF query languages. Currently, SPARQL [12] is becoming the prominent RDF query language, so we have chosen it for our work.

3.1   SPARQL Query Structure

A simple query in SPARQL consists of two parts: a SELECT clause and a WHERE clause. It is possible to further restrict query results by constraining the allowable bindings of variables to RDF terms using a FILTER clause.

Daplex query:

```
for each t in teacher
  for each s in has_lecturer_inv(t)
    for each c in has_course(s) such that level(c) = 4
      print(surname(t), section_name(s), code(c));
```

SPARQL query 1:

```
SELECT ?surname ?section_name ?code
WHERE
{
  ?t a unidb:teacher;
     unidb:surname ?surname.
  ?s unidb:has_lecturer ?t;
     unidb:has_course ?c;
     unidb:section_name ?section_name.
  ?c unidb:code ?code;
     unidb:level ?level.
  FILTER (?level = 4)
}
```

SPARQL query 2:

```
SELECT ?surname ?section_name ?code
WHERE
{
  ?t a unidb:teacher.
  ?s unidb:has_lecturer ?t.
  ?s unidb:has_course ?c.
  ?t unidb:surname ?surname.
  ?s unidb:section_name ?section_name.
  ?c unidb:code ?code.
  ?c unidb:level ?level.
  FILTER (?level = 4)
}
```

Fig. 4. Equivalent SPARQL queries

The same query can be written in different ways in SPARQL to produce the same results. Some of the equivalent alternatives make use of syntactic sugar to reduce the query length and improve readability. In the present work, however, it is important that the SPARQL query that is generated should have a simple structure, so that the code generation task is simplified. For example, Figure 4 shows two alternative versions of equivalent SPARQL queries that print the surnames of all teachers, together with the names of the sections that they teach, and the code of the course of which the section is a part, for fourth year courses only. The *subject* variables each appear only once when defining patterns using the same *subject* in query 1. While grouping together all parts of the query that relate to the same subject makes the query more readable, the flatter structure of query 2 is more uniform and, therefore, the second version was chosen as the target for automatic code generation from ICode. Comparing the SPARQL and Daplex queries (Figure 4) the relationship between these can be seen easily. All variables in the SELECT clause are related to variables in the *print* statement, all entities and functions used in Daplex are related with triples appearing in the SPARQL WHERE clause, and the condition expressed in *such that* clause of the Daplex query relate to an expression in FILTER clause of the SPARQL query.

Information about *person* instances are represented in RDF/RDFS at the most specialised level. Thus, for example, the names of some person instances might be represented at the person level, while others who are members of staff will be represented at the *member_of_staff* level, and others who are researchers will be represented at the *researcher* level (as shown in Figure 3) which, in this case, is a leaf class in the person class hierarchy. If a query requests the names of all persons, then information should be retrieved from all levels in

(a) Daplex query:

```
for each p in person
    print(forename(p), surname(p));
```

(b) SPARQL query 1:

```
SELECT ?forename ?surname
WHERE
{
{
  ?s a unidb:person.
} UNION {
  ?person1 rdfs:subClassOf unidb:person.
  ?s a ?person1.
} UNION {
  ?person2 rdfs:subClassOf ?person1.
  ?s a ?person2.
}
?s unidb:forename ?forename.
?s unidb:surname ?surname.
}
```

(c) SPARQL query 2:

```
SELECT ?forename ?surname
WHERE
{
{
  ?s a unidb:person.
} UNION {
  ?s a unidb:member_of_staff.
} UNION {
  ?s a unidb:student.
} UNION {
  ?s a unidb:researcher.
} UNION {
  ?s a unidb:teacher.
} UNION {
  ?s a unidb:undergrad.
} UNION {
  ?s a unidb:postgrad.
}
?s unidb:forename ?forename.
?s unidb:surname ?surname.
}
```

Fig. 5. Print the names of all persons

the person hierarchy. One approach to this is to examine the metadata of the schema to identify the names of all of the classes below *person* in the hierarchy automatically, and to generate a query that retrieves the names recorded with instances of each class in the data, taking the union of these sub-queries as the result of the original query. This gives rise to a query with many sub-queries (one for each class in the hierarchy), as shown in Figure 5(c). An alternative approach taken in this work is to examine the metadata of the schema to find the depth of the tree rooted at *person*, and to construct a query that retrieves the names of instances at each level of the class hierarchy, taking the union of these sub-queries as the result of the original query. This can result in a more compact SPARQL query, as shown in Figure 5(b).

3.2   Query Translation

Figure 7 illustrates how Daplex queries are translated to SPARQL. In the work described here, the existing Daplex compiler is used to construct an ICode version of the query. The ICode is then used to create three term lists that reflect the structure of the eventual SPARQL query: a SELECT list, a WHERE list and a FILTER list. These term lists are then used to build the SPARQL query. The query translation steps are described below with reference to the example query shown in Figure 6. The query translation system has been implemented in Prolog, and has benefited from Prolog's pattern matching and list processing facilities. The SPARQL queries generated in this work have been executed using the ARQ implementation of SPARQL for the Jena Semantic Web framework[1] to retrieve results from RDF/RDFS documents.

---

[1] http://jena.sourceforge.net/

(a) Daplex query:

```
for each u in undergrad
  for each c1 in takes(u)
    for each c2 in takes(u) such that
      level(c1)=level(c2)+2 or units(c1)=1
        print(code(c1), code(c2), surname(u));
```

(b) ICode:

```
[ var(evar8),var(evar9),var(evar10) ]
[
  generate(undergrad,var(uevar1)),
  generate(takes,[undergrad],[var(uevar1)],course,var(uevar2)),
  generate(takes,[undergrad],[var(uevar1)],course,var(uevar3)),
  logical_or([
      restrict(level,[course],[var(uevar2)],var(evar4)),
      restrict(level,[course],[var(uevar3)],var(evar5)),
      expression(var(evar6),[var(evar5)],expr(+,var(evar5),2)),
      expression([],[var(evar4),var(evar6)],expr(=,var(evar4),var(evar6)))
  ],[
      restrict(units,[course],[var(uevar2)],var(evar7)),
      expression([],[var(evar7)],expr(=,var(evar7),1))
  ]),
  restrict(code,[course],[var(uevar2)],var(evar8)),
  restrict(code,[course],[var(uevar3)],var(evar9)),
  restrict(surname,[undergrad],[var(uevar1)],var(evar10))
]
```

(c) SELECT list:

```
[ ?code=var(evar8),?code_1=var(evar9),?surname=var(evar10) ]
```

WHERE list:

```
[ gn(undergrad,obj1,var(uevar1)),
  gn(takes,undergrad,obj1,var(uevar1),course,obj2,var(uevar2)),
  gn(takes,undergrad,obj1,var(uevar1),course,obj3,var(uevar3)),
  rs(level,obj2,var(evar4)),
  rs(level_1,obj3,var(evar5)),
  rs(units,obj2,var(evar7)),
  rs(code,obj2,var(evar8)),
  rs(code_1,obj3,var(evar9)),
  rs(surname,obj1,var(evar10))
]
```

FILTER list:

```
[ or([ex(?level,=,?level_1+2)],[ex(?units,=,1)]) ]
```

(d) SPARQL query:

```
SELECT  ?code ?code_1 ?surname
WHERE {
?obj1 a unidb:undergrad.
?obj1 unidb:takes ?obj2.
?obj1 unidb:takes ?obj3.
?obj2 unidb:level ?level.
?obj3 unidb:level ?level_1.
?obj2 unidb:units ?units.
?obj2 unidb:code ?code.
?obj3 unidb:code ?code_1.
?obj1 unidb:surname ?surname.
FILTER ( ( ?level=?level_1+2 || ?units=1 ) )
}
```

Fig. 6. A Daplex query is first translated to ICode. The SPARQL code generator constructs a SELECT list, a WHERE list and a FILTER list from the ICode elements, then uses these three lists to build the SPARQL query.

Processing ICode. ICode is represented in Prolog as a list containing different qualifiers. An example of a Daplex query and its equivalent ICode is presented in Figure 6.

The **generate** qualifiers result from clauses that generate entity instances, either by iterating over instances of a named class (**generate/2**):

```
generate(Class, InternalVarForClass)
```

or evaluating a relationship function (**generate/5**):

```
generate(Function, [ArgumentType], [InternalVarForArgumentType],
         ResultType, InternalVarForResultType)
```

The ICode in Figure 6 has one **generate/2** qualifier that iterates over the *undergrad* class, and two **generate/5** qualifiers that apply the relationship function *takes* to the given *undergrad* instance.

A **restrict/4** qualifier is present for each scalar attribute mentioned in a query, and has the form:

```
restrict(ClassAttribute,[Class],[InternalVarForClass], InternalVarForClassAttribute)
```

In this example, different instances have attributes with the same name (in this case, *code* and *level*). Care is taken when generating the SPARQL query to ensure that different variables (*?code, ?code_1, ?level, ?level_1*) are used to ensure that the correct values are retrieved.

For each condition expressed in the query, one or more **expression/3** qualifiers will be generated. An **expression** qualifier can take different forms depending on the condition complexity. The **expression/3** qualifiers in Figure 6 represent equality tests and a simple arithmetic expression in the original Daplex query. Inequality tests are represented in a similar way (not shown in this example). Disjunctions in a query give rise to **logical_or/2** qualifiers in the ICode, like the one shown in Figure 6. Conjunctions can be represented by similar **logical_and/2** qualifiers, but these are normally flattened in a preprocessing step, since a list of qualifiers is implicitly understood to be a conjunction of qualifiers.

Processing Term Lists. The SPARQL query is built from the contents of the three term lists: a SELECT list, a WHERE list and a FILTER list. Examples of these are shown in Figure 6(c). These three lists are generated automatically from the ICode, which is processed one element at a time. As each ICode qualifier is processed, one or more of the SELECT, WHERE and FILTER lists are updated, as shown in Figure 7.

There is a very close correspondence between the SELECT, WHERE and FILTER lists, and the eventual SPARQL query. This can be seen by comparing (c) and (d) in Figure 6. The SELECT clause is the first clause of a SPARQL query, and is built from the elements in the SELECT term list that originate from **restrict** qualifiers corresponding to attributes that feature in the *print* part of a Daplex query. Statements in the WHERE clause are issued from all instances, relationships and attributes present in a Daplex query. In SPARQL, all variables used in the SELECT and FILTER clauses must be instantiated

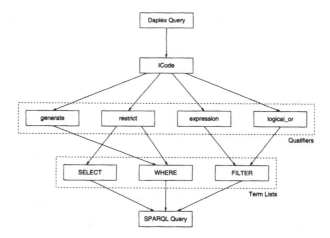

Fig. 7. Query translation flow. The **generate** qualifiers can cause the WHERE list to be updated, **restrict** qualifiers can cause both the SELECT and WHERE lists to be updated, and **expression** and **logical_or** qualifiers can cause the FILTER list to be updated.

(a) Daplex query:

```
for each r in researcher
  for each p in employed_on(r)
      such that duration(p) > 2
print(title(p),surname(r));
```

SELECT list:

```
[ ?title=var(evar4),?surname=var(evar5) ]
```

WHERE list:

```
[ gn(researcher,obj1,var(uevar1)),
  gn(employed_on,
      researcher,obj1,var(uevar1),
      project,obj2,var(uevar2)),
  rs(duration,obj2,var(evar3)),
  rs(title,obj2,var(evar4)),
  rs(surname,obj1,var(evar5)) ]
```

FILTER list:

```
[ ex(?duration,>,2) ]
```

SPARQL query:

```
SELECT  ?title ?surname
WHERE {
?obj1 a unidb:researcher.
?obj1 unidb:employed_on ?obj2.
?obj2 unidb:duration ?duration.
?obj2 unidb:title ?title.
?obj1 unidb:surname ?surname.
FILTER (?duration>2)
}
```

(b) Daplex query:

```
for each p in project
    such that duration(p) > 2
  for each r in employed_on_inv(p)
    print(title(p),surname(r));
```

SELECT list:

```
[ ?title=var(evar4),?surname=var(evar5) ]
```

WHERE list:

```
[ gn(project,obj1,var(uevar1)),
  rs(duration,obj1,var(evar3)),
  gn(employed_on_inv,
      project,obj1,var(uevar1),
      researcher,obj2,var(uevar2)),
  rs(title,obj1,var(evar4)),
  rs(surname,obj2,var(evar5)) ]
```

FILTER list:

```
[ ex(?duration,>,2) ]
```

SPARQL query:

```
SELECT  ?title ?surname
WHERE {
?obj1 a unidb:project.
?obj1 unidb:duration ?duration.
?obj2 unidb:employed_on ?obj1.
?obj1 unidb:title ?title.
?obj2 unidb:surname ?surname.
FILTER (?duration>2)
}
```

Fig. 8. Query that makes use of the inverse relationship **employed_on_inv**

in the WHERE clause. All conditions in the FILTER clause are issued from *such that* statements in the Daplex query and correspond to terms derived from `expression` and `logical_or` qualifiers. When translating logical conjunctions and disjunctions, operator precedence is taken into account.

Handling Relationship Functions and Their Inverses. The queries in Figure 8 print information about projects lasting more than two years and the researchers employed on those projects. The Daplex query language supports the use of inverse relationships. The relationship function *employed_on* in Figure 8(a) is represented in the WHERE list as:

```
gn(employed_on,researcher,obj1,var(uevar1),project,obj2,var(uevar2))
```

whereas the query in Figure 8(b) uses the inverse function *employed_on_inv*, which is represented in the WHERE list as:

```
gn(employed_on_inv,project,obj1,var(uevar1),researcher,obj2,var(uevar2))
```

Both of these WHERE list elements are translated into SPARQL triple patterns with the predicate `unidb:employed_on`, a variable representing a researcher as the subject, and a variable representing a project as the object. Thus, we see that the notion of inverse function is implicit in the SPARQL language, arising naturally from the concept of an RDF triple.

4   Discussion

Daplex is a query language that was initially proposed for expressing queries against a semantic data model — the functional data model [14]. When using Daplex to express queries against a federated system, the user formulates queries that are expressed in terms of the entities, attributes and relationships in the conceptual model, and the organisation and format of data in the federation's component databases are not visible at this level. Thus, in the case of RDF/RDFS collections in a federation, neither the RDF triples nor the tree structure of an XML serialisation need to be considered by the user when writing queries. Subsequent translation into a SPARQL query that exposes the underlying triple structure is done automatically.

Risch [13] describes a different approach to working with RDF/RDFS in which RDF/RDFS data are imported into the Amos system, where they can be queried using the AmosQL language. In contrast, the approach taken here intentionally aims to make use of existing query processing systems for external data resources without importing and reformatting data. Other related work includes the functional query language RQL [10], which has been developed for querying RDF. While the functional design of RQL makes it an attractive language, the availability of implementations and standardisation efforts for SPARQL make it an attractive choice for the present work.

The code generator described here is designed to translate the limited set of ICode qualifiers described in Section 3.2 into SPARQL. The scope of the present implementation has, in part, been set by limitations of the SPARQL language. For example, we cannot currently translate Daplex queries that contain quantified sub-queries or aggregate functions (count, average, etc.). In order to overcome this limitation, it would be possible to query metadata in P/FDM and to use Prolog to post-process query results as needed. However, the SPARQL language is still under development, and continues to evolve. Future extensions to SPARQL might increase the range of Daplex queries that can be translated, or might present better alternatives for translating the queries that are currently handled by the system.

SPARQL is one of many query languages for web and Semantic Web querying [1,3]. Other languages could be used as the targets for query translation, possibly avoiding some of the limitations of SPARQL. SPARQL was chosen for this initial investigation since it is growing in popularity as a Semantic Web query language, and the similarities between ICode and SPARQL made query translation relatively straightforward.

5   Conclusions

We have taken a first step towards integrating RDF/RDFS collections with an existing database federation. The work described here provides a functional data model view of RDF/RDFS data. As in P/FDM, we are able to represent subclass/superclass hierarchies in RDF/RDFS, although, unlike with Daplex, it is not possible to retrieve inferred class instances using SPARQL. This can be overcome consulting the metadata in P/FDM, finding the depth of the subclass tree and checking for instances in all levels.

Daplex features that are natively supported by SPARQL were implemented when translating queries. SPARQL queries show similarities with the ICode that is used internally within P/FDM, and it is interesting to note that the ICode's structure resembles a SPARQL query more closely that it resembles the original Daplex query. The Daplex query language supports the use of inverse functions, and the same concept is implicit in a SPARQL triple pattern by reversing the roles of the subject and object.

A semantic data model, in this case the functional data model, provides an intuitive way of viewing and querying data in the Semantic Web. We believe that the work described here represents a useful step towards incorporating RDF/RDFS data resources within a federated system, enabling queries that combine data from relational and other databases with data from the Semantic Web.

Acknowledgements

We are grateful for support from the Swedish Foundation for Strategic Research and the Chalmers Foundation.

References

1. Bailey, J., Bry, F., Furche, T., Schaffert, S.: Web and Semantic Web Query Languages: A Survey. In: Eisinger, N., Małuszyński, J. (eds.) Reasoning Web. LNCS, vol. 3564, pp. 35–133. Springer, Heidelberg (2005)
2. Embury, S.M., Gray, P.M.D.: A Modular Compiler Architecture for a Data Manipulation Language. In: Morrison, R., Kennedy, J. (eds.) BNCOD 1996. LNCS, vol. 1094, pp. 170–188. Springer, Heidelberg (1996)
3. Furche, T., Linse, B., Bry, F., Plexousakis, D., Gottlob, G.: RDF Querying: Language Constructs and Evaluation Methods Compared. In: Barahona, P., Bry, F., Franconi, E., Henze, N., Sattler, U. (eds.) Reasoning Web 2006. LNCS, vol. 4126, pp. 1–52. Springer, Heidelberg (2006)
4. Kemp, G.J.L., Angelopoulos, N., Gray, P.M.D.: Architecture of a Mediator for a Bioinformatics Database Federation. IEEE Transactions on Information Technology in Biomedicine 6, 116–122 (2002)
5. Gray, P.M.D., Embury, S.M., Hui, K.Y., Kemp, G.J.L.: The Evolving Role of Constraints in the Functional Data Model. J. Intelligent Information Systems 12, 113–137 (1999)
6. Gray, P.M.D., Hui, K.Y., Preece, A.D.: An Expressive Constraint Language for Semantic Web Applications. In: Preece, A., O'Leary, D. (eds.) E-Business and the Intelligent Web: Papers from the IJCAI-01 Workshop, pp. 46–53. AAAI Press, Menlo Park (2001)
7. Gray, P.M.D., Kerschberg, L., King, P.J.H., Poulovassilis, A. (eds.): The Functional Approach to Data Management: Modeling, Analyzing, and Integrating Heterogeneous Data. Springer, Heidelberg (2004)
8. Gray, P.M.D., Kulkarni, K.G., Paton, N.W.: Object-Oriented Databases: a Semantic Data Model Approach. Prentice Hall Series in Computer Science. Prentice-Hall, Englewood Cliffs (1992)
9. Karjalainen, M.: A System for Integrating Heterogeneous, Autonomous Databases. Licentiate thesis, Chalmers University of Technology (2006)
10. Karvounarakis, G., Magkanaraki, A., Alexaki, S., Christophides, V., Plexousakis, D., Scholl, M., Tolle, K.: RQL: A Functional Query Language for RDF. In: Gray, P.M.D., Kerschberg, L., King, P.J.H., Poulovassilis, A. (eds.) The Functional Approach to Data Management: Modeling, Analyzing, and Integrating Heterogeneous Data, pp. 435–465. Springer, Heidelberg (2004)
11. Kemp, G.J.L., Angelopoulos, N., Gray, P.M.D.: A Schema-based Approach to Building a Bioinformatics Database Federation. In: Proceedings IEEE International Symposium on Bio-Informatics and Biomedical Engineering, pp. 13–20. IEEE Computer Society Press, Los Alamitos (2000)
12. Prud'hommeaux, E., Seaborne, A.: SPARQL query language for RDF. W3C candidate recommendation, W3C (June 2007), http://www.w3.org/TR/2007/CR-rdf-sparql-query-20070614/
13. Risch, T.: Functional Queries to Wrapped Educational Semantic Web Meta-Data. In: Gray, P.M.D., Kerschberg, L., King, P.J.H., Poulovassilis, A. (eds.) The Functional Approach to Data Management: Modeling, Analyzing, and Integrating Heterogeneous Data, pp. 466–477. Springer, Heidelberg (2004)
14. Shipman, D.W.: The Functional Data Model and the Data Language DAPLEX. ACM Trans. Database Syst. 6(1), 140–173 (1981)

Ranking for Approximated XQuery Full-Text Queries

Giacomo Buratti[1] and Danilo Montesi[2]

[1] Department of Mathematics and Computer Science, University of Camerino,
Via Madonna delle Carceri 9, Camerino, Italy
giacomo.buratti@unicam.it
[2] Department of Computer Science, University of Bologna,
Mura Anteo Zamboni 7, Bologna, Italy
danilo.montesi@unibo.it

Abstract. Treating structural conditions included in an XQuery Full-Text expression as *desiderata* rather than *mandatory* constraints could be beneficial for better answering user's informational needs. Using an approximated semantics requires however a mechanism for calculating a score for each resulting tree, and an algorithm for efficiently finding the best results. Both these issues are explored in this paper. We present algorithms for query evaluation that uses a *threshold* approach in order to improve performance; the algorithms rely on some properties of the functions used to calculate the score. Moreover, we propose a method, based on the new concepts of *Path Edit Distance* and *Comparison Satisfaction Ratio*, for calculating the structural score of a tree that partially satisfies conditions over tree structure and element values.

Keywords: XQuery Full-Text, Approximation, Score, Ranking, Optimization.

1 Introduction

XQuery Full-Text [1] is a recent W3C proposed query language that extends XQuery with full-text operators. It is an answer to the necessity of integrating semi-structured and unstructured data into a more general framework, towards the so-called *Structured Information Retrieval* which is the area of investigation of many research works in the last years [2]. XQuery Full-Text, however, treats basic conditions (i.e. navigational expressions and constraints on value of elements or attributes) and full-text conditions in a very different way. In fact, while full-text conditions can have a boolean semantics (e.g. `where $b ftcontains "cat"` means that $b *must* contain the word *cat*) or a ranked retrieval semantics (e.g. `let score $s := $b ftcontains "dog"` means that the presence of the word *dog* is not *mandatory*; it is rather the way to calculate a score for each element in $b, which could later be used for ordering the result), basic conditions are always treated as mandatory: in order to be retrieved, an element *must* be reachable by exactly following the specified path

A. Gray, K. Jeffery, and J. Shao (Eds.): BNCOD 2008, LNCS 5071, pp. 165–176, 2008.

expression, and all the conditions on values *must* be satisfied (e.g. `for $b in doc("bib.xml")/books/book[/year>1995]`).

The flexibility of the schema, one of the main characteristics of the semi-structured data model, poses interesting questions for what concerns answering queries that impose structural constraints on the XML fragments to retrieve; it could be the case that such constraints are satisfied by a very small part of input documents. Nevertheless, some fragments could be relevant to users, even if they do not closely respect some structure constraints.

For example, consider the XML document shown graphically in Fig. 1. Then the path expression `/bib/book/author` returns only those authors that are the single authors of at least one book, while the user need is probably to find all book authors; the less restrictive path expression `/bib/book//author` would include also co-authors in the result. Analogously, the path expression `/bib/book/title` finds all the book titles, but ignores paper titles; however some semantic relationship exists between the words *book* and *paper*, because both are hyponyms of *publication*. Moreover, the path expression `//paper[//section/title ftcontains "INEX"]` returns papers that include in a section title the word *INEX*; the less restrictive expression `//paper[//section ftcontains "INEX"]` would return also papers that instead include the word in a section content. Finally, the path expression `/bib/book[/price < 39]` could discard the vast majority of the books (in the document shown in Fig. 1 no book satisfies the constraint); consequently, the user could also be interested in books having price 39, or even in books having a price not much greater than 39.

This issue has been already investigated in [3]. The idea proposed there is to consider the searched path expressions and the specified conditions on values as

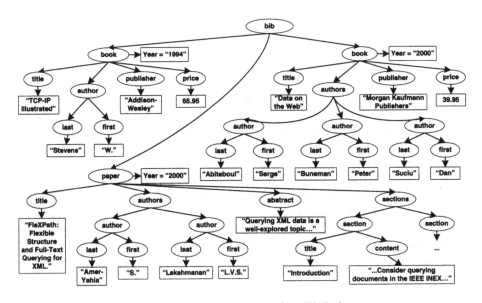

Fig. 1. Graphical representation of an XML document

desirable properties to enjoy for an element to be returned, instead of considering them as mandatory constraints. Queries are written as algebraic expression, where *approximated algebraic operators* are used and an outer *Top-k* or *Threshold* operator selects the best answers and presents them in score order. The algebraic framework developed in [3] is briefly reviewed in Sect. 3. This paper focuses instead on two interconnected issues, which are central for implementing an approximated XML system: 1) how to calculate the score to assign to an *approximated* answer, i.e. an element that does not perfectly respect query conditions? and 2) how to efficiently return the best answers to a query?

Section 4 deals with efficient query evaluation. We first present a naive evaluation algorithm and explain why it suffers serious performance problems. Then we define two useful properties of scoring functions and show that, if the functions we use enjoy these properties, query evaluation can be carried out using better performing algorithms that follow a *threshold* approach.

Though the algorithms presented are parametric with respect to the particular scoring function used, in Sect. 5 we propose a scoring model for non full-text conditions. We define the concepts of *Path Edit Distance*, a measure of the similarity between two path expressions, and *Comparison Satisfaction Ratio*, a measure of the satisfaction of a comparison expression. We do not deal with full-text score calculation, which is supposed to be done using some of the well known IR-like techniques.

Finally, Sect. 6 concludes our work by reviewing the main results achieved and outlining future research directions.

2   Related Work

Historically, Information Retrieval was born as a subject dealing with unstructured documents. The adaptation of its classical concepts to the management of semi-structured documents requires a considerable research effort, and many papers have been written on this issue. Particularly relevant is INEX [2] (INitiative for the Evaluation of XML retrieval), a series of conferences actively working on the so-called *Structured Information Retrieval (SIR)*, i.e. Information Retrieval over XML repositories. Participants to this initiative present SIR systems which are able to answer to *Content and Structure (CAS)* queries, i.e. queries that contain constraints on both the content and the structure of a document. A question arises regarding the way to interpret such queries: should conditions be interpreted *strictly* or *vaguely*? Moreover, should it be some difference between the interpretation of conditions on *target* elements, i.e. elements to be returned, and those on *support* elements, i.e. paths followed to reach the target elements? INEX does not dictate a choice; it rather proposes [4] different possible interpretations. Among them, we decide to use the *Strict-Vague (SVCAS)* semantics. This means that structure conditions concerning internal steps are interpreted as *vague* constraints, while structure conditions concerning target nodes are interpreted as *semi-strict* constraints, in the sense that we allow (with a penalty) only a limited number of relaxation on conditions over target nodes.

Defining a scoring method for approximated query answers is the focus of [5] and [6]. These papers propose an accurate scoring method, *twig scoring*, and two approximations of it: *path scoring* and *binary scoring*. Twig scoring is inspired by traditional *tf*idf* measure used in Information Retrieval [7].

TopX, an algorithm for processing queries expressed using the NEXI [8] query language, is presented in [9]. The algorithm returns the top-k results by combining a structure score, calculated as the ratio between the number of satisfied conditions and the total number of conditions, and a content score, calculated using a variation of classical *tf*idf* measure. The focus of the paper is on efficiently computing answers; a threshold algorithm makes probabilistic pruning of candidates and avoid as much as possible random access to indexes. With respect to TopX, our proposal does not use probabilistic pruning; however, we pay more attention to structural score calculation by carefully calculating the level of satisfaction of structural conditions.

3   The Approximated Algebraic Framework

Let us now review the algebraic framework presented in [3]. As already said, approximate queries are represented through algebraic expressions. Algebraic operators take as input a *forest*, i.e. a list of trees, and return a forest. Each output tree has a *global score* which is the combination of two sub-scores: a *structural score* and a *full-text score*. Each query is of the form $O_R(O_n(O_{n-1}(\cdots(O_1(F)))))$, where: F is the input forest; O_i is an *approximated operator* that somehow manipulates the input forest; O_R is a *ranking operator* that extracts from the input forest the trees with highest scores and returns them in descending score order.

The algebra is equipped with four approximated operators: projection, selection, full-text selection, full-text score assignment.

Approximated projection $\pi_\lambda^\star(F)$ returns subtrees of the input trees that can be reached by following a (more or less precise) approximation of the *path expression* λ. For example the algebraic expression $\pi_{/\text{bib}/\text{book}}^\star(\text{"bib.xml"})$, where *bib.xml* is the XML document shown in Fig. 1, would probably return a forest whose highest score trees are the two subtrees rooted at the two **book** elements (no approximation, so maximum score) and the subtree rooted at **paper**.

Approximated selection $\sigma_{\lambda[\gamma]}^\star(F)$ assigns to each input tree a structural score reflecting: 1) the availability of a subtree reachable by following an approximation of λ; 2) the degree to which that subtree satisfies the selection condition γ. For example the expression $\sigma_{/\text{book}[/\text{author}/\text{last.v}=\text{"Amer-Yahia" OR }/\text{price.v}<60]}^\star$ $(\pi_{/\text{bib}/\text{book}}^\star(\text{"bib.xml"}))$ should assign a non-zero score not only to the book *Data on the Web*, which is an exact answer, but also to: 1) the book *TCP-IP Illustrated*, which slightly fails to respect the price constraint; 2) the paper, which slightly fails to respect document structure and element names constraints.

Approximated full-text selection $\varsigma_{\lambda[\gamma]}^\star(F)$ searches one or more words or phrases into the content of a subtree reachable by following an approximation of

λ. If the words are found, the full-text score is set to 1, otherwise it is set to 0; the structural score, as usual, represents the degree of approximation applied to λ. For example the algebraic expression $\varsigma^*_{/book/title["INEX"]}(\pi_{/bib/book}(\text{"bib.xml"}))$ should assign a full-text score of 1 to the paper about *FleXPath*, because it contains the searched word into the subtree reachable by following the approximated path expression /bib/paper; in this case the approximation enables to: 1) reach also paper elements and 2) broaden the search scope from the content of title to the content of paper (that includes the content of title).

While full-text selection performs a full-text search using a *boolean* model (a tree either satisfies the selection condition or it does not satisfy the condition at all), **full-text score assignment** $\xi_{\lambda[\gamma]\ f_F}(F)$ assigns to each tree a full-text score (calculated by the function f_F) between 0 and 1. As in full-text selection, the structural score represents the degree of approximation applied of λ.

Usage of approximated operators is motivated by the consideration that a strict interpretation of conditions imposed by the user query could discard trees which could be of interest for the user. However a way to filter results (retaining only those that best match the user needs) is needed, otherwise the user would be overwhelmed by a huge amount of answers. This is the reason why queries always have an outer **Top-K selection** $\top$ or **Threshold selection** ω operator. They return, respectively, the k trees with highest global scores and those trees whose global score is higher than a defined threshold τ; in both cases trees are returned in descending score order.

4   Query Evaluation

Writing a naive algorithm to evaluate a query is straightforward. First of all the algebraic operators are executed (using the operator-specific algorithms) from the inner one O_1 to the outer one O_n, passing O_i's output forest as input to O_{i+1}; then, according to the ranking operator's semantics, the trees with lowest scores are pruned; finally the resulting forest is ordered by descending value of combined score. This algorithm suffers however of an evident performance problem: the size of intermediate results tends to increase along query evaluation, until the ranking operator is executed.

In order to understand this point, let us analyze the behavior of approximated projection. One could expect that it returns exact answers plus *reasonable* approximated answers (e.g. paper elements when looking for book elements); actually it returns a forest containing a tree for each element in the input forest. In fact, any original path expression can be relaxed into $//\beta$, where β is any element name. Hence approximated projection transforms a forest containing n elements into a forest containing n trees and the following number of elements:

- in the best case n, when each input tree is composed by only one element, as shown in Fig. 2(a);
- in the worst case $n(n+1)/2$, when each input tree is actually a *list*, like the one shown in Fig. 2(b) (the result is the input tree itself, plus those shown in Fig. 2(c));

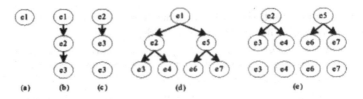

Fig. 2. Examples of approximated projection

- in the average case $n \log_k n$, when each non-leaf element has k child elements, as in the tree shown in Fig. 2(d) (the result is the input tree itself, plus those shown in Fig. 2(e)).

Therefore any projection multiplies, in the average case, by $\log_k n$ the number of elements, while any other approximated operator leaves it unchanged: selection, full-text selection and full-text score assignment does not discard any input tree, they just assign structural and full-text scores to the input trees.

4.1   A Threshold Approach

The naive algorithm did not take into account the fact that the ranking operator is supposed to cut off most of the trees. In order to take advantage of this characteristic of the queries, we must reason about the scoring function we use and the way the score is calculated. According to the semantics illustrated in Sect. 3, we can assume that each approximated operator calculates a *local* structural score SS_L (using a function f_S) and a *local* full-text score FS_L (using a function f_F), reflecting the level of satisfaction of its own structural / full-text constraints; such scores are then combined (using a function f_C) with the structural / full-text score returned by inner operators to form the *current* structural score SS and the current full-text FS; SS and FS are then combined (using a function f_G) each other to form the *current global score* S. The process goes on until the outermost operator is executed and the final global score is calculated; then Top-K / Threshold returns the query answer.

Suppose the ranking operator is Threshold. After executing m of the n query steps, we know that a tree will surely be discarded by Threshold if 1) the current global score of the tree is lower than τ and 2) we are sure that, after executing the remaining $n - m$ operators, the global score will not raise. In order to satisfy the second condition, the only things we need are that 1) the function f_C that calculates current structural / full-text score is a *left decreasing function*; 2) the function f_G that calculates the current global score is a *monotonic function*.

Definition 1. *Let* $f : R \times R \rightarrow R$ *be a function.* f *is a **Left Decreasing Function** if* $\forall x \in R, y \in R: f(x, y) \leq x. f$ *is a **Monotonic Function** if* $\forall (x_1, y_1) \in R \times R, (x_2, y_2) \in R \times R, x_1 \leq x_2, y_1 \leq y_2: f(x_1, y_1) \leq f(x_2, y_2).$

Being f_C a left decreasing function, SS and FS tend to decrease during the query evaluation: $f_C(SS, SS_L) \leq SS$ and $f_C(FS, FS_L) \leq FS$. Then, if f_G is monotonic, current global score S tends to decrease as well. Therefore, a Threshold query $\omega_{f_S, f_G, \tau}(O_n(O_{n-1}(\cdots(O_1(F)))))$ can be evaluated as follows. Initially both SS and FS are set to 1, and $F_1 = O_1(F)$ is evaluated; the algorithm implementing the operator O_1 calculates, for each tree to return, SS_L (using structural scoring function f_S) and FS_L (using some full-text scoring function). Then, for each returned tree, the algorithm implementing Threshold calculates: $SS = f_C(SS, SS_L)$; $FS = f_C(FS, FS_L)$; $S = f_G(SS, FS)$. Then each tree whose current combined score $S < \tau$ is removed from F_1. Now the query evaluation goes on evaluating $F_2 = O_2(F_1)$, calculating scores and discarding trees as before. After O_n is executed the resulting trees are ordered by descending S value.

It should be noted that the limitation imposed over the choice of f_C and f_G functions is not an issue. In fact a natural choice for f_C is multiplication (i.e. $SS = SS * SS_L$ and $FS = FS * FS_L$), and multiplication of reals in the range $[0, 1]$ is a left decreasing function ($xy \leq x$, being $xy = x$ when $y = 1$). Similarly a natural choice for f_C is weighted sum (i.e. $S = \theta * SS + (1 - \theta) * FS$, where $0 \leq \theta \leq 1$), which is a monotonic function. Though not strictly necessary for the threshold approach to work, a good f_C should be a continuous function of the weight θ, as discussed in [10].

The advantage of this Threshold evaluation method is that the size of intermediate results decreases, because a (hopefully large) part of the resulting trees are discarded. Note that, in order to achieve this result, we do not make any assumption about local scores calculation functions; we just require some common-sense properties: 1) an exact answer must have score 1; 2) an approximated answer must have a score $0 \leq s < 1$; 3) non full-text operators (projection and selection), are supposed to assign a local full-text score of 1 to each resulting tree.

The performance gain obtained using this approach depends on the ratio of discarded trees, which could be quite high, especially on the projection steps. As an example, consider the XML document in Fig. 1 and a query whose inner operator is $\pi_{/\text{bib}/\text{book}}(\text{"bib.xml"})$. The input tree contains 39 elements, so approximated projection returns a forest containing 39 trees; the threshold approach would probably retains just the three trees rooted at *book* and *paper* elements, thus reaching a 92% discard ratio.

Let us now consider Top-K queries. This time we do not have a defined threshold τ that allows to discard trees with a lower score. In order to use a threshold approach also for Top-K queries we must change the way query is evaluated: instead of using a *set-oriented* evaluation strategy, in which each operator is executed over the entire input forest, we follow a *mixed* evaluation strategy. This strategy tends, in a first phase, to *fill* the temporary resulting forest with the first k results, then to gradually *replace* trees with lower scores with trees with higher scores. Once the resulting forest contains k trees the threshold approach starts to work: if the (presently found) k-th score is higher than the score of a tree in an intermediate result, that tree can be safely discarded without completing query evaluation.

The performance is highly influenced by the order in which trees are evaluated. The optimal situation occurs when the first k trees that are included in the (temporary) resulting forest are also those which turn out to have the highest scores; in this case, in fact, all the other trees are immediately discarded. According to this consideration, it would be worthwhile thinking of a *pre-processing step* which tries to locate trees having high chances to be included in the Top-K result and process them first.

5   Structural Score Calculation

In Sect. 4 we have defined the query evaluation strategy to follow. The algorithms rely on left decreasingness of f_C and on monotonicity of f_G, while no assumption is necessary about local scores calculation. In this subsection we present a possible way to calculate structural scores in the presence of relaxations on both path expressions and comparison predicates.

5.1   Path Relaxations

Let us consider a subtree T' of an input tree T, reachable from $root(T)$ by following a path λ', that is returned by the approximated projection $\pi_\lambda^\star(F)$. In order to assign a structural score to T', we need a way to measure the *similarity* between λ' and the searched path λ. For example, suppose we are executing $\pi_{/\text{bib/book/author}}^\star$ over the XML document in Fig. 1. Which structural score should be assigned to the subtree rooted at author representing *Serge Abiteboul*? In other words, which is the similarity between the searched path /bib/book/author and the path /bib/book/authors/author? In order to answer this question, we define a novel similarity measure, called *Path Edit Distance* (*PED*).

Let us first introduce the concept of *Path Transformation System*, which is the tool that allows to transform a path expression into another one and to calculate the transformation cost. It is defined as a set of *transformation types*, each one having a cost. The Path Transformation System we propose includes three transformation types: *Insert*, *Delete*, and *Substitute*.

Insert adds a step into λ. For example /bib/book/author can be transformed into /bib/book/authors/author by inserting the step /authors just before the step /author. The cost of an *Insert* is: 1 when inserting a step just before another step which has a child axis, because such a transformation extends the result space (e.g. inserting /authors before /author in /bib/book/author); 0 when inserting a step just before another step which has a descendant axis, because such a transformation does not extend the result space (e.g. inserting /authors before //author in /bib/book//author).

Delete removes a step from λ. For example /bib/book/authors/author can be transformed into /bib/book/author by deleting the step /authors. The cost of a *Delete* is always 1, because in any case an application of this transformation potentially includes new elements in the result.

Substitute replaces a name β with β'. For example /bib/book can be transformed into /bib/paper by substituting book with paper. The cost of a *Substitute* is $1 - x$, where x is the similarity between the approximated and the original element name; therefore the cost ranges from 0 (β is equal to β') to 1 (β and β' are completely unrelated). It could seem strange that the cost of a substitution is not equal to the cost of an insertion followed by a deletion. However we defined this transformation in terms of similarity, making it a first class citizen, while in classical string edit distance it can be viewed as a derived one.

These basic transformations can be composed in order to operate more complex transformations. In general there are more than one strategy (i.e. sequence of transformations) that can be followed for transforming a path expression λ into λ', and each of those sequences has a cost, given by the sum of the costs of the included basic transformations. The Path Edit Distance between λ and λ' is defined as the cost of the *cheapest* transformations sequence from λ to λ'.

Definition 2 (Path Edit Distance). *Let λ and λ' be two path expressions. Let PTS be a Path Transformation System and let $O_{\lambda,\lambda',PTS}$ be the set of transformations sequences from λ to λ'. The Path Edit Distance $PED(\lambda, \lambda', PTS)$ is defined as $min\{cost(o_i) \mid o_i \in O_{\lambda,\lambda',PTS}\}$.*

PED clearly resembles classical String Edit Distance [11], with a difference: while in String Edit Distance we have a boolean judgement about equality between two letters, in PED we associate to each pair of element names (the equivalent of a letter in String Edit Distance) a score value representing the similarity between the names. A similarity of 1 means that the two names are equal, while a similarity of 0 means that the two names are completely unrelated.

The algorithm that calculates PED is a straightforward adaptation of the classical bottom-up dynamic programming algorithm for computing string edit distance; there is however a point to notice. We must recall that queries must be evaluated using a SVCAS semantics. The PED between a path expression $\alpha_1\beta_1\alpha_2\beta_2 \cdots \alpha_n\beta_n$ (where α_i is either '/' or '//', and β_i is an element name) specified in the query and a path expression $/\beta'_1/\beta'_2 \cdots /\beta'_m$ from the root of a tree to an element (only child axes can be found in a *real* path between two elements) is consequently calculated as the sum of: 1) the minimum distance between $\alpha_1\beta_1\alpha_2\beta_2 \cdots \alpha_{n-1}\beta_{n-1}$ and $/\beta'_1/\beta'_2 \cdots /\beta'_{m-1}$; 2) 1 minus the similarity between β_n and β'_m.

```
function PED(query pattern a[1]b[1]a[2]b[2]...a[n]b[n],
   element pattern /c[1]/c[2].../c[m]
     for i=0 to n-1
         d[i,0]:=i;
     for i=0 to m-1
         if a[1]='/' then d[0,i]:=i else d[0,i]:=0;
     for i=1 to n-1
         for j=1 to m-1
             if a[i+1]='/' then  InsCost:=1 else InsCost:=0;
             d[i,j] := min(d[i,j-1]+InsCost, d[i-1,j]+1,
```

```
        d[i-1,j-1]+(1-Similarity(b[i],c[j]));
return d[n-1,m-1] + (1 - Similarity(b[n], c[m]));
```

The algorithm takes as input the two path expressions (note that $a[i]$ corresponds to α_i, $b[i]$ to β_i, $c[i]$ to β_i') and involves the use of an $n \times m$ matrix d, where n and m are the lengths of the two path expressions. The invariant maintained throughout the algorithm is that we can transform the initial segment $a[1]b[1] \ldots a[i]b[i]$ into $/c[1] \ldots /c[j]$ using a minimum of $d[i,j]$ operations. At the end, the bottom-right element of the matrix contains the the minimum distance between $\alpha_1\beta_1\alpha_2\beta_2 \cdots \alpha_{n-1}\beta_{n-1}$ and $/\beta_1'/\beta_2' \cdots /\beta_{m-1}'$.

For example, consider the path expressions $\lambda = $ /bib/book//author and $\lambda' = $ /bib/paper/authors/paperauthor. Suppose that Similarity(*book, paper*)= 0.7, Similarity(*author, paperauthor*) = 0.9, while the similarity between any other element name is 0.05. The function *PED* returns 0.4. In fact λ can be transformed into λ' by: 1) substituting *book* with *paper* (cost 0.3); 2) inserting *authors* before //*author* (cost 0); 3) substituting *author* with *paperauthor* (cost 0.1).

The concept of Path Edit Distance is well suited for representing the structural score of a tree returned by an approximated projection. However we need a score value between 0 and 1, so we should divide *PED*'s output by the maximum possible *PED* value, which is $\max\{|\lambda|, |\lambda'|\}$, where $|\lambda|$ is the number of steps in λ. In fact it is always possible to transform λ into any λ' by: 1) substituting any β_i in λ with β_i' in λ' (in the worst case the cost is 1 for each substitution); 2) inserting the remaining steps of λ' in λ or deleting the remaining steps in λ.

5.2   Comparison Relaxations

We have seen that comparison predicates can be subject to relaxation. For example the predicate `price <= 50` can be relaxed into `price <= 60`. In this case, which structural score should be assigned to a book whose price is 59?

First of all, the scoring function should enjoy a common-sense property: the more a value is close to the searched value, the more the score should be high; in the previous example, if a book costs 51 and another one costs 58, the first one should have an higher score. Moreover, scoring should take into account the magnitude of the values; for example, if books have prices varying from 10 to 1000, a difference of 8 between searched price and found price is more acceptable than a difference of 0.1 in a domain having values varying from 0 to 1.

Taking into account these consideration, let us informally define the concept of *Comparison Satisfaction Ratio* (*CSR*). If a condition is satisfied, CSR is obviously equal to 1. If a condition is not satisfied CSR is 1 minus the ratio between 1) the difference between the found value and the searched value; 2) the maximum difference that can be found in the input set of values. The searched value is the *borderline* value that satisfies the condition; for example if the condition is $x \leq 50$ the borderline is 50, if the condition is $x \geq 80$ the borderline is 80.

Now suppose that the original selection predicate is `/book[/price.v <= 50]` and that we are considering an element named `totalprice`. In this case the input set is the set of elements named *price* or *totalprice* in the input forest. If the highest value in the input set is 100 and the value of the *totalprice* element is 60, then *CSR* is $1 - (60 - 50)/(100 - 50) = 0.8$.

If the values to compare are two strings and the comparison operator is $=$, CSR is instead the similarity between the two strings, as usual calculated using an ontology. An evaluation function must be defined for each kind of operator and values; for the sake of simplicity we do not discuss each possible case.

5.3   Putting Things Together

We have already noticed that the Path Edit Distance can be used for calculating the structural score of trees returned by approximated projection. Let us now discuss the other approximated operators.

The simplest form of selection predicate is $\lambda[p\theta x]$, where λ is a path expression, p is an element property (typically its value), θ is a comparison operator, and x is a constant. The system must find, for each input tree T, a subtree reachable by following an approximation of λ that satisfies an approximation of $p\theta x$. If F is the set of subtrees reachable by following an approximation of λ, a natural choice is to set the structural score of T to the maximum value among those calculated by combining (e.g. multiplying) the normalized PED between λ and λ', where λ' is the path from the root of the original tree to the root of the subtree we are considering, and the CSR of the predicate $p\theta x$.

In the case of full-text selection, where the predicate is of the form $\lambda[\gamma]$, we must check, for each input tree T, if there is some subtree that satisfies the full-text condition γ. If this is the case, the full-text score of T is set to 1, and the structural score is set to the maximum normalized PED among those of the subtrees that satisfies γ. In no subtree satisfies γ, the full-text score of T is set to 0, and the structural score is set to the maximum normalized PED value.

Finally, in the case of full-text score assignment, the full-text score assigned to each tree must range from 0 to 1, according to the level of satisfaction of the full-text condition. As in the case of full-text selection any subtree of an input tree T is analyzed, and T's full-text score is set to the maximum value of its subtree's full-text score, while T's structural score is set to the maximum structural score value among those of the subtrees with maximum full-text score.

6   Conclusions and Future Work

Using an approximated semantics in answering XQuery Full-Text queries may allow to best satisfy the user needs, as many presented examples suggest. However dealing with approximation requires a good scoring method and efficient algorithms; in this paper we have tackled these two issues.

The algorithms that evaluate a query returning the best k results or the results with a sufficiently high score rely on the assumptions that: 1) the function that calculates current structural / full-text scores enjoys the *left decreasingness* property; 2) the function that combines these scores to form the current global score enjoys the *monotonicity* property. These assumptions permits to follow a *threshold* approach to the query evaluation, i.e. to early discard some possible answer. We have also made some examples of valuable scoring functions, though the algorithms developed do not depend on a particular scoring system, thus leaving the freedom to make different choices. In particular we have defined the concepts of *path edit distance* and *comparison satisfaction ratio*.

The most obvious future research direction is the implementation of a working prototype of XML approximated query engine, based on the algebraic operators presented in this paper. Such a prototype is needed in order to test the efficiency of the threshold approach to query evaluation, as well as the effectiveness of the proposed score calculation functions. The issue of query optimization also involves the availability of ad-hoc index structures. Choosing a valuable indexing method is not a trivial issue, especially because those presented in literature are only suitable for exact query evaluation, so they should be re-thought for dealing with approximation. Finally we plan to support a more significant fragment of XQuery Full-Text. To this aim approximated algebraic operators should be supplemented with other operators, like the ones presented in [12], possibly augmented with some sort of approximated behavior.

References

1. W3C: XQuery 1.0 and XPath 2.0 Full-Text, W3C Working Draft (2006), http://www.w3.org/TR/xquery-full-text/
2. INEX: INitiative for the Evaluation of XML Retrieval (2007), http://inex.is.informatik.uni-duisburg.de/
3. Buratti, G., Montesi, D.: An Approximation-Aware Algebra for XML Full-Text Queries. In: Proceedings of ICSOFT 2007 (July 2007)
4. Trotman, A., Lalmas, M.: The Interpretation of CAS. In: Fuhr, N., Lalmas, M., Malik, S., Kazai, G. (eds.) INEX 2005. LNCS, vol. 3977, pp. 58–71. Springer, Heidelberg (2006)
5. Amer-Yahia, S., Koudas, N., Marian, A., Srivastava, D., Toman, D.: Structure and Content Scoring for XML. In: Proceedings of VLDB 2005, pp. 361–372 (2005)
6. Marian, A., Amer-Yahia, S., Koudas, N., Srivastava, D.: Adaptive Processing of Top-K Queries in XML. In: Proceedings of ICDE 2005, pp. 162–173 (2005)
7. Baeza-Yates, R., Ribeiro-Neto, B.: Modern Information Retrieval. Addison-Wesley, Reading (1999)
8. Trotman, A., Sigurbjörnsson, B.: Narrowed Extended XPath I (NEXI). In: Fuhr, N., Lalmas, M., Malik, S., Szlávik, Z. (eds.) INEX 2004. LNCS, vol. 3493, pp. 16–40. Springer, Heidelberg (2005)
9. Theobald, M., Schenkel, R., Weikum, G.: An Efficient and Versatile Query Engine for TopX Search. In: Proceedings of VLDB 2005, pp. 625–636 (2005)
10. Fagin, R., Wimmers, E.L.: A Formula for Incorporating Weights into Scoring Rules. Theoretical Computer Science 239(2), 309–338 (2000)
11. Levenshtein, V.I.: Binary codes capable of correcting deletions, insertions, and reversals. Soviet Physics Doklady 10(8), 707–710 (1966)
12. Buratti, G.: A Model and an Algebra for Semi-Structured and Full-Text Queries (Ph.D. Thesis). Technical Report UBLCS-2007-03, University of Bologna (2007)

Role Based Access to Support Collaboration in Healthcare

Alysia Skilton[1], W. Alex Gray[1], Omnia Allam[1], Dave Morry[2],
and Hazel Bailey[2]

[1] Cardiff School of Computer Science, Cardiff University, Queen's Buildings, 5 The Parade,
Roath, Cardiff CF24 3AA, UK
[2] Velindre Hospital, Whitchurch, Cardiff, CF14 2TL, UK
A.Skilton@cs.cf.ac.uk

Abstract. Traditional healthcare information systems have been developed and organized as silos. However, recent changes in healthcare delivery models have resulted in the widespread creation of MultiDisciplinary care Teams (MDTs). These teams consist of practitioners with a variety of specialties often sited at different locations [1, 2]. This collaborative approach has led to a significant shift in information needs. However, existing information systems are not designed to support this new level of collaboration and technical support for practitioners has not kept pace with changing needs [3]. As every case is different, one of the many information challenges of this new paradigm is that of providing appropriate views to practitioners based on the unique needs of the patient as well as the practitioner's role with that patient. This paper will describe an individualized role based approach to data views for healthcare providers using an independent system to access data stored in existing healthcare information systems.

Keywords. virtual organization, role based access, multidisciplinary care team.

1 Introduction

The traditional healthcare delivery model has been for practitioners with different specialties to work independently [4]. In keeping with this, legacy healthcare information systems are typically discipline organised silos [3]. In recent years, however, there has been an ongoing shift towards interdisciplinary collaboration in patient care resulting in the widespread development of MultiDisciplinary care Teams (MDTs) which consist of practitioners from a variety of specialties often working from different locations [1, 2]. This shift in working practice has led to significant changes in information needs and an increased need for information sharing among practitioners which has given rise to a variety of challenges with regard to appropriate and timely provision of information [5, 6]. In particular, exchange of information between practitioners at different sites is rarely handled by existing information systems, resulting in delays in information transfer or even a complete inability to access relevant information about a patient's condition. Additionally, practitioners with different specialties

A. Gray, K. Jeffery, and J. Shao (Eds.): BNCOD 2008, LNCS 5071, pp. 177–180, 2008.

will have varied information needs and these will again vary depending on the patient's condition. Medico-legal as well as data protection issues further require that information access be reasonable and traceable.

This paper will focus on the challenge of providing appropriate and flexible views to support collaboration between team members. The patient-centric nature of MDTs means that information from a variety of sources should be brought together and organized by patient, rather than by condition. Further, each member of the MDT will have different information requirements based on team role and patient condition. Because the move towards a collaborative approach is recent and ongoing, exact information requirements are not yet fully determined and are expected to continue changing as working practices are established and standardized. This paper will describe one approach to providing MDT members with flexible and appropriate access to patient records.

2 VOICCE Proposal

A virtual organisation (VO) approach that utilises existing healthcare information systems in a modified federation architecture is proposed [7]. The primary focus of the VOICCE (Virtual Organisation access to Information Sources and Services in a Collaborative Cancer care Environment) system is coordination of information and systems to provide appropriate, flexible, and comprehensive patient-centric information access to MDT members. This is achieved through applying a VO structure for existing MDTs and determining access to appropriate patient-focused information based on diagnosis, the nature or emphasis of the MDT, the member's team role, and the treatment stage. MDTs vary widely in structure and working style so the system must be flexible enough to support these variations.

The system consists of a management database, a software component, and included legacy databases. The management database stores access information- user, patient, and site information as well as associations between practitioners, patients, and care teams. The software component accesses the management database to determine information requirements and sources, retrieves required information from constituent systems, and displays the information to the user. A more complete description of the proposed system structure can be found in [7].

In addition to individual legacy healthcare information systems, the VOICCE project will be compatible with other systems including ISCO/CaNISC, the all Wales cancer information system [8] and the Welsh Clinical Portal [9]. Further stages of the project will also incorporate ongoing related research in our research group including an integrated care pathway workflow and provision of specific information to patients based on their individual diagnoses [10, 11].

3 Role Based Access

To increase flexibility of views we propose the inclusion of a small, local database at each site which will keep track of which items should be displayed for each role. This should allow significant flexibility in determining what information is provided while also allowing the system to be easily evolved when information needs change or new functionality is provided.

To achieve the desired flexibility the new database will associate interface components with specific roles. Interface components (windows, buttons, etc) will be classified as mandatory (always displayed) or optional. Mandatory items may be screens that are available to all users or items which are always displayed on a particular screen (whether or not the screen itself is always available). Optional items must then be assigned identifiers which can be associated with relevant team roles/views as illustrated in figure 1:

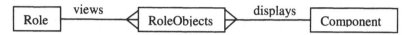

Fig. 1. ER diagram for proposed view definition database

Introducing this database will increase the adaptability and evolvability of the VOICCE system in several ways. First, it allows new functionality to be added to the system with minimal hassle. Rather than rebuilding each view, new services can be added by including a new class (or classes) into the software and simply adding a few rows to the RoleObject table for affected roles. Similarly, as information needs change views can be easily adapted or new views created by adding or removing rows from the RoleObjects table. By storing the databases locally there is potential for each site to develop site-specific (or individualised) roles to best support local working practices.

This work is in its early stages and potential challenges to continued development are currently being evaluated. First, administration and long-term maintenance of the system must be considered. For example, who will have rights to alter each view, who will be responsible for updating the database when new services are introduced, and can/should this be done automatically. Secondly, additional database retrievals will decrease overall system performance. While the small size and local hosting of the proposed database should minimize this problem, the actual impact must be evaluated. Finally, if local sites are allowed to alter pre-defined views, there must be some way of recovering or returning to these 'standard' views in case of problems.

4 Conclusion

This paper presents an outline design for a healthcare information system to support collaboration among healthcare teams. Because requirements for such a system will vary between practitioners, patients, and over time, evolvability and flexibility of the system has been emphasised. In order to provide maximum adaptability we propose that views should be determined through a simple local database which associates MDT members with appropriate information access.

This work is still in early stages and development of a prototype system is underway for purposes of evaluation. Potential benefits and challenges of the system have been considered. Benefits include increased flexibility and potential for personalisation of views. Challenges include maintenance of the database and potential impacts on overall system performance.

The emphasis on supporting collaboration while providing individualised and flexible access differentiates this work from other information sharing projects in healthcare. The work also concentrates on supporting the patient-centric view at the heart of the MDT and meeting the needs of the individual team members to access information about a patient from the available information resources.

References

1. Welsh Office, RCGP Summary Paper: Quality Care and Clinical Excellence, NHS Wales (1998)
2. Department of Health. The New NHS (1997) (accessed 10/01/2007), http://www.archive.official-documents.co.uk/document/doh/newnhs/forward.htm
3. Department of Health. Shifting the Balance of Power: The Next Steps, p. 55 (2002)
4. Informing Healthcare. Informing Healthcare Home (2007) (accessed 10/11/2007), http://www.wales.nhs.uk/IHC/
5. Allam, O.: A Holistic Analysis Approach to Facilitating Communication Between GPs and Cancer Care Teams, PhD Dissertation, Cardiff University (2006)
6. Street, A., Blackford, J.: Communication Issues for the Interdisciplinary Community Palliative Care Team. Journal of Clinical Nursing 10, 643–650 (2001)
7. Skilton, A., et al.: A New Approach to Connecting Information Systems in Healthcare. In: Proceedings of 24th Annual British National Conference on Databases, Glasgow (2007)
8. Allam, O., et al.: The ISCO Information System: a Model of Coexistence with the Integrated National Care Record. In: Proceedings of 9th International Symposium for Health Information Management Research (2004)
9. Informing Healtcare. Welsh Clinical Portal (2007) (accessed 23/01/2008), http://www.wales.nhs.uk/ihc/page.cfm?pid=23396
10. Ivins, W., et al.: Supporting Coordination of Integrated Care Pathways with Workflow Technology. In: 11th International Symposium of Health Information Management Research (2006)
11. Al-Busaidi, A., et al.: Personalising Web Information for Patients: Linking Patient Medical Data with the Web via a Patient Personal Knowledge Base. Health Informatics Journal 12, 27–39 (2006)

A Peer-to-Peer Database Server

John Colquhoun and Paul Watson

School of Computing Science, Newcastle University, Newcastle-upon-Tyne, NE1 7RU,
United Kingdom
{John.Colquhoun,Paul.Watson}@ncl.ac.uk

Abstract. Database systems have traditionally used a Client-Server architecture. If the server becomes overloaded, clients will experience an increase in query response time, and in the worst case the server may be unable to provide any service at all.

In the domain of file-sharing, the problem of server overloading has been successfully addressed by the use of Peer-to-Peer (P2P) techniques in which clients (peers) supply files – or pieces of files – to each other. This paper describes the Wigan P2P Database System, which was designed to investigate how P2P techniques for reducing server load and so increasing system scalability can be applied successfully in a database environment. Peers cache query results and use them to satisfy each other's queries. Wigan is based on the popular BitTorrent file-sharing protocol.

1 Introduction

In this paper we describe Wigan – a P2P database system designed to investigate whether the techniques used by file-sharing systems such as BitTorrent can be applied to building highly scalable database systems. We believe that this work is timely as almost all computers, including desktop PCs, now have significant quantities of spare resources (CPU, memory, disk, network bandwidth) that could potentially be used to reduce the load on a database server, if only algorithms to allow this could be designed. In Wigan, clients cache the results of their queries and these are then used to answer subsequent queries from themselves and other clients, so reducing the load on the server.

2 System Architecture

The Wigan system is derived from BitTorrent and hence the three major components in Wigan have the same names and basic roles as their counterparts in BitTorrent – the Seed, the Peers and the Tracker. Each is now discussed in turn.

The Seed: A Wigan seed possesses a complete copy of the database. Initially, the seed answers all queries (acting as if it were the server in a traditional client-server database). If at any time a downloading peer submits a query which cannot be answered by any of the other available peers, the query is answered by the seed.

A. Gray, K. Jeffery, and J. Shao (Eds.): BNCOD 2008, LNCS 5071, pp. 181–184, 2008.

The Peers: The peers send out queries and receive the results. However, they also cache the results of the queries in a local database server. This allows them to answer each other's queries, so taking the load away from the seed and providing greater scalability.

The Tracker: The central component in the Wigan system is the Tracker. This performs the same basic functionality as its namesake in BitTorrent in that it provides the downloading peers with a list of possible uploaders for the query they are requesting. However, due to the increased complexity of database queries when compared to file access, the Wigan Tracker has much more functionality and complexity. When a peer issues a query, it is sent first to the Tracker. This holds information on all the queries that have already been executed, along with the id of the peer that is caching the result. These "adverts" are stored in a canonical form representing the tables, columns and conditions on these columns for each query.

When a query arrives at the Tracker from a peer, it checks these adverts to see which other peers could answer the query. In Wigan, it is possible for a downloader's query to match exactly with an advertisement. It is also possible that the query is a proper subset of one or more advertisements. An example in SQL would be:

Query: `SELECT item FROM parts WHERE cost <= 10`
Advert1: `SELECT item FROM parts WHERE cost <= 10`
Advert2: `SELECT item FROM parts WHERE cost <= 15`

Both adverts can satisfy the query. On arrival at the Tracker, the downloader's query is converted into the same canonical form as is used to store the adverts. The Tracker then retrieves all adverts which contain the tables and columns in the downloader's query. This initial selection process removes the advertisements which do not have all of the required columns or contain none of the tables that appear in the downloader's query. The Tracker then examines all of these advertisements to check that the conditions in the "WHERE" clause of the advertisement do not prevent the advertisement from resolving the downloader's query. The result of the final part of the selection process is a collection of adverts which can all resolve the downloader's query.

This collection of adverts may include a selection of different queries, given that we have already shown how one query may be resolved by an advert for a different query, providing that query is a proper subset of the advert. To enable a downloader to distinguish between adverts for different queries, the Tracker will group the adverts by query, stating for each query how many pieces the downloader should receive. This ensures the downloader is aware of when it can stop sending requests for data.

The process of downloading and uploading in Wigan will now be described. A new downloader must contact the Tracker with the SQL query that it wishes to execute. The Tracker, using the processes described above, will return a list of suitable adverts grouped by query and the downloader must first select a group. For performance reasons, the downloader will choose those queries which exactly match the one it is searching for if this is possible or if it is not, start with the closest to an exact match.

The downloader contacts a randomly selected uploader peer from its chosen query group and submits a query for the first piece. If the uploader is able to accommodate a new downloader, it will perform the query and return all tuples from the first piece which matches the conditions of the query. A header with the query, piece number and a query ID is included so that if a downloader is receiving multiple queries simultaneously it can correlate responses to requests. Note that if there is no data in the first piece which matches the conditions of the query, the uploader will still send a response, containing just the header and no tuples. This prevents the downloader from assuming the response has gone missing due to a network or peer failure.

Once the first piece has arrived, the downloader stores the data in its local database and then makes a request for the next piece (potentially to a different peer). This process continues until the downloader has received all of the pieces. The downloader knows when this point occurs because the Tracker has informed it of the number of pieces. To improve performance, query requests for different pieces can be sent to a set of peers in parallel.

3   Evaluation

We have developed a simulator of the Wigan system using the SimJava tool [1] alongside a simulator of a Client-Server database system. This has enabled us to explore the differences in behaviour for systems with up to several thousand clients. This simulator was connected to a SQLServer database storing the data from the Transaction Processing Council's TPC-H benchmark [2]. The Wigan simulator was initially developed as a simulation of BitTorrent, calibrated against experimental results from real BitTorrent systems [3]. It was then developed into a simulation of Wigan. In the simulator, query execution itself was not simulated. Instead, each peer that received a query contacted the underlying database and executed a real query. This saved considerable implementation effort. The experiment we present here examined the behaviour for workloads consisting of multiple queries. In this experiment, there were five different small queries. The same set of queries was used for both the P2P and the Client-Server experiments. In Wigan, 2,600 peers were used. One of these was the seed and the first five warmed the cache. These five peers each submitted one of the five queries. There was a two minute gap to allow these five peers more than enough time to download and begin advertising. The remaining peers picked one of the five queries at random and submitted queries at a rate of six queries per second.

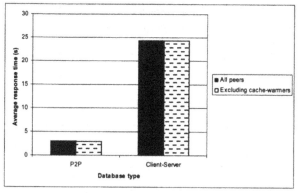

Fig. 1. Average response times for the warm-cache experiments with five repeating queries

In the Client-Server system, there was one server and 2,599 clients. To make a fair comparison with Wigan, the first five peers each submitted one of the five queries and there was a two minute gap before the remaining peers began submitting one of the five queries chosen at random. The rate was kept at six queries per second.

The response times are shown in Fig. 1. Two sets of response times are shown for each system in Fig. 1 – including and excluding the cache-warmers.

The cache-warming peers are able to host the first rush of downloaders when the continual query stream begins and once these start advertising, they can also provide queries to future downloaders.

4 Conclusions

This paper has introduced the Wigan P2P Database System, a database architecture derived from the popular BitTorrent file-sharing protocol. This is, to our knowledge, the first P2P database system designed with a focus on scaling up the performance of a single database server, rather than on federating distributed databases. The combination of the Tracker and seed, described in this paper, ensures that peers will always receive a correct and complete set of results for their queries if that is possible.

The results obtained from simulation show that P2P techniques can be applied to scaling database servers, and can, in certain cases, outperform a client-server database. Interestingly, when a database is first published through Wigan, the initial performance characteristics match that of the "flashcrowd" effect found in filesharing through BitTorrent. However, once this initial period is over the system behaviour demonstrates the power of the P2P approach in achieving performance scalability.

Work on Wigan is continuing. This includes an investigation into the best algorithms for implementing joins in a P2P environment. We are also building a "native" (non-simulated) version of Wigan to support a further range of experiments.

References

1. The SimJava tool, http://www.dcs.ed.ac.uk/home/hase/simjava/
2. Transaction Processing Council TPC-H Benchmark, http://www.tpc.org/tpch/
3. Izal, M., Urvoy-Keller, G., Biersack, E.W., Felber, P., Hamra, A.A., Garcés-Erice, L.: Dissecting BitTorrent: Five Months in a Torrent's Lifetime. In: Barakat, C., Pratt, I. (eds.) PAM 2004. LNCS, vol. 3015. Springer, Heidelberg (2004)

Checking the Integrity Constraints of Mobile Databases with Three-Level Model

Hamidah Ibrahim[1], Zarina Dzolkhifli[1], and Praveen Madiraju[2]

[1] Department of Computer Science
Faculty of Computer Science and Information Technology
Universiti Putra Malaysia, 43400 Serdang, Selangor, Malaysia
hamidah@fsktm.upm.edu.my, zarinadzolkhifli@yahoo.com
[2] Department of Mathematics, Statistics, and Computer Science
Marquette University, USA
praveen@mscs.mu.edu

Abstract. In a mobile environment, due to the various constraints inherited from limitations of wireless communication and mobile devices, checking for integrity constraints to maintain the consistent state of mobile databases is an important issue that needs to be addressed. Hence, in this paper we propose Three-Level (3-L) model, wherein the process of constraint checking is realized at three different levels. Here, we use sufficient and complete tests together with the idea of caching relevant data items during the relocation period for checking the integrity constraints. This has improved the checking mechanism by preventing delays during the process of checking constraints and performing the update. Also, the 3-L model reduces the amount of data accessed given that much of the tasks are performed at the mobile host. Hence, our model speeds up the checking process.

Keywords: Mobile databases, integrity constraints, constraint checking.

1 Introduction

Recently, there has been an increasing interest in mobile computing due to the rapid advances in wireless communication and portable computing technologies. Massive research efforts from academia and industry have been put forth to support a new class of mobile applications such as just-in-time stock trading, mobile health services, mobile commerce, and mobile games as well as migrating the normal conventional applications to mobile applications. Users of these applications can access information at any place at any time via mobile computers and devices such as mobile phone, palmtops, laptops, and PDA [3].

While technology has been rapidly advancing, various constraints inherited from limitations of wireless communication and mobile devices remain primary challenges in the design and implementation of mobile systems and applications. These constraints include: limited client capability, limited bandwidth, weak connectivity and user mobility. Mobile devices generally have poor resources and thus it is usually

A. Gray, K. Jeffery, and J. Shao (Eds.): BNCOD 2008, LNCS 5071, pp. 185–188, 2008.

impossible for them to store all data items in the network. In addition, disconnections occur frequently, which may be intentional (e.g., to save battery power) or unintentional (e.g., due to signal interference). These constraints make the wireless and mobile computing environments uniquely different from a conventional wired server/client environment [3].

A general architecture of a mobile environment consists of base stations (BS) and mobile hosts (MH). The base station is a stationary component in the model and is responsible for a small geographic area called a cell. They are connected to each other through fixed networks. The mobile host is the mobile component of the model and may move from one cell to another. These mobile hosts communicate with the base stations through wireless networks. Since a mobile host is not capable of storing all data items in the network, thus it must share some data item with a database in the fixed network. Any update operation or transaction that occurs at the mobile host must guarantee *database consistency*. A database state is said to be consistent if the database satisfies a set of statements, called *integrity constraints*, which specify those configurations of the data that are considered semantically correct. The process of ensuring that the integrity constraints are satisfied by the database after it has been updated is termed *constraint checking*, which generally involves the execution of *integrity tests*. In a mobile environment, checking the integrity constraints to ensure the correctness of the database spans at least the mobile host and one other database (node), and thus the update is no longer local but rather distributed [4]. As mentioned in [4], the major problem in the mobile environment are unbounded and unpredictable delays can affect not only the update but other updates running at both the mobile and the base stations, which is clearly not acceptable for most applications. With the same intuition as [4], we address the challenge of extending the data consistency maintenance to cover disconnected and mobile operations.

This paper is organized as follows. In Section 2, the previous works related to this research are presented. Section 3 describes the Three-Level (3-L) model. Conclusions are presented in the final section 4.

2   Related Work

Much of the research concerning integrity constraint checking construct efficient integrity tests, for a given integrity constraint and its relevant update operation, but these approaches are mostly designed for a centralized environment. As centralized environment has only a single site, the approaches concentrate on improving the checking mechanism by minimizing the amount of data to be accessed during the checking process. Hence, these methods are not suitable for mobile environment as the checking process often spans multiple nodes.

Although there are a few studies that have been conducted to improve the checking mechanism by reducing the amount of data transferred across the network in distributed databases such as [2], but these approaches are not suitable for mobile databases. These approaches reformulate the global constraints into local constraints (local tests) with an implicit assumption that all sites are available, which is not true in mobile environment, where a mobile unit may be disconnected for long periods. Even though failure is considered in the distributed environment, but none of the approach cater failure at the node where the update is being executed, i.e. disconnection at the target site.

Other approaches such as [1] focus on the problems of checking integrity constraints in parallel databases. These approaches are not suitable for mobile databases as the intention of their approach is to speed up the checking process by performing the checking concurrently at several nodes. To the best of our knowledge, PROMOTION [4] is the only work that addresses the issues of checking integrity constraints in mobile databases. Our proposed model differs from the approach proposed in [4] since it is intended to cater for the important and frequently used integrity constraints, i.e. those that are used in database application. Mazumdar's approach [4] is restricted to set-based constraints (equality and inequality constraints).

3 The Three-Level (3-L) Model

The Three-Level (3-L) model consists of three distinct levels, as depicted in Figure 1. When a user submits an update operation through a mobile host, the list of constraints, IC, at the mobile host is checked. Violation of any of the constraints will abort the operation. Otherwise, if the checking process does not require information from the other sites, then IC is said to be satisfied and the update operation is safe to be performed. The second level is invoked if the information stored at the mobile host is not sufficient to validate whether the constraint IC is violated or not. At the first level, the process of checking the constraints spans only the mobile host, i.e. local to the mobile host. The type of test suitable for this level is the sufficient test with the existential quantifier since the mobile host has limited capacity and thus the information (relations) stored at the mobile host is limited. For example, the test $(\exists t \exists v \exists w)(employee(t, b, v, w))$ is a sufficient test, which checks the existence of at least an employee who is currently working in the department b. If such information is available at the mobile host, then we conclude that the initial constraint is satisfied. If there is no such information, then further checking needs to be performed. The properties of the sufficient test can be *upgraded* to be similar to the properties of the complete test if all possibilities of values for the required data item are cached to the mobile hosts. For example, referring to the above sufficient test one notices that comparison is performed against the values of the *dno*. Assuming that the company has four departments, and a vertical fragment of the *department* table consisting of the distinct *dno* is cached to the mobile host, then performing the test against these data items can verify whether the test is satisfied or not, and eventually verify if the initial constraint is satisfied or violated. Caching can be performed during the relocation period.

The second level commences if the mobile host failed to validate the truth of the IC. The base station in the current position of the mobile host is responsible for checking the constraints. The base station checks the validity of the constraints against the data stored at its location. At this level, the process of checking the constraints spans the current cell of the mobile host, i.e. local to a cell of the current location of the mobile host. The types of test suitable for this level are the sufficient test and the complete test with the existential quantifier. If the information stored at the base station is not sufficient then the next level is invoked. However, if violation is detected then the base station notifies the mobile host to abort the update operation. The update operation is safe to be performed if no violation is detected.

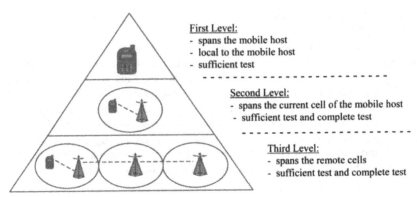

First Level:
- spans the mobile host
- local to the mobile host
- sufficient test

Second Level:
- spans the current cell of the mobile host
- sufficient test and complete test

Third Level:
- spans the remote cells
- sufficient test and complete test

Fig. 1. The Three-Level (3-L) model

The next level, third level, spans the remote base station(s), checks the validity of the constraints against the data stored at the remote site(s). Depending on the protocol of the mobile environment, either the flooding technique or the broadcasting technique is used to perform the constraint checking at this level. Here, the types of test that can be adopted are sufficient as well as complete test.

4 Conclusion

This paper has presented the Three-Level (3-L) model, which is designed for checking database integrity in a mobile environment. This model not only treats the issue of disconnection but also reduces the amount of data accessed during the process of checking the consistency of the mobile databases given that much of the tasks are performed at the mobile host. This is achieved by adopting the simplified forms of integrity constraints, namely: sufficient and complete tests, together with the idea of caching the relevant data items during the relocation period. Eventually the checking mechanism of mobile databases is improved as delay during the process of checking the integrity constraints and performing the update is reduced.

References

1. Hanandeh, F.A.H.: Integrity Constraints Maintenance for Parallel Databases. PhD Thesis, UPM, Malaysia (2006)
2. Ibrahim, H., Alwan, A.A., Udzir, N.I: Checking Integrity Constraints with Various Types of Integrity Tests for Distributed Databases. In: Proceedings of the Eighth International Conference on Parallel and Distributed Computing Applications and Technologies (PDCAT), pp. 151–152 (2007)
3. Ken, C.K.L., Wang-Chien, L., Sanjay, M.: Pervasive Data Access in Wireless and Mobile Computing Environments. Journal of Wireless Communications and Mobile Computing (2006)
4. Mazumdar, S., Chrysanthis, P.K.: Localization of Integrity Constraints in Mobile Databases and Specification in PRO-MOTION. In: Proceedings of the Mobile Networks and Applications, pp. 481–490 (2004)

Finding Data Resources in a Virtual Observatory Using SKOS Vocabularies

Alasdair J.G. Gray[1], Norman Gray[2], and Iadh Ounis[1]

[1] Computing Science, University of Glasgow, Glasgow, UK
[2] Physics and Astronomy, University of Leicester, Leicester, UK

Abstract. One problem faced by astronomers using the virtual observatory is finding which of the multitude of data resources is relevant for them. The current tool, VOExplorer, relies on matching searches against tags provided by the resources. This paper shows how SKOS encoded vocabularies can be used to improve the search results. The techniques are general and applicable to any loose collaborations sharing their resources.

1 Introduction

There are many astronomical distributed computing resources and data repositories, ranging from small per-instrument data centres to large specialist archives curating data from many instruments. Astronomers have traditionally focused on one part of the electromagnetic spectrum, and become familiar with that particular terminology and the associated data resources. One goal of the various Virtual Observatory (VO) projects, as mediated by the International Virtual Observatory Alliance (IVOA; www.ivoa.net), is to facilitate multi-wavelength astronomy—combining data taken in multiple wavelength domains, such as radio and X-ray. However, increasing the number of available resources, as curated in the IVOA repository, does not help if astronomers are unable to locate relevant ones.

This paper demonstrates how searches for relevant resources can be improved by (i) using controlled vocabularies to tag resources, and (ii) exploiting the semantic relationships that exist between the vocabulary terms. The first improvement eliminates the current situation of ambiguity between the meanings of tags associated with a resource and search terms, which should prevent irrelevant resources being returned. The second improvement will allow the application to explore alternative search terms available in the vocabularies that may have been used to tag relevant resources, including terms that are unfamiliar to the user.

2 Controlled Vocabularies in Astronomy

Vocabularies formalise and limit the terminology used within a domain of discourse, while defining the semantic relationships between them [2]. A vocabulary contains a set of *concepts* each of which captures the preferred label, alternative labels, definition, and notes about one term in the domain. A concept c_1

A. Gray, K. Jeffery, and J. Shao (Eds.): BNCOD 2008, LNCS 5071, pp. 189–192, 2008.

```
<#PlanetSatellite>
    a skos:Concept;
    skos:altLabel "Natural satellite"@en, "Celestial satellite"@en;
    skos:broader <#Planet>, <#Satellite>;
    skos:definition "A celestial body orbiting a planet."@en;
    skos:inScheme <>;
    skos:narrower <#Moon>, <#Titan>;
    skos:prefLabel "Planet satellite"@en, "Satellite planetaire"@fr;
    skos:related <#ArtificialSatellite> .
```

Fig. 1. The SKOS encoding, in turtle notation [1], for an astronomomic vocabulary concept. Note that "<>" refers to the current document.

Table 1. A summary of the astronomical vocabularies available in SKOS

Vocabulary	Publisher	Purpose	Number of Concepts
Journal Keywords	Journal publishers	Tagging articles to aid retrieval	311
Astronomy Outreach Imagery Metadata	IVOA	Tagging images for dissemination	208
The Astronomy Thesaurus	IAU	Library cataloguing	2551
The IVOA Thesaurus	IVOA	Update of the Astronomy Thesaurus	2890
Universal Content Descriptors	IVOA	Labelling data repository column headings	473

can be related to another c_2 as a *broader term* (c_2 is more general), a *narrower term* (c_2 is more specific), or a *related term* (c_2 shares an association). The broader/narrower relationships define a poly-hierarchical structure for the concepts. It should be noted that the broader/narrower terms do **not** prescribe a subsumption relationship, but are given the operational definition that any resource retrieved via a given term would also be retrieved via its broader term.

The Simple Knowledge Organisation System (SKOS) [7] is a mechanism to share taxonomies, thesauri, and vocabularies, in a machine understandable way. Information about a concept and its relationships are made as RDF statements [5] (see Fig. 1 for an example), allowing systems to appear to "understand" the concepts in a vocabulary by exploring the relationships between them. SKOS provides looser semantics than OWL [6], which are ideal for modelling a vocabulary.

There exist many astronomical vocabularies developed by a variety of organisations. Each vocabulary has been developed to address the needs of their users, which may include astronomers, librarians, or the general public. For example, the journal keywords vocabulary is used to tag research articles with descriptions of their content in order to aid retrieval. The IVOA is using SKOS to formalise these existing and future vocabularies, and we have embarked on the specification [4] and development work to support this (summarised in Table 1).

SKOS also provides relationships for mapping concepts between vocabularies. These are *exact match* (equivalent concepts), *broad match* (a more general concept), *narrow match* (a more specific concept), and *related match* (an associated concept). Suggested best practice within the SKOS community is to declare the mappings between pairs of vocabularies in a separate document, since the mappings tend to be less authoritative than the relationships within a vocabulary. It should be noted that there is a substantial cost in identifying and maintaining mappings between vocabularies. As such, mappings are not required for each pair of vocabularies. Rather, if vocabulary A is mapped to vocabulary B and vocabulary B is mapped to vocabulary C, then vocabulary exploration techniques can be applied to follow links from A to C via B.

3   Finding Relevant Resources

A major problem facing astronomers using the VO is identifying which of the 12,383 registry resources[1] are *relevant* for their research: that is, which archives contain data about celestial bodies they are researching. Currently, they use VOExplorer [8], a keyword search interface that relies on resources providing "tags" to describe their content. The provider is free to pick any keywords for their tags. However, no semantic information such as a definition is provided.

When an astronomer searches for resources using VOExplorer, they are also free to select their own terms. There are no guarantees that the astronomers will pick the same terms as the resource providers, resulting in no matches; or that the meanings that they imagine for the terms will be the same as those used by the resources, resulting in irrelevant resources being returned (*cf. the term mismatch problem* [3]). Additionally, if the search term and the resource tag are too generic, then the user can be swamped with thousands of results.

Instead, we propose that resources should select tags from one of the existing SKOS encoded vocabularies published by the IVOA [4]. This would provide a definition for each tag, so all users of the system can apply the same meaning for it. Additionally, a user's query term can be automatically expanded, or refinements suggested, by exploring the semantic relationships between vocabulary concepts.

Consider a resource about the satellites of planets which has been tagged with the term Natural satellite and an astronomer searching for resources about the Earth's moon using the search term Moon. Using the current VOExplorer, the astronomer would not see the resource as a result since the search term and the tag are different. However, if the information contained in the vocabulary concept Planet satellite presented in Fig. 1 were used, then by the alternative label the application would know that the resource is about Planet satellites. Additionally, due to the narrower term Moon, it could reason that the resource is relevant for the astronomer's search[2].

We have produced a web service for exploring the vocabularies using the same general principles[3]. We plan to add semantic search facilities to VOExplorer and,

---

[1] Checked on 21 January 2008.

[2] The example could equally have relied on some mapping between concepts in different vocabularies to find related terms for the astronomer's search.

[3] http://explicator.dcs.gla.ac.uk/WebVocabularyExplorer/

once that is completed, we will work with astronomers to produce an evaluation of the search results returned by the improved service.

4   Conclusions

This paper considered how astronomers can be helped in locating and identifying relevant resources in a virtual observatory by using SKOS encoded vocabularies. We showed that the existing approach can be improved by exploring the semantic relationships between vocabulary concepts. The proposed framework wraps the knowledge contained in the vocabularies and could provide (i) improved precision of results by providing definitions for tags, (ii) increased recall of results by expanding search terms using equivalent terms from multiple vocabularies, and (iii) result set refinement based on the semantic relationships in the vocabularies. The techniques used to model the vocabularies, and mappings, are not specific to astronomy and could be applied to any sets of vocabularies. Additionally, the results returned by the service only rely on the vocabularies and mappings that it has available. Thus, the service could be used in other application areas by loading in suitable vocabularies and allowing an application front end to make use of the returned information.

Acknowledgements. We would like to acknowledge the work of the IVOA semantics group and the funding of the EPSRC grant number EP/E01142X/1.

References

1. Beckett, D., Berners-Lee, T.: Turtle - Terse RDF triple language. Team submission, w3c (2008), http://www.w3.org/TeamSubmission/turtle/
2. Structured vocabularies for information retrieval–guide–definitions, symbols and abbreviations. British Standard BS 8723-1:2005, BSI (2005)
3. Furnas, G.W., Landauer, T.K., Gomez, L.M., Dumais, S.T.: The vocabulary problem in human-system communication. CACM 30(11), 964–971 (1987)
4. Gray, A.J.G., Gray, N., Hessman, F.V., Preite Martinez, A. (eds.): Vocabularies in the virtual observatory. Working draft, ivoa, February 22 (2008), http://www.ivoa.net/Documents/latest/vocabularies.html
5. Manola, F., Miller, E. (eds.): RDF primer. Recommendation, w3c, February 10 (2004), http://www.w3.org/TR/rdf-primer/
6. McGuinness, D.L., van Harmelen, F. (eds.): OWL web ontology language overview. Recommendation, w3c, February 10 (2004), http://www.w3.org/TR/owl-features/
7. Miles, A., Bechhofer, S. (eds.): SKOS simple knowledge organization system reference. Working draft, w3c, January 25 (2008), http://www.w3.org/TR/skos-reference
8. Tedds, J., Winstanley, N., Lawrence, A., et al.: VOExplorer: Visualising data discovery in the virtual observatory. In: ADASS XVII, London (September 2007)

Progressive Ranking for Efficient Keyword Search over Relational Databases

Guoliang Li, Jianhua Feng, Feng Lin, and Lizhu Zhou

Department of Computer Science and Technology,
Tsinghua University, Beijing 100084, China
{liguoliang,fengjh,dcszlz}@tsinghua.edu.cn,
lin-f@mails.tsinghua.edu.cn

Abstract. The existing approaches of keyword search over relational databases usually first generate all possible results composed of relevant tuples and then sort them based on their individual ranks. These traditional methods are inefficient to identify the *top-k* answers with the highest ranks. This paper studies the problem of progressively identifying the *top-k* answers from the relational databases. The approach of progressively identifying the answers is very desirable as it generates the higher ranked results earlier thereby reducing the delay in responding to the user query. We have implemented our proposed method, and the experimental results show that our method outperforms existing state-of-the-art approaches and achieves much better search performance.

1 Introduction

Keyword search is a proven and widely accepted mechanism for querying in textual document systems and World Wide Web. The database research community has recently recognized the benefits of keyword search and has been introducing keyword search capability into relational databases [2,3,6], XML databases [7,8], and graph databases [6], and heterogenous data sources [9,10].

Keyword search has been proposed as an alternative means for querying the underlying databases, which is simple and yet familiar to most internet users as it only requires the input of some keywords. Although keyword search has been proven to be efficient for textual documents (e.g. HTML documents), the problem of keyword search on the structured data (e.g. relational databases) and the semi-structured data (e.g. XML documents) is not straightforward nor well studied. The alternative approaches of keyword search over relational databases can be broadly classified into candidate network based [4],[5] and Steiner tree based approaches [1],[2],[6]. The Steiner tree based methods first model tuples in the relational database as a graph, where nodes are tuples and edges are primary-foreign-key relationships, and then identify the Steiner trees which contain all or a part of input keywords to answer keyword queries by discovering the structural relationships of primary-foreign-keys on the fly. However, the Steiner tree based methods have been proven to be an NP-hard problem [1]. The candidate network based methods identify the answers composed of relevant tuples by

A. Gray, K. Jeffery, and J. Shao (Eds.): BNCOD 2008, LNCS 5071, pp. 193–197, 2008.

generating and extending the candidate networks, such as the primary-foreign-key relationships. However, most of existing literatures always fist compute the answers and then rank them.

Alternatively, we propose to efficiently and progressively identify the Steiner trees from relational databases. Clearly, our proposed method is more desirable since it generates the higher ranked results earlier thereby reducing the delay in responding to the user query. Furthermore, users in general specify queries in the form: "Give me the *top-k* answers". Hence, the approach of progressive keyword-based query processing is more desirable to identify the *top-k* answers with the highest ranks. Another advantage of the progressive query processing is that in some applications, it is perhaps impossible to generate all possible answers. Based on above observations, in this paper, we emphasize on the search efficiency of keyword search over relational databases and study the problem of progressive keyword-based query processing.

2   Progressive Ranking for Efficient Keyword Search

We model the tuples in the underlying relational databases as a graph $\mathcal{G}(\mathcal{V}, \mathcal{E})$, where nodes ($\mathcal{V}$) are tuples and edges ($\mathcal{E}$) are primary-foreign-key relationships. The graph $\mathcal{G}$ is an undirected graph if the direction, either from foreign key to primary key or from primary key to foreign key, is not the main concern. Otherwise, the graph is a directed graph where there are two edges (u, v) and (v, u) in $\mathcal{E}$ such that $(u, v) \neq (v, u)$. Graph $\mathcal{G}(\mathcal{V}, \mathcal{E})$ is weighted with a node-weight $\omega(v)$ for every node $v \in \mathcal{V}$ and an edge-weight $\omega(u, v)$ for every edge $(u, v) \in \mathcal{E}$, both of which are non-negative numbers.

To model the problem of identifying the *top-k* relevant answers from relational databases, we introduce the traditional Steiner tree problem [1].

Definition 1. MINIMUM STEINER TREE: *Given a database graph $\mathcal{G}(\mathcal{V}, \mathcal{E})$ and a subset $\mathcal{V}'$ of $\mathcal{V}$, the connected subtree of $\mathcal{G}$ which includes all vertices in $\mathcal{V}'$ is called a Steiner Tree. The problem of finding the Steiner tree with minimum cost, is called the minimum Steiner tree problem.*

However, the Steiner tree based methods have been proven to be an NP-hard problem [1], we cannot find the minimum Steiner trees in polynomial time. Alternatively, we can progressively identify the most relevant Steiner trees and return them first, and thus reduce the response time.

For each keyword, there are some nodes which contain them, we call them *content nodes*. There are also some nodes which indirectly contain them if there is a path from the node to another content node which contain the keyword. Accordingly, we can maintain an inverted lists for each term t, the entries are the nodes which directly or indirectly contain t. For the node n, which indirectly contains the keyword, we also preserve the path from n to the content node, which have shortest path to n. We call such path Key-Node-Path.

Accordingly, the inverted list is composed of a triple <node,Key-Node-Path, weight>. We denote the inverted list for term t as $\mathcal{I}_t$. For example, in Figure 1, we have the inverted lists for terms k_1 and k_2 as follows:

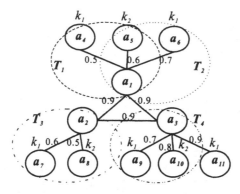

Fig. 1. A Running Example

$\mathcal{I}_{k_1}$=<$a_4, a_4, 0$>;<$a_6, a_6, 0$>;...;<a_1, a_1-$a_4, 0.5$>;<a_1, a_1-$a_6, 0.6$>;<a_2, a_2-$a_7, 0.6$>;<a_3, a_3-$a_9, 0.7$>;<a_3, a_3-$a_{11}, 0.9$>;...

$\mathcal{I}_{k_2}$=<$a_5, a_5, 0$>;<$a_8, a_8, 0$>;...;<a_8, a_8-$a_2, 0.5$>;<a_5, a_5-$a_1, 0.6$>;<a_{10}, a_{10}-$a_3, 0.8$>;...

Given a keyword query with n keywords, $k_1, k_2, ..., k_n$, we first identify the inverted lists of each k_i, and then identify the *top-k* nodes, which has the minimum weight sum. Finally, we combine the Key-Node-Paths to construct the Steiner tree and return the answers. Note that, we can employ the threshold-based techniques [10] to progressively and efficiently identify the *top-k* relevant nodes, thus we can employ progressive ranking for efficient keyword search over relational databases.

For example, given a keyword query with two input keywords $\{k_1, k_2\}$, we compute *top*-4 relevant results. We first retrieve the inverted lists for the two keywords. Then, we identify the *top*-4 relevant nodes with minimum weight sum, a_1, a_2, a_1, a_3 with cost respectively 1.1, 1.1, 1.3, 1.5. Finally, we combine the Key-Node-Paths to construct the *top*-4 relevant Steiner trees, i.e., T_1, T_3, T_2, and T_4. Accordingly, we can efficiently and progressively identify the answers.

Note that, we can find the accurate minimum Steiner tree for the keyword queries with the number of keywords no larger than 3. Even if the number of input keyword is larger than 3, we can approximately identify the answers and get the most relevant ones.

3   Experimental Study

We have implemented our proposed method. We report some experimental results in this section. We compared our algorithm with existing state-of-the-art algorithms BANKS-II [6] and DPBF [2]. We employed the DBLP[1] and IMDB[2](a movie database) datasets to compare these algorithms. The raw file of the DBLP dataset was about 420MB. IMDB contains approximately one million anonymous

---

[1] http://dblp.uni-trier.de/xml/

[2] http://www.grouplens.org/

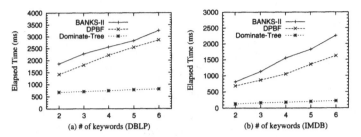

Fig. 2. Elapsed Time of Identifying Top-100 Results

ratings of 3900 movies made by 6040 users. We selected one hundred keyword queries with different numbers of input keywords to compare the algorithms. We computed the *top*-100 answers and compared the corresponding elapsed time. All the experiments were conducted on a computer with an Intel(R) Core(TM) 2@2.33GHz CPU, a 2GB of RAM and a 120G Disk running Windows XP, and all the algorithms were implemented in C++.

We evaluate the search efficiency for various algorithms. Figure 2 illustrates the experimental results, where KeyPath-Tree denotes our algorithm. We observe that our algorithm achieves much better search performance than the existing methods, which gives us rich confidence that the KeyPath-Tree based method can improve the search efficiency as we need not identify the answers by discovering the relationships between tuples in different relational tables on the fly. Alternatively, we adaptively identify the answer. Hence, our method leads to a significant improvement over the existing approaches. For instance, on IMDB dataset, KeyPath-Tree costs less than 200ms to answer the keyword queries with three input keywords while the other two methods involve more than 2000ms.

Acknowledgement

This work is partly supported by the National Natural Science Foundation of China under Grant No.60573094, the National High Technology Development 863 Program of China under Grant No.2007AA01Z152 and 2006AA01A101, the National Grand Fundamental Research 973 Program of China under Grant No.2006CB303103.

References

1. Bhalotia, G., Hulgeri, A., Nakhe, C., Chakrabarti, S., Sudarshan, S.: Keyword searching and browsing in databases using banks. In: ICDE, pp. 431–440 (2002)
2. Ding, B., Yu, J.X., Wang, S., et al.: Finding top-k min-cost connected trees in databases. In: ICDE (2007)
3. He, H., Wang, H., Yang, J., Yu, P.: Blinks: Ranked keyword searches on graphs. In: SIGMOD (2007)
4. Hristidis, V., Gravano, L., Papakonstantinou, Y.: Efficient ir-style keyword search over relational databases. In: VLDB, pp. 850–861 (2003)

5. Hristidis, V., Papakonstantinou, Y.: Discover: Keyword search in relational databases. In: VLDB, pp. 670–681 (2002)
6. Kacholia, V., Pandit, S., et al.: Bidirectional expansion for keyword search on graph databases. In: VLDB, pp. 505–516 (2005)
7. Li, G., Feng, J., Wang, J., Zhou, L.: Efficient keyword search for valuable lcas over xml documents. In: CIKM (2007)
8. Li, G., Feng, J., Wang, J., Zhou, L.: Race: Finding and ranking compact connected trees for keyword proximity search over xml documents. In: WWW (2008)
9. Li, G., Feng, J., Wang, J., Zhou, L.: Sailer: An effective search engine for unified retrieval of heterogeneous xml and web documents. In: WWW (2008)
10. Li, G., Ooi, B.C., Feng, J., Wang, J., Zhou, L.: 3-in-1: Efficient and adaptive keyword search on unstructured, semi-structured and structured data. In: SIGMOD (2008)

Semantic Matching for the Medical Domain

Jetendr Shamdasani*, Peter Bloodsworth, and Richard McClatchey

CCS Research Centre, CEMS Faculty, University of the West of England
Coldharbour Lane, Frenchay, Bristol BS16 1QY, UK
`firstname.lastname@cern.ch`

Abstract. This paper proposes some modifications to the SMatch algorithm that enables the semantic matching of medical terminologies using the Unified Medical Language System (UMLS) as a source of background knowledge. Semantic Matching is the process of discovering set theoretic relationships between differing data elements. Initial results from the domain of anatomy are presented that illustrate how semantic relationships can provide greater information during the ontology alignment process than equivalence relationships alone. The paper concludes by demonstrating how this is beneficial in the medical domain.

1 Introduction and Previous Work

Semantic Matching is the process of discovering set theoretic based relationships between differing concepts within two schemas or ontologies. The power of this approach is that it is able to identify a range of expressive relationships between concepts, in particular *less general* ($\sqsubseteq$), *more general* ($\sqsupseteq$) and *disjointness* ($\perp$) relations in addition to standard equivalence ($=$). In this paper we present a modification to the SMatch [1] system to make it applicable in the medical domain. The conventional SMatch method relies heavily on the use of the WordNet (WN) thesaurus [2]. The problem with using this resource is that it is too general, with an insufficient amount of medical terminology. This often leads to few meaningful relationships being returned when two medical ontologies are matched. A source of medical terminology is therefore required to drive the alignment process in a medical context. The UMLS [3] has been chosen for this purpose because of its wide coverage of clinical terms. We have modified the SMatch method to use the UMLS during the matching of medical ontologies. A prototype has been created and experimentation comparing the results from our extension to the output from the original SMatch system in a medical context has yielded promising results.

Research in the field of schema and ontology matching is active and several different approaches have been proposed. The work contained in [4] gives a more detailed review of the current research in this area. Semantic Matching involves the use of a structured background resource to extract matches between concepts

---

* Corresponding Author: This work has been funded by the Health-e-Child project (IST 2004-027749) Thanks to Tamas Hauer, Dmitry Rogulin and Andrew Branson.

A. Gray, K. Jeffery, and J. Shao (Eds.): BNCOD 2008, LNCS 5071, pp. 198–202, 2008.

in differing ontologies. Previous work has been conducted with use of a single background resource [5] or many background sources [6]. These approaches rely firstly on discovering terms in a background source, which they call "anchors" and then performing inferencing by using the knowledge gathered from the background knowledge by differing anchoring methods. Obviously this anchoring step relies on there being a certain amount of lexical overlap between the sources to be matched and the background resource. Our work concerns the modification of the SMatch approach by Ginunchiglia et al [1]. Section 2 presents our modifications to the SMatch system to incorporate the UMLS.

2   SMatch Applied to the Medical Domain

WN is primarily a *lexical resource* about the English language whereas the UMLS is a *conceptual resource* about the medical domain. WN contains information about the terms in the English language. Each term has a set of senses which denote a meaning of a term. The UMLS however is a collection of many different medical ontologies. Every concept has a CUI (Concept Unique Identifier) every CUI has high level relationships linking concepts. These are *PAR* (Parent), *CHD* (Child), *RB* (Broader Than), *RN* (Narrower Than), *SIB* (Sibling), *RO* (Other), *RL* (Similar), *SY* (Source Asserted Synonymy), *RQ* (Possible Synonymy). Every CUI is also annotated with a top level semantic type which is a high level categorization of the CUI. A full discussion of the UMLS is beyond the scope of this paper please see [3].

SMatch takes as input two trees and outputs a set of semantic relationships between concepts. Please see [1] for a detailed discussion of SMatch. In step one of their algorithm a label of a single node is taken and converted to an atomic formula in the Description Logics (DL) sense. This string is firstly preprocessed using normalisation and tokenization to be split into its corresponding parts. Individual tokens are looked up in WN and the corresponding senses are attached to create an atomic formula. Words in the English language denoting prepositions and conjunctions are ignored and are then converted to form logical connectives. These atomic formulae are then converted to DL based formulae. For example the string "Brain Stem" would be converted to $brain \sqcap stem$. A filter is applied according the relationships in WN to remove irrelevant senses. We firstly look up the whole label to see if a term does exist in the UMLS. If this is not so, then we search for tokens then we attach *concepts* (CUIs) from the UMLS. We also filter according to the semantic types of CUIs and disregard any CUIs which do not have the same semantic type. In step two a conjunction of the logical formulae to the root node is taken from a single node. There is also structural sense filtering performed, however this has not been implemented. Hence for the node in tree 1 which is labelled "Rhombencephalon", the formula for this node to its root would be $(rhobenchepalon \sqcap brain\ stem \sqcap brain)$. Each of these formulae would have corresponding CUIs attached.

In step three a variation of their WN matcher has been implemented which is the only matcher that is able to derive semantic relationships for this step. There

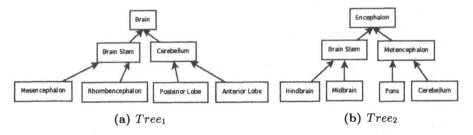

(a) $Tree_1$ (b) $Tree_2$

Fig. 1. The two input trees for our results comparison

is a mapping from the higher level relationships between CUIs and the semantic relationships which can be derived. The mappings are the following: (=) **Rule** - If A is connected via SY relationship to B or if A and B share the same CUI. (⊒) **Rule** - If a CUI of A is a PAR or RB of a CUI of B. (⊑) **Rule** - If a CUI of A CHD or a RN of B. (⊥) **Rule** - If a CUI of A is a SIB of B. At the end of this step a table of relationships is returned between concepts. If no relationship is found then a *null* relation is returned. In the fourth and final step we have kept their propositional reasoning approach to discover semantic relationships between different nodes. For an explanation of this step please see [1].

3   Results and Conclusion

Our preliminary evaluation is a comparison of our approach with our own implementation of the original SMatch approach. We have used the 2.0 version of WN and 2007AB version of the UMLS. Figure 1 shows our two tree inputs which are differing conceptualisations for the parts of the brain. $Tree_1$ (1a) and $Tree_2$ (1b) contain synonyms for medical terms as well as disjointness relationships between each other for this matching task. There are more and less general relationships present as well. The top half of table 1 shows the results from using the traditional SMatch approach using WN as a source of background knowledge and the bottom half of table 1 shows the results from our approach using the UMLS as a source of background knowledge. The *null* relationship states that there was no match found between the concepts.

The most interesting result is that the WN approach has not been able to discover disjointness (⊥) relationships between concepts at all. Although these terms do occur in the WN thesaurus, this is due to no appropriate relationships being present between the senses for these strings (antonymy) in the WN thesaurus. However the UMLS does not explicitly state antonymy between concepts therefore this is an interesting result. Several of the results generated by the pure SMatch approach are incorrect, for example Cerebellum is not = to Encephalon instead a ⊑ relationship should have been returned. Our approach does return this relationship correctly; this is also true with many of the other results in table 1. The SMatch approach was able to match Encephalon to Brain correctly as they are synonymous with each other, as did our approach. But these are very general terms in the English language, for example another synonym for

Table 1. These are the comparison of our results against the SMatch approach. The top half of the table shows the results from SMatch and the bottom half shows the results using the UMLS.

$Tree_1$ \ $Tree_2$	Encephalon	Metencephalon	Brain Stem	Midbrain	Hindbrain	Pons	Cerebellum
Brain	$=$	$\sqsupseteq$	$\sqsupseteq$	$\sqsupseteq$	$\sqsupseteq$	$\sqsupseteq$	$\sqsupseteq$
Brain Stem	$\sqsubseteq$	null	$=$	$=$	$=$	null	null
Mesencephalon	$\sqsubseteq$	null	$=$	$=$	$=$	null	null
Rhombencephalon	$\sqsubseteq$	null	$=$	$=$	$=$	null	$\sqsubseteq$
Cerebellum	$=$	$\sqsupseteq$	$\sqsupseteq$	$\sqsupseteq$	$\sqsupseteq$	$\sqsupseteq$	$=$
Posterior Lobe	$\sqsubseteq$	null	null	null	null	null	$\sqsupseteq$
Anterior Lobe	$\sqsubseteq$	null	null	null	null	null	$\sqsubseteq$
Brain	$=$	$\sqsupseteq$	$\sqsupseteq$	$\sqsupseteq$	$\sqsupseteq$	$\sqsupseteq$	$\sqsupseteq$
Brain Stem	$\sqsubseteq$	null	$=$	$\sqsupseteq$	$\sqsupseteq$	null	null
Mesencephalon	$\sqsubseteq$	$\perp$	$\sqsupseteq$	$=$	$\sqsubseteq$	$\perp$	$\perp$
Rhombencephalon	$\sqsubseteq$	null	$\sqsubseteq$	$\sqsupseteq$	$=$	null	null
Cerebellum	$\sqsubseteq$	$\sqsubseteq$	null	$\perp$	null	$\perp$	$=$
Posterior Lobe	$\sqsubseteq$	$\sqsubseteq$	null	$\perp$	null	$\perp$	$\sqsubseteq$
Anterior Lobe	$\sqsubseteq$	$\sqsubseteq$	null	$\perp$	null	$\perp$	$\sqsubseteq$

Brain in WN is Einstein which is incorrect for the medical domain. This clearly demonstrates that WN is a good source of lexical knowledge but not conceptual domain knowledge which is required in the medical world. The *null* relation does occur in our approach, this is mostly because this relationship could not be found using the UMLS Metathesaurus, as the UMLS grows our approach will yield more promising results. We also found that our predicted result for this test was identical to the results presented in table 1. The results have been verified by an expert in the medical domain and he was of the opinion that our approach was correct.

In this paper we have presented a modification of the original SMatch system for use in the medical domain. We have also shown that replacing a more general source of background knowledge with a more specific resource yields greater results. For our further work we are going to extend the SMatch algorithm to utilize differing forms of background knowledge which may yield interesting results. Differing reasoning schemes will also be investigated. An extensive evaluation against real world medical ontologies will be conducted following this.

References

1. Giunchiglia, F., et al.: Semantic Matching: Algorithms and Implementation. Journal of Data Semantics, 1–38 (2007)
2. Fellbaum, C.: WordNet: An Electronic Lexical Database. MIT Press, Cambridge (1998)
3. Brodenreider, O.: The Unified Medical Language System (UMLS): Integrating Biomedical Terminology. Nucleic Acids Research 32 (2004)

4. Euzenat, J., et al.: State of the Art on Ontology Alignment. Knowledge Web Deliverable (2.2.3) (2004)
5. Aleksovski, Z., et al.: Matching Unstructured Vocabularies using a Background Ontology. In: Staab, S., Svátek, V. (eds.) EKAW 2006. LNCS (LNAI), vol. 4248, Springer, Heidelberg (2006)
6. Sabou, M., et al.: Using the Semantic Web as Background Knowledge for Ontology Mapping. In: International Workshop on Ontology Matching (OM-2006) (2006)

Towards the Automatic Generation of Analytical End-User Tools Metadata for Data Warehouses*

Jesús Pardillo, Jose-Norberto Mazón, and Juan Trujillo

Department of Software and Computing Systems,
University of Alicante, Spain
{jesuspv,jnmazon,jtrujillo}@dlsi.ua.es

Abstract. Multidimensional models are used to obtain the required database metadata for implementing the data warehouse. Surprisingly, current approaches for multidimensional modelling overlook the necessity of additional data-cube metadata to allow end-user tools to query the data warehouse. To overcome this situation, we propose the use of the *Model Driven Architecture* (MDA) in order to automatically derive both kinds of metadata in a systematic and integrated way.

1 Introduction

A *Data Warehouse* (DW) is an integrated database that provides adequate information in a proper way to support decision making. The development of a DW is based on the *MultiDimensional* (MD) modelling [1,2] which structures data into facts and dimensions. The MD modelling resembles the traditional database design methods [3] because it is structured into a variety of steps during which a conceptual design phase is performed, whose results are transformed into a logical data model as the basis for the implementation. Actually, once a conceptual MD model is defined, two kinds of logical models must be derived tailored to specific technologies: (i) a model of the DW repository which determines the required database metadata for storing data in the DW, and (ii) a model of the data cubes which contains the necessary metadata to allow end-user tools to query the DW repository. Surprisingly, current approaches for MD modelling, only focus on the database metadata [3,4,5,6], thus overlooking the derivation of datacube metadata. However, current DW tools, such as *Oracle Warehouse Builder*, *Pentaho Business Intelligence*, or *Microsoft Analysis Services*, also need the definition of these metadata to properly analyse the DW. Therefore, the generation of end-user tool metadata is not properly integrated in the DW development process, thus being only tackled on an *ad-hoc* basis.

Considering these issues, an approach for DW development must provide mechanisms for enriching database metadata with end-user tool support in a

* This work has been partially supported by the ESPIA project (TIN2007-67078) and by the FPU grants AP2006-00332 and AP2005-1360 from the Spanish Ministry of Education and Science, and by the QUASIMODO project (PAC08-0157-0668) from the Castilla-La Mancha Ministry of Education and Science (Spain).

A. Gray, K. Jeffery, and J. Shao (Eds.): BNCOD 2008, LNCS 5071, pp. 203–206, 2008.

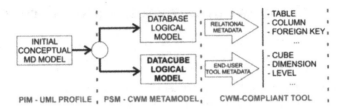

Fig. 1. Deriving both database and data-cube metadata from conceptual MD models

systematic and automatic way as pointed out in [7]. For this aim, we advocate the use of the *Model Driven Architecture* (MDA) for automatically deriving both database and datacube metadata (*Platform Specific Models*, PSM) from conceptual MD models (*Platform Independent Models*, PIM) as shown in Fig. 1. In our approach, we use the *Unified Modelling Language* (UML) [8] for specifying conceptual MD models by using our profile [9], and the *Common Warehouse Metamodel* (CWM) [8] for representing database and end-user tool metadata by means of several standard modelling languages.

2   Automatic Generation of End-User Tool Metadata

There are several business intelligence solutions to analyse data obtained from a DW: reporting, data mining, dashboards, and so on. In this paper, we focus on *On-Line Analytical Processing* (OLAP) tools since they are the foundation of data analysis for DWs. We consider the automatic generation of OLAP metadata from the conceptual MD models by extending our MDA-based approach presented in [10] for the database metadata derivation. To this aim, the *Query/View/Transformation* (QVT) language [8] is used to define a set of formal mappings between these modelling domains. These QVT transformations have been implemented by using the *medini QVT* tool[1] which is based on the *Eclipse* development platform.

To exemplify our approach, we have designed a PIM for analysing automobile sales. In Fig. 2, we show the *Autosales* MD model (left-hand side) which is transformed into the corresponding CWM OLAP metadata (right-hand side) by means of a QVT mapping (centre). The designed PIM consists of an *Autosale* fact (represented as ▦) and several dimensions (⌞): *Salespersons* involved on a sale, the sold *Auto*, the *Dealership*, the *Time* when the automobile is sold, and its *Customer*. Concerning the last one, we can establish a useful aggregation hierarchy (a roll-up sequence, ⊘, labelled with the same name, *e.g.*, *Standard*) based on places of residence (aggregation levels, ▰): customers (*CustomerData* level) can be aggregated into *Cities*, these into *Regions*, and finally regions into *States*. Moreover, we can specify two alternative paths to simplify the entire navigation: from customers to regions (*CityAlternate*) or directly from cities to states (*RegionAlternate*). We describe each aggregation level with dimension attributes (shown as ▱ᴬ), such as customer *BornDate*; or identifiers (▱), such

---

[1] URL: **http://projects.ikv.de/qvt** (March 2008).

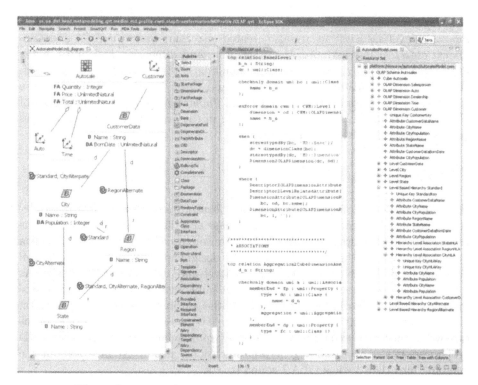

Fig. 2. Snapshot of the case study concerning automobile sales

as their own names. Moreover, we specify some analysis measures (FA) for the *Autosale* fact: *Quantity* of sold automobiles, their *Price* for sale, and their *Total* amount.

In order to map the PIM into a PSM for OLAP, firstly, the *Customer* OLAP dimension itself is generated and linked to the whole *Autosales* OLAP schema. Then, its *CustomerKey* unique key is created. For every level attribute, a CWM attribute is generated for the OLAP dimension, *e.g.*, *CityPopulation* and *RegionName*. Each descriptor is also attached to the *Customer* unique key. On the other hand, as an example of OLAP level generation, we focus on the *City* level. Typically, at first place, the *City* base in the MD model is mapped to the *City* level, attaching it to *Customer* OLAP dimension. Then, the descriptor relation is applied and the *CityKey* unique key and its *CityName* attribute (being part of the key) are created. In addition, the *Population* attribute in the PIM is mapped into its PSM counterpart.

Concerning the aggregation-hierarchy mapping, we only describe the *Standard* hierarchy. Once the *Customer* dimension has been mapped, the *Standard LevelBasedHierarchy* is generated to represent the whole *Standard* aggregation path. It is also created a *UniqueKey* and the *HierarchyLevelAssociations* related to the upper roll up: *StateHLA* and *RegionHLA* (also linked with their corresponding levels, *i.e.*, *State* and *Region*). Note that level associations are ordered, from the upper bound to the lower. Thus, the *StateHLA* is the first level (*i.e.*, the upper hierarchy level) and the *RegionHLA* the second one. Then, the other level associations are also created and connected: *CityHLA* and *CustomerDataHLA*. Furthermore, the descriptors and dimension attributes in the PIM must be mapped into their corresponding CWM attributes in the PSM. For instance, the *CustomerDataBornDate* and *CityPopulation* attributes in the PSM are created from the *BornDate* and *Population* dimension attributes of *CustomerData* and *City* levels, respectively. In this case study, their data types are omitted for the sake of simplicity.

3   Conclusions

Hitherto, no methodological approach has been proposed for the integrated development of DWs, considering both database and data-cube metadata. In this paper, we take advantage of using MDA to automatically derive these metadata from conceptual MD models. It allows DW designers to focus on the high-level description of the system instead of low-level and tool-dependent details. As a proof of concept, our proposal has been implemented in the *Eclipse* open-source platform, showing the feasibility of the automatic metadata generation in OLAP applications from the conceptual MD modelling. Our short-term future work consists of extending the proposed approach to consider advanced MD properties such as fact and degenerate dimensions, also investigating about the mapping into their logical OLAP counterparts.

References

1. Inmon, W.H.: Building the Data Warehouse. Wiley, Chichester (1996)
2. Kimball, R., Ross, M.: The Data Warehouse Toolkit. Wiley, Chichester (2002)
3. Hüsemann, B., Lechtenbörger, J., Vossen, G.: Conceptual data warehouse modeling. In: DMDW, p. 6 (2000)
4. Golfarelli, M., Maio, D., Rizzi, S.: The Dimensional Fact Model: A Conceptual Model for Data Warehouses. Int. J. Cooperative Inf. Syst. 7(2-3), 215–247 (1998)
5. Abelló, A., Samos, J., Saltor, F.: YAM^2: a multidimensional conceptual model extending UML. Inf. Syst. 31(6), 541–567 (2006)
6. Prat, N., Akoka, J., Comyn-Wattiau, I.: A UML-based data warehouse design method. Decis. Support Syst. 42(3), 1449–1473 (2006)
7. Rizzi, S., Abelló, A., Lechtenbörger, J., Trujillo, J.: Research in data warehouse modeling and design: dead or alive? In: DOLAP, pp. 3–10 (2006)
8. Object Management Group: Catalog of Specifications, http://www.omg.org
9. Luján-Mora, S., Trujillo, J., Song, I.Y.: A UML profile for multidimensional modeling in data warehouses. Data Knowl. Eng. 59(3), 725–769 (2006)
10. Mazón, J.N., Trujillo, J.: An MDA approach for the development of data warehouses. Decis. Support Syst. doi: 10.1016/j.dss.2006.12.003

The Hyperdatabase Project –
From the Vision to Realizations

Hans-Jörg Schek[1] and Heiko Schuldt[2]

[1] Professor Emeritus of the Swiss Federal Institute of Technology (ETH)
Zurich, Switzerland
[2] Database and Information Systems Group
Department of Computer Science, University of Basel, Switzerland

Abstract. In the future we expect an ever increasing number of data sources, reaching from traditional databases and large document and multimedia collections and information sources from the web, down to embedded information sources in mobile "smart" objects as they occur in a pervasive computing environment. Therefore not only the immense amount of information demands new thoughts but also the number of different information sources and their coordination poses a great challenge for the development of an appropriate information infrastructure. This was the starting point for the creation of the hyperdatabase project at ETH Zurich, almost 10 years ago. In view of this continuous, almost infinite "information space" that is distributed, heterogeneous, and changes continuously, the challenges for a new infrastructure for the information space were the following: First, it should provide convenient tools for accessing information via sophisticated search facilities and for combining or integrating search results from different sources. Second, the new infrastructure should facilitate distributed application development for analyzing and processing information. Third, transactional (workflow) processes should ensure consistent propagation of information changes and simultaneous invocations of several (web) services and data stream operations. Finally, the implementation of such an infrastructure should provide functions for recoverability, scalability, and availability by avoiding central global components and by self-configuration and adaptation features. In this paper we will elaborate some of the aspects in these areas and report on our hyperdatabase research and experiences with realizations in several projects such as ETHWorld. OSIRIS, PowerDB, and Digital Libraries started at ETH and are continued at the University of Basel.

Keywords: Middleware, Information Infrastructure, Hyperdatabases, Transactional Process, Digital Libraries.

1   Introduction

In the following we will describe the early driving forces that led us to establish our research vision and research directions. We first start with the situation from

A. Gray, K. Jeffery, and J. Shao (Eds.): BNCOD 2008, LNCS 5071, pp. 207–226, 2008.

the database perspective, summarized from [23]. A second main influence was clearly the demand coming from new media types such as images, audio, video and combinations and from the Web information explosion [22,25].

1.1   The Driving Forces from a Database Perspective

Relational database systems have been introduced more than thirty years ago. They have been considered as infrastructure and main platform for development of data-intensive applications. The notion of "Data Independence" [11] was a breakthrough because programmers were freed from low-level details, e.g., how to access shared data efficiently and correctly, given concurrent access. But already in the late nineties, the prerequisites for application development have changed dramatically. Storage and communication has become fairly cheap, and the internet dominates modern information infrastructures. Consequently, the role of database concepts had to be re-visited and newly determined. Undoubtedly, the database system has played and still plays an important role. However, it has more and more degenerated to a storage manager, far away from the applications. In this situation researchers at the turn of the century started to question the role of databases for future distributed information systems engineering ([34] and [1]). One conclusion was that we should rethink everything.

Beyond database systems we observed several interesting directions that were early attempts to support application developers and users in establishing and engineering their information systems: An important example for modern information management is Enterprise Resource Planning as for instance realized by SAP. We find the traditional DBMS at the storage level, but all application code is at the middle tier in so-called application servers. Application development is mainly the "customization" of the delivered system to the special needs of a given application. A TP Monitor is a further example for an additional product on top of databases and coordinates distributed databases. In a narrow definition a TP Monitor is an operating system for transaction processing. More generally and more recently it evolved into an infrastructure for developing and running applications, services, and components in a three-tier architecture. Another recent example for distributed application development is Workflow Management for business applications.

The VLDB Endowment in 1998 has established a future directions group which proposed to add "infrastructure for information systems" as the second main direction to the VLDB Conference in order to support application development [16].

1.2   Information beyond Databases, Information Explosion

So far we have considered the narrow field of "factual" data that are well represented by records or tuples in relational databases. However, other fields have evolved such us Information Retrieval, Geographical Information Systems, image, video, audio collections in special archives or in digital libraries. They demand support beyond databases. In the future, as a consequence of the immense progress in computer and communication technology, we expect an ever increasing number of data sources, reaching from traditional databases and large document and web page collections, down to embedded information sources in mobile "smart" objects in a pervasive computing environment. Not only the immense amount of information demands new thoughts but also the types of different information sources and their coordination poses a great challenge for the development of the appropriate information infrastructure. We talk about the continuous, "infinite" information, shortly called the "information space". Information in this space is distributed, heterogeneous, and undergoes continuous changes. Modern digital libraries, hospital information systems and patient records are prominent examples. Tools for accessing relevant information and further processing found information in a convenient manner are under-developed. Search clearly must go far beyond factual data retrieval. Content-based retrieval for images, audio or video must be combined with factual metadata and textual keyword search. We need tools that support personalization, context sensitive navigation, and visualization for intelligent browsing. Finally, entering queries is often a difficult task as the users have to have some common understanding about how the search engine works. Query by example and the usage of various relevance feedback mechanisms must be offered as an easy-to-use methodology to enter and to refine queries.

Another key problem with distributed information spaces, as they occur in intranets or digital libraries, is consistency of data stored at several places in the space. For instance, consider a query with some keyword x evaluated with a search engine. Since the search engine computed its indexes based on recently downloaded copies of the original data, a document d only means that it contained at some point in time the keyword x. In many situations, this retrieval quality is sufficient but it is unacceptable for applications requiring fresh results. Analogously, replicated information in the information space has to be kept consistent. For instance, an overview page with all current projects of a university should reflect the data provided by each research group. However, since the research groups may change their project data at any point in time, and often without notifying related authorities, the overview page will soon contain outdated data and becomes quickly useless. Consequently, the future infrastructure for a global information space has to provide some consistency guarantees [20]. The owner of an information space must be able to define rules how information from several sources has to be propagated to several destinations involving information extraction, aggregation, transformation and data integration. To this end, processes for the propagation of information have to be defined and to be linked to events that trigger a well-defined process to be automatically executed whenever necessary. The processes then correspond to the activities required to provide the desired consistency guarantees.

In view of these dramatic changes and new requirements it should become obvious that radically new thoughts and approaches for data and information management are necessary. The objective of this paper is to present a new vision, called hyperdatabase that we started at ETH Zurich and continue at the University of Basel, and we present resulting realizations of that vision. The contribution of this paper is the proof that an ambitious vision – going far beyond databases – has been realized by various related projects. We do hope that by this description other groups will be motivated to move their research into the hyperdatabase direction because much more needs to be done.

The paper is organized as follows: In Section 2 we will present our vision that we developed in view of the situation described above. Section 3, the main section will summarize the concrete realizations of this vision. Staying more in the realm of databases we report on the PowerDB project in Section 3.1. We continue in Section 3.2 with the more radical departure from databases and describe our service-oriented OSIRIS infrastructure for convenient application development. This is followed by ISIS and DelosDLMS (Section 3.3) in which digital library specific services for image, video, and audio retrieval and related indexing, for visualization, intelligent browsing and many more tasks are described. They have been developed together with partners in the large European Network of Excellence project DELOS. Section 4 summarizes the paper and briefly introduces ongoing research directions at the University of Basel.

2   The Hyperdatabase Vision

In summarizing the above observations we clearly see that functionality from many different disciplines must be combined and made available in a new infrastructure. We must combine data management with document, image, video, audio or 3D object management and retrieval. This requires document term extraction, ontology lookup for query term expansion, image feature extraction, or key frame detection from videos, just to give a few examples. Various indexing techniques for high-dimensional feature vectors such as the VA-file or the M-tree must be available in order to support multi-object, multi-feature queries. Visualization techniques by projections into the two or three-dimensional visual space such as Fastmap or Self Organizing Maps must be provided for intelligent browsing. These are again examples and therefore it is important to notice that one will never be able to define a complete list of necessary functionality. For example, new techniques for feature extraction from images will be developed by image specialists or new audio similarity functions may become available. Therefore, a new infrastructure must in general be extensible and adaptable to special applications. Any time a new type of object, a new indexing technique, or an improved feature extraction method must be added to the infrastructure and made be available to application developers and users. This should be as easy as adding a new object to a database.

Early attempts in the database field for an adaptation to new applications include extensible databases. Abstract data types (ADTs) extending the standard types in a database and providing indexing techniques for these ADTs where well-known attempts to apply databases more generally. Geometrical objects were a good example of this direction. However, in our opinion and in view of the above observations and requirements, these attempts were by far too narrow. Therefore, at ETH we established a much more radical research vision, called hyperdatabase research area. We departed much further from traditional database thinking in that we tried to move up to a much higher level of abstraction. Nevertheless we called our research direction hyperdatabase in order to express that we want to keep some important database properties that are well understood. In the following we will explain these early thoughts. In a narrow definition a hyperdatabase (HDB) is a database over databases[1] [23]. The hyperdatabase administers objects that are composed of objects and transactions that are composed of transactions. Hence, an HDB is a database, the primitives of which are again databases. This definition is still too narrow. In a more general definition, a hyperdatabase infrastructure administers not only many distributed databases but more generally distributed components and services with various functionality in a networked environment.

Remember that data independence was the main requirement of Ted Codd when he postulated relational databases. Now, similarly, the hyperdatabase infrastructure should provide a "higher order data independence". This, roughly, means that we must strive for immunity of application programs not only against changes in storage and access structure, but also against changes in location, implementation, workload, the number of replica of software components and their services.

What is the difference between a DB and an HDB? In a nutshell we say: a DB is a platform for clients concurrently accessing shared data. We need data definition, data manipulation, and transactions at the interface. The DB under the cover performs query optimization, correctness for parallel access, recovery, persistence, load balancing, availability. Similarly, an HDB is a platform for clients, concurrently accessing shared application services. As opposed to shared data in a DB, in an HDB we have shared components and services. At the interface of an HDB we need component and service definition and description, service customization, transactional processes encompassing multiple service invocations. The HDB, under the cover, performs optimization of client requests, routing, scheduling, and parallelization, correctness of concurrent accesses, flexible failure treatment, providing guaranteed termination (i.e., a generalized form of atomicity), availability, flexible recovery, and scalability. Table 1 summarizes the analogy.

Most importantly and in contrast to traditional database technology, a hyperdatabase infrastructure must not follow monolithic system architecture but must be fully distributed over all participating nodes in a network. Every node is equipped with an additional thin software layer, a so-called hyperdatabase (HDB layer) as depicted in Figure 1. This layer extends existing layers like the TCP/IP stack with process related functionalities. As such, the HDB layer abstracts from service routing much like TCP/IP abstracts from data packet routing. Moreover, while the TCP/IP protocol guarantees correct transfer of bytes, the HDB layer guarantees the correct shipment of process instances. Ideally, this layer comes together with the operating system much like the TCP/IP stack does.

---

[1] Similar to a hypermatrix which is a matrix that has matrices as elements.

Table 1. Analogy between a DBMS and the Hyperdatabase Infrastructure

Database Management	Hyperdatabase Infrastructure
Relational schema definition	Service definition and registration
Relational schema extension	New service registration
Relation	Service instance
Access to relation	Service invocation
Query and update language	Process definition language
Transaction	Transactional process
ACID Guarantees	Correct execution and guaranteed termination of process
Undo operation	Inverse service invocation
Redo operation	Repeatable service invocation
Indexing	Feature extraction and feature space organization
Query Optimization	Optimal process routing
Physical Database Design	Configuration Design by service allocation and replication

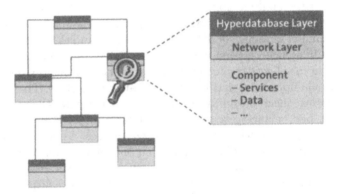

Fig. 1. Hyperdatabase Layers

3   Hyperdatabase Projects

3.1   PowerDB: Realization of the Narrow Hyperdatabase Vision

In the narrow definition a hyperdatabase is a database over databases. We followed this idea which led us to the "PowerDB" project. The goal was to build a high-performance database system by using as many database systems at the bottom layer as needed in order to achieve the desired throughput. In analogy to a computing cluster we called the set of component databases a database cluster, i.e., a network of PCs, and each PC runs an off-the-shelf DBMS. The challenge was to build the hyperdatabase infrastructure (PowerDB) that parallelizes and routes queries and updates to the appropriate component databases. Ideally, a database cluster allows for scale-out, i.e., meeting a (possibly very ambitious) performance objective by just adding more components to the cluster. Therefore, PowerDB follows a three-tier architecture with a database cluster as the bottom layer for storage management. Considering the middle tier we have focused on two directions within PowerDB, namely XML document management and Online Analytical Processing (OLAP) as it is used in data warehousing. In both cases we have introduced massive replication and partitioning in order to increase query throughput and query response times but still keeping update effort low.

PowerDB OLAP. With regard to OLAP, we have focused on the important question how to route complex OLAP queries to appropriate components in the cluster and how to propagate updates to the replicated databases in the cluster. Ideally, users should be able to ask for OLAP results based on fresh, i.e., up-to-date data. The state-of-the-art techniques in 2000 did not feature such functionality for performance reasons. Instead, OLAP warehouses were updated on a regular – for instance, weekly – basis. Our approach instead introduced a so-called freshness limit for the data OLAP queries operate on. A new protocol called FAS (short for Freshness-Aware Scheduling) ensured that the data is updated from the OLTP node(s) of the cluster on demand. Since updates are continuously processed at the OLTP production systems this usually requires to update the warehouse database before processing an OLAP query. Previous work on replication management with database systems has indicated that performance of such a setting will depend anti-proportionally of the number of replica introduced [15]. In other words, the expectations so far have been that performance goes down the more copies of a database have to be maintained. Using the TPC-R benchmark, we have conducted extensive experiments with FAS and up to 128 copies of the benchmark database. The bottom line of the experiments is surprising and a very positive one: the overhead for replication management with our new FAS protocol does not depend on the number of copies. Instead, it only depends on the update workload at the OLTP production system. This part of the project has resulted in a full prototype, and we have conducted numerous further experiments. [21] discusses these results in more detail, together with a more detailed description of the technical issues.

A further stream of research in the project has investigated different physical data organization schemes for efficient OLAP query processing on a cluster of database systems. The objective here is to investigate partitioning of the warehouse database across several cluster nodes with different degrees of replication at different granularities. The PowerDB middleware decomposes and routes OLAP query into one or several subqueries. These subqueries are optimized and processed locally at each cluster node. We investigated the trade-off between intra-query parallelism and inter-query parallelism with a fixed number of cluster nodes. This is an important issue with multi-user workloads where response time and throughput have to be considered jointly. [4] provides a more detailed discussion of the technical issues involved and the results. A significant improvement was obtained by introducing continuous update propagation in addition to the on-demand-refreshing as described above [6,3].

PowerDB XML Documents. Regarding document management, the middle tier (PowerDB-XML) consists of specialized components providing document-specific processing and update services. Object transaction monitors coordinate the database cluster and invoke document-specific components. PowerDB-XML decomposes services and transactions of services into concurrent short database transactions and lets them execute in the database cluster. We have demonstrated the speedup and scale-up characteristics mentioned before for a set of elementary services including Boolean retrieval and basic XML services, and for more sophisticated services including search according to vector-space retrieval [14,13]. Regarding effective retrieval on XML documents, the main innovation is support for flexible retrieval granularities with ranked and weighted retrieval models. This allows users to flexibly define the scopes of their queries. The infrastructure computes information retrieval statistics needed for result ranking and weighting dynamically on-the-fly, i.e., at query processing time. Consequently, users can leverage the full flexibility of XPath and XML document structures when formulating their document-centric queries.

Furthermore, PowerDB-XML allows bundling several XML service invocations to transactions. Conventional database transaction management techniques are not well-suited for concurrent XML processing. The reason for this is that the locking granularity with database systems, i.e., database row or page locking, does not reflect the semantics of XML processing which deals with tree-structured data. We therefore devised and implemented a new transaction manager called XMLTM that runs on top of the database cluster nodes. It follows the theory of multi-level transaction management. It relies on the underlying database systems at the cluster nodes as a transactional storage manager for XML. As extensive experiments have shown, using XMLTM improves performance of concurrent XML processing on a database cluster by up to an order of magnitude as compared to a setting with database transactions only. Furthermore speedup and scale up characteristics with a cluster of database and XML processing are convincing, and the orchestration overhead is negligible even for large overall database sizes of more than a terabyte striped across 128 cluster nodes. [12] provides an in-depth discussion of these results, together with a more detailed description of the technical issues.

3.2 Transactional Processes and OSIRIS: Foundations and Implementation of a Hyperdatabase Infrastructure

In the last years, the proliferation of service-oriented computing and in particular of Web services had a strong impact on information systems and middleware and has radically changed the way information processing takes place. System support for the invocation of single Web services is widely available, due to standardized protocols and formats (such as WSDL and SOAP). Beyond these basics, the most important challenges in service-oriented computing are the management of existing services and their evolution, the composition of existing services into a coherent whole by means of processes, the optimization of service requests, and reliability and correctness guarantees across service invocations.

All these challenges need to be met by novel hyperdatabase infrastructures. In addition, hyperdatabases need to be highly scalable so that they are able to deal with an increasing number of services, processes, and users.

In what follows, we briefly summarize the model of transactional processes which builds the foundation for novel hyperdatabase infrastructures and present a concrete implementation of the full hyperdatabase vision.

Transactional Process Management. Hyperdatabases draw upon the model of transactional processes [28] which provides process support with transactional guarantees over distributed components using existing services as a generalization of traditional database transactions. Essentially, transactional processes consider the termination semantics of the individual services they contain. Each service is either *compensatable, retriable,* or *pivot,* following the model of flexible transactions [40]. The effects of compensatable services can be semantically undone after the invocation has successfully returned. Retriable services are guaranteed to terminate correctly, even if they have to be invoked repeatedly. In this case, the last invocation succeeds while all previous invocations of this service do not leave any effects. [27] presents a more advanced distinction between termination classes, based on execution costs of services. Pivot services are those that cannot be compensated, due to the lack of an inverse service, or which are not appropriate for compensation due to their high costs.

Transactional processes contain two orders on their constituent services: a (partial) precedence order for regular execution and a precedence order for failure handling purposes. The latter specifies alternative executions i.e., services and the order of their execution order which will be used when the regular execution leads to a failure situation – similar to exception handlers in programming languages.

Based on the termination guarantees of services and the two intra-process orders, it can be verified already at built-time whether or not a process can be executed correctly. This is the case when all failures that may occur during execution can be resolved either by complete compensation, by partial compensation until a point is reached from where an alternative execution path can be followed (according to the preference order), or by forward recovery using only retriable services. All services preceding the first pivot service have to be compensatable. Each pivot service in a process (there might be several pivots in a process) must be succeeded by at least one execution path that consists only of retriable services, i.e., an execution path whose correct execution can be guaranteed. According to the model of transactional processes, a process that is correctly defined has *guaranteed termination* property. This means that it is guaranteed that exactly one out of a set of possible execution paths is effected correctly (or the effects of all services that have been invoked are completely undone) while all other executions paths do not leave any effects. Since guaranteed termination allows to choose exactly one out of possibly several executions, it extends and generalizes the well-known all-or-nothing semantics of transactions. More details on the model of transactional processes can be found in [26].

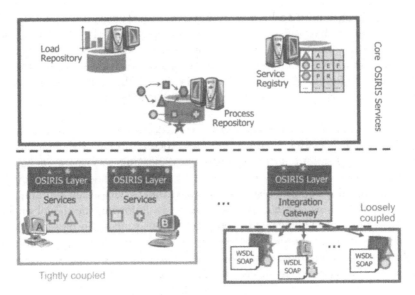

Fig. 2. OSIRIS Architecture

OSIRIS: A Complete Hyperdatabase Implementation. The hyperdatabase vision of a novel infrastructure for distributed service-oriented applications has been implemented in OSIRIS (Open Service Infrastructure for Reliable and Integrated process Support) [32,33]. The OSIRIS platform itself does not provide any application functionality but, by combining specialized application services, supports the definition and reliable execution of dedicated processes, according to the paradigm of programming in the large [39]. Thus, it can be used as underlying infrastructure for a very wide variety of application domains. The only prerequisite is that basic functionality of an application domain is available via services.

OSIRIS distinguishes between system services and application services. System services are used internally for coordinating the execution of processes in a distributed way, without relying on a central execution engine/scheduler. For application services, OSIRIS further distinguishes between loosely coupled and tightly coupled services. The hyperdatabase layer (called OSIRIS layer) runs on each host providing application services. This is the case for tightly coupled services. Loosely coupled application services are those that have to be called remotely, without a local ORISIS layer available. The integration/invocation is done via WSDL for service description and SOAP for invocation. The system architecture of OSIRIS is depicted in Figure 2.

OSIRIS provides a high degree of scalability [31]. This is based on a decentralized peer-to-peer approach for process execution [30] which considers several global repositories as part of the system services (core OSIRIS services) and services provided by the OSIRIS layers. While only the local OSIRIS layers are responsible for process execution, the global repositories collect metadata on the overall system and apply sophisticated replication mechanisms (based on publish/subscribe techniques) for control flow dependencies from the global repositories to the local OSIRIS layers. At run-time, this guarantees that no single point of failure is involved in the execution of processes. In addition, sophisticated load balancing is applied to distribute process load among available, suitable service provider peers. To benefit from load balancing over different service providers, application designers do not encode the service bindings of activities at development time. Rather, they only specify the type or class of a service to be invoked together with its parameters. The concrete service binding is selected at runtime depending on the load of machines and costs of invoking a particular service instance. At runtime, the OSIRIS layer selects a service provider based on costs, parameters, and conditions on its services.

In principle, each peer of the network could replicate all process information. However, this would require large amounts of data to be replicated over the entire network. Rather, we only want to have all the information on a peer that is needed to drive the execution of those process instances that potentially visit a peer. The OSIRIS approach divides each process specification into a set of *execution units*. Each execution unit contains the information to execute the corresponding service and to navigate the process depending on the result of the local service invocation. A peer only subscribes itself for those execution units of processes that invoke locally available service. Consequently, the amount of replicated data significantly reduces.

Among all core OSIRIS services, the following are the most important ones for distributed and decentralized process execution. The *Process Repository* holds the global definitions of all processes types. These types are the basis for decomposition into execution units. The *Service Registry* records a list of all available (tightly coupled) services, offered by all providers in the OSIRIS network. The *Load Repository* is storing information of the current load situation of providers in the OSIRIS network. Additionally, freshness parameters on subscriptions are used to avoid unnecessary propagation of minor load updates.

OSIRIS' decentralized and distributed approach to process execution is illustrated in Figure 3. Different service types are depicted with different shapes. The precedence order is represented by directed edges between the services of a process (i.e., the process on the left upper corner, whose execution is illustrated in the center of the figure, consists of three services which are invoked sequentially). The OSIRIS layer is available on top of all service providers and allows them to make available their services to OSIRIS processes. In the center, some of the core OSIRIS services are displayed. All these repositories are not needed for the execution of a process. Figure 3 also shows how a process description is divided into execution units and how these execution units are replicated to the local OSIRIS layers (dotted lines). Finally, after replication, enough process and service meta information is locally available to allow for peer-to-peer process execution. In particular, when a process is instantiated and executed, the local OSIRIS layers can decide on their own, based on locally replicated information, where to route a request to (solid lines between OSIRIS layers). This makes sure

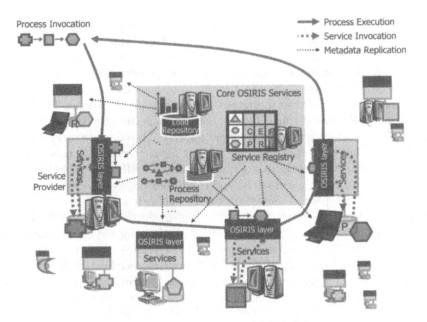

Fig. 3. Distributed Execution of OSIRIS Processes

that process execution takes place in a decentralized and distributed way and guarantees a high degree of scalability.

Finally, OSIRIS is equipped with the O'GRAPE (OSIRIS GRAphical Process Editor) [38] user interface for process definition. It allows for easy creation of process descriptions without programming skills. In addition, O'GRAPE supports the integration of existing application services by leveraging existing Web service standards like SOAP and WSDL.

There are two versions of OSIRIS: one has been implemented at ETH Zurich in C++ which runs on Microsoft platforms. The other version, developed at the University of Basel, is implemented in Java. The latter has a smaller footprint and can even be deployed on mobile devices. More details on the OSIRIS architecture and its implementation can be found in [29].

3.3   ISIS and DelosDLMS: Hyperdatabase Applications for Digital Libraries

ISIS: Services for Content-Based Search in Multimedia Collections. ISIS (Interactice SImilarity Search) is a concrete hyperdatabase application for information retrieval in multimedia collections [19], built on top of OSIRIS. It supports content-based retrieval of images, audio and video content, and the combination of any of these media types with text retrieval. Basically, ISIS consists of a set of pre-defined processes and several application services (like feature extraction, index management, index access, relevance feedback, etc.) that have been developed on the basis of the OSIRIS middleware. ISIS includes the

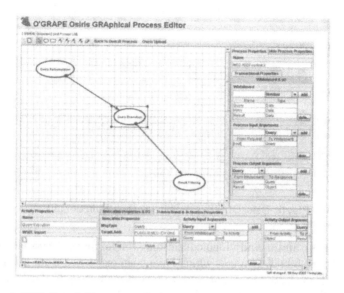

Fig. 4. ISIS Search Process including Relevance Feedback in O'GRAPE

VA-file [37], a sophisticated index structure for similarity search, which is particularly well suited for high-dimensional vector spaces. It also provides basic support for relevance feedback and visualization.

One of the main considerations in designing ISIS was to ensure high scalability and flexibility. Therefore, instead of implementing one monolithic application, ISIS consists of a set of specialized application services for similarity search which are combined using processes. The ISIS services can be easily distributed among several nodes in a network [36].

Figure 4 shows a sample process, shown in the design view of OSIRIS' O' GRAPE tool, which implements the refinement of a user query based on relevance feedback. The process specification just contains the details of all application services it encompasses (e.g., WSDL description) and their orders of invocation within the process. The actual service providers where the service is invoked are determined at run-time. Hence, each step of the process can be executed by any node providing the required service. After issuing the query a first time, a user can refine and re-issue her query. The query process (including user feedback) as depicted in Figure 4 consists of the steps *Query Reformulation* (based on relevance feedback the user has issued), *Query Execution* (index access), and *Result Filtering* (which may again take user feedback into account).

The process-based approach to application development also allows the definition of multi-object multi-feature queries, i.e., content-based similarity queries using different query objects and of possibly different types, and thus several services for index access.

ISIS has been successfully applied to the ETHWorld project, the virtual campus of ETH Zurich. It allows to effectively and efficiently search in several

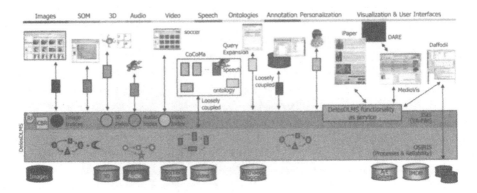

Fig. 5. DelosDLMS – Architecture & Functionality

large-scale image, audio, and video collections, the largest of them being a collection of more than 600'000 images which have been extracted from ETH websites.

More details on ISIS and in particular on content-based similarity search over multimedia collections can be found in [35] and [18].

DelosDLMS: A Next Generation Digital Library Management System.
The overall goal of the DelosDLMS is the implementation of a next generation digital library management system, which shows how text and audio-visual search functionality can be combined, which offers personalized browsing using new information visualization and relevance feedback tools, which allows annotation and processing of retrieved information, which integrates and processes sensor data stream, and finally, from a systems engineering point of view, which allows simple configuration and adaptation while being reliable and scalable [2,24]. DelosDLMS has been built in a joint effort of members of the DELOS Network of Excellence in Digital Libraries[2], funded by the EU in its 6th framework program. It shows a very wide variety of digital library functionality available as services provided by the DELOS partners which has been integrated into the OSIRIS/ISIS hyperdatabase infrastructure.

Figure 5 illustrates the DelosDLMS system and the wide variety of digital library functionality it provides to its users "out of the box". Most of the new services have been integrated in a loosely-coupled way, i.e., as Web services. Following the hyperdatabase concept, complete and sophisticated DL applications can be built starting from this collection of basic services by defining digital library processes. Table 2 summarizes all the digital library services DelosDLMS provides together with the DELOS partners which have contributed these services. Essentially, these services can be classified into six categories. DelosDLMS includes various generic multimedia *Content & Collection Management Services*, and *Search Support Services* to enable efficient metadata and content-based indexing and retrieval. In addition, DelosDLMS features *Annotation Management Services*, that provide extensive support for annotating content, including

---

[2] http://www.delos.info

Table 2. DelosDLMS Functionality and Contributors

DelosDLMS Functionality	Contributors
Hyperdatabase Infrastructure (OSIRIS)	University of Basel (ETH Zurich)
Content-based similarity search (ISIS)	University of Basel (ETH Zurich)
Self-Organizing Map Visualization	University of Konstanz
3D Feature Extraction & Similarity Search	University of Florence
Audio Feature Extractors	Vienna University of Technology
Semantic Video Retrieval	Technical University of Crete & University of Florence
Speech Interface	Technical University of Crete
Ontologies & Query Expansion	University of Glamorgan & Technical University of Crete
Annotation Management	University of Padua
Personalization	University of Athens
iPaper Interface	ETH Zurich
MedioVis User Interface	University of Konstanz
DARE User Interface	University of Rome 'La Sapienza'
Daffodil – Federated Search in DLs	University of Duisburg-Essen

annotation sharing to support collaborative environments. Furthermore, a set of *User Query Support Services* improves the user experience during searches, allowing query expansion based on controlled vocabularies, incremental refinement of query results, and personalized interaction with the system. *Advanced Visualization Services* offer a powerful alternative to the classical display of query results and also allow to visualize, browse and analyze in an effective way entire collections. Finally *Non-standard UI Support Services* give the possibility to interact with DL applications through non-traditional input-output devices.

In summary, DelosDLMS has been a nice showcase for the hyperdatabase vision and in particular for the high potential of hyperdatabase infrastructures in acting as the basic underlying infrastructure for a powerful, yet easy to extend, adapt and configure environment for the management of large-scale information spaces.

4   Conclusion and Outlook

The hyperdatabase concept has been introduced as reaction to the rapidly growing information spaces which contain information of different formats (such as, for instance, images, audio, video and combinations of these) and from different distributed sources. This information might even be subject to frequent changes and complex interdependencies.

The main objective of the hyperdatabase vision is to apply database system concepts outside of databases, especially in modern information systems which follow a three- or multi-tier architecture. This is based on a notion of higher order data independence, i.e., the independence of of application programs against changes in location, implementation, workload, the number of replica of software components and their services. In that sense, the hyperdatabase is a platform for clients that concurrently access shared application services. In this environment, the hyperdatabase has to optimize client requests (i.e., service invocations), to route and parallelize these requests and to guarantee the correctness of concurrent accesses to shared services.

Over the last ten years, the hyperdatabase vision has been implemented, exploited, and evaluated in a large variety of applications. The resulting systems such as PowerDB, OSIRIS, and ISIS have demonstrated the potential and adequateness of the hyperdatabase vision. In some applications, for instance in DelosDLMS, where these systems have been used in very demanding large-scale applications, they have strikingly passed the test of time.

Nevertheless, the systems we have presented in this paper do not cover the full hyperdatabase vision. Rather, they all focus on and realize selected parts of the vision. In addition, the hyperdatabase vision is not static but needs to evolve with the ongoing advancements and new trends in large-scale, distributed multimedia information spaces. In what follows, we conclude with a brief summary of current projects at the University of Basel which aim at taking this evolution into account by addressing novel challenges that are stemming from recent trends and developments.

Grid Data Management & Replication. Grid infrastructures are becoming more and more important, especially for data intensive applications (Data Grids). In particular, the almost unlimited storage resources of a Data Grid allow the replication of data and services across many potentially heterogeneous Grid nodes. This project aims at extending and generalizing replication protocols from PowerDB and applying them at Grid scale [5]. It includes the dynamic generation and removal of replicas based on the current load of the system, the distinction between updateable and read-only copies, the consideration of the special characteristics of data objects (some might be mutable, some others immutable so that a write access creates a new version of the object), etc. All this needs to be done by taking into account the distributed nature of the Grid which does not allow for any global component that guarantees serializability of concurrent accesses to several replicas.

Data Stream Management. The proliferation of sensor technology, especially in the context of embedded systems, has brought forward novel types of applications that make use of streams of continuously generated sensor data. Many applications like telemonitoring in healthcare particularly require reliable data stream management. This is even more important when data stream management applications are deployed in a failure-prone distributed setting including resource-limited mobile devices. In this project, we extend the hyperdatabase vision in two ways. First, by allowing to integrate mobile devices into a hyperdatabase network which requires an HDB implementation that comes with a small system footprint. Second, by extending the hyperdatabase vision from discrete service invocations in a request/reply style to the reliable processing of continuous streams of data [8,9].

Advanced Resource Reservation for Scientific Workflows. Many applications in eScience encompass a large number of highly sophisticated, resource intensive services which need to be integrated into processes or workflows [10]. Especially when these processes need to be executed with dedicated quality-of-service (QoS) guarantees (e.g., predefined response times), the resources required to execute a process in an optimal way must be reserved in advance (e.g., CPU share). In this project, we aim at providing an infrastructure for QoS-aware scientific workflows by addressing mechanisms for negotiating service level agreements for advanced resource reservation, for enforcing guarantees which have been subject to negotiations, and for dynamically adjusting resource reservations.

Context-Awareness & Semantics. At present, process-based applications are mostly defined by human experts. With the advent of semantic (Web) services, however, functionality comes along with a formal specification of their semantics [7,17]. This allows the application of advanced mechanisms for automatically creating ad hoc processes. In particular when considering the current context (e.g., location) of a user or her individual preferences, personalized process-based applications can be either newly created or existing ones can be automatically adapted. This project addresses the customizaiton and generation of processes using semantic Web services, the verification of these processes and their reliable distributed execution.

References

1. Abiteboul, S., Agrawal, R., Bernstein, P.A., Carey, M.J., Ceri, S., Croft, W.B., DeWitt, D.J., Franklin, M.J., Garcia-Molina, H., Gawlick, D., Gray, J., Haas, L.M., Halevy, A.Y., Hellerstein, J.M., Ioannidis, Y.E., Kersten, M.L., Pazzani, M.J., Lesk, M., Maier, D., Naughton, J.F., Schek, H.-J., Sellis, T.K., Silberschatz, A., Stonebraker, M., Snodgrass, R.T., Ullman, J.D., Weikum, G., Widom, J., Zdonik, S.B.: The Lowell Database Research Self-Assessment. Communications of the ACM 48(5), 111–118 (2005)
2. Agosti, M., Berretti, S., Brettlecker, G., Bimbo, A.D., Ferro, N., Fuhr, N., Keim, D.A., Klas, C.-P., Lidy, T., Milano, D., Norrie, M.C., Ranaldi, P., Rauber, A., Schek, H.-J., Schreck, T., Schuldt, H., Signer, B., Springmann, M.: DelosDLMS – The Integrated DELOS Digital Library Management System. In: Thanos, C., Borri, F., Candela, L. (eds.) Digital Libraries: Research and Development. LNCS, vol. 4877, pp. 36–45. Springer, Heidelberg (2007)
3. Akal, F.: Replication in a Database Cluster with Freshness and Correctness Guarantees. PhD Thesis, ETH Zurich (2007)
4. Akal, F., Böhm, K., Schek, H.-J.: OLAP Query Evaluation in a Database Cluster: A Performance Study on Intra-Query Parallelism. In: Manolopoulos, Y., Návrat, P. (eds.) ADBIS 2002. LNCS, vol. 2435, pp. 218–231. Springer, Heidelberg (2002)
5. Akal, F., Schuldt, H., Schek, H.-J.: Toward Replication in Grids for Digital Libraries with Freshness and Correctness Guarantees. Concurrency and Computation: Practice and Experience 19(16) (November 2007)

6. Akal, F., Türker, C., Schek, H.-J., Breitbart, Y., Grabs, T., Veen, L.: Fine-Grained Replication and Scheduling with Freshness and Correctness Guarantees. In: Proceedings of the 31st International Conference on Very Large Data Bases, Trondheim, Norway, August 2005, pp. 565–576 (2005)

7. Bergenti, F., Cáceres, C., Fernández, A., Fröhlich, N., Helin, H., Keller, O., Kinnunen, A., Klusch, M., Laamanen, H., Lopes, A., Ossowski, S., Schuldt, H., Schumacher, M.: Context-aware Service Coordination for Mobile e-Health Applications. In: Proceedings of the European Conference on eHealth (ECEH 2006), Fribourg, Switzerland, October 2006, pp. 119–130 (2006)

8. Brettlecker, G., Schuldt, H.: The OSIRIS-SE (Stream-Enabled) Infrastructure for Reliable Data Stream Management on Mobile Devices. In: Proceedings of the ACM SIGMOD International Conference on Management of Data, Beijing, China, June 2007, pp. 1097–1099. ACM Press, New York (2007)

9. Brettlecker, G., Schuldt, H., Schek, H.-J.: Efficient and Coordinated Checkpointing for Reliable Distributed Data Stream Management. In: Manolopoulos, Y., Pokorný, J., Sellis, T.K. (eds.) ADBIS 2006. LNCS, vol. 4152, pp. 296–312. Springer, Heidelberg (2006)

10. Candela, L., Akal, F., Avancini, H., Castelli, D., Fusco, L., Guidetti, V., Langguth, C., Manzi, A., Pagano, P., Schuldt, H., Simi, M., Springmann, M., Voicu, L.: DILIGENT: Integrating Digital Library and Grid Technologies for a new Earth Observation Research Infrastructure. International Journal on Digital Libraries 7(1-2), 59–80 (2007)

11. Codd, E.F.: The Capabilities of Relational Database Management Systems. IBM Research Report, San Jose, California, RJ3132 (1981)

12. Grabs, T.: Storage and Retrieval of XML Documents with a Cluster of Database Systems. PhD Thesis, ETH Zurich (2003)

13. Grabs, T., Böhm, K., Schek, H.-J.: High-level Parallelism in a Database Cluster: A Feasibility Study Using Document Services. In: Proceedings of the 17th International Conference on Data Engineering (ICDE 2001), Heidelberg, Germany, April 2001, pp. 121–130. IEEE Computer Society Press, Los Alamitos (2001)

14. Grabs, T., Böhm, K., Schek, H.-J.: PowerDB-IR – Information Retrieval on Top of a Database Cluster. In: Proceedings of the 2001 ACM CIKM International Conference on Information and Knowledge Management, Atlanta, Georgia, USA, November 2001, pp. 411–418. ACM Press, New York (2001)

15. Gray, J., Helland, P., O'Neil, P.E., Shasha, D.: The Dangers of Replication and a Solution. In: Proceedings of the 1996 ACM SIGMOD International Conference on Management of Data, Montreal, Quebec, Canada, June 1996, pp. 173–182. ACM Press, New York (1996)

16. Gray, J., Mylopoulos, J., Schek, H.-J.: Future Directions of Database Research — Changes in the VLDB Conference PC Structure (1999), http://www.vldb.org/future.html

17. Lopes, A., Costa, P., Bergenti, F., Klusch, M., Blankenburg, B., Möller, T., Schuldt, H.: Context-aware Secure Service Composition Planning and Execution on E-Health Environments. In: Proceedings of the European Conference on eHealth (ECEH 2006), Fribourg, Switzerland, October 2006, pp. 179–190 (2006)

18. Mlivoncic, M.: Efficient Evaluation Techniques for Complex Similarity Queries on Large Media Collections. PhD Thesis, ETH Zurich (2006)

19. Mlivoncic, M., Schuler, C., Türker, C.: Hyperdatabase Infrastructure for Management and Search of Multimedia Collections. In: Proceedings of the Sixth Thematic Workshop of the EU Network of Excellence DELOS: Digital Library Architectures – Peer-to-Peer, Grid, and Service-Orientation, S. Margherita di Pula, Cagliari, Italy, June 2004, pp. 25–36. Edizioni Libreria Progetto, Padova (2004)

20. Pu, C., Schwan, K., Walpole, J.: Infosphere Project: System Support for Information Flow Applications. SIGMOD Record 30(1), 25–34 (2001)
21. Röhm, U.: Online Analytical Processing with a Cluster of Databases. PhD Thesis, ETH Zurich (2002)
22. Schek, H.-J.: The Hyperdatabase Network – New Middleware for Searching and Maintaining the Information Space. In: Vojtáš, P., Bieliková, M., Charron-Bost, B., Sýkora, O. (eds.) SOFSEM 2005. LNCS, vol. 3381, pp. 42–46. Springer, Heidelberg (2005)
23. Schek, H.-J., Böhm, K., Grabs, T., Röhm, U., Schuldt, H., Weber, R.: Hyperdatabases. In: Proceedings of the First International Conference on Web Information Systems Engineering (WISE 2000), Hong Kong, China, June 2000, pp. 14–25. IEEE Computer Society Press, Los Alamitos (2000)
24. Schek, H.-J., Schuldt, H.: DelosDLMS – Infrastructure for the Next Generation of Digital Library Management Systems. ERCIM, Special Issue on European Digital Library (66) (July 2006)
25. Schek, H.-J., Schuldt, H., Weber, R.: Hyperdatabases: Infrastructure for the Information Space. In: Proceedings of the Sixth IFIP Working Conference on Visual Database Systems (VDB 2002), Bisbane, Australia, May 2002, pp. 1–15. Kluwer, Dordrecht (2002)
26. Schuldt, H.: Transactional Process Management over Component Systems. PhD Thesis, ETH Zurich (2000)
27. Schuldt, H.: Process Locking: A Protocol based on Ordered Shared Locks for the Execution of Transactional Processes. In: Proceedings of the 20th ACM SIGACT-SIGMOD-SIGART Symposium on Principles of Database Systems (PODS 2001), Santa Barbara, CA, USA, May 2001, ACM, New York (2001)
28. Schuldt, H., Alonso, G., Beeri, C., Schek, H.-J.: Atomicity and Isolation for Transactional Processes. ACM Transactions of Database Systems (TODS) 27(1), 63–116 (2002)
29. Schuler, C.: Distributed Peer-to-Peer Process Management – Realization of a Hyperdatabase. PhD Thesis, ETH Zurich (2004) (in German)
30. Schuler, C., Schuldt, H., Türker, C., Weber, R., Schek, H.-J.: Peer-to-peer Execution of (Transactional) Processes. International Journal on Cooperative Information Systems 14(4), 377–406 (2005)
31. Schuler, C., Türker, C., Schek, H.-J., Weber, R., Schuldt, H.: Scalable Peer-to-Peer Process Management. International Journal of Business Process Integration and Management (IJBPIM) 1(2), 129–142 (2006)
32. Schuler, C., Weber, R., Schuldt, H., Schek, H.-J.: Peer-to-Peer Process Execution with OSIRIS. In: Orlowska, M.E., Weerawarana, S., Papazoglou, M.P., Yang, J. (eds.) ICSOC 2003. LNCS, vol. 2910, pp. 483–498. Springer, Heidelberg (2003)
33. Schuler, C., Weber, R., Schuldt, H., Schek, H.-J.: Scalable Peer-to-Peer Process Management – The OSIRIS Approach. In: Proceedings of the IEEE International Conference on Web Services (ICWS 2004), San Diego, CA, USA, June 2004, pp. 26–34. IEEE Computer Society Press, Los Alamitos (2004)
34. Silberschatz, A., Zdonik, S.B.: Database Systems - Breaking Out of the Box. SIGMOD Record 26(3), 36–50 (1997)
35. Weber, R.: Similarity Search in High-Dimensional Vector Spaces. PhD Thesis, ETH Zurich (2000)
36. Weber, R., Bolliger, J., Gross, T.R., Schek, H.-J.: Architecture of a Networked Image Search and Retrieval System. In: Proceedings of the 1999 ACM CIKM International Conference on Information and Knowledge Management, Kansas City, Missouri, USA, November 1999, pp. 430–441. ACM Press, New York (1999)

37. Weber, R., Schek, H.-J., Blott, S.: A Quantitative Analysis and Performance Study for Similarity-Search Methods in High-Dimensional Spaces. In: Proceedings of 24th International Conference on Very Large Data Bases (VLDB 1998), August 1998, pp. 194–205. Morgan Kaufmann, San Francisco (1998)
38. Weber, R., Schuler, C., Neukomm, P., Schuldt, H., Schek, H.-J.: Web Service Composition with O'GRAPE and OSIRIS. In: Aberer, K., Koubarakis, M., Kalogeraki, V. (eds.) VLDB 2003. LNCS, vol. 2944, pp. 1081–1084. Springer, Heidelberg (2004)
39. Wiederhold, G., Wegner, P., Ceri, S.: Toward Megaprogramming. Commununications of the ACM 35(11) (1992)
40. Zhang, A., Nodine, M.H., Bhargava, B.K.: Global Scheduling for Flexible Transactions in Heterogeneous Distributed Database Systems. IEEE Transactions on Knowledge and Data Engineering (TKDE) 13(3), 439–450 (2001)

From Schema and Model Translation
to a Model Management System

Paolo Atzeni, Luigi Bellomarini, Francesca Bugiotti, and Giorgio Gianforme

Dipartimento di informatica e automazione
Università Roma Tre
{atzeni}@dia.uniroma3.it,
{bellomarini,bugiotti}@yahoo.it,
{giorgio.gianforme}@gmail.com

Abstract. Model management addresses problems dealing with forms of collaboration among heterogeneous databases. This collaboration may include exchange of data, schema integration, synchronization, translation and, in general, any issue characterized by a data evolving scenario. It provides a structured framework allowing standard solutions to data programmability problems in terms of the application of some recurring operators. The main mid-term target in this field is the definition of a model management system, a software platform providing the data architect with a complete set of tools addressing a wide spectrum of possible problems. In this paper we recall MIDST, a platform that works as an applicator of schema transformations. It was firstly conceived to perform model-independent schema and data translation. Then it has been extended to an applicator of general schema transformations including model management operators. Leveraging on MIDST rich representation of models, schemas and data based on a metalevel approach, we reason about potentialities and possible developments of this platform with the target of laying the basis for a real runtime model management system.

Keywords: model management, model management system, model-independent schema and data translation, data programmability.

1 Introduction

The management of heterogeneous databases, in integrated or collaborative contexts, always involves the need for solutions to *data programmability* issues. In general, data programmability addresses problems dealing with evolving scenarios: changes in a database which collaborates in a heterogeneous environment often implies a sequence of propagating changes in related databases at any level, model, schema and data [8,13,14]. Heterogeneity means that on the one hand systems are developed by different people, fostering different data models and technologies; on the other hand it recalls problems involving different software components using shared and interoperating data.

A. Gray, K. Jeffery, and J. Shao (Eds.): BNCOD 2008, LNCS 5071, pp. 227–240, 2008.

Moreover, business requirements which guided the design of the data model are not static but change in time, leading to an intensive refactoring, redefinition and migration of data. This even complicates data programmability, opening to a range of further problems including change propagation, synchronization, data exchange, integrity constraint satisfaction, data provenance memorizing and so on [7,6].

Model management provides a structured framework to encompass all these problems and establishes standard solutions based on the application of a finite set of operators [7].

There is the tendency to recognize the need for a model-independent solution to model management problems. Our approach had been pursuing model-independent schema and data translation [3,5,22,24] and led to the platform MIDST [3,4]. It was originally conceived only as an implementation of the MODELGEN operator (the one responsible for schema translation), but to a wider extent MIDST can be now considered as a general purpose applicator of schema transformations. By proposing a model-independent but model-aware definition and implementation of most common model management operators, we are working on a blueprint for standard solutions to recurring problems such as round-trip engineering and forward engineering [1]. These solutions refer to an off-line approach and not to a real runtime environment in which they are actually needed.

In the perspective of turning MIDST into a real model management system (MMS) [8], providing the data architect with a complete suite of tools to cope with data programmability problems in a real runtime context, here we address the main challenges in this migration.

We focus on the major scenarios where MIDST may be applied, as well as on the complementary issues that such a change of perspective raises. We underline how MIDST metalevel representation of models and schemas supports meaningful potentialities. We show how the main challenges can be either directly addressed by the platform, or faced through appropriate extensions that benefit from the metalevel expressivity.

We discuss the application of MIDST to the handling of evolving scenarios. Hence we explain possible approaches towards problems such as update propagation, schema synchronization and data exchange: reasonings about how model-independent solutions to simpler problems can be combined and successfully applied to these situations are provided. Complementary problems and refinements providing the data with higher quality are described as well. Special attention is devoted to data provenance treatment and integrity constraint handling, where MIDST metalevel expressivity is particularly effective.

Reasonings dealing with a concrete and advanced application of the framework to an object-oriented scenario is provided. We introduce a possible development of the platform, enabling a transparent handling of object-oriented structures.

The remainder of the paper is organized as follows. In Section 2 we describe the approach to data model handling used by MIDST; in Section 3 we outline the fundamental challenges in turning MIDST into a real MMS; in Section 4 and 5 we introduce some data programmability issues that can be addressed exploiting

MIDST metalevel potentialities; Section 6 illustrates an object-oriented scenario; finally Section 7 concludes the paper.

2   Background

In previous papers [3,4] we proposed MIDST, a platform for model-independent schema and data translation. The framework is based on the fundamental observation that any existing data model can be represented with a finite set of constructs [17]. Therefore MIDST handles a *metamodel* allowing the definition of general purpose constructs called *metaconstructs*. They are then used to assemble models, meaning that a model is thus defined as a collection (a subset) of all the existing metaconstructs. Schemas are consequently defined with respect to the model they belong to and have concrete constructs which inherit their properties from the metalevel.

Metaconstructs are characterized by a unique identifier (OID), a defining name, a set of properties coding details of interest and a set of references relating them to one another. Graphs of interrelated constructs build a model. For example we have a construct named abstract which models any "abstract" conceptual entity, such as objects (of the object-oriented model), entities (of the ER model), and so on. MIDST also manages aggregations which are constructs representing table-like entities (like tables in the relational model). Instead a lexical is a metaconstruct representing a lexical value independently of the model of interest. Then, whereas an abstract is simply characterized by its name, a lexical also has some defining properties such as whether it is identifier or not, whether it is nullable or not and so forth. We emphasise that many constructs are related to other constructs: an example is the lexical which can be linked either to an abstract (coding for example an attribute of entity) or to an aggregation (representing a relational column) by means of typed references.

The metalevel is implemented by means of a *multilevel relational dictionary* [2] which models all the mentioned concepts as relational tables: metaconstructs, properties and references.

Another important concept in MIDST is that of *supermodel*: it represents the most general model, including all the possible metaconstructs. Hence any other model is a specialization of it. The supermodel is the component that actually allows the model-independent schema translation that can be formulated in three phases: the schema (instance of the source model) is copied into the supermodel; a translation into the target model takes place in this environment; the result schema is finally downcast into the destination model. Translations are specified by means of datalog rules defined over MIDST metaconstructs.

3   Towards an MMS

3.1   Model-Independent Operators

MIDST was conceived in order to provide an implementation of MODELGEN, the operator responsible for schema translation. More formally, given a schema S_1

of a model M_1 and a target model M_2, MODELGEN computes a schema S_2 of model M_2 which corresponds to S_1. The translation process may be divided into two phases: the first one where the appropriate datalog translation rule is chosen and the second one, where the manipulations are actually performed.

We are currently working on the extension of this platform [1] to implement most important model management operators. In fact we can consider a datalog translation rule as a general transformation that can be applied to schemas. As a consequence, MIDST can be thought of as a platform capable of performing transformations that are not necessarily translations, but general model management operators.

These operators are coded with datalog rules, expressing manipulations directly in terms of the metaconstructs. This implies that they do not depend on the specific model of application. In particular, these datalog rules can be written to implement the DIFF and the MERGE operator: the first one computes the difference between two given schemas, while the second one performs a set-oriented union.

The general datalog implementation of the operators is composed of two phases. The first one works out the correspondences among the constructs of the source schemas. Then the second performs the specific operations. The DIFF, given two input schemas, copies into the target all the constructs belonging to the first, but not to the second one on the basis of the computed correspondences. Similarly, the MERGE copies into the target schema the constructs of both the source schemas; it uses the correspondences in order to avoid duplicates in the result.

Moreover the operators can be automatically generated from the currently available supermodel. We have a procedure that detects all the possible constructs and their relationships by interacting with the metalevel, and thus generates globally valid operators.

Solutions to most common model management problems can be expressed as scripts composed of a sequence of operators. Indeed, MIDST can be currently used to provide an off-line solution to some important problems such as *forward engineering* and *round-trip engineering*. As for the former, given a specification schema S_1 and an implementation schema I_1 which derives from S_1, changes in S_1 leading to a modified specification S_2 have to propagate to I_1 in order to obtain a coherently modified implementation I_2. Instead, as for the round-trip engineering: given a specification schema S_1 and an implementation schema I_1 which derives from S_1, changes in I_1 leading to a modified implementation I_2 have to propagate backwards to S_1 in order to obtain a coherently modified specification S_2.

Moving from Bernstein's solving procedures [7], we can build scripts for the cited problems in terms of the DIFF, MERGE, MODELGEN and in some sense MATCH operators.

3.2   Larger Scale and Complementary Issues

Solutions to model management problems are built in terms of scripts involving the application of several operators. Indeed, this is still a simplified version of what is actually needed in a concrete application context. In that wider perspective, issues are composed of sets of elementary model management problems whose solutions have to be coordinated.

We may consider several levels of abstraction: model management operators (such as DIFF and MERGE) belong to the lowest one, then we have simple problems (such as forward and round-trip engineering) with solutions in terms of simple operators; the top level contains more complex scenarios, such as ETL processes, whose solutions can be obtained only by coordinating procedures addressing simpler problems. Therefore, the ability to solve model management problems by building scripts in terms of simple operators is only the first requirement of an MMS, it is only the implementation of the lowest abstraction level. A meaningful MMS must cope with every level and then allow for high-abstraction environments that coordinate several model management problems.

This might seem only a change of scale issue, however it also raises collateral requirements and complementary problems that must be separately faced. Some examples of these issues include: the need for information about the provenance of data; a coherent handling of integrity constraints; a fine-grained access control; an efficient indexing mechanism for the data sources; triggers and business logic integration.

Besides, there are several quality requirements a real MMS should also consider: first of all runtime support but also availability, supportability, performance, security. As far as quality requirements are concerned, we can assume that in a research project they do not represent the riskiest element, in fact a good architectural definition phase can cope with them, leading to the design of the appropriate components.

However a simple off-line characterization of model management problems, although within a well-designed architecture, is not functionally sufficient. Indeed, MIDST currently implements the lowest abstraction layer, so it represents the first phase of the development of a real MMS.

Our aim is to discuss the most meaningful issues in the process of turning MIDST into a full-featured MMS. Hence in the following section we deal with some larger-scale problems to exemplify our approach; moreover we give details about possible directions to address complementary requirements.

4   Handling Evolving Scenarios

Evolving scenario problems [8] subsume issues dealing with changes performed over some given schemas or instances. In general, changes imply a complex net of propagations updating a set of interrelated databases.

Update propagation problems can be considered as a generalized and runtime extension of the forward engineering, involving that a change on a given database leads to modifications in another one. From a technological point of view, whereas currently MIDST solves the round-trip and forward engineering with respect to imported schemas (and hence off-line), this problem needs an on-line binding of two schemas so as to propagate changes during the execution.

A more complete definition of such a problem is *schema synchronization* which actually involves a propagation of the changes between two schemas in both directions. It may be worked out by MIDST either with a reversed application of the forward engineering solving script, or through the application of it in the one direction and by the use of round-trip in the other.

Peer to peer mappings define a net of databases whose schemas are inter-related. Therefore changes on one schema induce a chain of possibly different modifications in other schemas. This problem can be dealt with by MIDST as well: the core point is the definition of relations between databases (mappings) that can be directly applied to target schemas; it is important to point out that MIDST already solves something similar when performs a chain of schema trans-lations. Beacause of the general treatment of transformations, such an approach may be suitable in this context as well.

Data exchange problem is aimed at transforming a mapping between two schemas into a directly executable query actually moving data. With respect to this problem, MIDST paradigm supports advantageous preconditions [8]: only relational schemas are treated and the mappings are conjunctive queries. In fact here a relational meta-representation of any model is possible due to the dictionary generality, besides we use datalog mappings that are declarative rules in the form of conjunctive queries.

However, some remarkable issues in facing these problems are still open. In the general solution to round-trip and forward engineering provided by MIDST, we assume a substantial coincidence between schema and data evolution. It means that modifications between two different databases are mainly schema-driven. The migration of instances is handled as a consequence of the evolution of schemas. Datalog rules defining manipulations on the schemas are syntactically translated into transformations on the corresponding instances.

It implies that if a logical coherence between them exists, then operators correctly perform; otherwise the tight coupling between the two levels could become a drawback. In addition there are problems, such as data exchange, that are specifically instance-oriented. In both the cases we need to loosen that coupling.

The schema-instance coupling problem is closely related to representing map-pings. Many model management operators need information about schema corre-spondences in order to operate on them. For instance a difference operator must know those matches in order to correctly subtract constructs. In our platform, we do not currently handle an explicit representation of mappings. We move from a *unique name assumption* stating that metaconstructs with equal lexical properties are equal themselves. Under this assumption, model management op-erators perform a hierarchical comparison between input schemas in order to correctly treat them.

Again, this outlines the fact that our operators are schema oriented. Certainly it is a remarkable strength of the approach, providing generality thanks to the model-independent approach. Yet when data-oriented problems are faced or the treatment desired for instances differs from the one wanted for schemas, the need for some kind of decoupling arises.

One solution may involve the adoption of two different transformation languages: one for schemas and one for instances. It would involve a complete decoupling between the two layers, forcing the platform to separately deal with two levels of abstraction and, as a consequence, with two types of transformation rules. The opposite strategy is the one currently adopted by MIDST (with the cited drawbacks): one unified language for both schema and instances that, actually, causes schema rules to be initially translated into instance rules.

The two extreme views can be reconciled in two ways: designing an intermediate language allowing for greater expressivity on instances or modelling an engineered representation for mappings.

The first branch of solutions can be again split in two different approaches. One could think of an extension to schema transformations rules involving a set of functions specifying expressive manipulations for instances. In this way a more straightforward generation of data rules from schema rules would be allowed: it would not be a merely syntactical translation anymore. Instead, due to these functions, the semantics of data rules could be customized and strongly differ from schema rules. In this way, data rules generated from the schema level ones would be much more powerful.

It would be also possible to support two different languages for translations in a framework where the one for instances is a lower level translation of the one for schemas (in the specific case it would imply datalog being translated to SQL for schemas, and straightly SQL for instances). Then the data architect would be allowed to write specific SQL rules for instances whenever the automatically generated ones are not detailed enough.

Adopting an engineered representation of mappings is the most standard solution, since it guarantees a greater expressivity and flexibility. As dealt with in the literature [8], defining an engineered mapping is an open problem and a global approach has not been recognized yet. The main point is that of generating those mappings, hence the implementation of a sufficiently general MATCH operator. Many heuristic algorithms have been proposed in this field, also adopting sophisticated structures for mappings, however their weakness is the absence of an explicit and rich representation of models. This both complicates the process of similarity recognition and leads to model-dependent mappings. MIDST metalevel approach, supporting a complete and extendible meta-representation of models, can lead to simpler definitions of engineered mappings and to more effective matching algorithms. For instance, let us consider the *similarity flooding algorithm* [19,20], an advanced implementation of MATCH. It compares two graphs representing schemas and returns pairs of similar nodes. The similarity of nodes is evaluated both on the basis of heuristic criteria and on a similarity propagation assumption: if two nodes are similar, their neighbors also tend to be similar. Finally a user-aided pruning phase allows to discard the false positives.

The first step of the similarity flooding is the translation of the schemas into graph models. Currently some kind of generality in this field has been achieved by means of *SQL DDL to graph* translating tools [19,20]. Then the nodes are compared with one another independently of the logical function they have in the model of interest. MIDST rich representation of models and schemas would allow for a less syntactical implementation of the algorithm. One would no longer need to pass through the DDL specification of a given database in order to obtain the graph version, since it is already explicitly managed in the metalevel. In addition the graph model over which the algorithm operates could be enhanced with some kind of model-awareness. For example, given a subgraph of the first schema, the algorithm could perform a fake translation in order to isolate the correspondent subgraph in the second schema. Then the similarity flooding comparison might be limited to that portion and, therefore, yield less false positive pairs and involve less user effort.

5   Data Provenance and Quality Problems

The growing number of heterogeneous data together with a uniform access mechanism tend to increase their availability, while inducing a potential decrease in quality. Large and complex workflows involving the integration of pieces of information coming from different data sources present the need for provenance[1] metadata [25]. They enhance data quality under several aspects: possibility to verify whether the data meet the business requirements, establishing creational context, protection of intellectual property and so on.

The shared and uniform access mechanism provided by modern infrastructures makes data prone to losing quality and coherence. Therefore integrity constraints acquire more and more significance in these environments.

A modern approach to these issues should be model-independent and operate at runtime. Whereas there are many proposals for runtime provenance and integrity constraints handlers, to the best of our knowledge, MMS managing this kind of issues model-independently are not currently available.

Here we argue that MIDST metalevel can be extended to cope with these problems with a general approach. It is not worth analyzing possible strategies in detail, however brief explanations should get the idea across.

5.1   Data Provenance

MIDST manages migration of data expressed with directly applicable datalog rules. These rules are coded with respect to MIDST metaconstructs and define manipulations over them. Here it would not be useful to pursue the details of transformation rules, yet some concrete aspects are necessary to outline the main ideas. We adopt a variant of datalog where the unique identifiers (OIDs) of metaconstructs are generated by means of Skolem functions. For a given construct, we define a set of Skolem functions generating OIDs for it from different sets of strongly-typed parameters. These parameters may be other constructs identifiers or constants. Skolem functions are bijective and, for a given construct, the ranges of all the functions defined over it are disjoint. This approach allows to

---

[1] In the literature *data provenance* is sometimes referred to as *data lineage* or *data pedigree* [25].

easily handle some kind of *where-provenance*. It means that for a given construct occurrence we can track back the whole path leading to it. A construct occurrence is characterized by an OID which is the unique output of a specific Skolem function defined over the construct itself. MIDST handles a global materialization including every function. It is then sufficient to query that materialization to determine the parameters which generated the OID under examination. What is more is that, even though several functions are defined for a given construct, since their ranges are disjoint, one could infer which function has been applied on the basis of the OID value.

A detailed description of the possible implementations of strategies for the data provenance would not be noteworthy here. However the key point is that MIDST handles strongly-typed functions and strictly relates every construct instance to its specific OID. This supports the design of procedures capable of exploring the whole provenance graph. This exploration proceeds as long as a the construct under examination is derived from another construct. When a construct has an OID which derives from the application of a Skolem function to a constant value, the current branch of the exploration terminates.

This idea assumes that MIDST works as a runtime MMS managing the whole net of data migration; in that case pieces of information about *why* and *how provenance* might be useful as well. They convey domain information about the reason why a piece of data is present in a database. In some sense this information is already managed by means of constant parameters of Skolem functions, meaning that they store domain-level notions about the provenance. Anyway an extension to the multilevel dictionary might include a richer description of Skolem functions allowing for an expressive characterization of the *why* and *how* provenance given in a user-chosen language. The power of this approach lays both in the relational representation of metadata and in the strong connection between a metaconstruct and the generating function. While the former aspect is fundamental to guarantee a model-independent handling of data provenance, the second enables an increasingly rich ontological representation of domain information that will be inherently related to the appropriate construct.

So far we have been describing the approach towards data provenance with respect to metaconstructs; in fact MIDST proposes a mechanism allowing for a two-fold definition of transformations: they are valid both for schemas and for instances. Coherently, the platform adopts Skolem functions to define the OIDs of data which are treated alike. So we store a tuple of metadata for each value of each metaconstruct. For example, take the lexical that describes any string-like conceptual element such as entity attributes or table columns. We have one tuple of metadata for each value of every lexical. This representation may seem too fine-grained, yet here it allows for an extremely detailed recording of data provenance based on instance-level Skolem functions that work as we have described for schemas.

In addition, we are not bound to adopt a specific language for transformations, nevertheless it has to guarantee two major points: it must support Skolem functions and have rules acting on metaconstructs. For sake of simplicity we might choose to enrich the SQL language with the possibility of specifying functions for the OID generation. Even its standard version could be used if we interpose a query preprocessing phase applying Skolem functions to generate identifiers.

5.2 Integrity Constraints

In a model management system we may state that handling integrity constraints mainly involves three aspects: definition, application and management. The definition recalls the need to design a language and a metadata representation for constraints; the application is the satisfaction verification, while the management represents the need for an integrated handling in a heterogeneous environment.

It is clear that in a simple context which is usually model-dependent, a well-defined constraint only needs mechanisms for its validation. By contrast, a more complex environment, with translations and migrations among different data models, needs further strategies.

MIDST currently allows for a syntactical definition of both internal and external[2] constraints. As for the first ones, simple *SQL CHECK* conditions are expressed in the metaconstructs by means of their properties. Since the metalevel describes what properties a construct has and potentially their structure, more sophisticated and expressive internal constraints may be defined as well.

External constraints do not even need an explicit definition in terms of properties. For example, we handle a metaconstruct (foreign key) that connects lexicals on the basis of a foreign key constraint. Thus, since lexicals belong to conceptual entities, such as abstracts or aggregations, then the foreign key also models the relationships (and the dependences) between them.

As for the constraint verification, currently MIDST does not offer any effective solution. A syntactical test on instances based on constraints defined over schemas might be implemented, however it would not be the best choice. Integrity constraints allow for an enduring data consistence that must be verified at runtime. Thus, the architectural definition of a more complex MMS should point out what software component is responsible for that verification. Probably, if we consider an MMS as a mediator in a heterogeneous context, the responsibilty for this test will belong to the client database management systems. Instead, if the MMS concentrates the whole responsibility for the data management, it will include a dbms performing integrity checks. Hence an expressive representation of models and effective strategies to import and export constraints should be sufficient for our needs.

A real MMS deals with several models and performs translations among them. One main feature is that of preserving integrity constraints in those transformations. Here the potentialities of MIDST are particularly remarkable since constraints could be managed in a model-independent way. During translations internal integrity constraints are treated as propositional formulas. For example, consider a column of a relational table; in MIDST it is represented by a lexical. Suppose that a *not-nullable* constraint is defined over it. We have a datalog

---

[2] Constraints are similarly classified as *intra-relational* or *inter-relational* according to the relational terminology.

rule that translates columns into attributes of ER entities. The lexical has the property *isNullable: false* that models the constraint with a simple propositional formula. Normally, before the creation of the new lexical the translation rule does not need to alter the formula that is simply copied. Alternatively, if one wanted to invert that constraint and allow null values in entity attributes, the datalog rule would insert a negation.

In general it means that a datalog rule can involve a complex expression coding the translation of constraints when inter-model translations are performed. Foreign keys work alike. Suppose a foreign key links two lexicals of two different relational tables. When the schema is translated into the ER model, tables turn into entities and specific rules support the translation of integrity constraints into relationships.

This means that a possible direction is using MIDST for constraint definition. Constructs coding them could be defined in the metamodel and would be independent of the specific model. Translations for constraints could be written as well as normal translations currently allowed by the platform and, in a long-term perspective, could be even automatically generated from the metamodel.

6   An Object-Oriented Scenario

In object-oriented applications, the modern approaches towards persistence tend to recognize the benefits of adopting object-to-relational mapping (ORM) strategies [16,18,21,23,27]. Let us briefly define how an application can be considered in terms of schema and instances. Classes define the general structure of the objects: name, attributes and references. Then, the graph of the classes of an application represents its schema. At runtime, on the basis of the definition of the classes, a graph of objects is built. That graph is an instance of the class-based schema.

ORM frameworks are based on the specification of mappings between the object schema (the classes) and the relational schema (the one on the actual database) by means of annotations or other mechanisms involving metadata. In the software development process, the relational database and the software components are not designed at the same time and change independently. These frameworks, implementing a *meet-in-the-middle* approach [11,9], decouple the lifecycles of the two layers by leveraging on mappings. In fact, when the application logic or the database change, it is sufficient to redefine the mappings between them. One research key point in this field is of course the efforts in defining working solutions to the data exchange problem that makes the object instances migrate into the database. Moreover the definition of sophisticated mappings to correctly represent object structures (such as nested classes and hierarchies [10]) is relevant.

An innovative scenario may arise by using MIDST in order to support simple mappings between the object graph and the metalevel. In MIDST metamodel it is possible to determine a set of metaconstructs which represents a complete object-oriented model. Therefore the class schema of an application can be mirrored (imported) into MIDST supermodel and instances can be made to migrate by adopting extremely simple mappings. Unlike traditional ORM, the approach would not handle a static correspondence between two given schemas, instead it would implement a simple import of the object graph into the appropriate subset of the supermodel defining the object-oriented model. It is important to point out that this imports both the schema and the data of the application into MIDST metalevel and treats the result as a normal schema. Therefore model management operations as well as translations can be applied to it.

This introduces a great flexibility allowing for model-independent persistence handling. From another point of view, the described approach represents a sophisticated ORM where instances are memorized in an articulated relational structure (the multilevel dictionary) modelling general object graphs.

What is remarkable is that the explicit representation of schemas leads to a higher level of abstraction. Whereas in ORM we specify correspondences between classes and relations, instance variables and columns, references and foreign keys, here those very concepts are modelled in general in the metalevel and are equally valid for any application.

With traditional ORM only data exchange problems can be used to manage the relationship between the object graph and the database schemas. It also comes as a consequence of the strict pursuing of the meet-in-the-middle approach. In a complete MMS, the adoption of such a strategy would be less tight because of the availability of the whole spectrum of model management solutions.

Besides, MIDST does not only address the meet-in-the-middle approach. If the database is firstly developed (*database-first*), the application logic could benefit from an object graph directly derived from it (export) with a simple (copy) mapping. Conversely, if the application logic is an early activity (*application-logic-first*) in the development process, persistence can be achieved by importing meaningful entities. Finally if meet-in-the-middle is promoted, more sophisticated interrelating mappings can be defined.

Moreover, we could exploit the potentialities of the solutions to model management problems for complex tasks. Advanced relationships between the data model and the program instance itself could be addressed: a change in the data model induces changes in the memory object graph (forward engineering), while objects modifications propagate backwards to the database (round-trip engineering).

Although the illustrated approach has a greater significance in a runtime scenario, from many points of view, an off-line version is meaningful as well. Once an object-oriented graph has been imported into MIDST metalevel, it can be used for a wide variety of targets. First of all, possible applications involve the translation of these schemas into other models not only for persistence reasons, but also to facilitate sharing, integration, migration of data. General purpose model management operators (such as the ones already defined in MIDST) can be then applied to the object schema in the metalevel and modified versions of it can be obtained. The model-independent representation of an object-oriented application could be also used for visualization [15], structural and behavioral analysis.

Examples of specific applications of the structural analysis are anti-pattern detection and dependence verification [26]. On the other hand, behavioral analysis [12] could be based on the fact that an instance obtained from an object graph at a given time is a snapshot of the execution of the process. Different snapshots of an executing program allow to define a track of the execution states that could be related to mappings, handled by means of model management operators and used for debugging reasons.

7 Discussion

This paper, moving from MIDST approach towards schema and data translation, has recalled how the platform can be considered as a general applicator of transformations to schemas. On this basis, reasonings about a possible development of MIDST into a full-featured model management system have been provided. Major problems and research directions for the main challenges have been explained.

References

1. Atzeni, P., Bellomarini, L., Bugiotti, F., Gianforme, G.: A platform for model-independent solutions to model management problems. VLDB Journal (to appear, 2008)
2. Atzeni, P., Cappellari, P., Bernstein, P.A.: A multilevel dictionary for model management. In: Delcambre, L.M.L., Kop, C., Mayr, H.C., Mylopoulos, J., Pastor, Ó. (eds.) ER 2005. LNCS, vol. 3716, pp. 160–175. Springer, Heidelberg (2005)
3. Atzeni, P., Cappellari, P., Bernstein, P.A.: Model-independent schema and data translation. In: Ioannidis, Y., Scholl, M.H., Schmidt, J.W., Matthes, F., Hatzopoulos, M., Böhm, K., Kemper, A., Grust, T., Böhm, C. (eds.) EDBT 2006. LNCS, vol. 3896, pp. 368–385. Springer, Heidelberg (2006)
4. Atzeni, P., Cappellari, P., Gianforme, G.: MIDST: model independent schema and data translation. In: SIGMOD Conference, pp. 1134–1136. ACM Press, New York (2007)
5. Atzeni, P., Torlone, R.: Management of multiple models in an extensible database design tool. In: Apers, P.M.G., Bouzeghoub, M., Gardarin, G. (eds.) EDBT 1996. LNCS, vol. 1057, pp. 79–95. Springer, Heidelberg (1996)
6. Bernstein, P., Haas, L., Jarke, M., Rahm, E., Wiederhold, G.: Panel: Is generic metadata management feasible? In: VLDB, pp. 660–662 (2000)
7. Bernstein, P.A.: Applying model management to classical meta data problems. In: CIDR Conference, pp. 209–220 (2003)
8. Bernstein, P.A., Melnik, S.: Model management 2.0: manipulating richer mappings. In: SIGMOD Conference, pp. 1–12 (2007)
9. Cabibbo, L.: Objects meet relations: On the transparent management of persistent objects. In: Persson, A., Stirna, J. (eds.) CAiSE 2004. LNCS, vol. 3084, pp. 429–445. Springer, Heidelberg (2004)
10. Cabibbo, L., Carosi, A.: Managing inheritance hierarchies in object/relational mapping tools. In: Pastor, Ó., Falcão e Cunha, J. (eds.) CAiSE 2005. LNCS, vol. 3520, pp. 135–150. Springer, Heidelberg (2005)

11. Cabibbo, L., Porcelli, R.: $M^2 orm^2$: A model for the transparent management of relationally persistent objects. In: Lausen, G., Suciu, D. (eds.) DBPL 2003. LNCS, vol. 2921, pp. 166–178. Springer, Heidelberg (2004)

12. Giguette, R., Hassell, J.: A relational database model of program execution and software components. In: ACM-SE 38: Proceedings of the 38th annual on Southeast regional conference, pp. 146–155. ACM Press, New York (2000)

13. Haas, L.M.: Beauty and the beast: The theory and practice of information integration. In: Schwentick, T., Suciu, D. (eds.) ICDT 2007. LNCS, vol. 4353, pp. 28–43. Springer, Heidelberg (2006)

14. Halevy, A.Y., Ashish, N., Bitton, D., Carey, M.J., Draper, D., Pollock, J., Rosenthal, A., Sikka, V.: Enterprise information integration: successes, challenges and controversies. In: SIGMOD Conference, pp. 778–787 (2005)

15. Hamer, J.: Visualising java data structures as graphs. In: ACE 2004: Proceedings of the sixth conference on Australasian computing education, pp. 125–129 (2004)

16. Hibernate, http://www.hibernate.org/

17. Hull, R., King, R.: Semantic database modelling: Survey, applications and research issues. ACM Computing Surveys 19(3), 201–260 (1987)

18. Java Data Objects, http://www.jdocentral.com/

19. Melnik, S.: Model management: First steps and beyond. In: BTW, pp. 455–464 (2005)

20. Melnik, S., Garcia-Molina, H., Rahm, E.: Similarity flooding: A versatile graph matching algorithm and its application to schema matching. In: ICDE, pp. 117–128 (2002)

21. Microsoft ObjectSpaces, http://msdn.microsoft.com/library/default.asp?url=/li-brary/en-us/dnadonet/html/objectspaces.asp/

22. Mork, P., Bernstein, P., Melnik, S.: A schema translator that produces object-to-relational views. Technical Report MSR-TR-2007-36, Microsoft Research (2007), http://research.microsoft.com

23. Oracle AS TopLink, http://otn.oracle.com/products/ias/toplink/

24. Papotti, P., Torlone, R.: Heterogeneous data translation through XML conversion. J. Web Eng. 4(3), 189–204 (2005)

25. Simmhan, Y., Plale, B., Gannon, D.: A survey of data provenance in e-science. In: ACM SIGMOD International Conf. on Management of Data, vol. 34(3), pp. 31–36 (2005)

26. Structural Analysis for Java, http://www.alphaworks.ibm.com/tech/sa4j/

27. The Java Persistence API - A Simpler Programming Model for Entity Persistence, http://java.sun.com/developer/technicalarticles/j2ee/jpa/

XtreemOS: Towards a Grid-Enabled Linux-Based Operating System

Domenico Laforenza

Information Science and Technologies Institute (ISTI)
The Italian National Research Council (CNR)
Area della Ricerca
Via Giuseppe Moruzzi, 1
I-56126 Pisa Italy
domenico.laforenza@isti.cnr.it

Extended Abstract

The term Grid computing was introduced at the end of 90s by Foster and Kesselman; it was envisioned as "an important new field, distinguished from conventional distributed computing by its focus on large-scale resource sharing, innovative applications, and, in some cases, high-performance orientation" [1].

Defining Grids has always been difficult but nowadays there is a general agreement that Grids are distributed systems enabling the creation of Virtual Organizations (VOs) [2] in which users can share, select, and aggregate a wide variety of geographically distributed resources, owned by different organizations, for solving large-scale computational and data intensive problems in science, engineering, and commerce. Those platforms may include any kind of computational resources like supercomputers, storage systems, data sources, sensors, and specialized devices.

From the end of 90s a lot of water has passed under the bridge, and several researchers proposed to revise the initial definition of Grid. More recently researchers belonging at the European Network of excellence "CoreGrid" (http://www.coregrid.net/) reached an agreement on the following definition: a Grid is "a fully distributed, dynamically reconfigurable, scalable and autonomous infrastructure to provide location independent, pervasive, reliable, secure and efficient access to a coordinated set of services encapsulating and virtualizing resources (computing power, storage, instruments, data, etc.) in order to generate knowledge".

This is a more modern service-oriented vision of the Grid that stems from the conviction that in the mid-long term the great majority of complex software applications will be dynamically built by composing services, which will be available in an open market of services and resources. In this sense, the Grid will be conceived as a "world-wide cyber-utility" populated by cooperating services interacting as in a complex and gigantic software ecosystem.

In order to manage Grid platforms several approaches were proposed. Some of those, which for simplicity we might call it "á la Globus" [3], are based on middleware layers that link in a loosely-coupled way the user applications and

A. Gray, K. Jeffery, and J. Shao (Eds.): BNCOD 2008, LNCS 5071, pp. 241–243, 2008.

the underneath distributed multi-domain heterogeneous resources. The adoption of Grid middleware is one of the most widely adopted approaches. Those middleware layers are used to address the complexity of Grid platforms and to help the user to use Grid resources in an integrated way. In some of the current Grid middleware systems (e.g. Globus [3], EGEE gLite [4], UNICORE [5]) the operating system support for Grid computing is quite minimal or non-existent because they have been developed with different goals in mind. The á la Globus approaches are designed as "sum of services" infrastructures, in which tools are developed independently in response to current needs of users. In particular, Globus started out with the bottom-up premise that a Grid must be constructed as a set of tools developed from user requirements, and consequently its versions (GT2, GT3, GT4) are based on the combination of working components into a composite Grid toolkit that fully exposes the Grid to the programmer.

While Grid Computing has gained much popularity over the past few years in the scientific contexts, it is still cumbersome to effectively use in business and industrial environment. In order to overcome most of mentioned difficulties before several researchers proposed to build a true Grid Operating System (GOS) [6,7,8,9,10]. A GOS is a distributed operating system targeted for a large-scale dynamic distributed architecture, with a variable amount of heterogeneous resources (resource may join, leave, churn). A GOS should be virtual organizations-aware, spanning multiple administrative domains without no central management of users and resources (multiple administrators, resource owners, VO managers). This GOS should be composed of a consistent set of integrated system services, providing a stable Posix-like interface for application programmers. Moreover, abstractions or jobs (set of processes), files, events, etc. should be provided by a GOS.

This talk will present XtreemOS [11], a first European step towards the creation of true open source operating system for Grid platforms. The XtreemOS project aims to address this challenge designing, implementing, experimenting and promoting an operating system that will support the management of very large and dynamic ensembles of resources, capabilities and information composing virtual organizations. Recognizing that Linux is today the prevailing operating system, XtreemOS started an effort to extend Linux towards Grid, including a native support for the VOs management, and providing appropriate interfaces to the GOS services. As it will be explained in this talk, the result is neither a "true" Grid operating system nor a Grid middleware environment, but rather a Linux operating systems with tightly integrated mechanisms for the quick and user-friendly creation of distributed collaborations which share their resources in a secure and user-friendly way.

References

1. Foster, I., Kesselman, C. (eds.): The Grid: Blueprint for a new computing infrastructure. Morgan Kaufmann, San Francisco (1999)
2. Foster, I., Kesselman, C., Tuecke, S.: The anatomy of the Grid: Enabling scalable virtual organizations. International Journal of Supercomputer Applications (2001)

3. Globus, http://www.globus.org/, http://www.univa.com/
4. EGEE gLite, http://glite.web.cern.ch/glite/
5. Unicore, http://unicore.sourceforge.net/
6. Vahdat, A., Anderson, T., Dahlin, M., Belani, E., Culler, D., Eastham, P., Yoshikawa, C.: WebOS: Operating system services for wide area applications. In: Proceedings of the Seventh Symposium on High Performance Distributed Computing (July 1999)
7. Krauter, K., Maheswaran, M.: Architecture for a Grid Operating System. In: International Workshop on Grid Computing, pp. 65–76 (2000)
8. Pike, R., Presotto, D., Dorward, S., Flandrena, B., Thompson, K., Trickey, H., Winterbottom, P.: Plan 9 From Bell Labs. Computing Systems 8(3), 221–254 (1995), http://plan9.belllabs.com/plan9dist/
9. Padala, P., Wilson, J.N.: GridOS: Operating System Services for Grid Architectures. In: Pinkston, T.M., Prasanna, V.K. (eds.) HiPC 2003. LNCS (LNAI), vol. 2913, Springer, Heidelberg (2003)
10. Mirtchovski, A., Simmonds, R., Minnich, R.: Plan 9: An Integrated Approach To Grid Computing. In: IPDPS 2004, Santa Fe, NM, USA, April 26-30 (2004)
11. The XtreemOS European Project, http://www.xtreemos.eu/

High-Assurance Integrity Techniques for Databases

Elisa Bertino, Chenyun Dai, Hyo-Sang Lim, and Dan Lin

Department of Computer Science
Purdue University
{bertino,daic,hslim,lindan}@cs.purdue.edu

Abstract. With the increased need of data sharing among multiple organizations, such as government organizations, financial corporations, medical hospitals and academic institutions, it is critical to ensure data integrity so that effective decisions can be made based on these data. In this paper, we first present an architecture for a comprehensive integrity control system based on data validation and metadata management. We then discuss an important issue in the data validation, that is, the evaluation of data provenance and propose a trust model for estimating the trustworthiness of data and data providers. By taking into account confidence about data provenance, we introduce an approach for policy observing query evaluation as a complement to the integrity control system.

1 Introduction

With the widely use of computer techniques, it is estimated that more than 90% of the business records being created today are electronic as reported by American Record Management Association (ARMA) [1]. The need for sharing data within and across organizations is also more critical than ever. The availability of comprehensive data makes it possible to extract more accurate and complete knowledge and thus supports more informed decision making. However reliance on data for decision making processes and other critical data-intensive tasks requires data to be of good quality and trusted. We refer to such requirements as *high-assurance data integrity*.

While there have been some efforts to ensure confidentiality when sharing data, the problem of high-assurance data integrity has not been widely investigated. Previous approaches have either addressed the problem of protection from data tampering, through the use of digital signature techniques, or the problem of semantic integrity, that is, making sure that the data is consistent with respect to some semantic assertions. However, even though these techniques are important components of any solution to high-assurance data integrity, they do not address the question on whether one can actually trust certain data. Those techniques, for example, do not protect against data deception, according to which a malicious party may provide on purpose some false data, or against the fact that a party is unable, for various reasons, to provide good data. Techniques, like those developed in the area of data quality [4], may help; however they often require the availability of good quality data sources against which one can compare the data at hand and correct them.

A. Gray, K. Jeffery, and J. Shao (Eds.): BNCOD 2008, LNCS 5071, pp. 244–256, 2008.

It is clear that in order to address the problem of high-assurance data integrity we need comprehensive solutions combining several different techniques. In this paper, we first present an architecture for comprehensive integrity control systems [7] which is mainly based on metadata management and data validation. Then we discuss issues concerning data validation and propose an approach to evaluate the trustworthiness of data provenance as well as a framework that evaluates queries based on the confidence about data provenance. In what follows, we discuss our work in more details.

Integrity is generally understood as "the prevention of unauthorized and improper modification of data" [5], but this definition is not rigorous since the term "improper" could mean many things [16]. In order to provide a comprehensive approach, we define a set of meaningful requirements by examining various integrity models. We introduce a notion of metadata template by which various types of metadata related to integrity requirements can be specified. We also present a flexible integrity control policy specification language that is able to support not only access control policies but also data validation for preserving data integrity. In our integrity assurance system, data validation is carried out based on metadata values including the data sources. The trustworthiness of data resources largely affects the trustworthiness of the data. For example, a malicious data source provider may announce that a small company has successfully signed a big contract which is not true in reality. This information is then passed to a stock analysis agent, based on which the agent infers that the stock prize of that company will go up with high probability and send this information to the data users. If those users, based on such information, decide to acquire stocks of such company, they may end up with severe financial losses. In contrast, the data users may avoid such risks if they are aware that the source provider is not very trustworthy. Therefore, we propose a data provenance trust model that takes into account various factors affecting the trustworthiness. According to those factors, we assign trust scores to both data and data providers. Such trust scores represent key information based on which data users may decide whether to use the data and for which purposes.

If the trust score of the data is very low, users may require better data. There are many approaches for improving the data quality but the cost for obtaining accurate data can be very high in some situations. However, we observe that accurate data is not always necessary. For example, if a user just wants to compute some statistical summary of the data, data with low confidence may be sufficient since providing data with high confidence is usually very expensive. On the other hand, if the user has to make a critical decision, data with high confidence may be required. Therefore, we propose a data provenance-aware access control policy, referred to as *confidence policy*. As a complement to the integrity control mechanism that applies to the database before any operation, the confidence policy restricts the access to the query results based on the provenance confidence levels of the query results.

The rest of the paper is organized as follows. Section 2 briefly reviews related work. Section 3 discusses integrity requirements and an architecture for a comprehensive integrity control system. Section 4 presents a data provenance trust model. Section 5 presents a framework for policy observing query evaluation based on provenance confidence. Finally, Section 6 concludes the paper.

2   Related Work

Work related to our approach falls into three categories: (i) integrity models, (ii) access control policies, and (iii) lineage calculation.

Biba [6] has proposed an approach based on a hierarchical lattice of integrity levels so as to ensure integrity by blocking transmitting low-integrity objects to high-integrity subjects. However, the approach is not easy to use because it is not clear how to determine the appropriate integrity levels. Clark and Wilson [8] have proposed a model for data integrity in commercial environments. The model consists of two key notions: well-formed transactions and separation of duty. A well-formed transaction is one that only manipulates data in trusted ways so to preserve the consistency of data. Separation of duty mandates separating all operations into several subparts and executing each subpart by a different subject. The model has however some limitations in that it categorizes data integrity only according to two levels: valid and invalid. Our approach to integrity control systems is more comprehensive than those models in that it provides mechanisms driven by integrity policies and provides an approach to determine the data trust level based on data provenance information. As for access control in a relational database system, most existing access control models, like Role-Based Access Control [11] and Privacy-aware Role-Based Access Control [15], perform authorization check before every action on the database. Our confidence policies apply to query results and thus they are complementary to access control.

Data provenance, also referred to as lineage or pedigree in databases [20], has been widely investigated. Approaches have been developed for tracking the provenance of the query results, i.e., recording the sequence of steps taken in a workflow system to derive the dataset, and computing confidence levels of the query results [2,3,12,13,14,18]. For example, Widom et al. [21], have developed the Trio system which supports management of information about data accuracy and lineage (provenance). Sarma et al. [19] have developed an approach to compute lineage and confidence in probabilistic databases according to a decoupled strategy. However, very few approaches have been proposed for evaluating trust of data sources and provenance paths.

The most relevant work concerning the evaluation of data provenance is by Yin et al. [22], which however only deals with conflicting information provided by different websites. They assume an identifier that links different items corresponding to the same entity which seems unrealistic. Their trust model contains a large number of parameters that are hard to determine. Compared to their work, we do not assume the existance of identifiers for the entities of interest and take into account several aspects that can affect the trustworthiness of the data.

3   Architecture for Comprehensive Integrity Control Systems

We have devised a set of relevant integrity requirements and a comprehensive framework for integrity control systems in our previous work [7]. In this section, we briefly discuss the requirements and the framework. The proposed framework includes a system architecture for integrity management systems and a flexible integrity control policy specification language.

3.1 Integrity Requirements

As we mentioned before, the meaning of data integrity varies according to different people and applications [16]. Therefore, the first task in designing an integrity management system is to precisely identify what requirements are most essential. We have investigated various existing integrity models, and then, summarized the core requirements for integrity control system as follows.

- **Information-flow control** is needed to prevent lower integrity data from contaminating higher integrity data. The *Strict Integrity* and the *Low Water-Mark* models [6] are representative integrity models based the notion that integrity is achieved by controlling the flow of information from objects to subjects. These models assign integrity levels to subjects and objects, and then, prevent information from flowing from low to high integrity levels.
- **Data verification** ensures that only verified data are presented to certain transactions. Clark and Wilson [8] propose an integrity model ensuring that well-formed transactions only receive valid data to guarantee that the results of the transactions preserve their valid states.
- **Prevention of fraud and errors** is necessary to ensure that only legitimate data are introduced in information systems. Such requirement is usually addressed by enforcing separation of duty between users and system administrators. Separation of duty has been widely investigated in access control community, especially in the context of role-based access control models [11,17].
- **Autonomous data integrity validation** is essential for maintaining and/or enhancing integrity of data. Data validation is different from data verification since data validation mechanisms continuously monitor and validate data objects independently from access control. It also tries to enhance the integrity of data according to dynamic changes in the data environments.

Although these requirements do not address integrity in all its aspects, we believe that they are the most relevant also because each one of them requires the deployment of different techniques. We note that those techniques should be combined in order to achieve a systematic method for preserving integrity to some significant level.

3.2 System Architecture

We now briefly discuss a system architecture designed to harmonize the integrity requirements with conventional access control systems. Figure 1 shows a high level view of the proposed architecture.

As shown in Figure 1, the *integrity controller* is transparent to subjects who send access requests and receive access control results since it is integrated with the conventional access controller. The role of integrity controller is to specify and enforce integrity based on metadata and integrity policies. The integrity controller consists of the following four components.

- *Integrity policy supplier.* It provides information related to integrity policies and metadata values to integrity policy repository and integrity metadata repository.

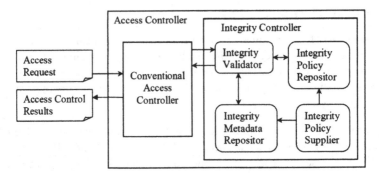

Fig. 1. Architecture for Integrity Management System

This is the key component of the architecture in that it interact with the external environment and applications in order to gather all information needed to assign trust values to data, to their provenance,and their providers.

- *Integrity policy repository* and *integrity metadata repository.* They maintain and manage various information about policies, users, and data for the integrity valida-tor. Among other functions, this component provides an editor for specifying poli-cies and metadata templates, that is, intensional definitions of metadata required for each data for which integrity is crucial.

- *Integrity validator.* It carries out integrity validation functions for access requests and data objects in database. The integrity functions of the integrity validator are invoked when access requests arrive from the conventional access controller or are autonomously executed by data integrity validation procedures.

3.3   Integrity Control Policies

We now describe a language for specifying metadata managed in the integrity matadata repository and then present our integrity control policy language which supports both data validation and integrity-related access control.

Metadata specification language
The metadata specification language is used to describe data structures and values of information by which data integrity is determined. Precisely specifying such informa-tion is important for integrity control since such information can vary according to the application requirements. For this we introduce a notion of metadata template.

Definition 1. Metadata template [7]. Let OT be the set of data types and R be the set of roles existing in the system. A metadata template for a particular data type $ot_i \in OT$ or a particular role $r_j \in R$ is specified as follows.

> **MD-TEMPLATE** *template-ID* **FOR** *target* {
> $attr_1$: *attribute-description*;
>   . . .
> $attr_n$: *attribute-description*;}

where $target$ is either ot_i or r_j and represents the entity that is associated with the specified metadata template. $attr_i$, $i = 1, ..., n$, is the name of the i-th attribute, and *attribute-description$_i$*, $i = 1, ..., n$, is the registered method for the i-th attribute, which may be a specific value, a function, or a system-variable.   □

An instance of metadata template is associated with a data item according to the metadata template specified for the type of the data item. The metadata instance is used in integrity control policies whenever the associated data item is accessed.

Integrity policy specification language

An integrity control policy is specified for a particular data type and enforced on all its instances. There are two kinds of policies in our framework: Access Control Policy (ACP) and Data Validation Policy (DVP). In order to preserve data integrity when a data item is read, modified, or deleted, ACP specifies what actions on the data are permitted under which conditions. On the other hand, independently from data accesses, DVP specifies autonomous processes for monitoring and/or enhancing the integrity. ACP and DVP are formally defined as Definition 2 and 3 respectively.

Definition 2. Access Control Policy (ACP)[7]. Let OT be the set of data types existing in the system and $ot_i \in OT$ be a data type. Let R be the set of roles existing in the system and $r_j \in R$ be a role. Let $ot_i.attrs$ be the set of attributes specified in the metadata template of ot_i. Similarly, let $r_j.attrs$ be the set of attributes specified in the metadata template of r_j . Then an ACP which governs access to the instances of ot_i by subjects with role r_j is specified as follows.

> **AC-POLICY** *ACP-ID* **FOR** (ot_i, r_j) {
>   **WHEN**   *AC-Event$_1$*, . . . , *AC-Event$_i$*;
>   **IF**   *Condition*;
>   **THEN**   *Decision$_1$*: *Action$_1$*, . . . , *Action$_m$*;
>   **ELSE**   *Decision$_2$*: *Action$_1$*, . . . , *Action$_n$*; }
> where:

- *AC-Event$_k$*, $k = 1, ..., l$, represents an access request {Read, Insert, Update, Delete}.
- *Condition* is a set of boolean-expression primitives which may be conjuncted, disjuncted, or negated with the boolean operators $\land$, $\lor$, and $\neg$, respectively. A boolean-expression primitive is of the form $(x \otimes y)$, where x (or y) is $attr_p \in ot_i.attrs$, $attr_q \in r_j.attrs$, a constant, or a function that returns *true* or *false*, and $\otimes \in \{<, \leq, >, \geq, =, \neq\}$.
- *Decision$_k$*, $k = 1, 2$, is an access control decision which is one of {Allow, Deny}.
- *Action$_k$*, $k = 1, \ldots, m$ (or n), represents an action to be taken as a consequence of the corresponding access control decision. An action is either a procedure invocation or a metadata update.   □

Definition 3. Data Validation Policy (DVP)[7]. Let OT be the set of data types existing in the system and $ot_i \in OT$ be a data type. Let $ot_i.attrs$ be the set of attributes specified in the metadata template of ot_i. A DVP for data type ot_i is specified as follows.

> **DV-POLICY** *DVP-ID* **FOR** ot_i {
>   **WHEN**   *Event$_1$*, . . . , *Event$_l$*;

```
IF          Validation-procedure;
THEN        Action₁, . . . , Actionₘ;
ELSE        Action₁, . . . , Actionₙ; }
```

where:

- $Event_k$, $k = 1, \ldots, l$, represents either an access request {Read, Insert, Update, Delete} or a user-defined event such as a specific time or a particular situation that triggers the specified validation policy.
- *Validation-procedure* is a designated function which validates the data instances of ot_i. It returns *true* if the validation succeeds; otherwise, it returns *false*.
- $Action_k$, $k=1,...,m$(or n), represents an action to be taken as a consequence of the data validation. An action is either a procedure invocation or a metadata update. □

The following examples illustrate how metadata templates, ACP, and DVP are used for addressing integrity requirements.

Example 1. In our example scenario, we assume that there are a role "USER" and a data type(i.e., table) "DATA". Whenever a subject activates USER role, a trust level is assigned to the subject using a function *getTrustLevel ()* with *USERID* of the subject. Also, whenever a DATA item is created, a default confidence level, 0 and a default verified value, *false* are assigned to the data item. To meet these integrity requirements, metadata templates for USER and for DATA are specified respectively as follows.

MD-TEMPLATE *template-USER* **FOR** *USER* {
    trustLevel: *getTrustLevel($USERID)*; }

MD-TEMPLATE *template-DATA* **FOR** *DATA* {
    confidenceLevel: 0;   // a default value
    verified: *false*;   // a default value }

USER can create a DATA item only if its trust level is greater than *threshold*. The confidence level of the DATA item is determined by the trust level of the USER who creates it. This integrity requirement is specified as an ACP, *ACP-INSERT*.

AC-POLICY *ACP-INSERT* **FOR** *(USER, DATA)* {
```
    WHEN        Insert;
    IF          (USER.trustLevel > threshold);
    THEN        Allow: (DATA.confidenceLevel ← USER.trustLevel);
    ELSE        Deny: −; }
```

The integrity of DATA may be influenced by changes on certain data items. Upon such an event(namely, *ChangeOnData*), DATA is autonomously revalidated by a predefined function, *revalidateDATA ()*, and then, the result is recorded on the metadata. This validation requirement is specified as a DVP, *DVP-VALIDATION*.

DV-POLICY *DVP-VALIDATION* **FOR** *DATA* {
```
    WHEN        ChangeOnData;
    IF          revalidateDATA(this);
    THEN        (DATA.validated ← true);
    ELSE        (DATA.validated ← false); }
```
    □

We believe that our integrity control policy language with metadata template sufficiently satisfies the various integrity requirements discussed above since it provides generic and intuitive methods to specify various integrity policies. In particular it can represents different integrity models previously proposed,like the models by Biba and by Calrk and Wilson.

4 Trust Evaluation of Data Provenance

As we already mentioned, one important issue in determining data integrity is the trustworthiness of data provenance. Data provenance includes information about the process through which data have been generated and the input and output data of these processes. Figure 2 shows a common scenario in which there are multiple parties characterized as data source providers, intermediate agents and data users. Data source providers could be sensor nodes or agents that continuously produce large volumes of *data items*. Those data items describe the properties of certain entities or events. Intermediate agents can simply pass the data items obtained from data source providers to data users, or make use of the data items to generate *knowledge items* consumed by data users or other intermediate agents. Data users are the final information consumers who expect to receive trustworthy data. For representation simplicity, we will refer to a data item or a knowledge item as an item when the context is clear.

To evaluate the trustworthiness of data provenance, we need to answer questions like "Where did the data come from? How trustworthy is the original data source? Who handled the data? Are the data managers trustworthy?" Due to the possible presence of malicious source providers and inaccurate knowledge generated by intermediate agents, the information provided to the data users could be wrong or misleading. Therefore, it would be very helpful that each piece of information received by data users be rated by a trust score indicating the trustworthiness level of the information. By using the trust

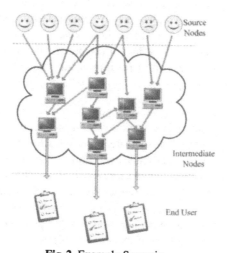

Fig. 2. Example Scenario

score, data users can determine whether they want to directly use the received information or need to further verify the information. Moreover, each data source provider (intermediate agent) is also assigned a trust score based on the amount of correct information it has provided. In the following, we present formal definitions of the level of trustworthiness for data items, knowledge items, data source providers and intermediate agents.

Definition 4. *Trust of data items and knowledge items. The trustworthiness of a data items f (or a knowledge item k), denoted as $t(f)$ (or $t(k)$), is the probability of f (or k) being correct.*

Definition 5. *Trust of source providers and intermediate agents. The trustworthiness of a source provider s (or an intermediate agent a), denoted as $t(s)$ (or $t(a)$), is the expected trustworthiness of the data items provided by s (or a).*

Our model takes into account various aspects that may affect the trustworthiness of an item. In particular, these aspects are *data similarity*, *data conflict*, *path similarity* and *data deduction*.

- **Data similarity** refers to the likeness of different items. Similar items are considered as supportive to each other and they can be obtained by using clustering algorithms. Then the trust score of an item tends to be higher when an item in a larger cluster, i.e., there are more similar items.
- **Data conflict** refers to inconsistent descriptions or information about the same entity or event. A simple example of a data conflict is that the same person appears at different locations during the same time period. It is obvious that data conflict has a negative impact on the trustworthiness of items.
- **Path similarity** refers to the likeness of the data generation paths. It affects the importance of supports obtained from similar data. If several independent sources provide the same data, such data is most likely to be true; otherwise, the support from similar data are not of much value. Therefore, if the path similarity among a group of similar items is low, we increase the trust scores of corresponding items; otherwise, we add a negative effect to the scores.
- **Data deduction** measures the effect of the process (e.g. data mining) on the data. Usually, the trustworthiness of the resulting data depends on the trustworthiness of input data and the on the parties that process the data.

We also observe that a data is likely to be true if it is provided by trustworthy data providers, and a data provider is trustworthy if most data it provides are true. Due to such inter-dependency between data and data providers, we have developed an iterative procedure to compute the overall trust scores. Initially, we assign each source provider and intermediate agent an initial trust score by querying the information that the end users already knew. The initial *trustworthiness* of each data item and knowledge item is then set to the *trustworthiness* of its source providers and intermediate agent. Then, we start the iteration. At each iteration, we compute the trustworthiness of the data based on the combined effects of the aforementioned four aspects, and recompute the trustworthiness of the data provider by using the trust scores of the data it provides.

When a stable stage is reached, that is, when the changes of trust scores are negligible, the trust computation process stops. We have carried out experimental activities to assess our trust score computation algorithm and our experimental results demonstrate its efficiency [9].

5 Policy Compliant Query Evaluation Based on Provenance Confidence

In this section, we discuss how to integrate the knowledge of data provenance with the query evaluation. We have developed a framework that evaluates queries according to confidence policies. An overview of the framework is shown in Figure 3. Our framework consists of three main components: query evaluation, policy evaluation and provenance evaluation. The main task of the query evaluation component is to evaluate queries and compute confidence levels of query results. The policy evaluation component filters out the query results that do not satisfy the confidence threshold as stated in confidence policies. The provenance evaluation component finds an optimal strategy to increase provenance confidence level of base tuples so that more useful results can be reported to users.

The data flow in the framework is described as follows. A user, or application, enters Q, pu, $perc$ and mon, where Q is a normal query, pu is the purpose of such a query, $perc$ is the percentage of results that a user expects to receive after policy checking, and mon is the maximum amount of cost he would like to pay to obtain more useful information. Then, the query evaluation component computes the query Q and the provenance confidence level of each tuple in the query result. These intermediate results are sent to the policy evaluation component. The policy evaluation component first selects the confidence policy regarding the role of user U, the data U wants to access and the purpose for which such access is required, and then checks each query result according to the selected confidence policy. Only the results with confidence level higher than the threshold specified in the confidence policy are returned to the user. If no result satisfies the confidence policy, the policy evaluation component sends a request message to the provenance evaluation component. The provenance evaluation component adjusts the confidence level of the base tuples involved in the query in order to obtain more

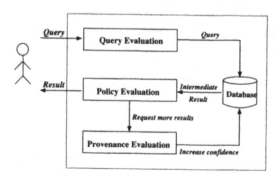

Fig. 3. System Framework for Policy Compliant Query Evaluation

candidate results that meet the confidence requirements stated in the confidence policy. Meanwhile, the provenance evaluation component needs to take into account the cost introduced during the confidence level increment and calculates a plan that can minimize such cost. The result tuple with the minimum cost will then be returned to the user.

We now proceed to present more details about confidence policy and provenance confidence increment.

5.1 Confidence Policy

A confidence policy specifies the minimum confidence that has to be assured for certain data, depending on the user accessing the data and the purpose for which the data are accessed. In its essence, a confidence policy contains three components: a subject spec-ification, denoting a subject or set of subjects to whom the policy applies; a purpose specification, denoting why certain data are accessed; a confidence level, denoting the minimum level of confidence that has to be assured by the data covered by the policy when the subject (set of subjects) to whom the policy applies requires to access the data for the purpose specified in the policy. Two example policies are shown as follows.

Example 2
- Pol_1: ⟨Secretary, analysis, 0.3⟩.
- Pol_2: ⟨Manager, investment, 0.8⟩.

Pol_1 states that a secretary can use the data with confidence level higher than 0.3 for analysis purpose; Pol_2 states that a manager can use the data with confidence level higher than 0.8 for investment purpose.   □

5.2 Provenance Confidence Increment

In some situations, the policy evaluation component may filter out all intermediate re-sults if their confidence levels are all lower than the threshold specified in the associated confidence policy. To enhance the chance for users to obtain more useful information, our system allows users to specify a minimum percentage (denoted as θ) of results they want to receive or a maximum amount of cost (denoted as c) they can afford. The prove-nance evaluation component will compute the cost of increasing the confidence levels of tuples in the base tables so that at least θ percent of query results will have the confi-dence level above the threshold or at most cost c is needed. If the user agrees with such additional cost, he will receive the query results. The problem can be formalized as a nonlinear constraint optimization problem which can be solved by using either heuristic or greedy algorithms. We refer the readers to [10].

6 Conclusion

In this paper, we analyzed various types of integrity models and identified a set of data integrity requirements. Based on these requirements, we have developed a framework for comprehensive integrity management, which includes metadata management, data validation and integrity control policies. An important part of data validation is the evaluation of data provenance. Therefore, we have developed a trust model for data provenance evaluation which estimates the trustworthiness of both data and data providers. Information about data provenance confidence is then taken into account during the query evaluation. In particular, we have introduced the notion of confidence policy that specifies the minimum confidence level about provenance that query results should have in order to be returned to the user based on the user current task and integrated the enforcement of such policy in query processing.

Acknowledgements

This work is supported by Air Force Office of Scientific Research under the project "Systematic Control and Management of Data Integrity, Quality and Provenance for Command and Control Applications".

References

1. http://www.arma.org/erecords/index.cfm
2. Abiteboul, S., Kanellakis, P., Grahne, G.: On the representation and querying of sets of possible words. Theoretical Computer Science 78(1) (1991)
3. Barbará, D., Garcia-Molina, H., Porter, D.: The management of probabilistic data. IEEE Transactions on Knowledge and Data Engineering 4(5), 487–502 (1992)
4. Batini, C., Scannapieco, M.: Data quality: Concepts, methodologies and techniques. Springer, Heidelberg (2006)
5. Bertino, E., Sandhu, R.: Database security - concepts, approaches, and challenges. IEEE Transaction on dependable and secure computing 2(1), 2–19 (2005)
6. Biba, K.: Integrity considerations for secure computer systems. Technical Report TR-3153, Mitre (1977)
7. Byun, J.-B., Sohn, Y., Bertino, E.: Systematic control and management of data integrity. In: Proceedings of the 11th ACM symposium on Access control models and technologies, pp. 101–110 (2006)
8. Clark, D., Wilson, D.: A comparison of commercial and military computer security policies. In: Proceedings of IEEE Symposium on Security and Privacy (1987)
9. Dai, C., Lin, D., Bertino, E., Kantarcioglu, M.: Trust evaluation of data provenance. In: CERIAS Technical Report (2008)
10. Dai, C., Lin, D., Kantarcioglu, M., Bertino, E., Celikel, E., Thuraisingham, B.: Policy observing query evaluation based on provenance confidence and lineage propagation (under preparation, 2008)
11. Ferraiolo, D.F., Sandhu, R., Gavrila, S., Kuhn, D.R., Chandramouli, R.: Proposed nist standard for role-based access control. ACM Trans. Inf. Syst. Secur. 4(3), 224–274 (2001)
12. Fuhr, N.: A probabilistic framework for vague queries and imprecise information in databases. In: Proc. VLDB, pp. 696–707 (1990)
13. Fuhr, N., Rölleke, T.: A probabilistic relational algebra for the integration of information retrieval and database systems. ACM Transactions on Information Systems 15(1), 32–66 (1997)
14. Green, T.J., Tannen, V.: Models for incomplete and probabilistic information. In: Proc. IIDB Workshop (2006)

15. Ni, Q., Trombetta, A., Bertino, E., Lobo, J.: Privcy aware role based access control. In: Proceedings of the 12th ACM symposium on Access control models and technologies (2007)
16. Sandhu, R.: On five definitions of data integrity. In: Proceedings of the IFIP WG11.3 Workshop on Database Security (1993)
17. Sandhu, R.S., Coyne, E.J., Feinstein, H.L., Youman, C.E.: Role-based access control models. IEEE Computer 29(2), 38–47 (1996)
18. Sarma, A.D., Benjelloun, O., Halevy, A., Widom, J.: Working models for uncertain data. In: Proc. ICDE, page 7
19. Sarma, A.D., Theobal, M., Widom, J.: Exploiting lineage for confidence computation in uncertain and probabilistic databases. Technical Report, Stanford InfoLab (2007)
20. Simmhan, Y.L., Plale, B., Gannon, D.: A survey of data provenance in e-science. SIGMOD Record 34(3), 31–36 (2005)
21. Widom, J.: Trio: A system for integrated management of data, accuracy, and lineage. In: Proc. CIDR, pp. 262–276 (2005)
22. Yin, X., Han, J., Yu, P.S.: Truth discovery with multiple conflicting information providers on the web. In: Proceedings of the 13th ACM SIGKDD International Conference on Knowledge Discovery and Data Mining (KDD 2007), pp. 1048–1052 (2007)

Towards General Temporal Aggregation

Michael H. Böhlen[1], Johann Gamper[1], and Christian S. Jensen[2]

[1] Free University of Bozen-Bolzano, Italy
{boehlen,gamper}@inf.unibz.it
[2] Aalborg University, Denmark
csj@cs.aau.dk

Abstract. Most database applications manage time-referenced, or temporal, data. Temporal data management is difficult when using conventional database technology, and many contributions have been made for how to better model, store, and query temporal data. Temporal aggregation illustrates well the problems associated with the management of temporal data. Indeed, temporal aggregation is complex and among the most difficult, and thus interesting, temporal functionality to support. This paper presents a general framework for temporal aggregation that accommodates existing kinds of aggregation, and it identifies open challenges within temporal aggregation.

1 Introduction

In database management, aggregation refers to the process of consolidating, or summarizing, a database instance; this is typically done by creating so-called *aggregation groups* of elements in the database and then applying an aggregation function, e.g., *avg*, *count*, or *min*, to each group, thus obtaining an aggregate value for each group.

In early work, Klug [6] put forward a formal relational database framework that encompassed aggregation. In his framework, aggregation is performed according to two parameters: (1) a set of attributes drawn from an argument relation, termed grouping attributes, and (2) pairs of a new attribute name and an aggregation function. The tuples in the relation are partitioned so that tuples with identical values for the grouping attributes are assigned to the same group. For each of the resulting aggregation groups, each aggregation function is evaluated on the tuples in the group, and the result is stored as a value of the associated attribute for each tuple in the group.

In temporal databases, tuples are typically stamped with time intervals that capture the valid time of the information, or facts, they record. During the 1980's, aggregation was incorporated in several query languages, e.g., Ben-Zvi's Time Relational Model [1], Navathe and Ahmed's TSQL [7], Snodgrass' TQuel [8], and a proposal by Tansel [10]. Some of these advances were subsequently consolidated in the TSQL2 proposal [9].

When aggregating temporal relations, it is meaningful to also group the tuples according to their timestamp values. With temporal grouping, groups of values from the time domain are formed. A tuple is then assigned to each group that overlaps with its timestamp, this way obtaining groups of tuples. When an aggregation function is applied to the groups of tuples, a temporal relation results. Different kinds of temporal groupings have emerged as being important. In *instant* temporal aggregation, the time

A. Gray, K. Jeffery, and J. Shao (Eds.): BNCOD 2008, LNCS 5071, pp. 257–269, 2008.

domain is partitioned into time instants, or points. In *moving-window* (or cumulative) temporal aggregation, additionally a time period is placed around each time instant to determine the aggregation groups. With *span* aggregation, the time line is partitioned into user-defined time periods.

This paper presents a general model for temporal aggregation that extends Klug's framework and that subsumes the temporal approaches mentioned above. The model provides orthogonal support for two aspects of aggregation: (a) the definition of *partial result tuples* for which to report one or more aggregate values, and (b) the definition of *aggregation groups*, i.e., the collections of argument tuples that are associated with the partial result tuples and over which the aggregation functions are to be computed. Aggregation then takes three parameters: a partial result relation, g; a mapping function, θ; and a set of pairs of an aggregation function and an attribute name, f_i/C_i.

The most related, past works are due to Vega Lopez et al. [11] and Böhlen et al. [3]. The former offers a framework that enables the analysis and comparison of different forms of temporal aggregation based on various mechanisms for defining aggregation groups, which all take advantage of different granularities. This leads to a point-based view that is not capable to preserve lineage information, and the resulting aggregation groups are contiguous in the time dimension, i.e., the union of the timestamps of all tuples in an aggregation group forms a convex set of time points. The latter offers a framework that decouples the partitioning of the time domain from the specification of the aggregation groups. This paper's proposal builds on this work and extends it in several directions. We elaborate on the relation to Klug's and SQL's framework, show how to express previous forms of temporal aggregation in the general model, and discuss by examples the additional expressiveness of the general model.

We proceed to introduce a running example. Section 3 then defines the new model, and Section 4 illustrates how important kinds of temporal aggregation can be defined using the model. Section 5 proceeds to identify directions for further research in temporal aggregation. Section 6 summarizes the paper.

2 Aggregation Example

Consider a temporal relation **emp** that captures work contracts with employees, recording for each contract the name of the employee (N), a contract identifier (CID), the department to which the employee is assigned for the duration of the contract, the monthly salary for the contract period (S), and the valid time of the contract (T). An instance of this relation is shown Fig. 1(a) and illustrated graphically in the upper part of Fig. 2, where the horizontal lines indicate the valid-time intervals of the tuples.

We consider the following three temporal aggregation queries over the relation:

- Q_{ITA}: *For each month and department, what is the number of contracts?*
- Q_{MWTA}: *For each month, how many contracts have been in effect during this month and the preceding two months?*
- Q_{STA}: *For each half-year period and department, what is the number of contracts?*

Q_{ITA} exemplifies instant temporal aggregation, for which the aggregation is applied to each database state, in this case to each month. To compute the aggregate result for

	N	CID	D	S	T
r1	Jan	140	DB	1200	[1,12]
r2	Dan	141	DB	700	[1,5]
r3	Dan	150	DB	700	[6,15]
r4	Tim	143	AI	2000	[4,9]

(a) Relation emp

D	Cnt	T
DB	2	[1,5]
DB	2	[6,12]
DB	1	[13,15]
AI	1	[4,9]

(b) Q_{ITA}

D	Cnt	T
DB	2	[1,5]
DB	3	[6,7]
DB	2	[8,14]
DB	1	[15,17]
AI	1	[4,11]

(c) Q_{MWTA}

D	Cnt	T
DB	3	[1,6]
DB	2	[7,12]
DB	1	[13,18]
AI	1	[1,6]
AI	1	[7,12]

(d) Q_{STA}

Fig. 1. Temporal Relation emp and Different Aggregation Queries

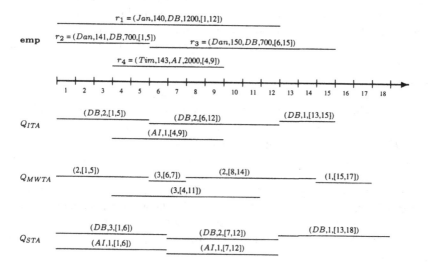

Fig. 2. Graphical Representation of the emp Relation and Aggregation Queries

a specific month, all tuples that are valid for that month are considered. Coalescing is used to get an interval-timestamped result relation. Coalescing yields result tuples over maximal time intervals, also called *constant intervals*. For forming maximal intervals two options exist. Either, the coalescing is performed wrt. the aggregate value alone, or it is performed wrt. the aggregate value and the lineage, i.e., the set of argument tuples used for computing the aggregate value. Coalescing with lineage preservation is the most general approach and is thus used here [2]. The result of Q_{ITA} is shown in Fig. 1(b) and graphically illustrated in Fig. 2. Note that without lineage preservation, $(DB, 2, [1, 5])$ and $(DB, 2, [6, 12))$ would have been merged.

Q_{MWTA} illustrates moving-window aggregation. Here, the aggregate value for each month is computed over all tuples that overlap this month or one of the preceding two months. Thus, the last result tuple extends beyond the end point of the last argument tuple. To obtain result tuples over maximal intervals, coalescing is applied similarly to how it is done for ITA. The result of Q_{MWTA} is shown in Fig. 1(c) and graphically illustrated in Fig. 2.

Q_{STA} is a span aggregation query. The time domain is first partitioned into half-year intervals independently of the argument relation. Then, for each half-year interval, the aggregation function is computed over all argument tuples that overlap that half year. The result of Q_{STA} is shown in Fig. 1(d) and graphically illustrated in Fig. 2.

3   General Temporal Aggregation

3.1   Preliminaries

We assume a discrete *time domain*, Δ^T, consisting of a totally ordered set of elements, termed time points (or instants). We assume a data model in which a timestamp, T, is assigned to each tuple that captures when the corresponding fact was, is, or will be true in the modeled reality. A timestamp is a convex set over the time domain and is represented by two time points, $[T_s, T_e]$, denoting its inclusive starting and ending points, respectively. In short, we assume a valid-time data model in which tuples are timestamped with intervals.

A *relation schema* is a three-tuple $R = (\Omega, \Delta, dom)$, where Ω is a non-empty, finite set of attributes, Δ is a finite set of domains, and $dom : \Omega \rightarrow \Delta$ is a function that associates a domain with each attribute. A *temporal relation schema* is a relation schema with at least one timestamp valued attribute, i.e., $\Delta^T \in \Delta$. A *tuple r over schema R* is a function that maps every $A_i \in \Omega$ to a value $v_i \in dom(A_i)$. A *relation r over schema R* is a finite set of tuples over R.

For notational simplicity, we assume an ordering of the attributes and represent a temporal relation schema as $\mathbf{r} = (A_1, \ldots, A_n, T)$ and a corresponding tuple as $r = (v_1, \ldots, v_n, [T_s, T_e])$. For a tuple r and an attribute A_i we write $r.A_i$ to denote the value of the attribute A_i in r. For a set of attributes $A_1, \ldots, A_k$, $k \leq n$, we define $r[A_1, \ldots, A_k] = (r.A_1, \ldots, r.A_k)$.

3.2   A General Model of Temporal Aggregation

Recall that Klug's (and SQL's) conventional framework for non-temporal aggregation performs aggregation on an argument relation according to two parameters [6]:

1. A set of attributes drawn from the argument relation, termed grouping attributes
2. A set of pairs of a new attribute name and an aggregation function

The tuples in the argument relation are partitioned according to their values for the grouping attributes. Then for each partition, each aggregation function given in the second parameter is computed on the tuples in the partition, and the result is stored as a value of the associated attribute for each tuple in the partition. The non-grouping attributes of the argument relation may be eliminated from the result by means of a projection using relational algebra.

The new model for temporal aggregation extends Klug's framework to the temporal context and generalizes it to provide orthogonal support for two important aspects of aggregation: (a) the definition of partial result tuples for which to report one or more aggregate values, and (b) the definition of aggregation groups, i.e., collections of argument tuples that are associated with the result groups and over which the aggregation functions are computed.

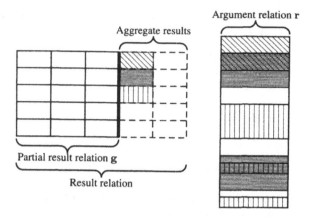

Fig. 3. General Temporal Aggregation

We assume that the aggregation is applied to a relation **r**, as described earlier. The new temporal aggregation model allows then to specify the following three parameters: (1) a *partial result relation*, **g**, (2) a *mapping function*, θ, from **r** to **g**, and (3) a set of *aggregation functions*, **F**. The aggregation model is illustrated in Fig. 3.

Instead of partitioning the tuples in the argument relation according to their values for certain of their attributes, we introduce a separate *partial result relation*, **g**, that contains a partial result tuple for each tuple that will be included in the result relation; i.e., these tuples will be extended with the aggregate results to form final result tuples. The partial result relation has schema $G = (B_1, \ldots, B_m, T)$, where the B_i are non-temporal attributes and T is a timestamp attribute that specifies a time interval (or time point, as a special case of an interval) over which to report an aggregation result. This relation generally has as attributes a subset of the attributes of the argument relation, the timestamp attribute being one of them. Thus, it can typically be specified as a relational algebra expression over the argument relation, i.e., $\mathbf{g} = RA(\mathbf{r})$. In general, however, the attributes B_i and the timestamp T in the partial result relation may also be obtained from relations other than **r**.

The second parameter, *mapping function*, $\theta : \mathbf{r} \to \mathbf{g}$, maps tuples from the argument relation, **r**, to tuples in the partial result relation, **g**. It may assign the same argument tuple to zero, one, or many partial result tuples. In other words, function θ associates with each partial result tuple a set of argument tuples, termed its *aggregation group*, over which to compute the aggregates to be reported for that tuple. This differs from the conventional framework, where each input tuple is mapped to exactly one group, based on equal values over all grouping attributes.

The third parameter is retained from the conventional framework and specifies the *aggregation functions*, $\mathbf{F} = \{f_1/C_1, \ldots, f_k/C_k\}$. Each f_i is some aggregation function that takes a (temporal) relation as argument and applies aggregation to one of the relation's attributes. The resulting value is stored as the value of an attribute named C_i. For instance, the pair $count_{CID}/Cnt$ states that $count_{CID}$ counts the CID values in the argument relation and returns the count, which is stored as a value of attribute Cnt. Using this notation, we allow for a family of count functions, one for each attribute of the argument relation. For example, $count_N$ and $count_S$ counts over the name and the salary attribute, respectively.

Definition 1 (General Temporal Aggregation). Let g be a partial result relation, θ a mapping function, and $\mathbf{F}$ a set of aggregation functions, as introduced earlier. The *general temporal aggregation* is then defined as follows:

$$\mathcal{G}^T[\mathbf{g}, \theta, \mathbf{F}]\mathbf{r} = \{g \circ f \mid g \in \mathbf{g} \wedge \mathbf{r}_g = \{r \in \mathbf{r} \mid \theta(r) = g\} \wedge f = f_1(\mathbf{r}_g), \dots, f_k(\mathbf{r}_g)\}$$

The schema of the result relation is $(B_1, \dots, B_m, C_1, \dots, C_k, T)$.

The mapping function, θ, defines and associates an aggregation group, $\mathbf{r}_g \subseteq \mathbf{r}$, with each partial result tuple, $g \in \mathbf{g}$. The aggregation functions are computed over these aggregation groups. The final result tuples are given as the partial result tuples extended ($\circ$, concatenation) with the results of the aggregation functions.

General temporal aggregation decouples the specification of the desired result tuples (i.e., the partial result tuples) from the specification of the aggregation groups (i.e., the mapping of argument tuples to the partial result tuples). In SQL and Klug's framework, the desired result tuples and the aggregation groups are determined by the grouping attributes only. Each different combination of grouping attribute values forms then a partial result tuple and—by equality on the attribute values—determines a corresponding aggregation group. We believe that the specification of the partial result tuples should be decoupled from the specification of the associated aggregation groups, and we find it natural to allow for the use of other operators than simply equality comparison for the specification of the aggregation groups. This yields a more flexible and expressive framework for temporal aggregation.

An important aspect of the framework is that the values for the timestamp attribute in the partial result tuples may be either fixed and provided by the user, or it may be inferred from the data in the argument relation. The use of *fixed intervals* corresponds to how the non-timestamp attribute values are treated: they must be provided explicitly. The use of *inferred intervals* is unique to the timestamp attribute. An inferred interval in a partial result tuple is calculated as the intersection of the intervals of the argument tuples that contribute to the aggregate results to be associated with that partial result tuple. These inferred intervals are termed *constant* because there are no changes in the argument relation during these intervals. Constant intervals are non-overlapping and maximal. Queries Q_{ITA} and Q_{STA} illustrate the difference between user-provided and inferred intervals.

The new model is quite general. The partial result relation, $\mathbf{g}$, is completely independent of the argument relation, $\mathbf{r}$, and its only purpose is to group the results. This provides extensive flexibility in arranging the results according to various criteria, and it makes it possible to express different forms of temporal aggregates including the ones proposed previously. We will show this next.

4   Different Forms of Temporal Aggregation

In part to explore the use and generality of the proposed aggregation framework, we show how three previously proposed forms of temporal aggregation can be expressed in a uniform manner using the framework. We also discuss aggregation queries that are difficult or even impossible to express in terms of the traditional temporal aggregation operators, but can be expressed easily in the new framework.

4.1 Instant Temporal Aggregation

In *instant temporal aggregation* (ITA), the time domain is partitioned into time instants, and an aggregation group is associated with each time instant t that contains all tuples with a timestamp that contains t. Then the aggregation functions are evaluated on each group, producing each a single aggregate value for each t. Finally, identical aggregate results for consecutive time instants are coalesced into the previously mentioned constant intervals.

In some approaches, the aggregate results for a constant interval must also have the same lineage, meaning that they are produced from the same set of argument tuples. Query Q_{ITA} and its result in Fig. 1(b) illustrate ITA. Without the lineage requirement, the result tuples $(DB, 2, [1, 5])$ and $(DB, 2, [6, 12])$ would become $(DB, 2, [1, 12])$.

Definition 2 (Instant Temporal Aggregation). Let r be a temporal relation, $\mathbf{F}$ be a set of aggregation functions, and $A = A_1, \ldots, A_k$ be the grouping attributes in r. Further, let $\mathbf{s} = \pi[A, T_s]r \cup \pi[A, T_e + 1 / T_s]r$ be the start points and $\mathbf{e} = \pi[A, T_s - 1 / T_e]r \cup \pi[A, T_e]r$ be the delimiting points of the constant intervals. Then the *instant temporal aggregation* for the aggregation functions in $\mathbf{F}$ over the argument relation r grouped by A can be expressed in the general temporal aggregation model as $\mathcal{G}^T[\mathbf{g}, \theta, \mathbf{F}]r$, where:

$$\mathbf{g} = \pi[A, [T_s, min(T_e) / T_e]](\mathbf{s} \bowtie [\mathbf{s}.A = \mathbf{e}.A \wedge T_s \leq T_e] \mathbf{e})$$
$$\theta(r) = \{g \in \mathbf{g} \mid g.A = r.A \wedge g.T \cap r.T \neq \emptyset\}$$

To express ITA, the partial result relation, $\mathbf{g}$, needs to specify the constant intervals of the result tuples, considering also the grouping attributes, $A_1, \ldots, A_k$. First, $\mathbf{s}$ and $\mathbf{e}$ collect all start and end points of the constant intervals together with the grouping attribute values. Each argument tuple, $r \in r$, induces two start points (the tuple's start point, $r.T_s$, and the successor of the tuple's end point, $r.T_e + 1$) and two end points (the tuple's end point, $r.T_e$, and the predecessor of the tuple's start point, $r.T_s - 1$). Second, those pairs of start and end points are selected that form a valid constant interval. This is the case if for each start point the closest end point that is greater than or equal to the start point is selected. This can be expressed as a join followed by a generalized projection.

Example 1. Consider Query Q_{ITA}. The start and end points of the constant intervals are given as $\mathbf{s} = \{(DB, 1), (DB, 6), (DB, 13), (DB, 16), (AI, 4), (AI, 10)\}$ and $\mathbf{e} = \{(DB, 0), (DB, 5), (DB, 12), (DB, 15), (AI, 3), (AI, 9)\}$, respectively. Substituting $\mathbf{s}$ and $\mathbf{e}$ in the expression for the partial result relation, we get $\mathbf{g} = \{(DB, [1, 5]), (DB, [6, 12]), (DB, [13, 15]), (AI, [4, 9])\}$. The aggregation functions are $\mathbf{F} = \{count_{CID} / Cnt\}$, and the mapping function is $\theta(r) = \{g \in \mathbf{g} \mid g.D = r.D \wedge g.T \cap \text{emp}.T \neq \emptyset\}$. To compute, for example, the aggregate value over the constant interval $[1, 5]$, the mapping function selects the two argument tuples r_1 and r_2.

This definition of ITA preserves lineage: adjacent result tuples with the same aggregate value are not coalesced if they are derived from different argument tuples (cf. the first two result tuples of Q_{ITA} for the DB department).

4.2   Moving-Window Temporal Aggregation

With *moving-window temporal aggregation* (MWTA) (first introduced in TSQL [7] and later also termed *cumulative temporal aggregation* [8,12]), a time window is used to determine the aggregation groups. For each time instant t, an aggregation group is defined as the set of argument tuples that hold in the interval $[t-w, t]$, where $w \geq 0$ is a window offset. In some work [11], a pair of offsets w and w' is used, yielding a window $[t-w, t+w']$ for determining the aggregation groups. After computing the aggregation functions for each aggregation group, coalescing is applied similarly to how it is done for ITA to obtain result tuples over maximal time intervals.

Query Q_{MWTA} and its result in Fig. 1(c) illustrate MWTA. To answer this query, a window is moved along the time line, computing at each time point an aggregate value over the set of tuples that are valid at some point during the last three months.

While both ITA and MWTA partition the time domain into time instants, they differ in how the aggregation groups for each time instant are defined.

Definition 3 (Moving-Window Temporal Aggregation). Assume the earlier definitions of $\mathbf{r}$, $\mathbf{F}$, and $A = A_1, \ldots, A_k$, and let w be a non-negative window offset. Further, let $\mathbf{s} = \pi[A, T_s]\mathbf{r} \cup \pi[A, T_e + w/T_s]\mathbf{r}$ be the start points and $\mathbf{e} = \pi[A, T_s - 1/T_e]\mathbf{r} \cup \pi[A, T_e + w - 1/T_e]\mathbf{r}$ be the end points of the constant intervals. Then the *moving-window temporal aggregation* for the aggregation functions in $\mathbf{F}$ over relation $\mathbf{r}$ grouped by A and using window offset w can be expressed as $\mathcal{G}^T[\mathbf{g}, \theta, \mathbf{F}]\mathbf{r}$, where:

$$\mathbf{g} = \pi[A, [T_s, min(T_e)/T_e]](\mathbf{s} \bowtie [s.A = e.A \wedge T_s \leq T_e] \, \mathbf{e})$$
$$\theta(r) = \{g \in \mathbf{g} \mid g.A = r.A \wedge [g.T_s - w + 1, g.T_e] \cap r.T \neq \emptyset\}$$

The expression of MWTA is similar to that of ITA; the only difference is that the effect of the window offset, w, must be considered both for the computation of the constant intervals that are stored in the partial result relation, $\mathbf{g}$, and in the mapping function, θ. Intuitively, each argument tuple affects the aggregation result beyond its own timestamp. Thus, to determine $\mathbf{s}$ and $\mathbf{e}$ to generate the timestamps of the partial result tuples, the window offset, w, is added to the end points of the argument tuples. The mapping function, θ, is modified similarly; the only difference is that the start point of the partial result tuple is decreased by w in order to collect also argument tuples that do not overlap with the timestamp of the result tuple, but have to be considered for the computation of the aggregates.

Example 2. Consider Query Q_{MWTA}, which has a window offset of 3. The start points of the constant intervals together with the grouping attribute values are $\mathbf{s} = \{(DB, 1), (DB, 6), (DB, 8), (DB, 15), (DB, 18), (AI, 4), (AI, 12)\}$ and the end points $\mathbf{e} = \{(DB, 0), (DB, 5), (DB, 7), (DB, 14), (DB, 17), (AI, 3), (AI, 11)\}$.

Substituting s and e in the expression for the partial result relation, we get $\mathbf{g} = \{(DB, [1,5]), (DB, [6,7]), (DB, [8,14]), (DB, [15,17]), (AI, [4,11])\}$. The aggregation functions are $\mathbf{F} = \{count_{CID}/Cnt\}$, and the mapping function is $\theta(r) = \{g \in \mathbf{g} \mid g.D = r.D \land [g.T_s - 2, g.T_e] \cap \mathbf{emp}.T \neq \emptyset\}$. To compute, for example, the aggregate value over the constant interval $[6,7]$, the mapping function uses the argument tuples $r_1, r_2,$ and r_3.

4.3 Span Temporal Aggregation

For *span temporal aggregation* (STA), the time domain is first partitioned into predefined intervals that are defined independently of the argument relation. For each such interval, an aggregation group is then given as the set of all argument tuples that overlap the interval. A result tuple is produced for each interval by evaluating an aggregation function over the corresponding aggregation group.

Query Q_{STA} and its result in Fig. 1(d) illustrate STA. The pre-defined intervals are 6-month periods.

Unlike in ITA and MWTA, the timestamps of the result tuples in STA are specified independently of the argument data. Most approaches consider only regular time spans expressed in terms of granularities, e.g., years, months, and days.

Definition 4 (Span Temporal Aggregation). Assume the earlier definitions of r, $\mathbf{F}$, and $A = A_1, \ldots, A_k$, and let $\mathbf{p}$ be a relation with a single attribute T that contains the time intervals over which to report result tuples. Then *span temporal aggregation* can be expressed as $\mathcal{G}^T[\mathbf{g}, \theta, \mathbf{F}]r$, where:

$$\mathbf{g} = \pi[A]\mathbf{r} \times \mathbf{p}$$
$$\theta(r) = \{g \in \mathbf{g} \mid g.A = r.A \land g.T \cap r.T \neq \emptyset\}$$

In the expression of STA, we assume that the timestamps of the result tuples are given in a relation $\mathbf{p}$. This relation is joined with the argument relation, $\mathbf{r}$, and projected to the grouping attributes, A, and the timestamp attribute, T, to form the partial result relation, $\mathbf{g}$. The mapping function, θ, is the same as for ITA.

Example 3. Consider Query Q_{STA}, which reports a result tuple for each six-month period. The time intervals of the result tuples are then given as $\mathbf{p} = \{([1,6]), ([7,12]), ([13,18])\}$, which gives a partial result relation $\mathbf{g} = \{(DB, [1,6]), (DB, [7,12]), (DB, [13,18]), (AI, [1,6]), (AI, [7,12]), (AI, [13,18])\}$. The aggregation functions are $\mathbf{F} = \{count_{CID}/Cnt\}$, and the mapping function is $\theta(r) = \{g \in \mathbf{g} \mid g.D = r.D \land g.T \cap \mathbf{emp}.T \neq \emptyset\}$. To compute, e.g., the aggregate value over the period $[1,6]$, the mapping function uses the tuples $r_1, r_2,$ and r_3.

Note that STA reports a result tuple for all predefined intervals. If the aggregate group is empty, the aggregate value is 0 or NULL. This behavior can be controlled by adjusting the definition of $\mathbf{g}$.

4.4   Aggregation over Non-contiguous Aggregation Groups

In ITA, MWTA, and STA the aggregation groups are defined over contiguous subsets of the non-temporal and timestamp domains. For the non-temporal attributes, each aggregation group is defined for a single attribute value; and for the timestamp, it is either divided into single time points, for ITA, or into contiguous sets of time points, for MWTA and STA.

It is desirable to also be able to compute aggregates over sets of argument tuples that are non-contiguous in some of the attributes. With general temporal aggregation, aggregation groups can be specified where the time domain is grouped into non-contiguous groups of time points and the timestamps of the tuples in an aggregation group do not necessarily overlap with the timestamp of the corresponding result tuple. Similarly, the aggregation groups need not be disjoint with respect to non-temporal attributes. We illustrate these capabilities by means of two examples.

Example 4. Consider the following query: *What is the total number of contracts in each quarter, summed up over the past two years?* In this query the argument tuples that contribute to a result tuple are temporally non-contiguous and do not overlap with the timestamp of the result tuple. This query can be formulated as $\mathcal{G}^T[\mathbf{g}, \theta, \mathbf{F}]$emp, where:

$$\mathbf{g} = \{([1,3]), ([4,6]), ([7,9]), ([10,12])\}$$
$$\theta(r) = \{g \in \mathbf{g} \mid g.T \cap [\text{emp}.T_s \bmod 12 + 1, \text{emp}.T_e \bmod 12 + 1] \neq \emptyset\}$$
$$\mathbf{F} = \{count_{CID}/Cnt\}$$

The partial result tuples simply specify the four quarters, whereas the mapping function associates the argument tuples with the correct quarters.

Example 5. Consider the following query: *For each department, what is the total number of contracts in the other departments?* Here, the aggregation group of a partial result tuple consists of tuples with a department value that is different from the department of the partial result tuple. This query can be formulated as $\mathcal{G}^T[\mathbf{g}, \theta, \mathbf{F}]$emp, where:

$$\mathbf{g} = CI(\pi[\mathbf{r}.D, \mathbf{s}.T](\mathbf{r} \bowtie [\mathbf{r}.D \neq \mathbf{s}.D] \mathbf{r}/\mathbf{s}))$$
$$\theta(r) = \{g \in \mathbf{g} \mid g.D \neq r.D \wedge g.T \cap \text{emp}.T \neq \emptyset\}$$
$$\mathbf{F} = \{count_{CID}/Cnt\}$$

where CI is a regular expression that computes the constant intervals as for ITA. Note that the aggregation groups are not disjoint. With each partial result tuple we associate all argument tuples with a different department value.

5   Open Challenges in Temporal Aggregation

The foundations of most temporal database technology were built in the 1980s and 1990s. In retrospect, much of that research seems to have focused implicitly on meeting the relational data management needs of administrative applications. (This paper's example database is a good representative of this class of application.) Over the last decade, new types of applications and technologies have gained in prominence, including ones that offer new challenges to temporal database technology and temporal aggregation. We proceed to discuss challenges, most of which are due to these developments.

Update-Intensive Applications Based on Sampled Continuous Functions. The class of update-intensive applications is gaining in prominence. For example, large populations of vehicles may report their speeds and other sensed data. These data are samples of continuous functions. For most times, a measured value of a function is not available. The samples may have been reported according to a scheme that offers accuracy guarantees, or they may have been reported at regular time intervals. This is unlike the salary attribute in our example, and this scenario suggests several challenges.

First, we may want to transform the sequences of samples to a representation where we have a value for each point in time so that we are back in known territory. Issues include how to accomplish this transformation, how accurately to do this, and how to capture the inaccuracy.

Next, when applying an aggregation function to the sensed data, it becomes relevant to take into account the inaccuracy of the data so that the inaccuracy of the result can be reported. Likewise, when using the sensed data for defining the partial result relation, the inaccuracy of the data is an important part of the equation.

Third, it may be observed that instant temporal aggregation and moving-window temporal aggregation may return result relations that contain up to twice as many tuples as the input relations, which seems counter to the goal of summarizing the data in order to obtain an overview. It thus becomes of interest to be able to "aggregate an aggregate." We believe that it would be attractive to enable the users to control the trade-off between result accuracy and result cardinality. For example, if the user specifies a certain required accuracy, the aggregation should return the smallest number of tuples needed to satisfy that accuracy.

Applications Involving Higher-Dimensional Temporal Data. Many application will involve bitemporal, spatio-temporal, or n-dimensional data. Supporting aggregation for such data offers several challenges. For example, with more than one dimension, it becomes necessary to define the 1+-dimensional equivalents of constant intervals. While constant intervals are unique, such constant regions are not. The definition as well as efficient implementation of maximal constant regions is a challenge.

Expressing General Temporal Aggregation in SQL. The SQL:2003 standard supports window functions. With these, aggregates may be computed by sorting and scanning the argument relation. While this is efficient, it does not support multidimensional groupings for which no single obvious ordering exists. Chatziantoniou's EMF-SQL extends the group by clause with grouping variables and introduces a such that clause for constraining the grouping variables [5]. Neither approach supports the specification of constant intervals, which is at the core of temporal aggregation. It would be interesting to extend these approaches with support for time. A survey of approaches to temporal aggregation in SQL-based temporal query languages is available [4].

Extension to Non-Relational Data Models. Far from all data is stored in SQL databases. Perhaps most notably, increasing amounts of data are stored in XML. Introducing temporal support, including support for temporal aggregation, calls for reconsidering many of the key data model and query language design decisions. For example: What is the equivalent of a tuple? Is there something comparable to tuple-timestamping and attribute-value timestamping? What are the implications of the hierarchical nature of the model for timestamping and aggregation?

Efficient Evaluation Algorithms. The general model covered in this paper defines temporal aggregation and offers a uniform way of expressing concisely the various forms of temporal aggregation that have been studied in the past. However, the definition does not imply an efficient implementation—a straightforward implementation would require costly operations such as joins and scans of the argument relation (4 scans for the delimiting points of the constant intervals and one for the aggregation). While efficient implementation of aggregation has been studied, solutions that integrate tightly with state-of-the-art relational database technology are in order. One specific challenge is to incrementally compute the partial result tuples as the argument relation is scanned, to avoid more than one scan of the argument relation.

6   Concluding Remarks

The framework for aggregation that has been available in SQL for several decades and that was formalized by Klug is very intuitive and has remained relatively unquestioned, at least in the context of on-line transaction processing. We believe that it is time to probe deeper. Specifically, the current framework is far from a panacea for all relational data management needs. We believe that aggregation can be rendered much more expressive.

This paper has elaborated on that view, by presenting a general framework for temporal aggregation, by illustrating how this framework accommodates existing forms of aggregation, and by pointing out new challenges that invite others to engage in further research—the general model proposed here is also not a panacea.

References

1. Ben-Zvi, J.: The Time Relational Model. Ph.D.thesis, Comp. Sci. Department, UCLA (1982)
2. Böhlen, M.H., Jensen, C.S., Snodgrass, R.T.: Temporal statement modifiers. ACM Transactions on Database Systems 25(4), 407–456 (2000)
3. Böhlen, M.H., Gamper, J., Jensen, C.S.: Multi-dimensional aggregation for temporal data. In: International Conference on Extending Database Technology, pp. 257–275 (2006)
4. Böhlen, M.H., Gamper, J., Jensen, C.S.: How would you like to aggregate your temporal data? In: Intl. Symposium on Temporal Representation and Reasoning, pp. 121–136 (2006)
5. Chatziantoniou, D.: Using grouping variables to express complex decision support queries. Data and Knowledge Engineering 61(1), 114–136 (2007)
6. Klug, A.C.: Equivalence of relational algebra and relational calculus query languages having aggregate functions. Journal of the ACM 29(3), 699–717 (1982)

7. Navathe, S.B., Ahmed, R.: A temporal relational model and a query language. Information Sciences 49(1-3), 147–175 (1989)
8. Snodgrass, R.T., Gomez, S., McKenzie, L.E.: Aggregates in the temporal query language TQuel. IEEE Transactions on Knowledge and Data Engineering 5(5), 826–842 (1993)
9. Snodgrass, R.T. (ed.): The TSQL2 Temporal Query Language. Kluwer, Dordrecht (1995)
10. Tansel, A.U.: A statistical interface to historical relational databases. In: International Conference on Data Engineering, pp. 538–546 (1987)
11. Vega Lopez, I.F., Snodgrass, R.T., Moon, B.: Spatiotemporal aggregate computation: a survey. IEEE Transactions on Knowledge and Data Engineering 17(2), 271–286 (2005)
12. Yang, J., Widom, J.: Incremental computation and maintenance of temporal aggregates. VLDB Journal 12(3), 262–283 (2003)

Distributed Systems and Automated Biodiversity Informatics: Genomic Analysis and Geographic Visualization of Disease Evolution

Andrew W. Hill[1] and Robert P. Guralnick[1,2]

[1] Department of Ecology and Evolutionary Biology, University of Colorado, Boulder,
Colorado, United States of America
[2] University of Colorado Museum, University of Colorado, Boulder, Colorado,
United States of America

Abstract. A core mission in biodiversity informatics is to build a computing infrastructure for rapid, real-time analysis of biodiversity information. We have created the information technology to mine, analyze, interpret and visualize how diseases are evolving across the globe. The system rapidly collects the newest and most complete data on dangerous strains of viruses that are able to infect human and animal populations. Following completion, the system will also test whether positions in the genome are under positive selection or purifying selection, a useful feature to monitor functional genomic characteristics such as, drug resistance, host specificity, and transmissibility. Our system's persistent monitoring and reporting of the distribution of dangerous and novel viral strains will allow for better threat forecasting. This information system allows for greatly increased efficiency in tracking the evolution of disease threats.

Keywords: Biodiversity Informatics, Geophylogenies, Google Earth, H5N1 Avian Influenza, Infectious Diseases, Human health, HyPhy, Viral evolution.

1 Introduction

A crucial task in biodiversity informatics is to build the computing infrastructure to provide rapid, real-time discovery, access, visualization, interpretation, integration and analysis of biodiversity information [1-5] at the ecosystem, species, and genetic levels. We provide a working example of an automated framework that greatly improves the speed of many preliminary analyses necessary to track lineages across the landscape, and decreases the man-hours necessary to gain useful information from current data warehouses. Our system currently targets combined genomic, geographic and ecological information.

There are many good reasons for providing tools to examine the relationship between geography and organismal and/or gene lineages. Although much information can be gleaned from just the sampled distribution of organisms across the landscape (e.g. species richness and diversity, predictive models of species distributions [6-9]),

A. Gray, K. Jeffery, and J. Shao (Eds.): BNCOD 2008, LNCS 5071, pp. 270–279, 2008.

there are also limits. Patterns of species distribution have come about through historical processes, and inferring these processes through examination of morphological and molecular variation and sorting of this variation into distinct lineages provides a much richer set of information about biodiversity [10] and especially about how species may respond to future biotic and abiotic perturbations. Biogeographical perspectives provide information about past and present patterns necessary for making accurate predictions about the future.

Here we discuss an information system that focuses on tracking the evolution of a particular type of biodiversity – viruses. We focus on viruses for three reasons: 1) They represent a continued threat to human health and therefore monitoring of changes to viral genomes and the spread of different viral strains is of practical importance [11] 2) Viruses evolve very quickly, on the order of weeks to years as opposed to thousand or millions of years, and we can therefore use modern landscapes as a backdrop to monitoring viral evolution as opposed to reconstructed past landscapes; 3) Viral genomes and proteomes are relatively simple and much is known, from biomedical research, about how viruses infect organisms and which changes in the genome have led to functional changes in the virus (e.g. which mutations confer drug resistance) [12].

In order to document the continuing evolution of viruses, we have built an information system that provides users with a continually updating view of the spread of viral lineages. Here we focus on influenza A viruses but the system can be applied to other biological infectious agents that are of concern (e.g. West Nile, Tuberculosis, Malaria, etc). Influenza A viruses are a focus because they are a persistent human health concern. H3N2 and H1N1 strains are responsible for human transmissible seasonal influenza which affects hundreds of millions of people each year [13]. Another strain, the highly pathogenic H5N1 avian influenza, has been implicated as the next potential human pandemic. If this virus was to evolve human transmissibility, mortality could in the millions [14]. Determining containment strategies if an outbreak were to occur is an area of very active exploration and all containment strategies revolve around knowing where strains of the viruses are co-circulating. Especially important is tracking how influenza A viruses are evolving resistance to the main antiviral drugs that are used in prevention and treatment, and how drug resistant strains are proliferating across the landscape.

1.1 A System for Automated Monitoring of Disease Evolution

Our information system is built around a set of operations that we want to rapidly and automatically perform in order to provide near real-time results for monitoring purposes. As well, automation frees researchers from performing many of the necessary but repetitive and time-consuming tasks of preliminary analyses. Fig. 1 provides a summary view of the process and is explained in more detail in the Workflow section below. The process begins with periodically scraping (at a rate consistent with the generation of new data) of genomic data coming in from flu sequencing projects occurring around the globe. In the last ten years, the number of influenza A flu genomes has grown by orders of magnitude and that rate will likely continue or accelerate into the future. From there, we automate construction of alignments and phylogenetic analyses of these genomes, along with automated georeferencing of the locations where the genomes were isolated. We also can delimit known mutations that are of importance for tracking across landscape – in particular those mutations known to either affect the transmissibility or pathogenicity of the virus, or those that lead to resistance to antiviral drugs. Finally, we provide information on which types of animals are carrying which lineages and how the virus might be transmitted among different types of hosts. This information is particularly crucial for documenting increased transmissibility of H5N1, now a predominately avian disease, from birds to mammals.

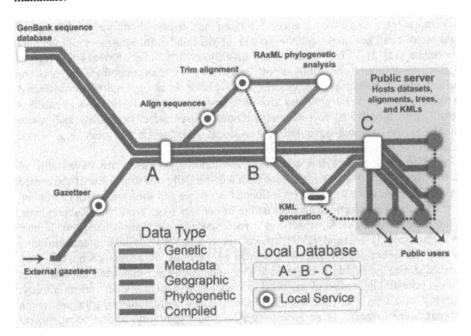

Fig. 1. Disease data, currently genomic data stored at NCBI GenBank, is automatically accumulated and passed through a set of analyses which are then compiled for download by the user through a web-service. Currently our system runs alignments, outsources phylogenetic inference, and generates Keyhole Markup Language (KML) files that allow for the visualization of disease spread. A user is then capable of downloading original sequences, metadata associated with each sequence, trimmed alignments, phylogenies, and complied/interactive KMLs.

Whereas other systems have been developed to provide web-enabled analysis of both user assembled genomic data (http://supramap.osu.edu/supramap) and occurence data (see ref. 15) the fundamental difference in our system is that it is an automated reporting system particularly useful for rapid assessment and preliminary analysis. By utilizing and integrating both influenza phylogenetic information (see ref. 16 for automated phylogeny) and geographic information, we can project the current evolutionary hypothesis for the virus onto a virtual global (e.g. Google Earth™) and use the rich visual symbology available in the visualization tool to show lineages and mutations of interest to the end user [17]. As well, we can use such a system to track movements of lineages with potentially worrisome mutations to any user, whether a scientist, policy-maker, health officials, or an interested member of the public. In the future, we will provide users with the means to extract useful subsets of data from our ever-growing database of influenza A genomes in order to generate new analyses for inclusion into our workflow. For example, if interested, a user could request a dataset of, *H3N2 isolates from between 2005 and present,* and then select a set of analyses that can be performed on that dataset. As well, each time new genome data becomes available, the user-defined dataset and analyses will be re-run and new results posted. All analyses will be stored so that ultimately the tool we are developing could be a community workbench for disease monitoring. In addition to these features, we include RSS feeds for individual datasets, allowing users to receive automated notification updates. Such subscription services are not required for updating Google Earth results since KMLs are already designed to update themselves with the most recent information each time a user loads the file in Google Earth.

The numbers of analyses that can be automated can also be expanded depending on user interest. We foresee several near future additions: First, we will include a channel for user generated annotations and corrections. This would, for example, allow users to improve the precision of sample locality for specific isolates, among other changes. Second, we will include amino-acid sequences and alignments for each dataset. Third, with the inclusion of amino-acid alignments, we plan to add several analyses performed in the HyPhy software [18], including codon-level selection measures. This would expand the degree to which a user could automate performing more specialized analyses. For example, a user might want to ask whether there is evidence for selection on mutations that lead to drug resistance for various different antiviral drugs. Since it is known which positions on which segments lead to resistance to different classes of drugs [19-21], the system can track those mutations and run codon-based selection tests to determine if there is evidence for positive selection or purifying selection, and how selection for resistance might be varying over time.

Below we discuss how we have constructed our automated monitoring system for influenza A. We also discuss features we would like to implement in the future and how the system can continue to grow both in terms of increased functionality and flexibility.

2 Workflow Description

Our workflow is designed to accumulate, link, and reformat numerous sources relevant to disease evolution and ecology. Currently we utilize only two main data sources: NCBI's GenBank for genomic data and metadata about viral isolation, and external gazetteers (e.g. the BioGeomancer workbench (http://bg.berkeley.edu/latest/) and the Getty Thesaurus of Geographic Names (http://www.getty.edu/research/conducting_research/vocabularies/tgn/index.html) for place names. From these genetic and geographic sources we can gain sufficient data to reconstruct both relationships among the viral isolates and their location on the globe, and then package that information for the user. Figs. 1 and 2 summarize the steps in creating meaningful outputs that can be used for disease monitoring. It is important to note that there are numerous places to utilize a distributed network of environmental and biological data resources and methods of analyses. We touch on a few of the obvious distributed resource and analysis tools that can be linked to our application below.

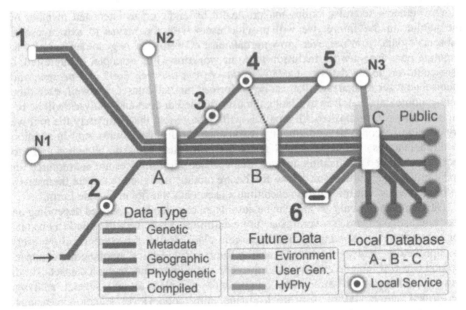

Fig. 2. The detailed data management and analysis workflow, where current elements are numbered and future elements are given the N prefix, is as follows: (1) Genetic data and linked metadata are collected from the GenBank ftp site. (2) Geographic place names for known disease occurrences are accumulated and linked to geographic coordinates. (3) Nucleotide sequences are aligned locally with MUSCLE and MAFFT multiple sequence alignment tools. (4) Alignments are programmatically trimmed to remove leading and trailing columns with only small amounts of sequences represented. (5) The alignments for each dataset are sent to the CIPRES web service to construct phylogenetic trees. (6) Phylogenies and geographic coordinates are combined to generate KML based framework for data visualization. Character optimizations can also be performed at this point using Phylip, Paup, or other capable tools. (N1) Environmental data. (N2) User generated dataset definitions, annotations, corrections. (N3) HyPhy analysis suite or Datamonkey service.

2.1 Data Accumulation

Because our system is currently designed for influenza A, data scraping is generally straightforward. Influenza genetic and associated data already organized and stored at the NCBI ftp site. Therefore, data scraping is a simple programmatic process of running cURL to transfer the files to a local repository. Following the transfer, the files are parsed into a local PostgreSQL database (Fig. 1, Database A). The parsed data includes the full genome sequence, date of collection, location of collection, the host from which the genome was isolated, and any other metadata that might be of interest. In order to allow for mapping, we then tie each isolate to the decimal degree latitude and longitude for its best locality description. In order to link locality strings to latitude and longitude, we currently use a hand assembled library of common localities of influenza isolation. This process is simplified by the fact that localities are a typical component of the influenza naming system. However, because these localities are generally very coarse, in the future we will allow users to update individual strain localities based on better available data such as latitude and longitude from primary literature. In addition, we will apply georeferencing best practices and associated geographic uncertainty to all isolates (as described in ref. 15). Pre defined datasets are all represented as *Views* (in some cases *Materialized Views* are used) within the PostgreSQL database, such that all data from beginning to end (Genbank data, alignments, trees, and KMLs) are stored in specific database tables and combined dynamically on lookup. Currently, our datasets are focused on complete genome sequences (those represented by all eight vRNA segments) for common influenza subtypes.

2.2 Data Analysis

Data analysis follows two main channels: The first is the phylogenetic analysis. We align the data for each dataset using MUSCLE (http://www.drive5.com/muscle/) [22] and MAFFT (http://align.bmr.kyushu-u.ac.jp/mafft/software/) [23] services available through the European Bioinformatics Institute (EBI; http://www.ebi.ac.uk/). Using local PHP scripting, raw sequences are uploaded and completed alignments are retrieved from the EBI web service [24]. Alignments are programmatically trimmed, simply removing as many leading and trailing columns as necessary until a certain threshold of the data is represented in the column. Trimmed alignments are stored in the PostgreSQL database (Fig. 1, Database B) and uploaded to a remote phylogenetic analysis service (http://www.phylo.org).

Remote phylogenetic analysis is run in much the same way as sequence alignment. To generate maximum-likelihood phylogenies for each or datasets, we use the RAxML [25] implementation available through a REST API service from the

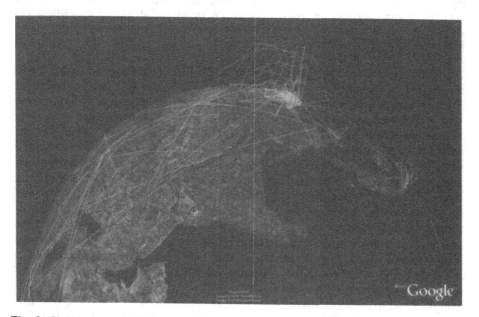

Fig. 3. Global view of H5N1 spread. Drug resistant isolates (and ancestors) highlighted in orange with non-resistant branches shown in white.

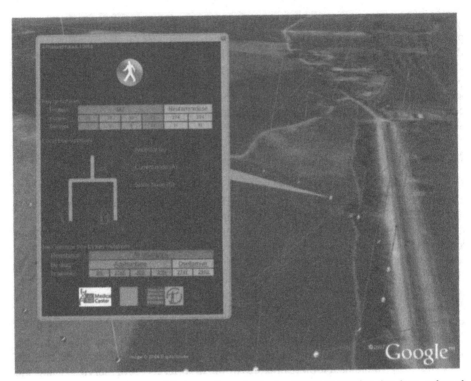

Fig. 4. Close-up view of several isolates. One, A/Thailand/1(KAN-1/2004), has been selected and a pop-up window shows the details of this isolate. Details include several key mutations in the viral genome as well as some information about its most phylogenetically closely related neighbors.

Cyberinfrastructure for Phylogenetic Research (CIPRES) project. In the future, it will be possible to include other potential user-specified analyses (e.g. parsimony or Bayesian analysis) as well as provide bootstrap values for phylogenetic hypotheses. After phylogenies are returned from CIPRES, we combine phylogeny and geographic information to form the structure of the KML visualization of disease spread. In short summary, each terminal taxon and hypothetical taxonomic unit (HTU) was assigned a set of geographical coordinates and altitude. Altitude is based on the phylogenetic depth of the node, where terminal taxa rest on the surface of the globe and HTUs are shown floating above the globe – the farther towards the base of the tree, the higher the altitude above the globe the HTU. For more information on the process of creating these KMLs, see ref. 17. By utilizing metadata on isolation date and the KML timespan function, we can add an explicit temporal component to the Google Earth visualization. Linking the phylogeny with time through the built in capabilities of Google Earth, we allow users to literally watch how the virus has likely evolved across the landscape through time.

Figs. 3 and 4 show such two such visualizations. Figs. 3 shows a global visualization of the spread of H5N1 avian influenza across the globe with a particular drug resistant mutation (colored in orange) optimized onto the tree. Fig. 4 shows a pop-up box that can be pulled up when a user selects any branch in the KML file. That pop-up box contains a rich set of information including all transformations that have occurred on that branch, the host, if any of the mutations are of interest due to known functional changes (e.g. increased transmissibility, drug resistance), and much more. Exemplar KML files are available for download at http://biodiversity.colorado.edu

2.3   Deployment of Application as a Web Workbench

The application and analyses we are currently running for monitoring influenza evolution is made available from our website, http://biodiversity.colorado.edu/. From the website, users can download original datasets, making it possible for them to use our preliminary analyses to formulate hypotheses and predictions, and then refine the datasets to test those predictions. Also available are files from each stage of the analysis, including alignment, RAxML trees, and KMLs. Furthermore, each stage and dataset is available to users through RSS feeds that allow users to easily monitor updates.

KML files will be the primary component for download from the website. As discussed above, opening these KML files in Google Earth, users will be able to explore the evolution of viruses across the globe and over time. Users will also be able to use the KMLs to interact directly with each of the other components of the analysis (GenBank record, alignment, and RAxML flat trees). Using the expiration features built into KML, each time a user opens the file, the newest and most complete dataset will be available for immediate interaction.

2.4   Future Workbench Directions

We foresee many future directions to expand our data visualization and analysis workflow. This includes using analysis of codons to provide information about functional changes to the virus. Such a process would be done by programmatically reconstructing the coding sequence from nucleotide sequences, and analyzing those through other programs developed elsewhere (i.e. HyPhy at http://datamonkey.org). An area of particular interest for monitoring purposes is detection of codon-level selection for known mutations that change how the virus functions. For example, it is already known which mutations give rise to antiviral drug resistance in influenza A populations, and monitoring those mutations may be of particular importance for pandemic planning. Such selection analysis could be run either locally or remotely. A local implementation would be to use the HyPhy software package which includes multiple tests for codon-level selection. Alternatively, we could use a remote service such as Datamonkey.org, to run many of the same analyses. In either scenario, we will be able to provide useful evolutionary information regarding host use potential, human transmissibility, or drug resistance.

Another direction we plan to take the system is incorporating more environmental data and information on host range and dispersal capabilities. Such information, when coupled to the genomic analyses described above, could be useful for better forecasting predicting where viruses may be spreading [26] and how viral transmissibility may be increased through host switching events, especially for the predominately avian H5N1 influenza. As well, coupling that information with characteristics of the human landscape (human population centers, poultry farms, etc.) will provide useful planning information in case of a pandemic.

3 Conclusions

By linking directly to the sources of sequence data and utilizing rapid alignment and phylogenetic algorithms (e.g. MUSCLE, MAFFT, RAxML) we can provide near real time visualizations of disease spread and evolution. Our application will allow researchers, medical professionals and policy makers to make more informed hypotheses and policies regarding the rapid spread and evolution of disease. Our current online web workbench is rudimentary right now, allowing users access to continually updating analyses of influenza evolution. Users may also select subsets of analyses to run depending on regions and time-frames of interest. In the near future, we will provide further flexibility and depth of analyses that can be run. All of our next steps are based on core functions for disease monitoring in the hopes that such applications can help us make informed decisions about how to respond to everything from seasonal influenza to pandemic influenza.

Acknowledgements. We thank Meredith Wilson for her efforts on the local gazetteer as well as design elements. Special thanks to the University of Colorado Museum and the Walker Van Riper for their generous grant to support this work.

References

1. Blackmore, S.: Knowing the Earth's Biodiversity: Challenges for the Infrastructure of Systematics Biology. Science 274, 63–64 (1996)
2. Cotter, G.A., Bauldock, B.T.: Biodiversity Informatics Infrastructure: An Information Commons for the Biodiversity Community. In: VLDB 2000, pp. 701–704 (2000)
3. Krishtalka, L., Humphrey, P.S.: Can Natural History Museum Capture the Future? Bioscience 50(7), 611–617 (2000)
4. Sugden, A., Pennisi, E.: Diversity Digitized. Science 289(5488), 2305 (2000)
5. Wilson, E.O.: A Global Biodiversity Map. Science 289(5488), 2279 (2000)
6. Kress, W.J., Heyer, W.R., Acevedo, P., Coddington, J., Cole, D., Erwin, T.L., Meggers, B.J., Pogue, M., Thorington, W.R., Vari, R.P., et al.: Amazonian biodiversity: Assessing Conservation Priorities With Taxonomic Data. Biodiver. Conserv. 7(12), 1577–1587 (1998)
7. Funk, V.A., Zermologlio, M.F., Nasir, N.: Testing the Use of Specimen Collection Data and GIS in Biodiversity Exploration and Conservation Decision Making in Guyana. Biodiver. Conserv. 8(6), 727–751 (1999)
8. Joseph, L., Stockwell, D.: Temperature Based Models of the Migration of Swainson's Flycatcher Myiarchus Swainsoni Across South America: A New Use for Museum Specimens of Migratory Birds. P. Acad. Nat. Sci. Phila. Sciences 150, 293–300 (2000)
9. Funk, V.A., Richardson, K.S.: Systematic Data in Biodiversity Studies: Use It or Lose It. Syst. Biol. 51, 303–316 (2002)
10. Wheeler, Q.D.: Systematics, the Scientific Basis for Inventories of Biodiversity. Biodivers. Conserv. 4(5), 476–489 (1995)
11. Morens, D.M., Folkers, G.K., Fauci, A.S.: The Challenge of Emerging and Re-Emerging Infectious Diseases. Nature 430, 242–249 (2004)
12. Rappuoli, R.: From Pasteur to Genomics: Progress and Challenges in Infectious Diseases. Nature Med. 10, 1177–1185 (2004)

13. Simonsen, L.: The Global Impact of Influenza on Morbidity and Mortality. Vaccine 17(1), S3–S10 (2000)
14. World Health Organization. Avian Influenza: Assessing the Pandemic Threat (2005), http://www.who.int/csr/disease/influenza/WHO_CDS_2005_29/en/
15. Guralnick, R.P., Wieczorek, J., Hijmans, R.J., Beaman, R., the Biogeomancer Working Group: Biogeomancer: Automated Georeferencing to Map the World's Biodiversity Data. PLoS Biol. 4(11), 1908–1909 (2006)
16. Hibbett, D.S., Nilsson, R.H., Snyder, M., Fonseca, M., Constanzo, J., Shonfeld, M.: Automated Phylogenetic Taxonomy: An Example in the Homobasidiomycetes (Mushroom-Forming Fungi). Syst. Biol. 54(4), 660–668 (2005)
17. Janies, D., Hill, A.W., Guralnick, R.P., Habib, F., Waltari, E.: Genomic Analysis and Geographic Visualization of the Spread of Avian Influenza (H5N1). Syst. Biol. 56(2), 321–329 (2007)
18. Kosakovsky Pond, S.L., Frost, S.D.W., Muse, S.V.: HyPhy: Hypothesis Testing Using Phylogenies. Bioinformatics 21(5), 676–679 (2005)
19. Suzuki, Y.: Natural Selection on the Influenza Virus Genome. Mol. Biol. Evol. 23(10), 1902–1911 (2006)
20. Gubareva, L.V., Kaaiser, L., Hayden, F.G.: Influenza virus neuraminidase inhibitors. Lancet 355, 827–835 (2000)
21. Hay, A.J., Wolstenholme, A.J., Skelhel, J.J., Smith, M.H.: The molecular basis of the specific anti-influenza action of amantadine. EMBO J. 4, 3021–3024 (1985)
22. Edgar, R.C.: MUSCLE: Multiple Sequences Alignment With High Accuracy and High Throughput. Nucleic Acids Res. 32(5), 1792–1797 (2004)
23. Katoh, K., Misawa, K., Kuma, K., Miyata, T.: MAFFT: A Novel Method for Rapid Multiple Sequence Alignment Based on Fast Fourier Transform. Nucleic Acids Res. 20(1), 3059–3066 (2002)
24. Labarga, A., Valentin, F., Andersson, M., Lopez, R.: Web Services at the European Bioinformatics Institute. Nucleic Acids Research Web Services Issue (2007)
25. Stamatakis, A.: RAxML-VI-HPC: Maximum Likelihood-based Phylogenetic Analyses with Thousands of Taxa and Mixed Models. Bioinformatics 22(21), 2688–2690 (2006)
26. Peterson, A.T., Benz, B.W., Papeş, M.: Highly Pathogenic H5N1 Avian Influenza: Entry Pathways into North America via Bird Migration. PLoSONE 2(2), e261 (2007), doi: 10.1371/journal.pone.0000261

Visualisation to Aid Biodiversity Studies through Accurate Taxonomic Reconciliation

Martin Graham, Paul Craig, and Jessie Kennedy

Centre for Information and Software Systems, Napier University, 10 Colinton Road,
Edinburgh, EH10 5DT, UK
{m.graham,p.craig,j.kennedy}@napier.ac.uk

Abstract. All aspects of organismal biology rely on the accurate identification of specimens described and observed. This is particularly important for ecological surveys of biodiversity, where organisms must be identified and labelled, both for the purposes of the original research, but also to allow reinterpretation or reuse of collected data by subsequent research projects. Yet it is now clear that biological names in isolation are unsuitable as unique identifiers for organisms. Much modern research in ecology is based on the integration (and re-use) of multiple datasets which are inherently complex, reflecting any of the many spatial and temporal environmental factors and organismal interactions that contribute to a given ecosystem. We describe visualization tools that aid in the process of building concept relations between related classifications and then in understanding the effects of using these relations to match across sets of classifications.

Keywords: Biodiversity, taxonomy, concepts, concept relationships, visualization.

1 Introduction

Consider a typical research scenario: a scientist is interested in analyzing the spread of invasive species in a certain region [1]. They are aware of pertinent results in the literature and have additional distribution records in their personal database, along with access to other potentially relevant datasets on-line. The researcher needs to be able to discover candidate datasets and be able to merge relevant and compatible information from these varied datasets. Simplistically, datasets might be retrieved and integrated on the basis of country and species name; however, just as country names and boundaries change over time, so do the definitions attached to species names. Unfortunately sufficiently sophisticated on-line taxonomic resources and tools to aid the biologist are not currently available to allow them to address these problems in legacy data sets or to adequately annotate new data sets. An essential step for reusability and longevity of these data is the documentation of the contents of such datasets, but effective documentation depends on the implementation of adequate practices and information technologies [2; 3] as well as adherence to defined data standards.

A. Gray, K. Jeffery, and J. Shao (Eds.): BNCOD 2008, LNCS 5071, pp. 280–291, 2008.

Ecological data may refer to organisms in a variety of ways: by their common name, by some internal code, or by scientific name. Although appearing to be less ambiguous than local common names, scientific names are also unstable and change in meaning over time and between authorities. The name used in one ecological study will reflect the classification context used by the authors at that time; datasets produced at different times or by different workers in different geographical locations might reference competing, if not conflicting, taxonomic standards [4; 5]. Hence the inconsistent meaning of taxonomic labels used to identify species or higher-level taxonomic groups necessitates semantic integration of the data for ecological analyses. Furthermore, if the context or source for a recorded name is not captured as part of the documentation of the dataset, it can be impossible for subsequent workers to accurately resolve relationships among taxa identified simply by name.

The exact meaning of taxonomic names can change over time due to the lumping, splitting, or redefinition of lineages as taxonomists revise their classifications [6], and might also vary significantly between contemporary treatments owing to differences in interpretation, (e.g. morphological versus genetic criteria) or circumscription (i.e. the limits or extent of a given taxon). The valid scientific names applied to taxa (i.e., species or other groups) in a given taxonomic classification are mechanistically determined according to codified rules of nomenclature via the method of typification and the principle of priority [7].   Because taxonomic opinion and classifications evolve, the names that are properly applied to revised taxonomic concepts may be *identical* to those used to refer to earlier and possibly quite different circumscriptions of taxonomic entities. To share a name, two taxon circumscriptions need only include the same type specimen. A further consequence of the application of the nomenclatural codes to the results of taxonomic revision is that different names may be used according to different taxonomic perspectives; yet refer to entities that appear indistinguishable. As a consequence of these problems of synonymy and homonymy it is impossible to integrate multiple datasets with any certainty of accuracy simply by matching the names of taxa they contain. Thus, taxonomic names are a significant and pervasive source of ambiguity when dealing with biodiversity data of mixed provenance [8].

An example serves to illustrate the problem. Alternative taxonomies arise with the discovery of new specimens and species, more information about shared traits and newly inferred phylogenetic relationships, and even new analytical tools [9]. Consider the example of gorilla taxonomy [10] (partially) in Fig. 1. Gorillas were first described and classified by Reverend Savage in 1847, based on a population found in West-Central Africa. He considered them similar to chimpanzees (named *Troglodytes niger* in 1812 by E. Geoffroy St. Hilaire) and grouped them into the same Genus calling them *Troglodytes gorilla*. However in 1816, Oken realized that the generic name Troglodytes had already been used in 1806 by Vieillot to name the bird wren, therefore the generic name for chimpanzees was changed to *Pan*, (strictly speaking Savage & Wyman should've named gorillas *Pan gorilla* in 1847). However, in 1852 I. Geoffroy St. Hilaire re-classified the gorillas, separating them from chimpanzees and renaming them *Gorilla gorilla*, the first use of the name for gorillas commonly used today. In 1902, they were found in East-Central Africa and in 1903 Matschie reclassified them and defined a new species of gorilla called *G. berengei*. Matschie continued his splitting of gorillas, resulting in several species including *G. graueri*

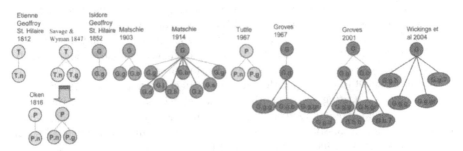

Fig. 1. Summary Gorilla Classifications showing genus, species and sub-species as classified by some of the primate taxonomists since gorillas were first discovered in 1847 through to 2004

from the Congo in 1914 and many others (*G. diehli, G. jacobi, G. schwarzi, G. hansmeyeri* and *G. zenkeri*). Other described species and sub-species not shown.

In 1967 Tuttle claimed that gorillas were related to chimps and put them back in the genus *Pan* while Groves claimed that there was only one species of gorilla, *G. gorilla* of which there were 3 sub-species: *G. g. gorilla, G. g. graueri and G.g.beringei* but by 2001 with more recent evidence Groves had reclassified Gorilla into two species (currently agreed by most experts in the field) and 5 sub-species: *G. gorilla, G. g. gorilla, G. g. diehli* and *G. beringei, G. b. beringei, G. b. graueri* and an un-named subspecies of *G. b*. However recent DNA analysis [11] is suggesting that four distinct evolutionary specific units of gorilla exist although it is not clear if these are species or sub-species. In addition to taxonomic treatments, if we consider the popular field guides for example Mammal Species of the World, in the 1993 revision it presented gorillas as one species *G. gorilla* with 3 subspecies, similar to Groves 1967. However in the 2005 edition they are adopting the Groves 2001 classification with 2 species and 4 subspecies. Apes of the World on the other hand adopt Tuttle's definition of gorilla and recognize 1 species *P. gorilla*.

It should now be clear that when we use the taxonomic name *G. gorilla* there may indeed be many different definitions of this name; what we refer to as taxon concepts (the taxon name as defined by a particular taxonomist in a particular classification). Just at species level in the gorilla example above we have 10 different taxon names that are used with varying meanings across 8 different classifications, (i.e. we have 18 different taxon concepts which have been described by the authors). However the current "accepted" treatment used varies between individuals and institutions, and therefore biologists undertaking analysis of data which may have been collected according to different field guides could end up with misleading results in their analysis unless they were knew if it was about *G. gorilla* Groves 1967, as compared to *G gorilla* Groves 2001 or *P. gorilla*. In databases and in the literature however authors are frequently vague about what taxon concept they are referring to, and simply cite a name such as *G. gorilla* thinking this makes it clear as to what they meant (and for something as well known as gorillas who wouldn't?). This can also have serious repercussions, for example, in conservation if the red list (and associated statute) cites *G. gorilla* (according to Groves 1967 but without explicitly specifying so) as endangered and illegal to trade, then a poacher might be able to legally argue that trading in *G. berengei* (according to Matschie or Groves 2001) is legal as it's a different species.

If ecological information is to be useful for future analyses, it should document against what treatment the original authors of the data identified the organisms, and long-term strategies to manage the legacy of ecological data must accept and accommodate this constraint [12]. Minimally, a reference to the source publication (e.g. field guide) used in making taxonomic identifications should be included, to indicate the taxonomic concept being identified. New or annotated data should record 'taxon concepts' which capture the differences in names shown by the case studies in Fig. 1, rather than simple scientific names. The adopted convention for referring to taxonomic concepts is to cite the name *sec.* author [4] where "*sec.*" stands for the Latin *secundum*, meaning "according to" a particular (team of) author(s). It provides (*inter alia*) a solution to the problems discussed. We can now refer to *Gorilla gorilla* Savage & Wyman sec. Groves (2001), for example and use this as a reference for the underlying definition. To this end, an abstract model, the Taxonomic Concept Schema (TCS) for representing taxonomic concepts and their relationships has been developed [13] and ratified by the International Biodiversity Standards (TDWG) as one of their standards. This standard will facilitate merging ecological datasets collected at different times and places by workers following varied taxonomic standards.

Research has been undertaken to determine the stability of names relative to taxonomic concepts [14] using Koperski et al's moss data set as example data [15]. It was revealed that only 13% of Koperski et al's taxa declared congruent relationships to concepts with the same name in different classifications and made no other relationships. Another 22% of the taxa had congruent relationships only, but this time to homotypic synonyms, a further 20% had doubtful stability and 45% had various incongruent relationship types, indicating instability between taxonomies.

Recent work [16] reports similar issues in weevil data, reinforcing the message that researchers can only depend on a minority of names in one classification actually meaning the same concept in another, and this ratio tends to diminish as time passes between classifications. Thus with names unsuitable as cross-taxonomy identifiers, concepts and concept relationships come to the forefront of linking and matching between taxonomies. What are needed now are tools to enable taxonomists to accurately mark up their data with concepts and relate new revisions to existing legacy classifications so vital for long term biodiversity studies, and for other specialists to be able to effectively use this data.

2 Visualisation

One approach for exploring and generating the structures formed through the concepts and their relationships is Information Visualisation (IV) [17] – the graphical display of and interaction with complex data sets. Essentially we have a set of multiple hierarchies – the classifications we are attempting to reconcile – along with a set of links that map between those hierarchies – which are the concept relations. To this end we have developed two complementary visualizations for our data; the first, TaxVis, allows users to explore relationships between multiple classifications, and the second, Concept Relation Editor, allows concept relationships to be placed between pairs of classifications.

2.1 TCS Relationship Data

Both visualisations take TCS data in the form of an XML file that contains descriptions of publications, names and relationships to generate a multiple tree model with the relations and names acting as links between the publications (the classifications). The relationships themselves are defined in the data set, and are assumed to be the work of taxonomists whose names are associated with those relations. Inferring further TCS relations from existing relationships is a subject that is approached formally in [18] and discussed informally in [19]. In short we do not infer relationships in our visualizations beyond enforcing reciprocality, i.e. if A includes B, we make a relationship that B is included in A, similarly if C overlaps D, then D must also overlap C.

Generally inferring relationships is problematic as it produces a relationship which is only as strong as its weakest link i.e. if A *is congruent to* B which overlaps C we can only conclude A has an overlap with C. Further, if A *is included in* B which overlaps C, we cannot even infer the overlap, as the part of B which overlaps C may not be the part which includes A. Add on top of that the difficulty of chaining relationships defined by different authors who may well have different opinions and the trustworthiness of inferred relations quickly deteriorates. Conceivably one workable scenario is to chain congruent relationships by the same author, but so far we leave further relation inferencing to the user to perform in the visualization.

2.2 TaxVis – A Visualisation for Exploring Multiple Classifications

We have developed a visual taxonomy explorer which allows matches between classifications to be explored through concept relationships [19]. The visualization itself consists of a number of types of different co-ordinated views applicable to a classification data set, known as a multiform visualization [20], though in the following discussion we will concern ourselves mainly with only one of the views in particular – the multiple tree view [21]. In this view, classifications are displayed as individual top-down hierarchies. Selections that are made in one hierarchy are reflected in the other hierarchies giving a measure of overlap and distribution between related classifications.

One of the most revealing tasks that can be performed in the application is to compare the differences in matches made through naïve name matching to those made through following concept relationships. Using a TCS version of Koperski et al's [15] moss concept data as input to the visualization we can show the numerous differences generated by the two approaches for a sample genus, *Eurhynchium*. Matching between just three of the classifications in the set, Koperski's recent revision and Smith's 1980 and Mönkemeyer's 1927 classifications, demonstrates the type of differences that can be observed.

Firstly, when matching strictly by name, it becomes obvious even before visualization that there will be no inter-genus relationships. The species *X.a* in one classification cannot be matched to anything other than *X.a* in another classification. At higher levels in a classification families, classes, and even genera themselves could freely be repositioned in higher taxa without necessarily requiring re-naming – which in itself can cause problems with homonymy as people assume the same name means the same thing in different classifications. This is not so with species, a species moved between two genera must take on the name of its parent genus as the first part of its binomial name. Thus, when matching *Eurhynchium* across the two classifications, from Koperski back to Mönkemeyer all that happens is that the *Eurhynchium* genus representation is highlighted in both classifications, as seen in Fig. 2. Differences in species naming and authoring means none of the *Eurhynchium* species match by name. Smith's 1980 classification fares better, being closer in time to Koperksi et al's revision, with several name matches highlighted, though there are still several nodes that remain unaffected, indicating no name match.

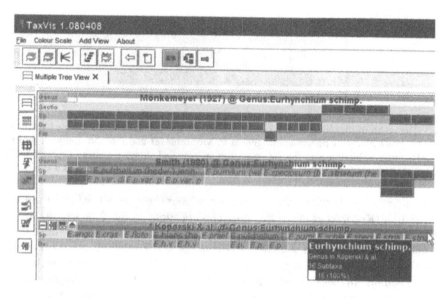

Fig. 2. *Eurhynchium* taxa selected by name in Koperski have little impact on Mönkemeyer

By contrast when matching by concept relations a completely different picture emerges, as seen in Fig. 3. Koperski et al's *Eurhynchium* has been selected and the visualization set to highlight matches by concept relationship. This reveals relationships to four different genera in Mönkemeyer, including its interpretation of *Eurhynchium*, so according to Koperski et al, their definition of the genus is made from parts of those four different genera, indicating that integrating data collected under these two classifications could be troublesome. Smith's classification contains three genera that overlap with Koperski et al's treatment of *Eurhynchium*. However, exploration of *Eurhynchium*'s species and varieties in Koperski et al shows that at a lower level many of the relationships are congruencies, albeit between concepts with different names. For example, in Fig. 3, the mouse is currently hovering over *Eurhynchium striatalum* in Koperski et al, and links and a tool tip reveal this name in Koperski is considered conceptually equivalent to a species of *Isothecium* in Mönkemeyer and Smith's classifications, though a differently named species in each.

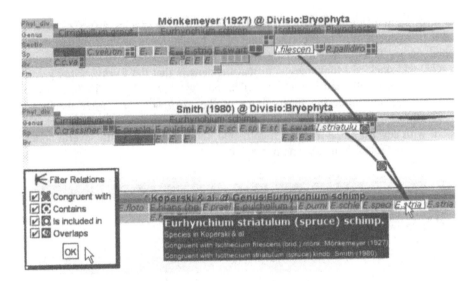

Fig. 3. The result of matching Koperski et al's *Eurhynchium* genus and its contents by concept relations reveal it is split between four genera in Mönkemeyer and three in Smith. A tool tip currently displays relationships for the *striatulum* species and shows matches to species in the *Isothecium* genus in the other classifications. A relation filter control is included as a key.

The moss set is simplified by the fact the relationships are all defined from one classification (Koperski et al) to the other classifications in the data set, and are all authored by the same people (Koperski et al). Other data sets may not assume these constraints, indeed we have a *Ranunculus* data set where relations are concentrated around two classifications and the relation set includes relations defined by two differing authors. In these circumstances it can be useful to filter out relations defined by one or more authors as taken as a whole the relationship set can contain apparently contradictory findings as seen in Fig. 4, or as stated in the previous section can lead to erroneous conclusions if relations defined by more than one author are chained together to deduce other relations.

Thus, we can visually match and explore the relationships between a set of classifications to reveal patterns that would be non-existent using naïve name matching. Using this tool, ecologists with names collected under more than one classification can match such data to be consistently based on just one of the referenced classifications. Another alternative is to use a third-party classification as seen in Fig.3 above, where data collected and named using Mönkemeyer and Smith's classifications can be integrated under Koperski et al's classification, the example above showing *Isothecium filescens* in Mönkemeyer and *Isothecium striatulum* in Smith to be conceptually equivalent. Obviously on a singular basis, finding such matches could easily be done by just processing the relevant TCS and XML, but the visualisation allows users to view the stability of whole classifications by concept relationships.

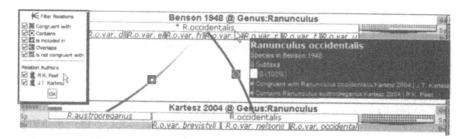

Fig. 4. Relations of *R.occidentalis* between Benson and Kartesz indicate an apparently contradictory situation - congruent with another species but containing another in the same classification. This is due to the relations being authored by two experts who have differing opinions. The authors and the types of relation can be filtered in or out through a pop-up menu (seen in the top left of the figure).

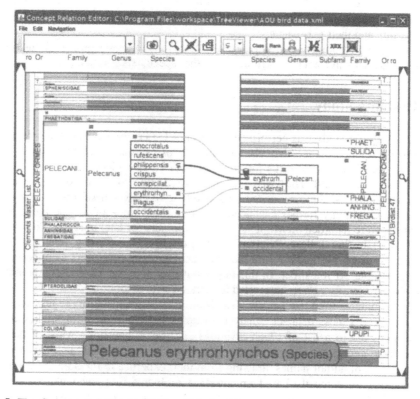

Fig. 5. The Concept Relationship Editor. Relationships are made by dragging links between taxa in opposite-facing classifications.

2.3 The Concept Relationship Editor

The concept-based matching used in TaxVis is of course only as reliable as the quailty of the relationship data used. In some cases there may be errors or contradictions, or just no relationship data defined at all A second visualization tool, the Concept Relation Editor (CRE) [22], was prototyped to allow taxonomists to intuitively add and edit their own relations between classifications. This could either be done for a classification the user has authored to relate it back to previous classifications, or as a third-party author inserting their own relationships between two pre-existing classifications.

In the visualization, as shown in Fig. 5, a pair of classifications is selected from the current data set and displayed facing each other on different sides of the application window. A focus+context effect [23] is applied to the trees such that selected taxa receive more space than unselected taxa, giving them room to display relationship information or for rendering child taxa. This effect can be replaced with a more traditional scroll and pan technique for large lists if the user so wishes.

Making relationships is simply a question of setting the author name and the type of relationship through the toolbar menu at the top of the display, and then dragging with the mouse a path between the taxa that are to be related. Links for selected portions of the classifications are displayed, with icons to represent the type of relationship and their permanency.

In this way taxonomists can link new classifications to legacy data, with the results being stored back in the TCS XML data for other specialists to examine.

3 Usability Study

An informal user study was performed at the TDWG (Taxonomic Databases Working Group) conference on the two visualizations to assess their usability. Users were asked to complete sample tasks for either or both visualizations, depending on their availability and interest. They were also asked to provide comments on any problems they encountered as they proceeded, and also to give their general impression of the visualization and any further enhancements they could think of for the tools. These comments were recorded on MiniDisc audio equipment for later analysis. This "think-aloud" [24] testing follows Nielsen's [25] prescription for using relatively small numbers of users, but making sure that they are *representative* users as opposed to a random sample off the street. In this case as attendees at the TDWG conference we could be sure our users were interested in working with taxonomic data.

Five volunteers tried the TaxVis visualization, attempting a scenario task based on Koperski et al's moss data set. Analysis of notes and audio recordings taken during the sessions led to a list of 17 observations and user suggestions. Most of the user suggestions and issues were based on taxonomic issues such as the incorrect capitalization of author names, drawing from their expertise in the domain, whilst the observations were mostly based on interface problems they encountered, such as being tricked by misleading colouring into attempting to select non-existent concepts.

For the Concept Relation Editor we had 8 volunteers use the visualization and attempt to complete a pair of tasks based on *Ranunculus* and Bird data sets. Again, notes and audio recordings were taken during the sessions, leading to 42 observations and user suggestions, many of which occurred with multiple users. The observations ranged from purely interface issues such as a drop-down list initializing with an empty selection, making users unsure as to its function, to issues that required the

Table 1. Most common issues found in testing of the Concept Relation Editor

Observation	Type	No. of users
1. Brushing on nodes not showing relationship lines	Observation	*****
2. Direction of contains and contained relationships unclear (one user did notice a set symbol was grey at one end of a link and black at the other but didn't know what this meant)	Observation	****
3. User not equating 'taxonomies' with 'classifications', error seen in labelling, ignoring button and exploring menu options instead (see 35)	Observation (use user's language)	***
4. Headers (name of classification) wanted on taxonomy/classification selection panel – and on main display (as well as / replacing the labels at the far left/right of the screen)	User suggestion	***
5. User doesn't use scrollbar in lens mode, just moves mouse up and down the classification and looks at the large tooltip at the top of the screen	Observation	***
6. Deduced congruent relationships cannot be confirmed nor deleted	Observation	***
7. Drop down list – selecting with mouse from list didn't work – had to press return on the keyboard	Observation	***
8. To make a relation requires dragging to the name text rather than the bounding box of the node (i.e. doesn't work when released over the set symbols)	Observation	***
9. User looked to open new taxonomies under 'File', not 'Edit'	Observation	***

domain expertise of taxonomists and taxonomic data managers to be flushed out. Amongst these were terminology usage (classifications versus taxonomies), default ordering of nodes (many classifications have what is known as a taxonomic ordering, which is not the default alphabetical ordering typically used) and the automatic downloading of pictures from the web to represent taxa (their accuracy was questioned). A summary of the issues that were observed or commented on by three or more users is given in the table below. For brevity we exclude the other 33 issues that were picked up by only 1 or 2 of the participants.

The discrepancy in the number of issues found between the two visualizations can be attributed mainly to the fact that the CRE tool had not been through any previous rounds of similar testing, unlike TaxVis, which as a result had many of its more glaring interface issues discovered and dealt with in previous incarnations. The unequal number of volunteers (8 for CRE compared to 5 for TaxVis) may also have contributed but as they are different interfaces we can't really compare like with like here. What we did notice in the CRE testing was the classic pattern of each additional user finding a smaller and smaller set of unique issues in an interface, but with reproduced issues reinforcing the findings of previous users. In any case, as pointed out by [26], what matters is not so much the number of issues found or users employed, but whether the findings are acted upon. In this case both TaxVis and CRE underwent significant re-engineering to address as far as possible the problems found.

4 Summary

We have described how a pair of related visualizations, TaxVis and the Concept Relation Editor, can be used to explore, follow and construct concept relationships across a data set of multiple classifications.

Visualising such operations offers advantages over a purely textual results service and text-based data entry approach. The most obvious being that relationships, both in their creation and in later exploration, can be viewed in the context of other relationships and concepts, and assessed in that light. This is important as concept-based matching is inherently more complex than naïve one-to-one name matching. In TaxVis, it is possible to select and follow relationships across multiple classifications and to use the related concepts found as the starting point for further queries. In the Concept Relation Editor, users can construct their own relationship sets and observe the gradual building-up of their efforts.

Acknowledgments. Thanks to Robert Peet and Xianhua Liu for determining and encoding the concept relationships in the *Ranunculus* data set. Also thanks to the volunteers at the TDWG 2007 conference who gave their time and expertise to our user testing.

References

1. Higgins, S.I., Richardson, D.M., Cowling, R.M., Trinder-Smith, T.H.: Predicting the landscape-scale distribution of alien plants and their threat to plant diversity. Conversation Ecology 13, 303–313 (1999)
2. Michener, W.K., Brunt, J.W. (eds.): Ecological Data: Design, Management, and Processing. Blackwell Science, Oxford (2000)
3. Foster, I., Kesselman, C. (eds.): The GRID 2: blueprint for a new computing infrastructure, 2nd edn. Elsevier Series in Grid Computing. Elsevier, Amsterdam (2004)
4. Berendsohn, W.G.: The concept of potential taxa in databases. Taxon 44, 207–212 (1995)
5. Pullan, M.R., Watson, M.F., Kennedy, J.B., Raguenaud, C., Hyam, R.: The Prometheus Taxonomic Model. Taxon 49, 55–75 (2000)
6. Peterson, A.T., Navarro-Sigüenza, A.G.: Alternate species concepts as bases for determining priority conservation areas. Conservation Biology 13, 427–431 (1999)
7. Minelli, A.: The status of taxonomic literature. Trends in Ecology & Evolution 18, 75–76 (2003)
8. Kennedy, J.B., Kukla, R., Paterson, T.: Scientific names are ambiguous as identifiers for biological taxa: their context and definition are required for accurate data integration. In: Ludäscher, B., Raschid, L. (eds.) DILS 2005. LNCS (LNBI), vol. 3615, pp. 80–95. Springer, Heidelberg (2005)
9. Schuh, R.T.: Biological Systematics: Principles and Applications. Cornell University Press, Ithica (2000)

10. Groves, C.P.: A history of gorilla taxonomy. In: Taylor, A.B., Goldsmith, M.L. (eds.) Gorilla biology, pp. 15–34. Cambridge University Press, Cambridge (2003)
11. Wickings, E.J., Clifford, S.L., Anthony, N.M., Jeffery, K., Johnson-Bawe, M., Abernethy, K.A., Bruford, M.W.: Gorilla mtDNA - Sequences Unravelled and Secrets Revealed. Gorilla Journal 29 (2004)
12. Kennedy, J.: Exploiting Diverse Sources of Scientific Data. Final Theme report, e-Science Institute (2007)
13. Kennedy, J., Bowers, S., Jones, M., Madin, J., Peet, R., Pennington, D., Schildhauer, M., Stewart, A.: http://www.tdwg.org/fileadmin/2007meeting/slides/ Kennedy_DataIntegrationIssuesSeek_abs231.ppt
14. Berendsohn, W.G., Geoffroy, M.: Networking taxonomic concepts – uniting without unitary-ism. In: Curry, G., Humphries, C. (eds.) Biodiversity Databases - Techniques, Politics, and Applications, pp. 13–22. CRC Taylor & Francis (2007)
15. Koperski, M., Sauer, M., Braun, W., Gradstein, S.R.: Referenzliste der Moose Deutschlands. LV Druck im Landwirtschaftsverlag GmbH, Münster-Hiltrup (2000)
16. Franz, N., Peet, R., Weakley, A.: On the use of taxonomic concepts in support of biodiversity research and taxonomy. In: Wheeler, Q.D. (ed.) The New Taxonomy. Systematics Association Special Volume Series, vol. 74, pp. 61–85. Taylor & Francis, Boca Raton (2008)
17. Card, S.K., Mackinlay, J.D., Shneiderman, B. (eds.): Readings in Information Visualization: Using Vision to Think, 1st edn. The Morgan Kaufmann Series in Interactive Technologies. Morgan Kaufmann, San Francisco (1999)
18. Thau, D., Ludäscher, B.: Reasoning about Taxonomies in First-Order Logic. Ecological Informatics 2, 195–209 (2007)
19. Graham, M., Kennedy, J.: Visual exploration of alternative taxonomies through concepts. Ecological Informatics 2, 248–261 (2007)
20. Roberts, J.C.: Multiple-View and Multiform Visualization. In: Erbacher, R., Pang, A., Wittenbrink, C., Roberts, J. (eds.) Visual Data Exploration and Analysis VII. SPIE, vol. 3960, pp. 176–185. SPIE Press, Bellingham (2000)
21. Graham, M., Kennedy, J.: Combining linking & focusing techniques for a multiple hierarchy visualisation. In: Banissi, E., Khosrowshahi, F., Sarfraz, M., Ursyn, A. (eds.) IEEE Conference on Information Visualization, pp. 425–432. IEEE Computer Society Press, Los Alamitos (2001)
22. Craig, P., Kennedy, J.: Concept Relationship Editor: A visual interface to support the assertion of synonymy relationships between taxonomic classifications. In: Visualization and Data Analysis. SPIE, vol. 6809, p. 12. SPIE Press, Bellingham (2008)
23. Cockburn, A., Karlson, A., Bederson, B.B.: A Review of Overview+Detail, Zooming, and Focus+Context Interfaces. ACM Computing Surveys 41 (to appear, 2009)
24. Tognazzini, B.: User testing on the cheap TOG on Interface, pp. 79–89. Addison-Wesley, Reading (1992)
25. Nielsen, J.: Guerrila HCI: Using Discount Usability Engineering to Penetrate the Intimidation Barrier. In: Bias, R.G., Mayhew, D.J. (eds.) Cost-Justifying Usability, pp. 245–272. Academic Press Professional, London (1994)
26. Wixon, D.: Evaluating Usability Methods. Interactions 10, 28–34 (2003)

Author Index

Lecture Notes in Computer Science

Sublibrary 3: Information Systems and Application, incl. Internet/Web and HCI

For information about Vols. 1– 4690
please contact your bookseller or Springer

Vol. 4872: D. Mery, L. Rueda (Eds.), Advances in Image and Video Technology. XXI, 961 pages. 2007.

Vol. 4871: M. Cavazza, S. Donikian (Eds.), Virtual Storytelling. XIII, 219 pages. 2007.

Vol. 4858: X. Deng, F.C. Graham (Eds.), Internet and Network Economics. XVI, 598 pages. 2007.

Vol. 4857: J.M. Ware, G.E. Taylor (Eds.), Web and Wireless Geographical Information Systems. XI, 293 pages. 2007.

Vol. 4853: F. Fonseca, M.A. Rodríguez, S. Levashkin (Eds.), GeoSpatial Semantics. X, 289 pages. 2007.

Vol. 4836: H. Ichikawa, W.-D. Cho, I. Satoh, H.Y. Youn (Eds.), Ubiquitous Computing Systems. XIII, 307 pages. 2007.

Vol. 4832: M. Weske, M.-S. Hacid, C. Godart (Eds.), Web Information Systems Engineering – WISE 2007 Workshops. XV, 518 pages. 2007.

Vol. 4831: B. Benatallah, F. Casati, D. Georgakopoulos, C. Bartolini, W. Sadiq, C. Godart (Eds.), Web Information Systems Engineering – WISE 2007. XVI, 675 pages. 2007.

Vol. 4825: K. Aberer, K.-S. Choi, N. Noy, D. Allemang, K.-I. Lee, L. Nixon, J. Golbeck, P. Mika, D. Maynard, R. Mizoguchi, G. Schreiber, P. Cudré-Mauroux (Eds.), The Semantic Web. XXVII, 973 pages. 2007.

Vol. 4823: H. Leung, F. Li, R. Lau, Q. Li (Eds.), Advances in Web Based Learning – ICWL 2007. XIV, 654 pages. 2008.

Vol. 4822: D.H.-L. Goh, T.H. Cao, I.T. Sølvberg, E. Rasmussen (Eds.), Asian Digital Libraries. XVII, 519 pages. 2007.

Vol. 4820: T.G. Wyeld, S. Kenderdine, M. Docherty (Eds.), Virtual Systems and Multimedia. XII, 215 pages. 2008.

Vol. 4816: B. Falcidieno, M. Spagnuolo, Y. Avrithis, I. Kompatsiaris, P. Buitelaar (Eds.), Semantic Multimedia. XII, 306 pages. 2007.

Vol. 4813: I. Oakley, S.A. Brewster (Eds.), Haptic and Audio Interaction Design. XIV, 145 pages. 2007.

Vol. 4810: H.H.-S. Ip, O.C. Au, H. Leung, M.-T. Sun, W.-Y. Ma, S.-M. Hu (Eds.), Advances in Multimedia Information Processing – PCM 2007. XXI, 834 pages. 2007.

Vol. 4809: M.K. Denko, C.-s. Shih, K.-C. Li, S.-L. Tsao, Q.-A. Zeng, S.H. Park, Y.-B. Ko, S.-H. Hung, J.-H. Park (Eds.), Emerging Directions in Embedded and Ubiquitous Computing. XXXV, 823 pages. 2007.

Vol. 4808: T.-W. Kuo, E. Sha, M. Guo, L.T. Yang, Z. Shao (Eds.), Embedded and Ubiquitous Computing. XXI, 769 pages. 2007.

Vol. 4806: R. Meersman, Z. Tari, P. Herrero (Eds.), On the Move to Meaningful Internet Systems 2007: OTM 2007 Workshops, Part II. XXXIV, 611 pages. 2007.

Vol. 4805: R. Meersman, Z. Tari, P. Herrero (Eds.), On the Move to Meaningful Internet Systems 2007: OTM 2007 Workshops, Part I. XXXIV, 757 pages. 2007.

Vol. 4804: R. Meersman, Z. Tari (Eds.), On the Move to Meaningful Internet Systems 2007: CoopIS, DOA, ODBASE, GADA, and IS, Part II. XXIX, 683 pages. 2007.

Vol. 4803: R. Meersman, Z. Tari (Eds.), On the Move to Meaningful Internet Systems 2007: CoopIS, DOA, ODBASE, GADA, and IS, Part I. XXIX, 1173 pages. 2007.

Vol. 4802: J.-L. Hainaut, E.A. Rundensteiner, M. Kirchberg, M. Bertolotto, M. Brochhausen, Y.-P.P. Chen, S.S.-S. Cherfi, M. Doerr, H. Han, S. Hartmann, J. Parsons, G. Poels, C. Rolland, J. Trujillo, E. Yu, E. Zimányie (Eds.), Advances in Conceptual Modeling – Foundations and Applications. XIX, 420 pages. 2007.

Vol. 4801: C. Parent, K.-D. Schewe, V.C. Storey, B. Thalheim (Eds.), Conceptual Modeling - ER 2007. XVI, 616 pages. 2007.

Vol. 4797: M. Arenas, M.I. Schwartzbach (Eds.), Database Programming Languages. VIII, 261 pages. 2007.

Vol. 4796: M. Lew, N. Sebe, T.S. Huang, E.M. Bakker (Eds.), Human–Computer Interaction. X, 157 pages. 2007.

Vol. 4794: B. Schiele, A.K. Dey, H. Gellersen, B. de Ruyter, M. Tscheligi, R. Wichert, E. Aarts, A. Buchmann (Eds.), Ambient Intelligence. XV, 375 pages. 2007.

Vol. 4777: S. Bhalla (Ed.), Databases in Networked Information Systems. X, 329 pages. 2007.

Vol. 4761: R. Obermaisser, Y. Nah, P. Puschner, F.J. Rammig (Eds.), Software Technologies for Embedded and Ubiquitous Systems. XIV, 563 pages. 2007.

Vol. 4747: S. Džeroski, J. Struyf (Eds.), Knowledge Discovery in Inductive Databases. X, 301 pages. 2007.

Vol. 4744: Y. de Kort, W. IJsselsteijn, C. Midden, B. Eggen, B.J. Fogg (Eds.), Persuasive Technology. XIV, 316 pages. 2007.

Vol. 4740: L. Ma, M. Rauterberg, R. Nakatsu (Eds.), Entertainment Computing – ICEC 2007. XXX, 480 pages. 2007.

Vol. 4730: C. Peters, P. Clough, F.C. Gey, J. Karlgren, B. Magnini, D.W. Oard, M. de Rijke, M. Stempfhuber (Eds.), Evaluation of Multilingual and Multi-modal Information Retrieval. XXIV, 998 pages. 2007.

Vol. 4723: M. R. Berthold, J. Shawe-Taylor, N. Lavrač (Eds.), Advances in Intelligent Data Analysis VII. XIV, 380 pages. 2007.

Vol. 4721: W. Jonker, M. Petković (Eds.), Secure Data Management. X, 213 pages. 2007.

Vol. 4718: J. Hightower, B. Schiele, T. Strang (Eds.), Location- and Context-Awareness. X, 297 pages. 2007.

Vol. 4717: J. Krumm, G.D. Abowd, A. Seneviratne, T. Strang (Eds.), UbiComp 2007: Ubiquitous Computing. XIX, 520 pages. 2007.

Vol. 4715: J.M. Haake, S.F. Ochoa, A. Cechich (Eds.), Groupware: Design, Implementation, and Use. XIII, 355 pages. 2007.

Vol. 4714: G. Alonso, P. Dadam, M. Rosemann (Eds.), Business Process Management. XIII, 418 pages. 2007.

Vol. 4704: D. Barbosa, A. Bonifati, Z. Bellahsène, E. Hunt, R. Unland (Eds.), Database and XML Technologies. X, 141 pages. 2007.